# The Impact of Illness on World Leaders

# THE IMPACT
# OF ILLNESS
# ON WORLD
# LEADERS

*Bert Edward Park* M.D.

**upp** UNIVERSITY OF PENNSYLVANIA PRESS
*Philadelphia 1986*

*Permission to reprint photographs used in the text and material from works cited in the text is acknowledged at the end of this volume, following the Index.*

*Printed in the United States of America*

*Designed by Adrianne Onderdonk Dudden*

*Library of Congress Cataloging-in-Publication Data*

*Park, Bert Edward.*
  *The impact of illness on world leaders.*

  *1. Heads of state—health and hygiene.*
*2. Nervous system—Illnesses.   3. History,*
*Modern—20th century.   I. Title.*
*D412.7.P37   1986      909.82      86-16136*
*ISBN 0-8122-8005-9 (alk. paper)*

*To Mom and Dad*

# Contents

# Illustrations

PLATES

# *Acknowledgments*

I am deeply indebted to a number of individuals who offered their insights, criticisms, and encouragement throughout the course of preparing this manuscript. As solitary an undertaking as this project has been, no one individual should presume to possess the breadth and depth of knowledge required to complete it without anticipating some mistakes in interpretation. Any errors that remain are my own. Those historians who have prevented me from falling prey to medical reductionism in what should be, after all, an historical analysis include James Giglio, Meredith Adams, William Hammond, and Wayne Bartee, all in the Department of History at Southwest Missouri State University. I owe a special debt of gratitude to Dr. Howard Mahan, Chairman of the Department of History at the University of South Alabama, whose kindness and encouragement in the early stages of my research gave me the confidence to try my hand at something rather far afield from neurosurgery. To my neurosurgical colleagues, many of whom I'm certain have questioned my choice of avocation, goes my gratitude for their understanding—among them, my Chief of Neurosurgery at Vanderbilt University Hospital, Dr. William Meacham.

I would like to acknowledge the role played by my friend and advisor Ed Quigley, without whose perseverance the project might never have reached the University of Pennsylvania Press. He also offered helpful suggestions for the title of the work. Three members of the Press deserve special mention: Tom Rotell, who had faith enough to push for the manuscript's acceptance; Janet Greenwood, who guided me through much unfamiliar ground in preparing it; and last, Alan Schroder, who copyedited the original draft with skill and precision.

A great debt is also owed to those individuals among the clerical staff who spent long hours in typing the revisions in the manuscript—Pat Phemister, Ann Herbst, and Mary Gorman. I also wish to recognize the talents of Viviana Harper, who is responsible for the medical illustrations that appear in the work, modified from the works of Frank Netter, the acknowledged doyen of medical illustrationists.

In some cases it has proved next to impossible to trace the original source of copyright property, although full acknowledgment has been given for excerpted material. To those authors whom I have occasionally taken to task, I trust that they might accept this in the scholarly spirit in which it is intended. To a man, each has taught me far more as a student of history than any minor criticisms I have made could possibly dispel. In particular, I wish to draw attention to the following scholars whose efforts have immeasurably enriched my training as a fledgling historian: Arthur Link, Edwin Weinstein, Alexander and Juliette George, Arthur Walworth, Robert Marquand, Werner Masser, Alan Bullock, Hugh Trevor-Roper, Robert G. L. Waite, Joachin Fest, David Irving, James MacGregor Burns, Jim Bishop, Hugh L'Etang, David Carlton, Clinton Rossiter, and Richard Neustadt.

Finally, my warmest thanks are reserved for my family who had to endure it all. Only those closest to a project such as this understand the price they have so graciously paid to see it completed. My wife, Judy, brought new meaning to the role of supporter and cheerleader, while my father, Dr. William I. Park, continues to fulfill his role as the kindest man, and best physician, I know.

# *Preface*

## FOR THE SAKE OF BALANCE:
## BIOHISTORY THROUGH
## JAUNDICED EYES

No attempt to write a book would be considered complete without some re-evaluation and second-guessing on the part of the author. My own efforts to do so have revolved around the motive behind my taking on the task, the methodology used, and the tenor of the finished work. With regard to the first, I am reminded of a pungent comment, once directed toward Arthur Burns, former chairman of the Federal Reserve Board: Like so many specialists, from relief pitchers to brain surgeons, he fancied himself a Renaissance Man.[1] If destined to remain among other frustrated mortals who have failed to fulfill that role, I still must ask myself what compelled me to cross the street to another discipline outside the protection of my degree in medicine. Intellectual hubris? A meager twenty-eight hours credit toward a master's degree in history? Or a need, like Adolf Hitler's, for a catastrophic failure worthy of my own "greatness"? Perhaps my motive stems from self-doubt after spending my formative intellectual years in the specialized training required to become a neurological surgeon. Is there a closet pseudo-intellectual hidden within me, anxious to demonstrate that despite the years of sacrifice, I am well rounded after all? Sad commentary, I suppose. Whatever the motive, the street crossing has been made. But was it done right, or have I run the risk of being cut off at the intersection by the esteemed historians and others I may have offended along the way?

Concerning the issue of tenor, many who read these pages will assert that I have left myself open to criticism by being more dogmatic than a retrospective study of this nature warrants. It is clearly difficult to justify dogmatism when some degree of reliance has been placed on secondary sources. Nevertheless, when only secondary accounts are available, I have taken great pains to document assertions by using more than one source. Hence the extreme annotation (which some may find tedious). Furthermore, one of my purposes in embarking on this task was not only to point out where criticism of some sources is justified, but to debunk certain myths that have been perpetrated by what Arno Karlen terms the Law of Repetition in biohistorical accounts.[2] Never in these pages has criticism been directed so as to impugn the skills or reputations of the esteemed list of scholars I have occasionally taken to task in this regard.

Undoubtedly, too, some will question what they perceive as reductionism in my eagerness to advance the medical side of the argument. For reductionism admittedly runs the risk of leaving one standing intellectually naked in the breeze—if not gales—of scholarly criticism. With three possible exceptions, I believe the diagnoses proposed in my review are sound enough to warrant the strong stand taken.

First, there is room for argument regarding the number and degree of hypertension-related strokes Woodrow Wilson suffered before going to Paris in 1919. This does not negate, in my view, the compelling evidence that illness later impacted on his leadership both during and after the Paris Peace Conference, though the wording of my argument regarding his compromises on Treaty issues from April 3 to April 14, for example, may suggest unifactorial causation (and of course such was not the case). Second, no primary sources are available (at least by name) to substantiate the amount of Benzedrine Anthony Eden was taking during the Suez crisis of 1956, though three separate secondary sources document his involvement with the drug. Limitations of space and emphasis precluded developing this argument further. Finally, by far the most controversial assertion in these pages is the claim that Adolf Hitler may have suffered from temporal lobe epilepsy. Skepticism has justifiably evolved over the alleged pervasiveness of such a condition, since it has been so often inappropriately applied to other tyrants of history. This controversial view is intended as but a beginning to an ongoing investigation of that possibility in Hitler's medical history. Only time and further medical investigation will validate or invalidate the claim; until then, a curt dismissal by skeptics is as unjustified as any dogmatic assertion in its favor.

The above reference to Arno Karlen brings me to a reconsideration of the methodology applied in my review of illness and aging as they have impacted on leadership. Reading *Napoleon's Glands and Other Ventures in Biohistory* compelled me, as did few other critics who reviewed my manuscript, to re-examine my conclusions for accuracy and credibility. Karlen's incisive and entertaining analysis of the place for biohistory as a scholarly endeavor implies that in many instances in the past we may have made too much of it. On those occasions where it is relevant, the evidence has often been misread to foster inaccurate—if still titillating—interpretations. To state the matter simply, there is a potential conflict between what sells and what enlightens, and the latter, cloaked in the staid apparel of scholarly methodology, is usually not as readable as the former. This situation explains why some less exacting accounts allow certain biohistorical myths to linger. It also says something about why scholars lose much of their reading audience: they are writing for each other, because their professional reputations hang in the balance. Only one who is truly gifted as both scholar and writer can approach the academic world and the general reading public to capture the attention of both.

Arno Karlen is such a writer. While reading his account of Napoleon as biohistory, I realized that there are some useful parallels to be drawn from that one case study that have individual application to each of the leaders discussed in my work. The most obvious of these is the way in which Karlen forces all of us to confront the way we view history. Is the past a product of Thomas Carlyle's Great Man theory? Does a great man's itch force millions to scratch?[3] Or, as Leo Tolstoy would have argued, do the forces of history arise from the masses, with its leaders merely swept along by its impulses and occasional excesses? By emphasizing the primacy of the physiological failings of a few selected leaders as one explanation for the devolution of power away from Europe in the first half of the twentieth century, I am perhaps swimming against the current of scholarly opinion, which today tends to de-emphasize the individual's impact on history. Karlen has made me at least aware of the limitations inherent in such an approach. With regard to the message implicit in the pages that follow, the reader must judge for him or herself.

BERT E. PARK
February, 1986

---

[1] Rather, Dan, and Gary Gates. *The Palace Guard*. New York: Harper and Row, 1974. p. 61.

[2] Karlen, Arno. *Napoleon's Glands and Other Ventures in Biohistory*. Boston: Little, Brown, and Co., Warner Books edition, 1984. p. 45; see Appendix 2, n. 11.

[3] Ibid., p. 33.

# Introduction

What possible value is there in a physician suggesting reinterpretations of history? Should a relative amateur be allowed a public forum in order to suggest modifications in traditional historical concepts? Is he not on unequal footing when he chooses to take on the best minds devoted to this distinguished discipline?

Four years of research into the primary and secondary source materials related to certain twentieth-century leaders reveals that two shortcomings of traditional scholarly efforts directed toward assessing their performance have become evident. The first is a relative indifference to aging and disease as they affect leadership skills. The second may in part explain the first: historians as a rule have felt uncomfortable using the tools required to investigate those effects, for here the historian is on unfamiliar ground. The former is correctable if sufficient emphasis is brought to bear in those cases where it is appropriate. The latter is unavoidable without the proper training. This entails an understanding of such concepts as the "clinical syndrome" and the "differential diagnosis," which are foreign to the historian but familiar to the clinician.[1] Physicians simply speak a different language than their professional counterparts in history. Yet, more than ever, new tools are elevating the study of the past to a more scientific level, and history is being rewritten in the process. The computer sciences have modified our thinking particularly in the fields of social and political history, where examination of demographics and voting patterns has prompted often startling reappraisals of time-honored beliefs. Biohistory, the study of the past through the eyes of the physician, the biologist, the behavioral scientist, and the anthropologist, has introduced the historian to some unfamiliar, yet very useful terminology.

Computer programming is one form of language; medical jargon is another. Both have relevance to the study of history in the proper circumstances. It would be unwise to expect a physician to be a credible diplomatic historian, for example, where a command of foreign languages is indispensable to the proper study of the subject. Similarly, medical terminology is sufficiently foreign to almost all historians that meaningful contributions to an understanding of disease would not be anticipated from them.

Not surprisingly, the study of illness and leadership has largely been left to the eclectics of our age—the journalist and the popular historian. This circumstance has fostered some peculiar and enduring myths. Not every despised leader, for example, has suffered from the ravages of syphilis, as some would have us believe, yet Stalin, Napoleon, Hitler, and Mussolini have all been placed among the list of sufferers. Even if such indefensible allegations have the dubious merit of sensationalism, they have contributed nothing to the serious study of history.

We can no longer afford to allow such unfounded assertions to pass uncontested. If one historical truth remains inviolate, it is this: reality is probably less influential than is the perception of reality, whether right or wrong. As such, popular perceptions of leaders have proven more enduring than historians are willing to admit, in spite of their best efforts to redress the balance. Biography lacks appeal to the general public unless it spurs insight into personality, including idiosyncrasies. The reader above all wishes to know what makes a given leader human. Such a preoccupation may not be appropriate to the study of history, but it nonetheless defines the basis on which the common man molds his opinions. And it is the man on the street, not the historian, who keeps the leader in office.[2]

The study of certain of these leaders has also uncovered molders of public opinion who have passed largely unnoticed. These are the physicians who ministered to the men in power, disguising their infirmities and prolonging their tenure in office long after leadership skills had become tarnished by age and disease. Perhaps a greater degree of credibility would result if these physicians were indicted by a member of their own profession. To mold these recurrent acts of deception into an indictment is one of the distasteful but necessary tasks of this study.

Another is to draw attention to the fact that, as disparate as they often prove to be, the popular and scholarly perceptions of leaders share one area of common ground: Images die hard. The present study seeks to alter, in varying degrees, both the popular and scholarly assessment of eight such leaders during a critical forty-year period of our recent history. Most readers are familiar enough with the images of Woodrow Wilson the Rigid Moralist, Franklin Roosevelt the Political Pragmatist, Adolf Hitler the Evil Genius, Winston Churchill the Inspirational Orator, and Anthony Eden the Esteemed Diplomat. Few are aware of the reverse sides of these respective portraits: Wilson the Progressively Demented, Roosevelt the Encephalopathy Victim, Hitler the Epilepsy Sufferer and Pharmacologic Dupe, Churchill the Aging Stroke Victim, and Eden the Amphetamine Abuser. Outlandish assertions? Perhaps, but not unfounded, as a review of the primary and secondary source materials shows. Each leader was considered among the greatest movers and shakers of his day, yet all were afflicted by neurologic illness that impacted negatively on their leadership skills and decision-making abilities. And none of the leaders was accurately perceived by the public they served.

Woodrow Wilson was afflicted with hypertension at a relatively early age and suffered numerous small strokes, which over a long period of time affected his behavior and thought processes. The aberrations and changes in his character became apparent at precisely the period during which he was carrying on negotiations at the Paris Peace Conference in 1919. Some disastrous diplomatic agreements may have resulted. Similarly, American membership in the League of Nations was lost largely on the basis of his inability to deal effectively with this issue as a leader while he was convalescing from a devastating stroke and his wife was, in effect, running the country.

Much has been made in the popular and scholarly literature on Franklin D. Roosevelt about his having been a very sick man while attending the Yalta Conference with Joseph Stalin and Winston Churchill. Probably before (and undoubtedly after) this conference, Roosevelt's health and occasionally his decision-making capacity were impaired by a combination of hypertension, diffuse atherosclerosis, chronic obstructive pulmonary disease, and congestive heart failure. He suffered from transient episodes of clouding of consciousness, termed "encephalopathy," which intermittently and adversely affected his political skills. Ironically, his illnesses were hidden from the American public, just as Woodrow Wilson's illnesses had been disguised some twenty-five years before. More ironic still, the very physician who denied Roosevelt's infirmities had been recommended to the President by the physician who had been in charge of dispensing information regarding Woodrow Wilson's health. Parallels between the two men are intriguing and deserve further emphasis than has been given them to the present time.

During his second term as Prime Minister of Great Britain from 1951 through 1955, Winston Churchill was afflicted by a significant dementia on the basis of two separate strokes and multiple episodes of transient cerebrovascular insufficiency. He was but a shadow of the extraordinary leader he had been during World War II. Furthermore, his waning skills and his performance at increasingly infrequent public appearances were bolstered by the use of central nervous system stimulants given to him by his physician. At the age of eighty he was still Prime Minister of Great Britain, but under the circumstances it is not surprising that his four-year term saw few significant accomplishments.

Churchill's successor in office, Anthony Eden, became embroiled in the Suez Canal crisis of 1956 shortly after becoming Prime Minister. The various accounts of the period characterize this as an exercise in duplicity and deception on his part. His own government did not know of the scheme that he had concocted with the French to instigate hostilities between Israel and Egypt to allow Great Britain to masquerade as a peace-keeping force in the area and thus to reassert its waning influence in the Middle East. What has not been recognized to date is that Anthony Eden demonstrated all the signs and symptoms of amphetamine toxicity during this period, and that his irrational and deceitful conduct was partially influenced by this central nervous system stimulant.

It has often been speculated by armchair historians that Adolf Hitler was insane, or at the very least only partially responsible for his actions. Unknown to most, he was a victim of several diseases, all of which affected his conduct from 1941 until his death. He was indeed victimized by Parkinson's disease, as has been suspected by some in the past. More significant, however, he probably suffered from the unrecognized malady of temporal lobe epilepsy, which may explain much of his rather bizarre behavior during his last three years in power. Not only did he manifest the disease intermittently, he also demonstrated all the abnormal personality features that accompany that phenomenon. What has further been neglected is the impact of over seventy different medications he was taking during his last four years in power. Several of these involved various combinations of injurious central nervous system stimulants—such as amphetamines, cocaine, strychnine, and belladonna—and many of these stimulants actually augmented his suspected underlying seizure disorder.

Three other members of the leadership fraternity during the thirties have been generally ignored by all but the professional historian. Paul von Hindenburg, Ramsay MacDonald, and Józef Piłsudski remain enigmatic examples of the failed leadership that characterized the interwar years. The ravages of age on intellectual performance may explain their lesser status, at least in part. Inasmuch as they personify the theme implicit in this work, their story must also be told.

Paul von Hindenburg was 86 at the time he surrendered Germany's political fortunes to Adolf Hitler—and he behaved accordingly. His last three years as President of the Weimar Republic were marked by political intrigue among his subordinates, largely as a result of his decreasing intellectual capacity. The instability of Germany's ostensibly democratic government in large measure reflected this aging octogenarian's erratic behavior.

During these same years, Ramsay MacDonald as Prime Minister of Great Britain fell victim to a pervasive depression, augmented in the end by a tragic encounter with Alzheimer's disease. As one of the original authors of Britain's fateful preoccupation with pacifism during the thirties, his inability to reassess that doctrine's tragic flaw as events unfolded reflected several aspects of the condition that afflicted him, most notably a failure to employ the abstract attitude in weighing alternative considerations.

His contemporary in Poland, Marshal Józef Piłsudski, was victimized to a lesser degree by the effects of premature aging on the brain, yet enough so that he retained certain delusions concerning Poland's military strength and her diplomatic position vis-à-vis the threatening powers of neighboring Nazi Germany and Soviet Russia. His impact on events as they transpired symbolized much of what was wrong with Central Europe during the interwar years.

Perhaps two of the most perplexing aspects of the impact of neurologic illness on leadership skills are, first, its extraordinary prevalence during such a brief period of modern European history and, second, the equally extraordinary nature of the period itself. The years 1918 to 1956 witnessed the movement of power and influence away from European capitals to two new superpowers on the world stage. Europe had lost control of its own affairs, not to mention its heretofore central role in world history. The eminent historian Hajo Holborn outlined this thesis in the introduction to his acclaimed work *The Political Collapse of Europe:*

> After 1919 . . . only the facades of a European system remained standing. In World War II, which was decided by the participation of the Soviet Union and the United States, the collapse of the traditional European system became an irrevocable fact. What is commonly called the "historic Europe" is dead and beyond resurrection.[3]

Holborn called for a reappraisal of traditional historical views regarding this transformation, and in so doing obliquely emphasized the contribution of some individual leaders to it. His reappraisal included some very non-European protagonists:

> For more than thirty-five years the United States has made herself a partner to all the great political decisions of Europe. This history of the political collapse of Europe contains, therefore, a long sequence of American participation and has to be reappraised in the light of our present situation.[4]

In large measure, America's participation was framed by the personalities of Woodrow Wilson and Franklin D. Roosevelt. Just as Adolf Hitler's perplexing decision in 1941 to extend the European conflict into Russia bore the stamp of a very personal perception of his own role in transforming Europe, so too did the efforts of these two American presidents reflect their own very personal imprint on planning that continent's future security. Yet the perceptions of all three were adversely influenced by diseases that colored their perspectives. Their respective conditions represented merely the tip of the iceberg of compromised leadership that characterized the years encompassing Europe's political collapse.

In analyzing leadership effectiveness, historians have largely ignored the medical factor. In certain instances where they have at least acknowledged it, they have misread some of the data to foster incorrect interpretations. These need to be corrected. Accordingly, this review includes a reappraisal of some of the pertinent sources and their contributions to the issue.[5] Medical jargon has been kept to a minimum, but not to the extent of compromising the credibility of the work. My intention is to present a comprehensive overview of the problem of neurologic illness among world leaders as it related to the transformation of Europe during the first half of the twentieth century.

## NOTES

1. The term "clinical syndrome" encompasses those symptoms and physical findings, that, when added together, allow the physician to make a diagnosis. The term "differential diagnosis" includes all of the possible disease processes that may account for the clinical syndrome described.

2. The professional historian will note, undoubtedly with some displeasure, that a few such popular accounts are included in this study in the analyses of the historiography of each leader. Their displeasure should not blind them to the formative role such works have played in influencing public opinion.

3. Holborn. *Political Collapse of Europe*, p. x.

4. Ibid., p. xi.

5. This is not the first attempt by a physician to address the issue. Hugh L'Etang has written two separate accounts of leaders and their illnesses during the twentieth century entitled *The Pathology of Leadership* and *Fit to Lead?* Two shortcomings of these works deserve comment. One was avoidable, the other not. Generally speaking, L'Etang deals

only briefly with the succession issue; the breadth of his coverage certainly identifies the problem, but in the main he has made no proposals in depth for dealing with it. The second shortcoming is unavoidable. Being the first of its kind, and truly a landmark in medical historiography, *The Pathology of Leadership* contains relatively little discussion of the merits of other investigators' analyses of the data. The myths created by some writers concerning these leaders' illnesses require debunking (when indicated) if the critical reader is to gain proper insight into where the medical factor had an impact and where it did not. These criticisms notwithstanding, the medical historiography of this period owes a great debt to Dr. L'Etang. His work has served as a catalyst for further investigation by his successors, and it remains the standard against which subsequent works will be judged.

# REFERENCES

**MEDICAL**

L'Etang, Hugh. *The Pathology of Leadership.* New York: Hawthorn Books, 1970.
————. *Fit to Lead?* London: William Heinemann Medical Books Ltd., 1980.

**SECONDARY**

Holborn, Hajo. *The Political Collapse of Europe.* New York: Alfred A. Knopf, 1954.

*The Impact of Illness on World Leaders*

*The Paris Peace lost an opportunity as unique as the great war itself. In destroying the moral ideation born of the sacrifice of the war it did almost as much as the war itself in shattering the structure of western civilization.*

*Jan Smuts*

# 1

# Wilson: Prelude to Collapse

That the death of Woodrow Wilson's aspirations for American participation in the League of Nations was virtually assured by his stroke in Pueblo, Colorado in late September, 1919 is a defensible historical thesis. What is less appreciated, and perhaps more germane to the implications of America's early postwar conduct, was his state of health before and after the stroke and the world's knowledge of this. Wilson scholars are aware that some degree of dogmatism and rigidity characterized the American President's approach to the negotiations at the Paris Peace Conference earlier that year. Some attribute this to the moralistic traits of the Calvinist sermonizer he is purported to have been, perceiving Wilson's methods as a reflection of his image as the prophet from the New World, educating mankind.[1] Others have used the tools of psychoanalysis to explain Wilson's behavior.[2] A few discern that his actions in Paris and during the subsequent Senate debate concerning the League reflected subtle alterations in his behavior not entirely consistent with his previous character. They ascribe the change to Wilson's deteriorating health,[3] although a detailed understanding of the true nature of the disease afflicting him has remained somewhat of an enigma to most of these writers, given their lack of formal medical education.

The first physician to assess the available medical data in a comprehensive fashion was Dr. Edwin A. Weinstein. This psychiatrist and neurologist published an article in 1970[4] and a book in 1981[5] suggesting that Woodrow Wilson suffered a series of strokes that adversely affected his behavior while President. Since the appearance of these publications, a storm of controversy has arisen over the acceptance of Weinstein's assertions by Arthur Link, the acknowledged doyen of Wilson scholars.[6]

The medical historiography of this issue has been blessed with an increasing degree of sophistication in recent years. Yet professional medical opinion remains sharply divided between two conflicting camps: those who accept the Weinstein thesis of large-blood-vessel strokes as originally proposed,[7] and those who strongly believe that Weinstein has misread the evidence and concocted an argument that does not withstand close medical scrutiny.[8] Any suggestion that the difference of opinion between the two camps is only a matter of degree and lacks significance is dismissed by the publication of the opposing views in the March 1984 issue of the *Journal of American History.*[9]

The strong positions taken by the two sides of the argument have obscured the admittedly small but extremely significant common ground they share. They agree that Wilson was victimized by high blood pressure at a relatively young age. Therein lies the key to an assimilation of the wealth of otherwise conflicting data supporting a new thesis: Woodrow Wilson suffered from a slowly progressive disease, the initial cause of which (hypertension) may have been in evidence as early as the turn of the century. The nature of his chronic illness, broadly speaking, was a heretofore unrecognized mild but progressive dementia possibly occurring on the basis of multiple small-vessel lacunar infarctions (strokes) related to high blood pressure, accentuated in the end by a devastating atherosclerotic occlusion of a large vessel supplying the right side of the brain. A recent medical review of aging in the nervous system corroborates the contribution of both atherosclerosis and hypertension to the development of dementia. According to Dr. Donlin M. Long: "Most of these patients will have relatively large infarcts [such as Wilson experienced in Pueblo, Colorado, in 1919] . . . but smaller infarcts may occur to explain the history of progressive intellectual decline. . . . An elevated blood pressure accentuates the situation."[10]

One may understandably feel uncomfortable with this allegation that the nation's twenty-eighth Chief Executive and one-time president of a major American university was suffering from dementia late in his career, with all of the distasteful implications such an assertion implies. Perhaps much of the public is unaware that the medical definition of the word "dementia" has changed through the years. The 1969 *Psychiatric*

*Glossary* implies as much: "The old term denoted madness or insanity; now it is used entirely to denote an organic loss of intellectual function."[11] In this respect the term is now synonymous with what is known medically today as an "organic brain syndrome" (OBS). In such a condition the so-called cognitive functions are impaired, recent memory is compromised, and emotional responses are easily elicited and are disproportionate and inappropriate to the stimulus.[12] Many of these changes may be subtle and may escape the notice of the casual observer. Dr. Zbigniew Lipowski, a noted authority on dementia, gives a more detailed definition of this malady:

> The hallmark of dementia is the deterioration of efficiency in intellectual or cognitive performance of sufficient severity to interfere with social or occupational function or both. . . . [This includes] deficits in the areas of memory, abstract thinking, problem solving, and learning of new skills. Additional essential features include the impairment of judgment, defective control of impulses and emotions, and personality change—that is, either an accentuation or an alteration of [underlying] personality traits. [Lipowski further points out that] diagnosis depends on establishing a change in the person's customary behavior and identifying an organic cause judged responsible. Since the patient usually lacks insight into his altered behavior and may deny any awareness of it, statements by reliable witnesses are usually indispensible.[13]

Every aspect of these essential features fits into an inclusive description of Woodrow Wilson during his second term as President of the United States. Furthermore, this review will document not only that such changes occurred but also a probable cause for them, and will glean much of its evidence from observations by reliable witnesses close to Wilson. That the true nature of Wilson's illness was largely unappreciated by his contemporaries, however, is certain. That historians and journalists have not done a great deal to clarify the issue will be argued (see Appendix 1).

Regardless of the nature of Wilson's neurologic condition, Weinstein identified subtle changes in his behavior as early as 1896, after an alleged stroke involving his right arm. He became seemingly more energetic and less relaxed, assuming a very businesslike air in his daily work. Of equal importance was his increasing penchant for criticizing people, both subordinates and opponents—a trait that Weinstein concluded was to have sinister implications for his tenure as president of Princeton University from 1902 to 1910.[14] With the appearance of a second "lighter stroke" in 1904, he demonstrated "impulsive, oversensitive, and arbitrary" behavior during his period of disability.[15] In the aftermath of this illness, he became embroiled in a power struggle con-

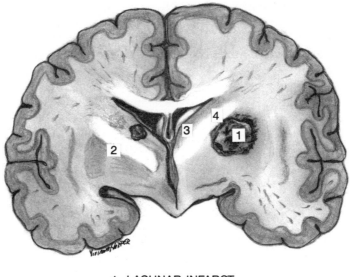

1. LACUNAR INFARCT
2. BASAL GANGLIA
3. THALAMUS
4. INTERNAL CAPSULE

*Fig. 1.1   Cross-section of an abnormal brain, showing two separate lacunar in-
farcts and their relationship to deep basal-ganglionic structures.*

cerning the quadrangle plan for dormitories, many aspects of which foreshadowed the behavior he would demonstrate over the League fight years
later. Weinstein asserted that this incident and others might not have occurred, at least in the form that they did, if Wilson had not had a stroke
in 1904.[16]

There followed a serious encounter with near-total blindness of Wilson's left eye in 1906 that Weinstein argued had equally telling effects on
the Princeton controversy. The esteemed ophthalmologist Dr. George de
Schweinitz told his patient that he had sustained a blood clot in the eye,
and Wilson still had a weak right hand at the time. Given this information, Weinstein concluded that "The clinical neurologist would say that
Wilson's stroke in 1906 and his previous history clearly defined the nature of his illness."[17] Indeed they do, but the nature of the problem was
more likely related to systemic hypertension with recurrent small-vessel
strokes (termed "lacunar infarctions") and a hypertension-related retinal
hemorrhage, rather than large-vessel strokes and atherosclerosis, as
Weinstein asserted (see Appendix 1 and Fig. 1.1).

The fact that Wilson may have met defeat at Princeton partially on account of postulated neurologic disease might be viewed as an omen of his future crisis over the League of Nations while serving as President. Yet the role his illness played prior to entering office is not as unassailably defensible as its incontrovertible impact after that time. Indeed, Weinstein was forced to admit:

> It is difficult to evaluate the respective roles of so-called psychogenic and organic factors in Wilson's changed conduct after the strokes of 1906 and 1907. Alterations in social and emotional behavior appear following strokes, but they endure only if there is extensive brain damage. Wilson's clinical history indicates that his pathology was confined to a limited area in the left cerebral hemisphere.[18]

Rigidity and obstinacy had always been a distinguishing feature of Wilson's personality, and some might argue that his behavior in this earlier period was merely consistent with his character. Nonetheless, the later pathologic and self-destructive augmentation of this personality trait during the second half of his tenure as President of the United States cannot be dismissed so easily, and this phenomenon was, in large measure, disease induced.

In spite of these antecedent events, Woodrow Wilson entered the office of the presidency allegedly in good health, according to his personal physician, Dr. Cary Grayson. "Careful examination and all the medical tests," Grayson later wrote in his memoirs, "revealed that there was no organic disease."[19] A perusal of this source, however, suggests an element of either denial or naiveté on the part of Wilson's new physician. To his way of thinking, the medical management of the President was merely "a clear case for preventive medicine," even though he was aware that while at Princeton alone he had suffered three significant illnesses.[20]

Grayson's suggested treatment for the President's medical condition is of interest more for what he omitted than for what he proposed. "This," Grayson wrote, "was the beginning of my diagnosis of his general condition and my systematic treatment which depended very little upon drugs. Indeed, when I took his medicines away from him he accused me of being a 'therapeutic nihilist.'"[21] It would be useful to know just what these medications were, particularly in relation to any perceived treatment at the time for systemic hypertension.[22] Few, if any, truly useful medications for such an affliction existed at this time, but the fact that Wilson was on medication at least underscores his previous physician's belief that treatable disease did in fact exist.

Some of Wilson's contemporaries certainly had reservations concerning his health. Even such an admiring supporter of the President as

Joseph Tumulty, who repeatedly denied the infirmities of his mentor, wrote in 1921:

> Here was a man sixty-three years old—a man always delicate in health. When he came to the White House in 1913, he was far from being well. His digestion was poor and he had a serious and painful case of neuritis in his shoulder. It was even the opinion of so great a physician as Dr. Weir Mitchell, of Philadelphia, that he could probably not complete his term and retain his health.[23]

During his first term Wilson began to suffer intermittently from severe, blinding headaches for days on end—possibly common tension headaches related to stress, but just as plausibly a manifestation of a significant acceleration of his known systolic hypertension. Neurologists recognize that headaches in the hypertensive state are unusual except in severe cases. Ominously, by 1915 there were physical changes to suggest that Wilson was in fact severely afflicted by this disease. In January, Grayson acknowledged signs of kidney failure. This is often seen with severe hypertension of a chronic or longstanding basis. Then, too, the significant changes found on examination of Wilson's retinae[24] at this time, described by Dr. Edward Gifford, are again seen most commonly in poorly controlled cases of hypertension present for many years. Impairment of renal function and the presence of retinal hemorrhages and exudates are known to be extremely grave prognostic signs for patients with hypertension.[25] Both were documented at least as early as 1915, and the retinal changes began as early as 1906 with his hemorrhage in the left eye (see Appendix 1, n. 36). As a leading medical authority of Wilson's day succinctly concluded: "At this stage the damage is [already] done."[26]

Shortly after taking office, Wilson suffered a recurrence of his neurologic condition. Weinstein stated that on April 11, 1913, "he sustained a probable stroke affecting, this time, his left upper extremity." "'For the last forty-eight hours,'" Wilson volunteered, "'there has been a threat in my left shoulder of my old enemy, *neuritis*.'"[27] This attack continued for several weeks. Ignoring other clinical possibilities for the symptoms described, Weinstein asserted that "the most likely diagnosis is that he had developed an ulcerated plaque in his right carotid artery from which an embolus had broken off."[28]

Regrettably, the descriptions in the Weinstein work and the available primary sources are not ample enough to substantiate the claim of either a cerebrovascular accident or the alleged subsequent transient ischemic attacks. Weinstein himself drew attention to the fact that the term "neuritis" was an imprecise catchall for all manner of ailments in this era's medical terminology. What is absent in this episode is that specific description of a reversible ischemic neurologic deficit (RIND)[29] or transient ischemic attack (TIA)[30] which are the neurologist's precise criteria for making a diagnosis of cerebrovascular insufficiency. Viewed in concert with his previous symptoms, as well as his documented hypertension, the supposition by prospective and retrospective evidence of a cerebro-vascular event is possible—but by no means a certainty—given the available clinical description. Nevertheless, Weinstein attaches great significance to the event:

> This meant [in conjunction with the earlier alleged stroke involving his right upper extremity] that the cerebral circulation has been impaired on the right, previously unaffected, side of the brain. This evidence of bilaterality of involvement not only increased the risk of further strokes, but also created the possibility that enduring changes in behavior, based upon insufficient blood supply and impaired oxygenation of the brain, might eventually occur.[31]

The essence of the matter from the historical prespective, Wilson's mild behavior changes notwithstanding, is that significant deleterious effects on his political leadership were simply not in evidence at this time.[32] The extraordinary track record Wilson compiled in domestic legislation during his first four years in office demonstrates that.

In a special session of Congress from April 17, 1913, to October 24, 1914, Wilson orchestrated the longest and one of the most successful such sessions in the nation's history to that time. He obtained a long-sought revision of the tariff with the signing of the Underwood-Simmons Bill. In Alexander and Juliette Georges' estimation "it was a tremendous victory for Wilson. He had overcome an array of interests, which two other Presidents had found invincible."[33] Equally skillful political ma-neuvering and the strong hand of executive leadership thereafter re-sulted in the signing of the Glass-Owen Bill, dealing with banking and currency reform. Concerning legislation on trusts and monopolies, Wil-son's admittedly coercive methods again proved successful, resulting in passage of the Clayton Antitrust Act. These successes, in conjunction with the bill establishing the Federal Trade Commission, underscored Wilson's domination of Congress. "The Sixty-Third Congress adjourned on October 24, 1914. Under Wilson's imperative leadership, it had been one of the most productive sessions in the nation's history," the Georges have concluded.[34] Whatever changes were manifest in Wilson's charac-ter by this time because of neurologic disease did not, then, significantly detract from his executive role. Most investigators, in fact, view Wilson's first term as a major stage in the evolution of the modern American presi-dency. As one writer has noted: "The present-day role of the President as policy-determiner in the legislative field is largely the creation of the two Roosevelts and Woodrow Wilson."[35]

Indeed, Wilson recapitulated his domestic feat in the final year of his first term when he embarked upon another round of progressive legislation. In many ways, the accomplishments of this new phase of progressivism surpassed what had already been done. Adopting the principles of Theodore Roosevelt's New Nationalism, the President pushed through unparalleled measures creating a national regulatory and welfare apparatus intended to promote liberal ends believed unobtainable at the time. This included, among other measures, direct aid to the farm community and protective labor laws. The esteemed scholar Arthur Link has argued that no period of executive leadership had been more productive than what Wilson accomplished in domestic legislation just prior to World War I.[36] Wilson's increasing rigidity and obstinacy in the face of opposition were real enough, yet his record on domestic legislation hardly reveals inconsistent political actions, as some have argued. Such personality traits were to serve him poorly during the ultimate crisis of his career, but to assume that they had any negative effects immediately prior to America's entry into World War I does not square with the facts.

Whatever the nature of the "stroke-like illness" a month after assuming office, its insignificance was underscored by the observations of those close to the President and by its omission from other sources covering the period. The memoirs of neither Grayson nor Tumulty make any significant reference to the event as a stroke. Indeed, Grayson's statement to Colonel Edward House in October that Wilson was in good health indicated that his primary physician was not aware of any sinister underlying disease process at this time.[37] Then, too, the treatment suggested for the "neuritis" of 1913 by the eminent neurologist Francis Dercum implies to the modern-day physician an illness perhaps as nondescript as bursitis or adhesive capsulitis of the shoulder, for Dercum assured Mrs. Wilson that the President's neuritis would respond to "baking and a hot climate," the recommended treatment of the day for aching joints and sore muscles.[38] The reader may recall that Tumulty referred only to a "painful neuritis" during this period, which again would be more suggestive of bursitis than a stroke.[39] Finally, the observation that the President continued to play golf during this period implies what must have been a rather insignificant difficulty with his left arm.[40] Lack of the services of one arm hardly lends itself to a proficient game of golf!

One final myth regarding Wilson's health needs to be dispelled prior to a discussion of those significant factors that did affect his leadership. This is the recurrent and mysterious twitching of his left eye, which plagued him on an intermittent basis for years, particularly when he became fatigued or distressed. All investigators to date have misjudged its significance. Arthur Walworth related the muscle twitching of the upper half of the left side of Wilson's face to the previously described hemorrhage involving his left eye—"the one that had been impaired in 1906"[41]—assuming that there had been some inferential clinical-pathological correlation. Ray Stannard Baker later made note of the facial tic during the Paris Peace Conference after a particularly grueling meeting of negotiations: "I went up to see him, in the evening after the meetings of the Four, . . . his face quite haggard and one side of it and the eye twitching painfully."[42] Wilson's inner circle during the President's later trip to the western states made frequent references to the same phenomenon. Finally, the most knowledgeable of medical observers, Edwin Weinstein, discussed the left facial twitching in some detail, but also failed to grasp its significance. "It seems likely that it was a nervous tic," Weinstein concluded, "rather than a sign of any organic brain involvement, since Wilson noted that the movements came on only when he was upset or overtired."[43]

In point of fact, the phenomenon represented a typical case of "hemifacial spasm." Ascribing any special significance to its occurrence in relation to its effect on Wilson's leadership is not justified, in spite of its well-known propensity to occur during periods of emotional distress. Today neurosurgeons recognize the characteristic clinical picture and are able to treat its cause by surgery to remove the elongated, redundant loop of blood vessel that is found to compress the facial nerve at its exit from the brainstem (see Fig. 1.2). This results in disappearance of the peculiar twitching episodes of the muscles around the eye in well over 85 percent of cases. The most recent medical paper to deal with this now well-known entity was published by Drs. Loeser and Chen in August 1983. They describe the malady in this way:

> Hemifacial spasm is characterized by the insidious development of paroxysmal, involuntary, unilateral, hyperkinetic facial movements. It commonly affects the left side more than the right, and presents typically during the fifth and sixth decades. [Wilson was thirty-nine at the time of its first occurrence in his case.] The abnormal movements are aggravated by emotional stress, fatigue, and facial movement. It almost always starts as a mild intermittent twitch of the orbicularis oculi [muscle of the eyelid], and there are no other associated neurologic deficits.[44]

The differential diagnosis for this phenomenon includes: (1) postparalytic hemifacial spasm (Wilson had never suffered facial paralysis, a necessary antecedent to this diagnosis); (2) habit spasm, which is under voluntary control (effectively dispelled in descriptions of Wilson's case); and (3) focal seizures, which present as brief but severe facial spasms,

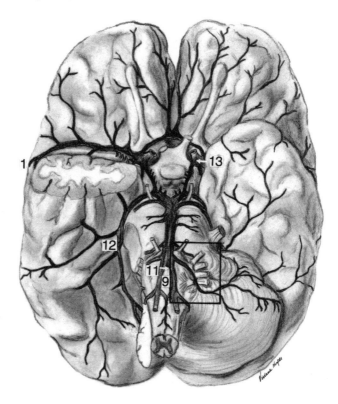

Fig. 1.2 This is a view of the brain and
its vascular supply from below.
The insert illustrates an artery
compressing the facial nerve, giving rise to hemifacial spasm. (8)
Facial nerve; (9) Brainstem; (10)
Compressing artery; (11) Ver-
tebrobasilar arteries; (12) Posterior cerebral artery; (13) Internal carotid artery.

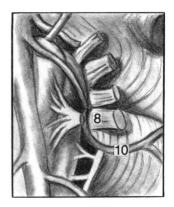

are not related to stress, and usually involve other parts of the same side of the body in concert. With regard to Woodrow Wilson, then, this peculiar, yet identifiable, phenomenon had no relation to his neurologic illness and later deterioration after 1916.

One event, however, undoubtedly did affect his emotional state and consequent leadership capabilities during his first term. In August 1914, his first wife, Ellen, died as a consequence of longstanding nephritis. The evidence is clear that for four to five months thereafter Wilson suffered from a severe reactive depression, the side effects of which include confused thinking and poor memory. Wilson confided to House during this period that "he was unfit to be President because he could not think straight."[45] A few near-disastrous diplomatic repercussions may have resulted from this condition, the most apparent of which was a contrived conflict with Mexico leading to some loss of American lives.[46] Fortunately, cooler heads prevailed, but the example stands as compelling evidence of the effect of an individual's emotional state at the time certain decisions are made.

His wife's death was equally significant in relation to Grayson's handling of the problem, and it presaged a recurrent incriminating scenario in this unique physician-patient relationship. When Mrs. Wilson's death was imminent, Dr. Grayson apparently lacked the courage to tell Wilson or the family the truth. It fell to Dr. Edward P. Davis to do so. Weinstein concluded that "Grayson's status as a virtual member of the family . . . made it difficult for him to act with professional detachment," and he served only to reinforce Wilson's denial of his wife's illness.[47] Later, Grayson was also unable to deal frankly with either Wilson or the nation, which had a right to know of its president's physical condition; his impotence at this juncture is disquietingly significant in retrospect.

By 1917, increasing intransigence and a penchant for personal isolation were becoming permanent features of Woodrow Wilson's leadership. Few of the constructive domestic policies that characterized Wilson's early years in office are found in the record of the second term. Certainly the United States' preoccupation with the war in Europe largely accounts for this absence of domestic legislation. Still, his immediate associates began to be alarmed by Wilson's behavior alone. Robert Lansing, the new Secretary of State after William Jennings Bryan's resignation in 1915 (a resignation spurred, in part, by Wilson's preference for negotiating with Germany and Britain behind Bryan's back), gave this telling assessment of his chief: "The impression made was that he was irritated by opposition to his views, however moderately urged, and that he did not like to have his judgment questioned even in a friendly way."[48] Colonel Edward House recorded in his diary that Grayson had told him:

> If one urges Wilson to do something contrary to his own conviction, he
> ceases to have any liking for that person. He does not like to meet people
> and isolates himself as much as anyone I have ever known. . . . His imme-
> diate entourage, from the Secretary of State down, are having an unhappy
> time just now. He is consulting none of them and they are as ignorant of his
> intentions as the man in the street.[49]

Was this self-imposed isolation and rigidity an early manifestation of
neurologic compromise? The observations of Dr. Lawrence C. Kolb, author of a noted psychiatric textbook, suggest that possibility by inference:

> A certain tendency to isolation occurs [with aging and early dementia]. . . .
> Altruistic sentiments are usually lost early, while egotistic, selfish ones are
> intensified. . . . As the patient with a mild organic brain syndrome becomes
> aware of the gradual impairment of his capacities, there is at first an inten-
> sification of already existing character defenses. . . . He becomes more like
> himself.[50]

Personality traits are exhibited in bolder relief. Rigidity of thought and a
preference for unwarranted discretion become characteristic of such individuals, who increasingly perceive limited alternatives to their own set
of values. Kolb has further observed that as the above "character defenses fail to protect the individual from anxiety, then . . . persecutory
symptoms emerge as a means by which the personality defends against
fears of death and impending loss of functions and satisfactions."[51]
Given what is now known of Wilson's later behavior in Paris and after, in
particular his extreme paranoia regarding Henry Cabot Lodge and the
opposition in the United States Senate, the implications for leadership
under such restrictions are bothersome, to say the least.

America's possible entry into World War I consumed most of the early
weeks of Wilson's second term. To ascribe American entry into the war
to alleged presidential infirmities is of course indefensible. In truth,
Germany's announcement of unrestricted submarine warfare eventually
left the President with no option but to break relations and prepare for
war. But once embarking upon an undeclared naval war, and unencum-
bered by congressional control, Wilson reverted to virtual character
assassination when encountering strong resistance in the Senate.[52] Heretofore, in the battles over domestic legislation, the President had exercised a very strong hand, but he had kept enough friends in appropriate
places to assure him dramatic successes in the legislative arena. With
the storm clouds of war gathering, however, the negative aspects of
Wilson's evolving character seemed to darken accordingly. "A little
group of willful men," he charged, "representing no opinion but their
own, have rendered the great Government of the United States helpless
and contemptible."[53] Such slander betrayed his political intuition. For

*Woodrow Wilson at the time of America's entry into World
War I, 1917*

here he was grossly misrepresenting the facts and cruelly impugning the
patriotism of his opponents. (He would do so again in the 1918 election
campaign; see p. 17.) In truth, the majority of senators believed that
they were upholding the country's tradition of not permitting the President to wage undeclared war without the consent of Congress.[54] Modern
medical thought in relation to cerebrovascular-induced dementia now
offers a plausible contribution to understanding Wilson's behavior: A
gradual decline is first seen in dementia suspects as defects of memory
and then errors in judgment. Some individuals become irritable, aggressive, and quarrelsome.[55] Moreover, there is virtually no insight into the
disease process in most of those afflicted.[56]

During this period Wilson was clearly troubled with illness. Along with his succession of possible TIA's on the basis of systemic hypertension, Wilson's headaches returned. The diaries of both Colonel House and Edith Wilson substantiate their increasing frequency during this period. He had, in fact, earlier experienced "four days of blinding headaches" during the events that precipitated William Jennings Bryan's resignation.[57] Although his blood pressure was not recorded in the medical record, Wilson was put to bed on several occasions, often for as long as ten days, on account of "a cold." Weinstein suspected that such a lengthy confinement would not be typical for a common cold, and that Grayson may have ordered him to bed on account of elevated blood pressure.[58] Irwin Hoover, Wilson's personal valet, is reported to have said on March 31: "I never knew him to be more peevish. He's out of sorts, doesn't feel well, and has a headache."[59]

Two days later Wilson reluctantly convened a special session of Congress to announce the United States' entry into the war. Having been assailed by doubt up to this point about the wisdom of doing so, he thereafter pursued his chosen course with a stubborn belief in the righteousness of America's cause. According to the Georges Wilson's "pattern of decision-making—replacing extreme uncertainty with extreme certainty—was characteristic of the man."[60] Perhaps so. Yet other subsequent displays of inflexibility began to suggest not only a recurrent but an unhealthy pattern in dealing with those opposed to his policies. Indeed, from the moment war was declared, Wilson's rigid thinking transformed itself into unbridled paranoia in dealing with the opposition.

The Overman Act, passed in May 1918 at Wilson's insistence to give sharply increased powers to the executive over the legislative branch in wartime, was but the first in a series of perhaps necessary but ultimately counterproductive measures that alienated the very support he would eventually require to bring his postwar visions for a League of Nations to fruition. Given the problems that confront any nation in wartime, such a call for broadened executive authority was not necessarily out of line. Following on the heels of other actions that had been perceived as autocratic, however, the vehemence with which Wilson pursued his goals aroused considerable bipartisan concern. According to the *New York Times*, "The measure, which came from the President . . . was criticized . . . as intended to provide assumption of the entire power of Government by the Executive. Leaders in the Senate, Democrats and Republicans alike, showed anger . . . over the proposal."[61] The Georges concluded that Wilson's purpose was to enhance his authority and to exercise it without any restrictions.[62] In response to a suggestion that he form a bipartisan Cabinet, Wilson wrote Tumulty that he was "utterly opposed to anything of the sort."[63] If he perceived that playing one party off against the other was a necessary evil in the face of the Lodge-Roosevelt forces aligned against him, his tactics nonetheless in one sense violated his obligation to maintain national unity in time of war—with consequent fateful implications at war's end.

Wilson further extended the concept that Democratic partisanship was synonymous with patriotism by his injurious call shortly thereafter in the midterm election campaign for a national referendum on his policies. He outlined this plan in a letter on October 26, 1918. Attorney General Thomas W. Gregory commented:

> The letter was not merely the worst political mistake that he could make, but it was utterly un-Wilsonian. . . . [It] seemed to stigmatize everyone who was not a member of the Democratic Party, and it immediately raised an electoral issue and gave an opportunity to the Republicans which up to then had been lacking. . . . It seems probable to me that Wilson decided to write the letter in a moment of extreme weariness . . . at the end of a long session when his nerves were taut and his intellectual sentinels were not on the lookout for danger. Otherwise I cannot conceive of his writing the letter which, . . . is so thoroughly un-Wilsonian.[64]

This represented his first great political mistake as President. Weinstein admitted that "the action itself was, of course, not indicative of any impairment of brain function, but that what was disturbing was the language."[65] Wilson proclaimed: "The leaders of the minority in the present Congress have been unquestionably pro-war, but they have been anti-Administration. . . . The return of a Republican majority to either House of Congress would . . . be interpreted on the other side of the water as a repudiation of my leadership."[66] The President's statement, when weighed against the backdrop of Republican support for the war effort up to this time (even if Lodge and Roosevelt had remained personally anti-Wilson), was perceived as a challenge and an insult to those Republicans who had put party affiliation aside to work for the common goal of victory.

Few statesmen of the day, or historians thereafter, viewed this appeal as a positive step. Even though Wilson had been goaded by the likes of a Lodge or a Roosevelt on a personal level since 1916, his alacrity in throwing down the gauntlet against all those of the opposing party was an exercise of shortsightedness if not self-destruction. Not only was he risking losing the good will of many Republicans who saw merit in his war effort and peace plan, but he was also ignoring the time-honored observation that midterm congressional elections traditionally revolve around local issues—not to mention the fact that the party out of power usually makes gains, regardless of the issues involved.

This was clearly an uncharacteristic failure of political intuition on

Wilson's part, for which he bore sole responsibility. The decision was his own. William McAdoo had not been consulted. Robert Lansing believed it "an injudicious and unwarranted attack upon the loyalty of his political opponents." Vance McCormick, the Chairman of the National Democratic Committee, warned the President that "if it went out as written, it would be misunderstood and react against him. He could not be made to see that it would be misconstrued."[67]

Wilson's insight failed him in three respects: first, in repudiating potential political friends; second, in ignoring historical trends of off-year elections; and, third, in failing to perceive that a defeat of local Democrats at the polls might be on some other basis than his leadership. Current knowledge of the "organic brain syndrome" offers some understanding of Wilson's behavior. According to Zbigniew Lipowski, "Impaired control of the expression of emotions and impulses is the cardinal feature of this disorder. Foresight and the ability to anticipate the social or legal consequences of one's actions are typically diminished."[68]

Other peculiar responses to stress had become commonplace in Wilson's behavior that year. In March, after the German breakthrough during the Second Battle of the Marne, the British made a public appeal for American reinforcements. Rather than carefully weighing the necessity and consequences of such an action, as would be in keeping with the spirit of Allied cooperation, Wilson quashed the appeal with a quick retort demanding the British Ambassador's recall. At least part of his motivation for doing so may have stemmed from his paranoid inference that the British were implying that prior American aid was insufficient. Wilson's anxiety appeared to reach new heights when he thereafter ordered the American embassy in London to deny the Prime Minister of Australia a visa after hearing of his desire to come to the United States on a speaking tour. Wilson feared that he might make pronouncements favoring economic sanctions against Germany, a position the President strongly opposed. Not only was Wilson being inconsiderate of reasonable Allied military requests, he was unable to allow the presentation in public of proposals ostensibly alien to his own thought in propagating the war effort and planning for the peace. That such improprieties may have been due to his changing character is suggested by the observations of Louis D. Brandeis in August 1918: "Wilson had been a bold and independent leader before then, but after that time, his judgment was not as good as it had been before," and "he did things which were 'unnatural' to him."[69]

Wilson's tunnel vision extended to other political developments of his day on the eve of the Armistice and the Peace Conference in Paris. First, David Lloyd George was swept to overwhelming victory on his pledge to the British people for "the Draconian peace demanded by a public full of hatred of the Germans."[70] Second, Georges Clemenceau received a resounding vote of confidence in the French Chamber of Deputies for his proclamation adhering to "the old system of alliances called the 'balance of power.'" In doing so, he had made it clear that he was unwilling to entrust French security to the proposals outlined with "noble simplicity (*noble candeur*)" by President Wilson.[71] Moreover, as Ray Stannard Baker observed on October 15, 1918, "The leaders in Europe are also secretly irritated by the preponderance of Wilson in diplomacy, the way in which the Germans talk over their heads to the man in the White House, and the way in which . . . he takes the responsibility upon himself of a kind of arbiter of the world's destiny."[72]

That Wilson may have been blind to these developments was implied by the Georges: "His evaluation of public opinion" they state, "seems not to have been affected one whit by these external events." He was swept along shortly thereafter on his arrival in Europe by cheering throngs of Europeans, who embraced his message of peace with enthusiasm. The height of his unrealistic appraisal of events would be reached with his arrival in Paris; establishment of the League, he believed, would cause other difficult problems to disappear.[73]

Wilson's decision to attend the Conference in the first place raised concern in the minds of some contemporaries then and many historians today. He apparently never gave any consideration to not going, fervently believing that any "dangerous and destructive agreements" reached beforehand by the other Allied leaders could only be prevented by his assumption of leadership there.[74] His response to Robert Lansing's unwelcome advice not to go was typical of the manner in which he dealt with opposition thereafter. He merely listened to Lansing's remarks without comment and then turned to other matters.[75] This behavior is consistent with that of many aging individuals, who either react defensively or ignore alternative points of view that do not square with their own narrow perceptions. Nor do they choose to explain themselves when challenged. It is significant that such a favorable chronicler of events as Ray Stannard Baker listed this characteristic as typical of Wilson: "He seemed incapable of presenting or dramatizing his own actions. . . . He can tell what he thinks and hopes and believes, . . . but he has no genius for telling what he did."[76]

Herbert Hoover also believed there were drawbacks to Wilson's decision to attend the Conference. He later asserted that a crucial American weakness at the peace table was one of lack of diplomats skilled and experienced in the art of diplomacy,[77] a weakness that Wilson insured when he preempted the diplomats' role. Hoover further observed that "the President was met with settings unfamiliar to him and obstacles he had never imagined," and concluded that "American idealism was unfit to participate in a game played with power as the counters."[78] From the medical perspective, Hoover's observation concerning unfamiliar surroundings and unexpected obstacles is of interest insofar as these conditions might impact on a neurologically compromised individual. Dr. Marcel Kinsbourne has graphically elucidated this theme:

> Thrusting the old person into a novel environment [has been observed to] so overburden his cerebral system . . . that he becomes over-aroused and disoriented, or will withdraw. It is well recognized that to take an old person out of his familiar home setting . . . may completely disorient him and render his behavior senseless.[79]

Not that Wilson was old chronologically, but physiologically the record suggests that he was experiencing rather rapid cognitive and emotional changes on the basis of hypertension and cerebrovascular disease. This is not to say that his behavior became "senseless" or his awareness "disoriented"; these are the extremes of that condition. But subtle changes consistent with an early dementia were becoming manifest at the time he ventured to Paris in an encounter with forces he was poorly prepared to understand. As a trained historian, Hoover asserted, Wilson was no doubt familiar with the age-old destructive European forces that operated at the negotiating table, but sadly, "he did not seem to realize their dynamism."[80]

One way in which a compromised individual defends against unfamiliarity and uncertainty is to prepare as assiduously as possible for any eventualities he might encounter in a new setting. It is on this basis of preparation in particular that Woodrow Wilson was found wanting. His failure to take advisors from outside his own party was but one example. No Republican senators accompanied him to Paris. Josephus Daniels defended Wilson's decision in this matter by asserting that his failure to appoint any Republican senators to the Peace Commission was based on the conviction that these senators should not frame a treaty that could go into effect only by their later voting on it.[81]

In this sense, Wilson's rigid morality adversely affected a situation that demanded both compromise and a sense of team play to accomplish the objective. The President failed to recognize that he needed a spokesman in the Senate to defend his interests, a self-defeating stance in view of his later proclivity to neglect that responsibility himself. Instead, he would choose to take his case to the people. If this was his plan all along, then his inability to foresee the need to cultivate such a spokesman in his absence represented a critical lack of foresight. As Daniels was forced to admit: "Experience has shown that Senators . . . resent exclusion from negotiation in framing treaties." He concluded that, "as matters turned out in Paris, it would have been wiser if Bryan and Taft had been named instead of House and Lansing."[82]

Not that the role of the commissioners was all that important in Paris. Even Ray Stannard Baker was critical of Wilson in this regard:

> Undoubtedly he did not take his own commissioners into consultation as much as he should have done; he is too much the solitary worker; he delegates authority with difficulty; he has too little appreciation of the need of explanation, conference, team play. . . . He had thought out his principles and set his course. . . . They were his faith. . . . And they were unchangeable.[83]

Wilson's colleagues must have wondered: Why obtain facts and information if they were to have no chance of changing the President's prevailing view? Alternatively, in reviewing the course of events, it might be asked whether Wilson may have obtained the facts but assimilated them poorly into his principles and opinions. His proposed plan of operation envisioned preliminary examination of specific issues by "dispassionate" technical commissions before they were considered by the Big Four. Yet even Baker noted the plan's limited effectiveness, given Wilson's proclivity for rigid adherence to views worked out largely by himself in isolation.[84]

Wilson had prepared himself for the Peace Conference with the help of The Inquiry, a group of experts assembled from the beginning of September 1917 to study the war aims of the belligerents and to advise him in developing an American peace program. The President undoubtedly benefited from their advice early on, enough to use their recommendations as a guide in preparing the Fourteen Points Address of January 4, 1918. In one sense, then, his willingness to take "common counsel," as he termed it, galvanized his thinking in formulating his planned program. In this respect, he was prepared. But subsequent events cast a new light on Arthur Link's assertion that "Wilson was the best-informed and on the whole the wisest man among the statesmen assembled there."[85] Observations by Baker and others, including Colonel House, reveal the reverse side of the coin: Once in Paris, and despite the presence of some individuals who had sat in on The Inquiry, the President rarely sought advice on what he perceived to be the substantive issues. He labored alone.

Wilson hoped to represent the "new order" against the "older order" of balance-of-power politics played by traditional diplomats preoccupied with accommodating their own limited programs of self-interest. Yet Baker acknowledged that at Paris "we find the old order in advance of the new in presenting its programme." The reason for this is clear, and it rests with the lack of preparedness in specifics by the spokesmen for the new order, including Wilson. "The Conference," Baker concluded, "improvised as it went along and met each problem as it arose."[86]

Others were even more critical of the President's lack of preparedness and absence of a defined program. Robert Lansing asserted that Wilson "talked a good deal about 'taking common counsel,' but showed no disposition to put it into practice." He firmly believed that both Wilson's lack of preparedness and his preference for isolation were out of character for him when compared with their working relations in the past and felt they reflected the President's inexplicable naiveté or denial of circumstances as they existed at the Conference. Concerning the former, Lansing acknowledged that "there was a general belief that Mr. Wilson was not open-minded . . . [yet] I had not found him so during the years we had been associated." With regard to the latter, he asserted before the Conference that "from the little I know of the President's plan, I am sure that it is impracticable. . . . No account is taken of national selfishness and the mutual suspicions which control international relations. It may be noble thinking, but it is not true thinking."[87]

Baker agreed: With the armistice, "the spirit of unity began to disintegrate. The Allies had not, after all, common purposes." The old governments and the old system were in control. The reasons for this development were painfully obvious to American participants at Versailles. The President knew his own convictions but failed to educate others to them. Nor had he prepared contingency plans for specific situations he was likely to encounter. While Lansing devoted an entire chapter in his memoirs to the lack of a specific American program (for which he viewed Wilson to be at fault), Baker succinctly observed in this respect that the President had not prepared for "the 'items' of the peace, but [only for] the creative principles of it."[88]

Indeed, it appears that it was not until Wilson arrived in Paris that he addressed himself to any consideration of specifics. As Baker perceived: "Any leader who rejects an old method of settlement must be able to assert and explain a new method. Thus President Wilson was forced . . . to defend a system which he and his commission on the League of Nations had not yet had time to work out!"[89] Wilson left such details to Colonel House in the early sessions, and only to him, a fact that left various other members of the United States Commission in consternation even before the Conference began. Henry White, Robert Lansing, and Tasker Bliss were at a loss as to how they were to contribute to the proceedings. Bliss wrote in December of being "disquieted to see how hazy and vague our ideas are," and in January "that he was disturbed because he did not know the President's exact views on various problems."[90]

The record reflects that in matters of detail, particularly economic matters, Wilson in fact had few definitive views; he admitted that such details did not interest him.[91] This observation may assume some significance when one recalls certain tactical ploys mildly demented individuals use when forced to assimilate new or unfamiliar material. He or she may try to conceal intellectual and memory deficits by directing the conversation to familiar and well-remembered themes, as efficiency falters when faced with a large pool of information.[92] Viewed from this perspective, the principles Wilson did espouse, such as acceptance of the League Covenant into the peace settlement, may arguably be said to have represented such "familiar and well-remembered themes" for him.

Perceiving most problems only in generalities, the President believed that a functioning League would resolve all the economic entanglements. But as Baker cogently observed, this assumption required two prior conditions that did not in fact exist: first, that all nations subdue their immediate political interests, and second, that clear and strong action be taken on economic problems that could not be ignored. Wilson was largely responsible for the failure to achieve the second prerequisite. The Conference, which he led from the beginning, "did its best," according to Baker, "to avoid both the immediate economic problems of relief and the permanent problems of international economic coöperation."[93] Insisting that Europe first put its own economic house in order before the United States would help further, the President's position became an exercise in delusion as he ignored the obvious: Europe could not possibly reconstruct its house without prior American economic aid. It is perhaps significant in the end that most of the meaningful gains on economic issues were made during the last two months of the Conference, after Wilson had departed for the United States.

On the logistical level, the problem of dealing with such mundane matters as paperwork underscored the theme of lack of preparedness. The President had made no arrangements for an adequate clerical staff at the Conference. "It was a constant grief to me," House later wrote in his diary, "to see him working in his lonely, inefficient way when there was so much depending upon the conserving of his strength and keeping his mind clear for sound judgment."[94] On a more strategic level, Wilson's consuming interest in establishing the League overrode all considerations of a more substantive nature—including the British and French preoccupation with negotiating specific territorial and economic settlements. Given such a limited perspective, the Georges conclude that Wilson ignored those "psychological characteristics of his negotiating adversaries" while planning obstinately to advance his own objectives.[95]

Robert Lansing later summarized the effect on the proceedings of Wilson's lack of preparedness, for which the President substituted inflexible generalities:

> President Wilson's inherent dislike to depart in the least from an announced course, . . . seems to me to have been the most potent influence in deter-

mining his method of work. . . . Even when there could be no doubt that in view of changed conditions it was wise to change a policy, . . . he clung to it with peculiar tenacity. . . . Mr. Wilson's mind once made up seemed to become inflexible. It appeared to grow impervious to arguments and even to facts. It lacked the elasticity and receptivity which have always been characteristic of sound judgement and right thinking. . . . This rigidity of mind accounts in large measure . . . for the President's failure to prepare or to adopt a programme at Paris. . . . He dealt in generalities.[96]

Given what is now known of neurologically restricted individuals, such a predisposition in Wilson's case is understandable, if not defensible. Acknowledging that Wilson's physical and mental compromise was to become accelerated at later phases of the Conference, what is disquieting to note, then, are the numerous examples of enforced isolation and inattention to detail even during the earliest stages of the Paris Peace Conference. These graphically portray the increasingly limited mental and psychological reserves of a President physically assaulted by hypertension and cerebrovascular insufficiency. Dr. Kurt Goldstein has designated this condition a "reduced ability to apply the abstract attitude":

Thinking is more or less impoverished, labored, superficial, and concrete. The patient finds it difficult to appreciate various aspects of a problem and to shift purposefully from one aspect of it to another. He displays perseveration and circumstantiality that reflect rigidity of thinking. The ability to reason logically and to make sound judgments is more or less defective.[97]

Failing to appreciate the close ties Lloyd George, Clemenceau, and Italy's Vittorio Orlando had developed during the war years, and discounting the fact that he was thrusting himself as an unknown quantity into their midst, Wilson chose to isolate himself from those assistants who would have been of invaluable assistance in educating him to other leaders' way of thinking and their goals. Instead, he had chosen as his only advisor an alter ego in Colonel House, who had achieved and maintained his prominent position only by making judiciously sycophantic responses to presidential whim and opinion. Ironically, this relationship in itself had limitations that would eventually surface, as House expressed some hidden dissatisfaction with his mentor, probably on the basis of his own desire to head the United States Peace Commission.[98] It was precisely this conflict, which blossomed during Wilson's later absence from the Conference, that ultimately drove the wedge between the two, assuring Wilson's isolation.

By the summer of 1918 his penchant for secrecy and increasing defensiveness served to paint the President into his own corner. He became even less discreet in his personal criticisms of others. In Arthur Link's estimation, Wilson not only had undergone a personality change but had lost his sense of timing. More petulant in his behavior and more ascerbic with his remarks, he was prepared to "bully the Council of Four" in Paris, if necessary, as his paranoia grew.[99] Nor could he feel free to consult with Gilbert Hitchcock, his designated party leader in the Senate, because he no longer felt he could trust him with information. Moreover, Wilson barred other key individuals from participation in upcoming proceedings, people who would have been of immense value to him in an advisory capacity. "I would not dare take Mr. Taft. I have lost all confidence in his character," he complained. "And the other prominent Republicans . . . are already committed to do everything possible to prevent the Peace Conference from acting upon the peace terms which they have already agreed to."[100]

During the latter part of 1918 there is substantial evidence that Wilson's memory was failing. He confided to House that his mind had become "leaky." Then, too, just before his departure for Paris, "he made decisions which he later forgot." Under such restrictions, his tendency to isolate himself was detrimental, as the presence of a structured personal staff would have at least kept him abreast of the lesser details that he chose to ignore. With respect to the increasingly complex issues bearing down upon Wilson during 1918, his behavior may be seen from the psychological perspective as, in Weinstein's words, "a defense against feelings of incapacity and a sense that he was no longer in control of his environment."[101] From the neurological perspective, on the other hand, his compromised memory and inattention to detail may have been a reflection of early dementia. "Memory impairment," according to Zbigniew Lipowski, "is typically an early and prominent feature of progressive dementia. There is usually forgetfulness or anterograde amnesia, reflecting difficulty in learning new material and in relating to current experiences."[102]

At the time of his arrival in Paris on January 7, the President was physically worn out, albeit emotionally bolstered by confidence that Walworth described as "all-possessing."[103] Wilson's belief in his own indispensability had been magnified by the cheering crowds that had greeted him throughout Europe just prior to the Conference. This was further augmented once he achieved a notable early success with the adoption of the Smuts Resolution, which in essence assured that the framing of a League Covenant took precedence over divisions of the spoils. What he failed to perceive, however, was that there were strong reasons for the British and French to have acquiesced to such an agreement as early as they did. As the Georges point out:

Plainly, the British Prime Minister had gained the impression in his first encounter with Wilson that he could trade his approval for the immediate formation of a league (not a very great concession on his part, since a league was part and parcel of the British program!) for Wilson's agreement to certain British proposals, the adoption of which would conflict with the Fourteen Points.[104]

Having read Wilson correctly, both Lloyd George and Clemenceau quickly realized that the President's deep personal involvement with the concept of the League was something they could successfully exploit. Indeed, one observer ruefully acknowledged the deep personal and psychological importance of the matter to Wilson by observing that "the League to Wilson was like a toy to a child—he would not be happy until he got it."[105]

As events developed, however, the French were soon to see Wilson as the main obstacle to a guarantee of their immediate security. The President perceived this as an affront, believing incorrectly that the increasingly intransigent French were acting disagreeably only on account of his suspected sympathy toward the smaller nations. Thereafter, according to Walworth, he "burned with resentment," and became "doubly secretive and suspicious."[106] In point of fact, European statesmen justifiably feared that they might be left to cope with their postwar economic problems without American assistance, and it was in their interest to make the League Covenant acceptable to the United States Senate. Yet it was this potential leverage that Wilson neglected to utilize later, due to his personal distaste for having to pay open deference to his Senate foes, who opposed America's entry into the League under Wilson's proposed format.[107]

To be sure, Woodrow Wilson's medical condition in relation to these events is but a part of the story. Ray Stannard Baker's account of the Paris Peace Conference substantiates that there were formidable differences and potential conflicts between the Old Order and the New, as embodied in the interests of France and the United States respectively. In order to understand the conflicts Wilson encountered during the first month of the Conference, one must recognize that, whereas America had no specific program other than the acceptance of the general principles of the New Order, the French were prepared to present very specific proposals grounded in Old Order concerns for self-interest and security. This is the theme developed in Baker's work *Woodrow Wilson and World Settlement*.[108]

Baker underscored the pervading problem that concerned Wilson during the opening sessions of the Conference. By November 1918 America had obtained the solemn promise of the Allies that peace would be made on the basis of the Fourteen Points.[109] Considering what transpired thereafter, Baker was compelled to make the following observation:

*Lloyd George, Clemenceau, Orlando, and Wilson in Paris, 1919*

> The President—and America—sincerely believed that the nations of Europe meant what they said. . . .
> But he did not then understand . . . how terribly the nations had suffered from the war, how bitter they had grown. . . . Nor did he realize that the same reaction—less violent, perhaps—was soon to take place in his own country.[110]

For a man who fervently believed that he knew and spoke for the people, Wilson's failure to perceive the evolution of such sentiment until the eleventh hour is telling. He was dismayed to find that the European allies wanted economic, reparational, and military settlements to be made first and to be in accord with the provisions of the treaties signed during the war. "The League," said Baker, "was to come afterward—if at all!"[111]

The French in particular arrived at Paris with a specific program, planned in advance and based on their deeply entrenched preoccupation with security against Germany. This program included the following salient features, most of which were ultimately gained by Clemenceau:

1. French military control of the Rhine.
2. A permanent alliance of the Great Powers to help France maintain this control.

3.  Smaller allies to menace Germany from the east.

4.  A territorial reduction of the German Empire.

5.  Crippling of German political organization.

6.  Disarmament of Germany, but not the Allies.

7.  Imposition of a crushing indemnity upon Germany.

8.  A strict reduction in German economic resources.

9.  Commercial agreements preferential to France.[112]

Add to this the Italian claims to portions of Austria-Hungary and Japanese claims in China and the Pacific, and it becomes readily understandable how the pious but intransigent American president found himself "almost alone to face enormous and overwhelming difficulties" during this "Dark Period."[113]

True, Wilson did achieve two major early victories. On January 25, the League of Nations was made an integral part of the treaty of peace, and on February 14 the concept of the Covenant was unanimously accepted. Yet Wilson's obstinate methods had irritated the opposition, and they would continue to do so. Even prior to arriving in Paris, he had refused to consent to a French proposal to include the costs of the war in Germany's planned payments. After arriving, he reminded his colleagues of his victory of January 25 by uncompromisingly reiterating on March 15 that the League must be an integral part of the Treaty. Two days later he effectively circumvented an elaborate French scheme to obtain perpetual control over the military and naval affairs of Germany. Shortly thereafter he was instrumental in defeating a proposal to make the League for all intents and purposes a military alliance for the defense of France.[114]

If Wilson had seemingly overcome the Old Order and the "slump in idealism" after the Armistice, he was still on unstable diplomatic ground.[115] The European allies felt they had been defeated. Great Britain did not get the immediate partition of German colonies it had sought, and the French had accepted the Covenant only with the hope of either obtaining the settlements they wanted before the League was brought into being or creating the kind of League they wanted, which would consist of a strong centralized organization backed by powerful military forces. Ultimately, they got neither.[116] More injurious still, Wilson's departure for the United States in February proved detrimental to the gains already achieved.[117] The forces of the New Order were left in their infancy to fend for themselves. The respite provided the opportunity for Lloyd George and Clemenceau to institute their own grand design "to commit the Conference with a *fait accompli* and so raise the expectations of the people for speedy settlements, that the President [on his return] would be unable to stem the tide."[118]

The battlelines between French self-interest and Wilson's idealistic principles were rapidly being drawn and fortified, with the effect that the negotiations entered what Baker termed the "Dark Period" of the Conference upon Wilson's return. This roughly encompassed the last three weeks in March, prior to another significant illness that afflicted Wilson on April 3. Progress came to a standstill as neither side would yield; Wilson fought for the New Order of open diplomacy, while Clemenceau defended the Old. In order to understand how this desultory state of affairs had evolved out of a very hopeful beginning, it is necessary to review certain critical developments during the weeks antedating the Dark Period.

Prior to Wilson's departure in mid-February, the President had actually accomplished the essence of what he was seeking. What disability he possessed at the time appears to have been only intermittently manifest on the surface, since he dealt with matters that interested him with clarity and conciseness in the early days of the Conference. "In contrast with the meetings of the Council of Ten that Wilson attended in the mornings," Arthur Walworth has noted, "the sessions of the League Commission were more delight than duty to a man whose lifelong hobby had been the study and the making of constitutions." [119] The content of the meetings affected his performance accordingly. Whereas his limitations were often made obvious to many during the tedious and often nonproductive morning sessions, his powers of intellect and persuasion did surface in relation to those matters that preoccupied him.

This observation does not negate the dementia thesis. Such an individual's limitations become obvious only when confronted with tasks that demand choice or assimilation of new information. With familiar themes he may remain comfortable, and his deficiencies are not so obvious. As Goldstein has described:

> A patient with impairment of the abstract attitude may not appear to deviate grossly from normal in everyday behavior. . . . In a variety of situations, however, he does not react like a normal individual. He appears more stereotyped and reserved; he seems to lack initiative and spontaneity. Tasks which demand choice or shifting particularly reveal the deficit. [120]

Wilson's abilities, therefore, may not have been grossly impaired during the first half of the Conference, yet his interests were limited, and he paid more heed to these than to the needs of the hour. In essence, he chose to ignore certain realities of Western Europe in order to deal with what was more familiar—a characteristic feature of aging individuals with limited intellectual reserves. Still, Walworth was to allude to "Wilson's presiding genius" during certain of these meetings. [121] If one accepts the definition of the word as representing a single-minded devotion to a limited problem, such a streak of "genius" may have reflected physiologically induced single-mindedness on Wilson's part, and nothing more. This intransigence would represent the first seed of frustration planted in the soil separating the battlelines drawn between Clemenceau and Wilson.

A second vexing problem arose that served to substantiate the impression that the President was becoming increasingly isolated. When Wilson departed from Paris on February 15, he left Colonel House in charge of affairs there. Illness once again played a major role in the events. As House wrote in his diary, "When I fell sick in January, . . . I lost the thread of affairs and I am not sure that I have ever gotten fully back."[122] The thread was critical, as House had been left in Paris to conduct negotiations without any specific instructions from Wilson, a situation never satisfactorily explained thereafter.

Nor can it be assumed that House would have performed well at any rate, given his limited experience. Herbert Hoover later asserted that at the beginning House had been "entirely ignorant of European politics and the forces behind the statesmen who were in control."[123] If such an inexperienced man was to represent America's interests in Wilson's absence, one would expect some guidance from above during the period. None was forthcoming. The record confirms that during this interlude Wilson responded negatively to his representative's messages. Dispatches from Paris, viewed through the President's increasingly distorted perspective, gave the impression that House had consented at one point to the heresy of separating Covenant and Treaty, when in actuality House had merely discussed with his secretary the possibility of doing so as a means of appeasing the Senate.[124] Under the doubly adverse circumstances of disease and distrust, House eventually fell from favor.

Others were to suffer identical fates. Wilson was noted to be relying more on the intense loyalty of his subordinates during the course of the negotiations than on the inherent worth of their advice. By way of example, Herbert Hoover's allegiance came into question when he advanced his views concerning the treaty's negative impact on the economic recovery of Europe; he was thereafter effectively barred from advising the President.[125] Similarly, Robert Lansing's occasionally critical comments and unsolicited advice became an increasingly onerous burden for the sensitive President to bear. With his rejection of House in particular, Wilson's isolation was now complete.

Why then had Wilson dramatically turned against his most trusted friend and advisor? Certainly House's unsatisfactory relationship with the President's second wife, Edith Galt Wilson, was one factor. Her persistently negative appraisal of House was bound to sow seeds of discord. Vice-President Thomas R. Marshall stated the problem another way: "I am not going to get myself entangled with Mrs. Wilson. No politician ever exposes himself to the hatred of a woman, particularly if she is the wife of the President of the United States."[126] She was a force to be reckoned with, and the nation would discover this after Wilson's devastating stroke later the same year.

More important is an understanding of the unique relationship between the two men and how it had changed. House's capacity for enhancing the President's self-esteem by accepting his opinions at face value was the catalyst of Wilson's affection. Only now House began to give unwelcome advice regarding Wilson's relationship to the Senate, urging a course of moderation and compromise. As the Georges point out, "So far from serving as a purveyor of psychological tranquility, then, House now added to Wilson's burdens."[127]

House was given an official position in Paris and undertook policy negotiations in Wilson's absence. Even though he had been instructed to do so by the President, this may have aroused Wilson's jealousy, as the Colonel "was 'feeling his oats' and greatly enjoyed his new role as a statesman in his own right."[128] Wilson therefore felt he had grounds for distrust and isolated himself from that discomfiture. Baker nevertheless implied that Wilson's distrust of House's motives, at least, may have been misplaced: House "never intended for a moment to be disloyal to the President. . . . But the real effect of his action here . . . was to confuse everything." On February 24, for example, House expressed the naive conviction that "in reality no difference of opinion existed between the Members of the Conference." As Baker's account made clear, however, "the deepest and the most vital differences did exist, . . . it was a naked difference of principle."[129]

If perceived disloyalty from his own delegation mortified Wilson, Lloyd George's shifting allegiance appeared to erode his potential support even further. The Prime Minister's lack of guiding principles was a great disappointment to the President. Baker accused Lloyd George of having "failed the President utterly while he was absent in America." Their respective approaches to the French were different, and Wilson found no solace in the Prime Minister's proclivity to "whittle down each French demand as it was presented,"[130] rather than to oppose the demands in toto on the basis of principle, as Wilson preferred. It appears, then, that the President's isolation from his closest advisors, his transient absence from the proceedings, and his philosophical divorce from his negotiating allies all combined to represent the second seed of the discord that blighted any common ground of the Dark Period.

The third seed derived from Wilson's penchant for secrecy; he simply rejected the potentially useful tool of publicity. This was exemplified on the home front by the President's failure to improve his public relations.

He failed to convince his detractors that a League was needed, or that the Covenant agreed to was the best obtainable.[131] The American public fervently desired some knowledge of what had actually transpired thus far at the Conference. This he failed to give them. Baker firmly believed that "one of the greatest mistakes made at the conference . . . was a want of better understanding of what happened there and the exact reasons why . . . the President decided as he did." Baker also thought that "a much broader publicity, a constructive publicity, could have been had at the conference, and this view was frequently urged upon the President."[132]

One of Wilson's most inexplicable qualities, as has been described, was his inability to explain himself or his actions. His failure to take advice on this issue, then, was tragically consistent. Here is one cogent example of the "failure of the abstract attitude" that Goldstein has described in relation to neurologically compromised individuals: "The individual fails if he has to give an account to himself (and others) for acts and for thoughts."[133] Baker himself recognized the implications of Wilson's medical condition in relation to this issue:

> One element in this aloofness that grew more pronounced . . . was the state of his health. . . . Often at the close of the day . . . he seemed utterly beaten down, worn out. . . . At Paris, where so much depended upon the right publicity and the support of world public opinion, these temperamental and physical limitations were costly indeed.[134]

Bear in mind that this was not an observation tendered by a detractor in the mold of a Lansing or a Lodge. This was the assessment of a close confidant and admirer of the President. As telling an indictment as this proved to be, there remains a contradiction in Wilson between the image and the reality of the man that cannot pass without comment: Here was a leader ostensibly speaking for the people, yet inexplicably restricting their access to the facts they required to judge the case their spokesman was championing! A failure of the abstract attitude on the basis of a subtle yet progressive restriction of the intellect might well explain this contradiction. It may represent one measure of that progression that Wilson's failure to perceive the benefits of constructive publicity in educating his following was to become more obvious thereafter. Even greater restrictions were placed on what was revealed after the President's return from America in March.[135]

These, then, were three of the most recognizable seeds of discord that restricted any meaningful progress in the negotiations following Wilson's return. From the medical perspective, it is noteworthy that these three factors—obstinacy and intransigence, increasing isolation, and a predisposition to secrecy—also frequently characterize patients suffering from an evolving dementia or organic brain syndrome. Their influence was negative, if not self-destructive, during the first two months of the conference.

Several other aberrations from Wilson's established policies became manifest during the period coinciding with the President's physical decline. Early on, Wilson had in effect violated his principle of "open covenants, openly arrived at" by urging that a small council composed of England, France, Italy, and the United States meet secretly over the question of their commitment to the League.[136] Later, in response to Orlando's support for the League, Wilson sinned against his doctrine of self-determination by approving the cession of the Trentino to Italy.[137] These actions represented contradictions Robert Lansing could not ignore, and he described the negative impact of these apparent breaks with Wilsonian principle. "His secret negotiations," Lansing declared, "caused the majority of the delegates . . . and the public at large to lose in a large measure their confidence in the actuality of his devotion to 'open diplomacy.'"[138]

If the above compromises were necessarily motivated by the inevitable give-and-take required in diplomatic negotiations, they nonetheless were advanced by a President who appears to have been compromised by neurologic disease. Some of the diplomatic settlements at least suggest Wilson's inattention to detail concerning the realities of the postwar European situation. He confessed in May 1919 that the giving away of the Trentino was "based on insufficient study." He now regretted his decision, but declared that he had been ignorant about the situation at the time.[139] Since the President negotiated in isolation, one wonders what other critical matters may have been similarly neglected. This suggestion merits careful scrutiny when one considers the protestations of Colonel House. He had warned Wilson not to continue to deal with the other leaders without someone from his staff there to record the conversations. "To the chagrin of his colleagues on the American delegation," the Georges note, "the President not only ventured into these all-important meetings without either a secretary or an assistant, but also issued express instructions that the minutes not be circulated to anyone in the American delegation—not even to House."[140]

His associates' greatest concern, however, was that Wilson during the Dark Period was a man due for a complete breakdown. That breakdown occurred on April 3, 1919. He was struck down by a significant viral illness that may have been complicated by encephalitis. The superimposition of an acute delirium associated with this viral infection upon the previously described symptoms of a subtle dementia perhaps assured his permanent intellectual and emotional deterioration thereafter. The

salient features of delirium include a rapid onset, with concurrent disturbances of attention, memory, and thinking, all of which Wilson demonstrated during the first week of his illness in April. By definition, delirium
is a transient disorder, yet it does not follow that its outcome will always
reflect a restitution of prior mental function in the elderly. High fever
alone may induce this, even in the absence of encephalitis.[141]

Wilson's symptoms during this illness were compatible with those
seen in patients afflicted with either an influenza virus or the virus of
encephalitis lethargica. Yet any systemic virus associated with delirium
may cause personality changes. For example, patients infected by the
virus of encephalitis lethargica are known for their impulsive behavior
and occasional aggressiveness, even though they usually make adequate
emotional contact and can discuss things quite clearly.[142] In some viral
illnesses, sequelae have been shown to be even more severe in the presence of preexisting cerebrovascular disease. Under such circumstances,
a chronic brain syndrome may evolve, in which earlier fluctuating levels
of awareness are replaced by relatively stable cognitive impairment. The
two syndromes of delirium and dementia may therefore be seen to shade
into one another and overlap.[143]

We have seen that some suggestive aspects of dementia already characterized many of Wilson's activities prior to April 1919 on the basis of
hypertension and probable cerebrovascular insufficiency.[144] His behavior
following the April affliction fits the description of that condition to the
letter. Moreover, the diplomatic logjam of conflicting interests that characterized the Dark Period broke up *precisely* during the period of
Wilson's illness beginning on April 3, 1919, and this is of singular importance from the historical perspective.

Not that investigators have been able to agree on the specific nature
of the illness itself. Hugh L'Etang reviewed the data and was unable to
arrive at a firm decision:

> If any one factor stands out it was an episode early in April 1919 when
> Wilson was prostrated by an illness, the nature of which has never been
> entirely or satisfactorily explained. . . . Suffice it to say that an exhausted
> man . . . had an infective illness that may or may not have been accom-
> panied by a stroke.[145]

Walworth and Weinstein have also underscored the significance of the
timing of this setback, although they originally misconstrued the nature
of the illness itself. Walworth asserted (as Gene Smith had before him
and Weinstein would initially reiterate) that "experts on arteriosclerosis
. . . have questioned Grayson's diagnosis of the illness at Paris as influenza and have concluded that it was caused by a slight vascular occlu-

sion . . . brought on . . . by prolonged high pressure on brain and nerves."[146]

This imaginative view is incorrect, as the President's symptoms from April 3 through April 6 are in no way compatible with that diagnosis. Grayson's memoirs (and the descriptions of others) reveal that Wilson was felled by extreme lethargy, spiking temperatures, a severe cough, and diarrhea—no symptoms of which support a diagnosis of cerebral thrombosis.[147] The absence of transient paralysis, speech disturbance, or visual deficits further refutes the assumption of a stroke. Disorders of perception and mentation did occur during and after that event, the superficial analysis of which has led some investigators to believe these sequelae to be the result of a cerebrovascular event. More to the point, high temperature, cough, diarrhea, and changes in mentation, associated with lethargy and fitful sleeping, are strong evidence for a significant viral illness with secondary effects on brain function.

Interestingly enough, Dr. Grayson may have cited the correct diagnosis of "influenza," but failed to realize (or admit) the ancillary effects of the virus on the President's thought processes. The criticism here is that he used a blanketing term such as "influenza" to account for this multitude of symptoms, without giving proper attention to the concurrent changes in mentation that were obviously of critical importance for a President engaged in delicate negotiations. Whether this represented a genuine oversight on the physician's part or, as is suggested by the later record, an attempt to cover up Wilson's mental insufficiencies, remains unclear.

What is clear is that Grayson's noncommittal stance represents the dangerous norm for physicians who minister to individuals in leadership positions. Those involved with health care recognize that individuals often choose their physicians for peculiar reasons, sometimes with little regard for their training or experience. All too often, such "credentials" as social polish, engaging conversation, loyalty, or even a subservient nature count for more than a physician's experience or skills. Dr. Grayson was a case in point. Having been connected by marriage to Presley Marion Rixey, Surgeon-General of the Navy and White House physician to both Theodore Roosevelt and William Howard Taft, the personable young physician enjoyed visibility within the White House medical orbit. He had served in the Taft administration. Not surprisingly under the circumstances, Wilson later appointed Grayson to be his White House physician partly on the basis of Taft's recommendation. Sadly, there is no evidence to suggest that the young naval physician had any special skills in hypertension or cerebrovascular disease, having served but an internship at the Columbia Hospital for Women in Washington and a brief stint at the Naval Hospital.[148]

Grayson had first been brought to Wilson's attention during a White House reception in which he administered prompt but minor first aid to the President's sister, who had taken a fall. Thereafter Wilson was captivated by the young man's highly personable nature, and the physician-patient bond was solidified accordingly. As Weinstein notes, "Like Wilson, the Doctor was an excellent story teller, and the men enjoyed exchanging anecdotes. They developed a close friendship far exceeding the usual doctor-patient relationship."[149] This circumstance is often not beneficial to a physician's objectivity in dealing with disease. There was likewise much to suggest that Wilson attempted to treat many of his immediate subordinates as members of the family. As a member of the inner circle, Grayson would have found it even harder to be objective. Later, his subservience and loyalty to Wilson would in fact supercede his duty to give the nation a truthful explanation of the circumstances of Wilson's health during the last four years of his administration.

Nor was Grayson, perhaps, alone in his professional guilt. After Wilson's later stroke in September 1919, Dr. Francis Dercum, a noted Philadelphia neurologist, allegedly advised the President's wife to allow him to remain in office because he would lose his greatest incentive to recover if he resigned.[150] Perhaps this represents reasonable advice for the patient, but it is highly inconsiderate of the nation's best interests. In attempting to mount a defense for this particular physician, it is disquieting to learn that his medical records were destroyed, as were those of Dr. de Schweinitz.[151] If professional guilt was collective later, the record suggests it to have been an individual phenomenon while Wilson was in Paris. Grayson acknowledged the President's illness in April but ignored its overriding significance.

Whatever the effects of Wilson's viral illness upon his thought processes, the setback represented the critical turning point in his behavior. A review of the record reveals that, at least on an intermittent basis, Woodrow Wilson was no longer fully capable, mentally or emotionally. This observation is in keeping with Lipowski's discussion concerning delirium, which is often seen in the acute stages of a febrile viral illness. "An elderly patient," Lipowski observes, "may be well-compensated and only begin to display intellectual deterioration during a physical illness, usually one complicated by delirium that clears up, but the patient's mental abilities fail to return to the premorbid state."[152]

Not only are the clinical descriptions of Wilson's illness suggestive of viral delirium, but from 1917 through 1919 a veritable epidemic of what has been termed von Economo's encephalitis (encephalitis lethargica) swept through much of Europe and the United States. Dr. Henry Brill has described the cognitive and emotional effects on thousands of individuals stricken with the illness, of which Wilson could have been one so afflicted: "There was often a marked discrepancy between good intellectual capacity and primitive behavior. Such a patient often was a 'master of what he said,' but in his compulsive actions, was a 'slave of what he did.'"[153] Considering further that by this time Wilson probably had cerebral arteriosclerosis of an advanced degree, Dr. Lawrence Kolb's observations regarding the effects of any viral illness superimposed on this condition are important: "Patients with cerebral arteriosclerosis are peculiarly apt, on the occasion of a mild infection (*such as encephalitis*) to suffer from episodes characterized by confusion, disorientation, misidentification of persons, anxiety, fear, suspiciousness, and delusional trends."[154]

Of course, in order to postulate permanent effects on cognitive and behavioral functions secondary to viral impact superimposed on diffuse cerebrovascular insufficiency, one must substantiate more than only prior left hemisphere dysfunction in Wilson's case. Weinstein has argued that Wilson had experienced intermittent symptoms of cerebrovascular disease for sixteen years before becoming President, citing episodes suggestive of alleged left carotid disease occurring in 1896, 1897, 1904, 1906, and 1907. It was not until 1913 that signs of bilateral hemisphere involvement became apparent, with the episode of neuritis involving the left arm. As has been indicated above, his argument for diffuse or bilateral brain involvement on the basis of large-vessel atherosclerosis involving both carotid arteries is not entirely convincing.

What is certain, however, is that Wilson was afflicted by significant hypertension, and it has been proposed above that the ischemic events he experienced may have been on the basis of lacunar infarctions, many of which are known to be subclinical or inapparent.[155] It is this condition of small-vessel arteriosclerosis secondary to hypertension that more confidently assures us that Wilson's cerebrovascular disease was both bilateral and diffuse prior to April 1919. This argument regarding small-vessel lacunar infarctions notwithstanding, Wilson's large-vessel, atherosclerotically-induced stroke five months later, taken alone, is still enough to support the thesis of intellectual decline even before that catastrophic event took place. Men without cerebrovascular insufficiency symptoms, but who have atherosclerosis, exhibit marked reductions of cerebral blood flow and oxygen tension in the brain. In psychological and intellectual testing researchers have found *little difference* between men with asymptomatic atherosclerosis and patients with dementia.[156]

The mode of onset of dementia is recognized to be dependent upon its cause. Interestingly enough, according to Lipowski:

> The onset may be sudden or acute as a result of . . . encephalitis. More often, the onset is insidious or gradual. . . . The patient may attract atten-

tion by making mistakes, by forgetting appointments, by slips of judgment, by irritability. . . . Some patients begin to withdraw from social interactions because they find them frustrating or confusing. . . . Personality traits are exhibited in bolder relief. The patient becomes conspicuously more pedantic, self-righteous, petulant, . . . irascible, suspicious and withdrawn.[157]

Is there a better description of Woodrow Wilson at the Paris Peace Conference than this? Irwin Hoover, Wilson's personal valet, observed that after his illness Wilson "acquired the peculiar notion that he was personally responsible for all the property in the furnished palace he was occupying. . . . One thing was certain: he was never the same after this little spell of sickness."[158]

In addition to the changes in the President's neurologic system that were accelerating at this time, other organ systems of his body were also reaching critical levels of compromise. For example, Grayson recorded that, following the April illness in Paris, "asthmatic coughing" began to wake him at intervals all through the night.[159] The reader should not be misled by Grayson's imprecise use of the term "asthmatic." These were not asthmatic attacks as medicine recognizes them today. Wilson did not suffer from asthma. Rather, the description strongly implies that Wilson's heart was beginning to fail, probably on the basis of hypertension, which had also accounted for the series of lacunar infarctions beginning as early as 1896, the retinal hemorrhage of 1906, and possibly the renal failure that was first noted in 1915. That is to say, the attacks of coughing at night were representative of what physicians term "paroxysmal nocturnal dyspnea." The patient afflicted by this condition discovers that to increase blood return to the heart and out of the lungs he must sleep sitting up. Grayson acknowledged that thereafter the President assumed a semi-sitting position while sleeping. This was particularly evident during his later fateful trip to the western United States (see page 46).

With reference to Irwin Hoover's comment above, the psychiatrist would recognize the pleasure Wilson derived from rearranging the furniture in his room as perhaps an effort to maintain some control of his environment. Indeed, he demanded an itemization of all articles in the room and had an agent sit in the room while he was out.[160] The neurologist, on the other hand, would place more emphasis on the observation that demented individuals tend to become less confident in unfamiliar surroundings. Wilson's efforts might have represented a symbolic defensive gesture against this.

Similarly, if Wilson attributed his loss of confidence in Colonel House to House's perceived subversive activities, perhaps the President's disease-induced disorders of perception had unleashed a pathologic sense of paranoia unrestrained by reason—often a characteristic sign of neurologic compromise in the aged. "I am surrounded by intrigue here . . . the only way I can succeed is by working silently" he had confided.[161] He also became more and more certain that all of the French servants occupying his headquarters were spies.[162]

His emotional and mental instability was certainly apparent to his close associates. Gilbert Close complained: "I never knew the President to be in such a difficult frame of mind as he is now. Even while lying in bed he manifests peculiarities." Edmund Starling remarked that after this illness Wilson "lacked his old quickness of grasp, and tired easily."[163] Moreover, on March 23, just prior to the systemic viral illness in early April, Clemenceau sent agents to Colonel House suggesting that "too much activity had [already] dulled Wilson's mental processes."[164] Certainly the process of decline was suddenly and irrevocably accelerated by the viral infection the next month. Add an illness characterized by delirium, and there developed an acceleration in what was earlier only a mild dementia.

Ignoring the question of Wilson's infirmities, many historians have attributed his uncompromising stance to his idealistic faith. It is equally defensible that Wilson's ill health fostered this rigidity, augmented by paranoia. This behavior intensified his sense of isolation, first nurtured in Europe by plan, then accelerated to dangerous levels by illness, finally undermining his political support at home—not, perhaps, so much from a sense of honor and righteousness characteristic of the Calvinist sermonizer, but as a result of a disease that accentuated his tendency toward rigid thought and tunnel vision. It is typical for aging individuals with compromised neurologic function to develop both a single-minded approach to complex problems and an extreme rigidity and defensiveness when such devotion is thwarted. Defective control of impulses and emotions is noted. In one who was a leader and a spokesman for his nation's interests during difficult negotiations, such qualities would naturally have distressing implications.

As Weinstein has correctly surmised, however, impaired brain function itself does not necessarily translate into political inefficiency, since the "executive may respond to reduced capacity by accepting more help and delegating more responsibility."[165] Unfortunately, Wilson responded in just the opposite manner. Indeed, his complete devotion to the cause of the League left little enthusiasm for constructive domestic measures, even though he had formerly been a great progressive reformer. It is arguable that from 1919 on Wilson had lost touch with domestic realities and, recognizing his limited ability to deal with more than one issue effectively, had disguised his insecurity by a single-minded devotion to the League. More important, he did not guard against his own reduced capacity by accepting more help and delegating authority. His behavior during all phases of the negotiations in Paris, but particularly during the April illness, offers a dramatic case in point.

It may be recalled that prior to this event, negotiations had come to a virtual standstill. During the month following Wilson's return from the United States on March 13, with effective control of events slipping from his grasp, it became apparent that some concessions would have to be made. Baker argued that it was just such a consideration that ushered in the "era of compromise" in early April between Wilson and Clemenceau. For Wilson "accommodation became imperative." The League became the President's "irreducible minimum" in that accommodation. Given the temperament and principles of the man who made the decision to stand uncompromisingly for a League of Nations while satisfying the immediate French demands for security based on terms he considered temporary, Wilson "could not have done otherwise than he did."[166] So Baker asserted. Yet, as many others have done, this same observer apparently failed to recognize the significance of the illness that afflicted Wilson at precisely the same time as the "era of compromise" began in early April.

The critical point from the historian's perspective is that some of the most important decisions of the Paris Peace Conference were made during Wilson's April illness and the period immediately thereafter. Indeed, the treaty-makers made astounding progress in the next two weeks, in stark contrast to the near-deadlock before, for Wilson had continued to work during this time. The Council met in the room next to Wilson's sickbed, and House sat in his place, reporting each move to the bedridden President as he shuttled between the two rooms. From his bed Wilson tentatively approved a formula Clemenceau proposed as a basis for the reparations settlement.[167] He accepted the British and French demands that German reparations payments would have no monetary or time limits, a critical compromise with dire implications for postwar German economic development.[168] This was a position that a month before he had felt "bound in honor to forego."[169] On April 14 Wilson accepted the French Premier's scheme for making France secure along the Rhine, and a week later France obtained an Anglo-American guarantee of French security. Wilson, it seemed, perceived the problem only in generalities, claiming that "the League itself affords sufficient protection."[170] Nonetheless, he had seen his way clear at this time to make an uncharacteristic compromise in his previous stance against military provisions for the League. He also finally agreed to limiting the size of the German army, and reversed his previous moralistic stance by agreeing to the infamous "war guilt clause" making Germany responsible for the war and for Allied damages suffered. On April 2, prior to the onset of his viral illness, he refused to acknowledge either German war guilt or approve of a trial of the former Kaiser. By April 9, six days into his illness, he had agreed to both. Compromise on the war-guilt issue was followed shortly thereafter by a concession that confirmed the awarding of the Saar coal mines to France. It is not surprising, therefore, that Lloyd George charged: "After his illness, Wilson fell completely under the influence of Clemenceau." [171]

Historians will readily recognize that these decisions and others represented the crux of subsequent criticism of the agreements made at the Paris Peace Conference. In an unconvincing attempt to defend Wilson's actions, Baker observed that both sides gave much in the exchange during "those crucial five days of the Peace Conference, April 8–13." Wilson not only obtained an agreement on the League essentially as he had envisioned it, but also secured amendments "he considered necessary to meet home opposition." Moreover, the League was to be made "an 'integral part' of the Treaty of Peace, just as he had planned." Baker argued that "these things in themselves were . . . great concessions upon the part of the French." [172] This argument loses some of its persuasiveness when one perceives that American gains during this "era of compromise" were discussed in one paragraph, whereas French gains required thirteen pages to be fully outlined. Although Baker went to great lengths to defend Wilson's actions as politically necessary compromises in which the United States gained a great deal, he also made telling criticisms. The decisions in regard to war guilt and reparations, the Saar Valley, and the French occupation of the Rhineland were all examples, Baker concluded, of how the French had "contrived to put into the Treaty . . . many things that are irrational and inexcusable as judged by the accepted bases of the peace." [173] And they were agreed to by an American president during and immediately following an illness in which disorders of perception were arguably manifest.

Baker admitted that the Saar settlement "was forced into its existing form by the French desire for annexation" [174] because the region contained rich coal deposits. The decision to give France even temporary control of them was to yield to France's desire to cripple the German economy. It also violated Wilson's tenet of national self-determination. In addition, reparations and exorbitant costs of a dictated war guilt further added to the German burden. The reparations clauses so dissatisfied the American delegation that they made a concerted effort to overturn them after they were completed. And "as for the occupation of the left bank of the Rhine," Baker continued, "it is [not at all] the 'guarantee for the execution of the present treaty' which it professes to be." Historians cannot, and have not, ignored Baker's conclusion: "In all these arrangements the original French intent appears under various disguises, . . . labouring along through tortuous phrases under a load of idealistic expressions and restrictive conditions."[175] Viewed another way, the Old Order had again managed to triumph over the New, even though its impact was disguised—but not restricted—by the wording of the Treaty. Yet it was just such tortuous phrases and idealistic expressions that Wilson depended upon to assuage his conscience, to enable him to believe that the concessions he had made were the least possible under the circumstances. Arthur Link argues that Wilson perceived the Treaty's shortcomings realistically: "He signed the Versailles Treaty in the conviction that the passage of time . . . and the League of Nations, would almost certainly operate to rectify what he knew were the grievous mistakes of the Peace Conference."[176] If so (and the point is arguable), his later role in the League fight assumes even more tragic significance. In the end, Wilson rationalized his position by declaring that "all the questions of the present great settlement are parts of a single whole."[177]

Returning again to Goldstein's observations concerning the failure of the abstract attitude in the dementia state, Wilson's statement alone intimates a great deal. The afflicted individual fails if he is required to grasp the essentials of a given whole. This is precisely what the President failed to do with reference to many of the concessions made during and immediately after this brief illness. He refused to acknowledge the negative impact such agreements would surely have in relation to selling the whole package to the United States Senate at a later date. Nor did he apparently consider the possibility that the concessions might lead to repudiation of the whole treaty on principle. That possibility seemed obvious to other participants at the Conference. P. B. Noyes, an American delegate on the Inter-Allied Rhineland Commission, observed that the basic principle of a fifteen-year occupation of the area "is bad, [in that] the quartering of an enemy army in a country as its master in time of peace . . . will insure hatred and ultimate disaster." On a still broader philosophical plane, the British general G. B. Smuts spoke for most of the victors when he asserted that "the Treaty should not be capable of moral repudiation by the German people hereafter. . . . The final sanction of this great instrument must be the approval of mankind."[178] Ironically, the treaty was never morally accepted by the Germans, and the approval of mankind was soon withdrawn. The ultimate cost of that repudiation would prove extremely high.

There were other aspects of Wilson's behavior at Versailles that suggested a rather abrupt deterioration in his mental faculties after his illness. On May 3 he admitted to Grayson and Baker that he was so fatigued that he had difficulty remembering what had transpired. For example, he later insisted that he did not know of the numerous secret treaties concluded between the Allies prior to going to Paris, an allegation known to be false.[179] Whether his amnesia was politically or physiologically induced is open to question. Baker, for one, felt the President must have been aware of the treaties but had never made any attempt to study them in detail. Baker ruefully admitted: "Here was an opportunity neglected through failure to appreciate its importance." [180] Whether Wilson was either dissimulating or truly forgetful, it is at least apparent that the significance of the treaties' existence was lost on him. Indeed, the Bolsheviks had published texts of the agreements as early as November 17, 1917, and the State Department received a cablegram from the British on January 15, 1918, that detailed them in a communication to the President. On the same day, Lloyd George made public reference to certain of the treaties. [181] For Wilson to claim ignorance under these circumstances either borders on dishonesty (not a likely consideration, given his staunch morality) or serves to underscore true deficits in cognitive function—deficits he himself was acknowledging by this time.

During May 1919, as noted earlier, Wilson confided to Charles Seymour that he had been unaware of the implications of his decisions concerning the surrendering of the Trentino to Italy. [182] This decision stemmed from yet another secret treaty, in which Italy had been guaranteed this territory as her price for entering the war. Although Wilson accepted this arrangement, it directly contradicted the ninth of his Fourteen Points: "A readjustment of the frontiers of Italy should be effected along clearly recognizable lines of nationality." [183] Italy also demanded the port of Fiume, another area in which not all the people were Italian. When Wilson made a public statement of his opposition on April 23, 1919, it backfired. In Baker's words, his ideas and principles were described by this time as being "so far removed from the traditional thought of Europe on international affairs as to seem bizarre and impractical." [184] This Wilsonian ploy of "going to the people" was a recurring failure in the President's political methodology. It had failed in the off-year elections of 1918, and it would fail again in his later proposal to hold a referendum on the League issue—not to mention the ineffectiveness of his speaking campaign in support of the League after leaving Paris. He was, in essence, immune to the lessons of experience, which is yet another failure of the abstract attitude, as identified by Goldstein: "The affected individual fails if he is required to voluntarily evoke previous experiences." [185]

A final reference to the secret treaty issue will serve to demonstrate Wilson's failure to appreciate the implications of his actions while inadvertently compromising his principles. The Japanese had obtained prior agreements with the Allies concerning certain interests in the Pacific and the Chinese province of Shantung, although they were required both to "exercise restraint" and to join the League. Just as Wilson had done with the French and the Italians, he compromised his principle of national self-determination and acquiesced to imperialistic demands of the Old Order to gain acceptance of the one issue that occupied him to the exclusion of all other considerations. He had failed the Goldstein test once again: "To grasp the essential of a given whole."[186] Herbert Hoover's assessment of Wilson's intellect before and after April is telling. Before the illness he was "quick and incisive"; after it, he "groped for ideas."[187]

Primarily because the President had compromised many of his principles during the period of his brief illness, the treaty-makers had made enough progress by April 14 to allow the German representatives to come to Versailles to receive the terms of the peace. Such rapid progress in a two-week period on key controversial issues is astounding, given the limited gains made by the Big Four up to that point. Astonishment merges with distress when applying Zipowski's observation concerning neurologically impaired individuals to Woodrow Wilson: "Foresight and the ability to anticipate social or legal consequences of one's actions are typically diminished."[188]

Wilson did not respond to the German objections to certain aspects of the treaty, however reasonable, nor would he reappraise his own work. Lloyd George had urged the President to work with him toward modifying some of the concessions made to France. Wilson refused to do so, and the Georges portrayed his rigidity in psychological terms: Such modifications "would reactivate his crises of conscience of March and April. Indeed, so distressing to Wilson had been his earlier concessions to the French and to others that he seems to have lost track in his own mind of the extent to which he had been forced to compromise his principles."[189] It might likewise be argued that the nuances and vagaries associated with making even more revisions presented obstacles Wilson no longer had the emotional or intellectual fortitude, on the basis of physiologic compromise, to undertake. According to Lipowski:

> In mild or early cases of dementia one may observe difficulties in sustaining mental performance, with early appearance of fatigue and a tendency for the patient to fail when the task is novel or complex. This also applies if circumstances require shifts in problem-solving strategy. Faced with a new or complex problem . . . the patient tends to become frustrated and flustered, and performance fails.[190]

Of equal importance, Wilson had inexplicably hardened against all perceived adversaries, Allied and German alike. Before the illness he had been considerate of the German delegates. Afterwards he treated them with increasing disdain.[191] Regarding the revisionist bloc in the Senate, Walworth made the observation that he was "completely mired in emo-

tional revulsion toward men whom he could think of only as devils."[192]
This statement ostensibly referred to Lodge and his allies, yet during the
latter half of the Paris Peace Conference Wilson privately expressed the
same opinion of Clemenceau, and to a lesser degree Lloyd George. Isolation was never more manifest in a leader in office than during this period
from the second half of the Paris Peace Conference through the remainder of the Wilson presidency.

Following his return to the United States after the Conference, Wilson
began to suffer yet again from increasingly frequent headaches. When
William Bullitt, Wilson's personal envoy to Russia, returned to Washington, he was delayed in seeing the President, being told that Wilson was
suffering from a headache. The President himself admitted in September
that "'for the past weeks I have been suffering from daily headaches.'"[193]
His wife registered her concern during Wilson's speaking tour through
the western states that same month: "He grew thinner and the headaches
increased in duration and in intensity until he was almost blind during
the attacks," she recalled.[194] Grayson corroborated this: "From the time
we reached Montana," Grayson related in his memoirs, "the President
suffered from asthmatic attacks and severe headaches."[195]

This symptom was but one facet of Wilson's failing health, which had
concerned the inner circle (Grayson, Tumulty, and Mrs. Wilson) from the
moment the President proclaimed his resolve to make the trip west. He
vowed to take his case to the people in order to save the League, in spite
of everyone's warnings against the plan. Both Grayson and Tumulty knew
enough of his unstable condition to advise him against going. "Admiral
Grayson . . . stood firm in his resolve that the President should not go
West," Tumulty recalled, "even intimating to me that the President's life
might pay the forfeit if his advice were disregarded. Indeed, it needed
not the trained eye of a physician to see that the man . . . was on the
verge of a nervous breakdown."[196]

Wilson was aware of this danger and may even have sought to martyr
himself for his cause: "Even though it might cost him his life," Josephus
Daniels related, "he would," in Wilson's words, "'willingly make the
sacrifice to save the Treaty.'"[197] Alexander and Juliette George are among
those who imply that Wilson's quest for martyrdom was not merely a hollow valedictory. He assuaged his guilt for having provoked his own impending defeat over the League, while portraying himself again martyred
in a great cause by seeking vindication from 'the people.'[198]

Not only did such peculiar notions reveal Wilson's tenuous emotional
state; his physical condition likewise deteriorated significantly during
the trip. Episodes of diplopia (double vision) occurred, and his cardiac
decompensation (congestive heart failure) accelerated. Grayson related
in his memoirs that "frequently I was summoned during the night to . . .

assist him in breathing. It was necessary for him to sleep a good part of the time sitting up."[199] This represented an apparent progression of the paroxysmal nocturnal dyspnea first noted in April 1919. And then there were the headaches.

Headaches occurring on a daily basis are only rarely a manifestation of diffuse cerebrovascular insufficiency. Most often such a symptom is indicative of muscle tension. Occasionally it can be an ominous response to markedly elevated levels of systolic blood pressure, as described earlier. Retrospective evidence in Wilson's case suggests this latter factor to have been the cause of his extreme discomfort during this time. Indeed, for the entire ten-day period prior to his stroke in Pueblo, Colorado, the President is known to have suffered daily from severe headaches.[200] If marked elevations of blood pressure are sustained, much more serious symptoms than headaches alone appear: the afflicted individual may experience a pre-stroke warning known as "hypertensive encephalopathy," during which transient periods of unawareness or clouded thought processes become evident. That Wilson probably experienced at least one such episode is suggested in the description of his speech in Pueblo, Colorado, the night prior to the onset of the first signs of his devastating stroke. During that particular speech, his voice was weak and his sentences were punctuated with long pauses, as if he were having difficulty in maintaining his train of thought. As Gene Smith described it:

> He did well enough until suddenly he stumbled over a sentence. "Germany must never be allowed—" he stopped and was silent. "A lesson must be taught to Germany—" He stopped again and stood still. "The world will not allow Germany—"[201]

It is not clear from the record whether Wilson was reading his speech or speaking extemporaneously. If reading, a transient bout of cortical blindness related to hypertension-induced constriction of vessels supplying the visual cortex may have prevented him from seeing the words on the page. Alternatively, if speaking extemporaneously, he may have been suffering from a form of word-finding difficulty termed "expressive dysphasia" for the same reason. In either instance, in conjunction with the headaches he is known to have been experiencing, the underlying cause would be the same: a marked and rapid rise in blood pressure culminating in a hypertension-related transient ischemic attack.

Cerebral thrombosis is often presaged by uncontrolled hypertension, and evidence is nearly conclusive that it was a thrombosis of the right internal carotid artery that caused the fateful stroke on September 29 (see Fig. 1.3). A description of that event draws close attention to the

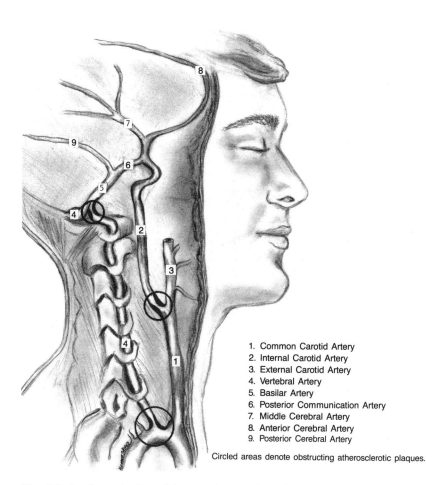

1. Common Carotid Artery
2. Internal Carotid Artery
3. External Carotid Artery
4. Vertebral Artery
5. Basilar Artery
6. Posterior Communication Artery
7. Middle Cerebral Artery
8. Anterior Cerebral Artery
9. Posterior Cerebral Artery

Circled areas denote obstructing atherosclerotic plaques.

*Fig. 1.3  A schematic view of the vascular supply to the brain, including the large feeding arteries in the neck. The circled plaques denote areas most commonly affected by atherosclerosis.*

severe headache initiating the first ischemic manifestations early that morning. Mrs. Wilson related that "I found him sitting on the side of his bed. . . . He said he had tried to sleep but the pain had grown unbearable and he thought I had better call Dr. Grayson." [202] Shortly thereafter he suffered obvious initial physical signs of a stroke, though one learns little from Dr. Grayson's account of that particular event. "Early the next morning," Grayson recounted, "I was awakened . . . and told that the President was suffering very much. I went at once and found that he was on the verge of a complete breakdown." [203] Inexplicably, there was no specific description of those physical findings of left-sided weakness to which all others referred: "As he spoke saliva came down from the left side of his mouth and they saw that the left half of his face was fallen and unmoving. His words were mumbled and indistinct." Shortly thereafter "his left arm and leg refused to function." [204]

The speaking tour was abruptly cancelled and plans were hurriedly made to return to Washington. Grayson's explanation to the reporters was typically vague, emphasizing that nothing serious had occurred: "He hoped the President would need only a short rest and that it was certain he was not seriously ill. He added there was nothing organically wrong with the President's physical or nervous system. He would say no more than that." [205]

Severe headaches accompanying such neurologic deficits as left-sided weakness and slurred speech might suggest an intracranial hemorrhage of the right side of the brain. This consideration is effectively dispelled by the observation that his symptoms improved rapidly within twenty-four hours. During the return to Washington, Wilson regained some use of his arm and leg. [206] The effects of a hemorrhage would not clear so rapidly. By medical definition, then, the first episode represented a transient ischemic attack, even though its severity is indicated by the fact that the facial weakness did not completely clear. Three days later Wilson awoke with a weak left hand, followed shortly thereafter by extension of the weakness to the entire left arm and leg. The involvement of face, arm, and leg implicates an occlusion of the carotid artery, as no other vessel supplies such a wide area of the cerebral cortex. [207] (See Fig. 1.4.)

A reconstruction of the events of the stroke, then, suggests that on September 29 the President suffered a right internal carotid artery thrombosis, but the attack was transient on the basis of sufficient collateral circulation to protect the function of the arm and leg until three days later, at which time an extension of the clot (thrombus) in the vessel occurred. Another possible scenario is that the first attack was caused by the fragmentation of a piece of clot (embolus) from a proximal thrombus developing in the carotid artery that carried itself to the distal middle

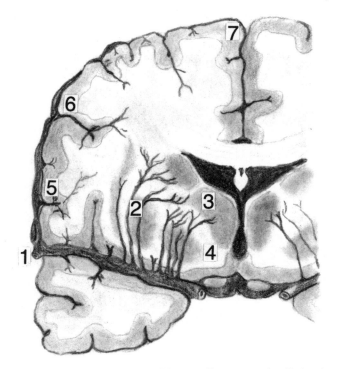

*Figure 1.4 A cross-section of a normal brain, illustrating the distinction between the deep (basal-ganglionic) and superficial (cortical) blood supply. (1) Middle cerebral artery; (2) Lentriculostriate arteries; (3) Thalamus; (4) Internal capsule; (5) Face; (6) Arm; (7) Leg.*

cerebral artery and then resolved. Three days later the evolving thrombus completed its occlusion of the right internal carotid artery. There remains a third possibility—that Wilson had suffered yet another lacunar infarction on the basis of hypertension.[208] This is an attractive proposition to the clinical neurologist, in that a second disease process (large-vessel atherosclerosis) would not have to be postulated. However, the severity and longevity of the stroke, its stuttering progression, the left-sided visual field deficit, and the presence of anosognosia (denial of the affected side) are all observations more consistent with large-vessel thrombosis or embolism. In any case, a devastating stroke had occurred, which significantly compromised both Wilson's vision and the use of his left side.

From that point on, of course, any effectiveness the speaking tour may have had was lost. Yet even up to that point, its impact had been largely negative. Few of the forty speeches Wilson made during the trip were well prepared, and he really said nothing new to aid his cause.[209] Above all, the trip itself had demonstrated his poor judgment. The Treaty's acceptance hinged on the mild reservationists in the Senate, not on the people, and any effort to carry the fight to them took him away from the critical happenings in Washington. Not only was he attempting to capture the wrong audience, but the poorly prepared speeches of a rigidly paranoid, ill man were counterproductive. Wilson implied that opposition to the treaty sprang either from "downright ignorance" or some "malicious private purpose." This led the Georges to conclude: "In Washington, the President's contemptuous references to his opponents raised practically everyone's hackles."[210] The *New York Times* reported that "the mild reservationists were rapidly moving toward the Lodge camp. Wilson had done more than any other man to drive them there."[211] In retrospect, Wilson's cerebrovascular accident may be viewed as a tragic yet symbolic finale to a singularly unproductive enterprise.

Yet it was not the end of his presidency. A chosen few (Grayson, Tumulty, and the President's wife) had no doubt that Wilson had suffered a severe stroke, but events immediately following his breakdown raised more questions than were answered by the administration's public statements. The rumors began during Wilson's trip from the train station in Washington to the White House. As Gene Smith has described the incident:

> Because it was Sunday morning the streets were practically empty. But as they rode the President reached up and took off his hat and bowed as if he were returning the greetings of a vast throng. Enough people saw what he had done to send flying through Washington the information that the President is physically all right but salutes empty sidewalks. He has lost his mind.[212]

What knowledge did the American public have of this devastating turn of events? In a word, none. Was Wilson's disability sufficient to compromise his leadership abilities? Yes. If so, was this disability certifiable? Yes. Was he so certified? No. Then who was in effect running the executive branch? No one. Let us develop this disconcerting situation more fully.

With regard to the public's knowledge of Wilson's illness, the evidence is irrefutable that the administration divulged very little. Grayson related to the press only such statements as "the President has suffered a complete nervous breakdown," and "his condition is not alarming."[213] Nothing more could be learned. For weeks thereafter, the country remained completely in the dark. Even those close to power but still not within the chosen circle had no precise knowledge of what had happened. Rumors spread which Grayson could not dispel. As Colonel House recorded in his diary for October 21, 1919: "There is much discussion in Washington and elsewhere as to whether the President has suffered a stroke. McAdoo, who has seen him, declares Grayson says he has not had one."[214] The official medical reports referred only to a "nervous breakdown, indigestion, and a depleted system."[215] Wilson's condition was described to the Cabinet in precisely those terms on October 6. The reason for such circumlocution was obvious. Grayson admitted that at that time he did not want the illness disclosed.[216]

The entry in Colonel House's diary cited above brings the situation in the government into sharp focus for posterity, though it remained blurred to contemporaries. Aside from Mrs. Wilson, Grayson, and Tumulty, no one was allowed to see the President. The Cabinet was dismayed that no executive business was being transacted. As late as three months after the cerebrovascular accident, House recorded that Lansing did not believe the President to be writing any of the papers purported to be coming from him.[217]

The essential features of Wilson's disability are hardly in question. Indeed, his physical limitations were painfully obvious to those chosen few allowed to see him. For the first month after his stroke, Wilson was unable to read so much as a newspaper.[218] In attempting to dictate a letter, his articulation would gradually become more indistinct until "finally losing the thread of his thought, he would stare into space." He could write a poor imitation of his signature only with help.[219] His left arm, a useless appendage, was carefully disguised under the bed sheets.[220]

Wilson's mental faculties were also significantly compromised. He felt inadequate, which affected his judgment of men and events. After the stroke, according to Weinstein, "his metaphors often controlled his thinking . . . [He] reduced complex issues to all-or-none questions of right or wrong, and of morality or immorality. . . . [As such, his language] became maladaptive and self-isolating."[221] He also manifested wide swings of emotion. He wept easily. Unable to examine a subject too deeply, the President was incapable of grappling with the problems raised by his new disability.[222]

Edith Wilson and Dr. Grayson attempted to justify their public silence during this period by arguing that attempting to remove the incapacitated President from the White House would emotionally disturb him and might prove fatal.[223] This observation was punctuated by Dr. Dercum's plea to Mrs. Wilson that the President not resign.[224] Such observations may serve to substantiate Wilson's unstable emotions at the time, but the claim made that any psychological duress might be fatal was excessive. No reasonable medical opinion today substantiates it.

Emotional disturbance alone is not a recognizable cause of death in the stroke patient.

Undoubtedly, though, Wilson's disability was sufficient to compromise his leadership abilities. As executive activities came to a virtual standstill, Lansing called a special meeting with the Cabinet to discuss presidential disability from the medico-legal standpoint. The constitutional provision is unequivocal on this point: "In case of the removal of the President from office, or of his death, resignation, or inability to discharge the powers and duties of the said office, the same shall devolve on the Vice President."[225] Grayson and Tumulty both refused to certify disability. Tumulty's account of how this decision was made revealed the limited thought that went into such a judgment on the part of Grayson.

> Mr. Lansing sought a private audience with me in the Cabinet Room. He informed me that he had called diplomatically to suggest that in view of the incapacity of the President we should arrange to call in the Vice-President to act in his stead as soon as possible, reading to me . . . [the] clause in the United States Constitution. . . .
>
> Upon reading this, I coldly turned to Mr. Lansing and said: "Mr. Lansing, the Constitution is not a dead letter with the White House. I have read the Constitution and do not find myself in need of any tutoring at your hands of the provision you have just read." When I asked Mr. Lansing the question as to who should certify to the disability of the President, he intimated that that would be a job for either Doctor Grayson or myself. I immediately grasped the full significance of what he intimated and said: "You may rest assured that while Woodrow Wilson is lying in the White House on the broad of his back I will not be a party to ousting him. He has been too kind, too loyal, and too wonderful to me to receive such treatment at my hands." Just as I uttered this statement Doctor Grayson appeared in the Cabinet Room and I turned to him and said: "And I am sure that Doctor Grayson will never certify to his disability. Will you, Grayson?" Doctor Grayson left no doubt in Mr. Lansing's mind that he would not do as Mr. Lansing suggested. I then notified Mr. Lansing that if anybody outside of the White House circle attempted to certify to the President's disability, that Grayson and I would stand together and repudiate it. . . .
>
> It is unnecessary to say that no further attempt was made by Mr. Lansing to institute ouster proceedings against his chief.[226]

The issue, then, was decided on the basis of personal loyalty and not on what was in the nation's best interest. The same small group of loyalists who had accompanied Wilson westward were now circling the wagons—"stonewalling," in modern journalistic parlance—under the banner of loyalty. The question of disability had been sprung upon Grayson quickly, with his reply apparently almost an afterthought. Nor had Grayson stated that Wilson was *not* disabled; he had merely acquiesced in the refusal to acknowledge the fact. This was done in spite of his private comment to a party leader, Robert Woolley, on June 13 that Wilson was "'permanently ill physically,' was gradually weakening mentally, and could not recover." [227] In view of Wilson's efforts to convince those around him to conceal his infirmities, such a refusal might seem justified as a physician's duty to his patient. But from the professional standpoint, Grayson's refusal to certify the President as disabled bordered on dissimulation; his silence thereafter compounded that offense. More important, his responsibility to Wilson stopped far short of his ultimate accountability to the American people.

The record is irrefutable that Wilson was not an effective head of state for at least the first seven months after his cerebrovascular accident, although a few would have the reader believe otherwise. [228] During this entire period the executive arm, to use an unpleasant metaphor, was effectively paralyzed. Emergency communications vanished, letters sent to the executive office were not returned, bills were allowed to become law without Wilson's signature. Everything was cleared through either Grayson, Tumulty, or Wilson's wife, none of whom were elected officials and none, except Tumulty, who were remotely familiar enough with executive or legislative matters to assume the position of responsibility they preempted.

An early political casualty of the illness was Secretary of State Lansing, who found himself *persona non grata* following the disability controversy. His resignation was sought shortly thereafter. According to Tumulty, the President claimed he had given Lansing everything, only to be repaid by his Secretary's repudiation of the Treaty. Wilson perceived this as a personal affront. "It is never the wrong time to spike disloyalty," he later charged. "When Lansing sought to oust me, I was upon my back. I am on my feet now [seated as he was in his invalid's chair on the White House portico] and I will not have disloyalty about me." [229]

Yet the accusation that Lansing attempted to spike Wilson's peace initiatives does not withstand scrutiny. He did not repudiate anything. Rather, he merely pointed to the aspects of the settlement that the Senate might have difficulty supporting. His political instincts certainly were sharper than Wilson's primitive, rigidly espoused positions. Not only had Lansing asserted that "nothing ought to be done to prevent the speedy restoration of peace by signing the Treaty," but also that "anything which was an obstacle to ratification was unfortunate because we ought to have peace as soon as possible." [230] Such recorded sentiments (described by a participant unsympathetic to Lansing) hardly represented a desire for repudiation. Moreover, Herbert Hoover held Secretary Lansing in high esteem and pointed out that Lansing "did not publicly oppose the President. He signed the Treaty and supported its ratification by the Senate."

Hoover greatly regretted the Secretary's break with the President and asserted that "the President's action was that of a very sick man."[231] As described earlier, Hoover himself was a casualty of Wilson's definition of loyalty, being barred from the inner circle for warning them about the harm he thought the Treaty might do to the European economy.[232] The circle protecting the beleaguered President now included none of the very able advisors whom Wilson had chosen at an earlier time.

Appreciating a woman's influence is critical to any understanding of who really was the keeper of the keys in Wilson's disease-induced asylum. "There was a filter through which all public business functioned," Herbert Hoover observed. "The President . . . certainly did not have the advantage of personal contacts and information upon which to form judgments. His mind may have been clear but in his seclusion his judgment must have been uncertain."[233] This "filter" was the First Lady. Evidence indicates she performed her protective tasks exceptionally well—if not in the best interests of the office itself.

By way of example, during the early phase of Wilson's illness, certain officials insisted upon seeing him personally because they felt they were bringing information "absolutely necessary that the President of the United States should have."[234] Edith Wilson's response defined the problem for executive leadership at this time: "I am not interested in the President of the United States. I am interested in my husband and his health."[235] As Grayson himself noted, "she stood like a stone wall between the sickroom and the officials."[236] Numerous imploring letters never received Wilson's attention. Colonel House also felt the effects of the filter. He penned two critical letters regarding the Senate fight during a three-day period in November, neither of which was acknowledged. In fact, few letters reached the President at all during this critical period before and between the votes on the Treaty of November 19, 1919, and March 19, 1920. "His lack of contact with the people and their leaders," Hoover concluded, "separated him from the reality of which sound compromises are made."[237]

Even with such artificial barriers to communication, there was much to support the belief that Wilson's illness prevented him from assessing viable alternatives in any case. Ray Stannard Baker spoke for many when he asserted: "I feel so strongly that if the President were not ill—if he were himself—he could and would save the situation."[238] Possibly so; but the President was now a drastically changed and increasingly restricted entity. Illness—not pious, unrelenting virtue—would be the harbinger of the Treaty's defeat.

Mrs. Wilson attempted to shield herself from blame by citing the advice of others, most notably the physicians in attendance. Her explanation, however, was porous, if not naive. "I, myself, never made a single decision," she said, "regarding the disposition of public affairs. The only decision that was mine was what was important and what was not, and the *very* important decision of when to present matters to my husband."[239] The critical importance of control over accessibility seems not to have entered into her thinking. The reasons she gave for acting as she did were equally naive: "It is always an excitement for one who is ill to see people. The physicians said that if I could convey the messages of Cabinet members and others to the President, he would escape the nervous drain audiences with these officials would entail."[240]

It is not necessarily correct that neurologically compromised individuals should receive the minimum of intellectual and interpersonal stimulus. Precisely the opposite is true in medical thinking today. In the words of a noted authority on the treatment of patients with dementia: "The maintenance of social contacts is important. Social isolation tends to increase the patient's disability and needs to be counteracted."[241] As a rule, those patients who seem to achieve a more rapid reentry into a cognitive recognition of their milieu are those who receive adequate environmental contacts. Those whose contacts are restricted are usually slower to progress. This is common knowledge to any clinical neurologist or neurosurgeon, and it is questionable whether such an esteemed neurologist as Francis Dercum would have suggested anything else—the claims of Mrs. Wilson to the contrary notwithstanding.

Isolation also begets depression in elderly individuals—particularly those suffering from cerebrovascular disease. Perhaps one of the most frequently overlooked factors in the differential diagnosis of the arteriosclerotic brain syndrome is the complicating depressive reaction of aging. Anthony Storr, an eminent British psychiatrist, observed that "if a man is taken from his family, his job, and his social circle, and put into a situation of uncertainty and fear, he will become profoundly depressed. . . . It takes but a few weeks . . . to reduce most people to a state of profound dejection and an apathetic stupor."[242] Considering Wilson's isolation in at least one sense—that which prevented him from performing his routine public duties—there is little wonder that executive function became so ineffective.

On rare occasions, political audiences were granted. A description of them goes far toward explaining how the inner circle hid the President's disability. More than one account described Wilson's left arm as carefully tucked under the sheets, with his right arm left visible. Visitors were allowed to approach the bed only from the right side. Since Wilson could see only out of his right peripheral field of vision, this arrangement allowed him to see the visitor despite the semidarkened room, kept poorly illuminated to prevent the observer from perceiving the left-sided facial weakness of the president, which was still very much in evidence.

Equally significant was his new growth of beard and moustache, probably deemed useful in disguising his twisted facial features. Finally, Mrs. Wilson and Grayson were always in attendance, lest Wilson's fatigue or inappropriate emotional reactions become too obvious to the visitor.[243] Again, Mrs. Wilson claimed much of this charade was assumed at the behest of Wilson's physicians. This may have been characteristic of Grayson, as the previous record suggests, but that Dercum, too, was a moving force in this regard, as Mrs. Wilson claims, cannot be so readily accepted. It is perhaps significant that Dercum had already passed away by the time Mrs. Wilson's memoirs were published.

Deception became the order of the day. Although the President was still unable to sit unsupported, false reports of his heavy workload and his work habits were published by Grayson and others.[244] The Cabinet met regularly to transact interdepartmental business, but there was little if any guidance in domestic or, more important, international affairs. Individual Cabinet members had little contact with the President except through Tumulty, and his description of how business was conducted between the two of them during the first month is disquieting in the extreme:

> Even when he lay seriously ill, . . . I conferred with him and discussed every phase of the fight on the Hill. . . . *Though hardly able*, because of his physical condition, *to discuss these matters with me*, [italics mine] he evidenced in every way a tremendous interest in everything that was happening . . .
>
> One of the peculiar things about the illness . . . was the deep emotion which would stir him when word was brought to him that this senator or that senator on the Hill had said some kind thing about him or had gone to his defense . . .[245]

Many contemporaries were later to witness this same inappropriate emotionality, which is recognized today as a manifestation of frontal lobe dysfunction quite typical of such patients. Stockton Axson later recounted how in the autumn of 1920, "I would be reading to him, . . . [and] (he would begin sobbing, when there didn't seem to be anything particular in the text to call for it)."[246]

According to Tumulty, "never would there come from him any censure or bitter criticism of those who were opposing him in the [League] fight."[247] Such an assertion boggles the mind, ignores the record, and compromises Tumulty's reliability as a witness. Henry Cabot Lodge would not have believed this; nor have the countless descriptions of their subsequent struggle even remotely supported such a claim.

The distressing condition of executive affairs became apparent in the conflict over the League of Nations. Under the circumstances, leadership in the Senate fell to Gilbert Hitchcock, who saw the wisdom of compromising with the mild reservationists on any modest changes that might command enough votes to frustrate Lodge. Briefly summarized, potential opposition in the Senate divided along the following lines. There were the "irreconcilables," who were of one mind to dispose of the League altogether, regardless of the circumstances. There was also a sizable group of "mild reservationists," who would vote for the League if certain limitations and safeguards on America's participation were included. [248] The record is clear that the mild reservationists worked in good faith for the passage of the Treaty, even trying to compromise with Wilson, but these efforts were completely ineffective. There is an element of tragic irony here: If Wilson had only dealt with the mild reservationists, he would have had his Treaty at any time during those months of indecision. Yet he refused to compromise, insisting that the treaty be accepted with no changes. [249]

Certainly there was ample room for compromise based on semantics alone. According to Alexander and Juliette George,

> In substance, Wilson's four interpretations and the four reservations then being sponsored by the "mild reservationists" were all but identical. Wilson authorized Hitchcock to use his interpretations in any way he saw fit . . . But Hitchcock could not make the one concession that was necessary. He could not say that Wilson would permit the interpretations or reservations to be included in the resolution of ratification. He could not say that Wilson was willing to make them binding upon the other signatories. [250]

It is important to highlight the great emphasis the stricken President placed on his perception of the difference between the words "interpretations" and "reservations." They really meant the same thing, but Wilson's refusal (or inability) to accept this suggests once again an impairment of the abstract attitude. Consider Dr. Kurt Goldstein's observations of compromised individuals who demonstrate this impairment:

> The patient's speech in everyday life may not show much deviation from the norm. He may in certain situations have a great number of words at his disposal. This is the case when the words belong concretely to the situation. He will fail concerning the same words, however, when the situation demands that he consider their meaning. . . . He cannot understand that the same word can have different meanings. [251]
> Or the corollary—that different words can have the same meaning.

Given this observation, it is doubtful that a more tragic example of the effects of illness can be found in twentieth-century diplomacy than the impact of Wilson's failure of abstraction with regard to this distinction.

Rather than a potential source for compromise, the semantics of the controversy paradoxically served to prevent an effective compromise. It was the form of the mild reservations rather than their substance to which Wilson stubbornly objected. Gene Smith observed that men outside the Senate acknowledged this, but "few if any of these pleas reached the man they were intended for. . . . [There was] no reply beyond the First Lady's statement that no compromise could be permitted."[252]

David Hunter Miller, who had played a large part in drafting the Covenant, believed that the President was attaching too much importance to the reservations. "So far as the Lodge reservations made changes in the League," he wrote, "they were of a wholly minor character, they left its structure intact, and they would have interfered with its workings not at all."[253] Herbert Hoover echoed this sentiment in his memoirs: "Whatever the reservations implied, they did not in my mind destroy the great major functions of the League. . . . I was convinced that the European League members were so anxious for American cooperation in world problems that they would accept the reservations."[254] Hoover expressed this view in a letter to Wilson, but the President did not acknowledge it. One may question whether he saw the letter, but even if he did, his position remained unrealistic and rigid. In essence, the President was enslaved by the wording of the argument, increasingly disposed to blind obstinacy, if not paranoia. He declared that "These reservations . . . represent a dishonorable attempt, on the part of leaders who do not speak for the people, to escape any real responsibility. . . . These evil men intend to destroy the League."[255] His political instincts had abandoned him. The rigidity fostered, in part, by his progressive organic brain syndrome prevented him from recognizing the usefulness of compromise in gaining his desired end. "Better a thousand times to go down fighting than to dip your colours to dishonourable compromise," he proclaimed.[256]

Few scholars, then or now, have characterized the innocuous amendments presented by the mild reservationists as "dishonorable." Failing once again to utilize the abstract attitude, the compromised President could not separate the identifiable parts from the whole. Whether by failed access to the facts or failed perception of them once presented, Wilson refused to acknowledge that the mild reservationists were a breed apart from Lodge and his band of irreconcilables. He therefore fatefully proclaimed that "the text of the Treaty must be approved as is. . . . Any *condition* to our ratification—reservations or amendments which would require the assent of the other signatories of the Treaty—would not constitute adoption of the Treaty."[257] In the absence of any new instructions from the President, then, Hitchcock could only stay the course by insisting on ratification without reservations.

Gilbert Hitchcock's extraordinarily difficult position was compounded by the fact that he was only the acting minority leader. The official minority leader of the Senate, Thomas S. Martin of Virginia, died shortly before the Treaty came up for a vote in November. [258] Yet even the skills of an accomplished minority leader would have been impotent in the absence of rational executive leadership. Nor had Hitchcock enjoyed Wilson's esteem prior to this period, a fact known to all. This weakened his position even further. During the entire month of October, Hitchcock had not been afforded a single meeting with the stricken President. When he was finally received by Wilson on November 6, the record indicates that the session hardly produced the cooperation required by the urgent necessity to plot a constructive course. Hitchcock's advice fell on deaf ears when he argued that unless the Lodge amendments were accepted it would be utterly impossible to get the United States into the League.

> "It *is* possible! It is possible!" the President gasped out.
> "Mr. President, it might be wise to compromise—" Hitchcock started to say.
> "Let Lodge compromise!"
> "Well, of course, he must compromise also. But we might well hold out the olive branch."
> "Let Lodge hold out the olive branch!"
> Hitchcock was shown out. [259]

The compromised President was still incapable of assimilating data when it was presented to him, and most facts were not even presented, given the logistics of the situation. Having been unable to make headway with Wilson or Hitchcock during this critical month of negotiations, the mild reservationists threw in their lot with the Lodge reservations, and the Treaty would eventually be left for dead.

The role of Henry Cabot Lodge in all this certainly deserves no praise. Yet in the Georges' assessment:

> It may be argued that Lodge's reservations were offensively worded . . . that his motives in presenting them were questionable. But the reservations did not nullify the Treaty. They did not even seriously embarrass full participation of the United States in the League of Nations. In practice they would have been of little significance. That is the consensus of a generation of scholars who have subjected the Lodge program to minute scrutiny. [260]

This is a very critical observation. Certainly Wilson's isolation partly explains his inability to perceive these facts, but isolation alone is hardly a sufficient explanation. Indeed, during this period Wilson was portrayed as having thought of little else than the Senate fight. He was consumed by it. A sense of righteous indignation and rigid thinking had always been a Wilsonian characteristic. Now such qualities were magnified manyfold under the stress of illness. There is, then, ample evidence to support a medical understanding of how, as the Georges observed, "a man might destroy his life's work . . . over a few paltry phrases."[261]

On November 19, 1919, the Treaty was defeated in the Senate, but ironically the issue was not yet dead. Public demand for the League persisted. Wilson was to be given a second chance. House (in exile in Paris) attempted to reach his old mentor by letter, emphasizing correctly that history's ultimate judgment of Wilson hung on a successful resolution of the issue. He wrote through Mrs. Wilson:

> Objectionable reservations could be corrected later: the essential thing was to make the President's great work live. . . . It would then be up to the Allies to decide whether or not to accept our ratification [of the Treaty with the reservations]. Wilson could feel that he had discharged his duty. . . . If the Allies rejected the Treaty with the Lodge reservations, Wilson's previous opposition to the reservations would be vindicated. If they accepted the reservations, we would [still] be in the League and time would vitiate their effect. [262]

Under the circumstances, this was a piece of very sage advice, and it offered Wilson a way out of the dilemma.

Nothing came of the proposal. The letter was not acknowledged in any way. Once again Mrs. Wilson may not have shown the letter to the President, considering her well-known dislike of House's previous influence on her husband. It is also possible that Wilson was aware of the proposal but was now refusing any advice from House because of his break with the man who had previously been his most trusted confidant. Whatever the explanation, Wilson's rigidity was not mollified. In fact, his own alternative proposals reflected a progressive degree of unrealistic thinking.

The cornered President suggested a national referendum on the issue. This recalled his appeal to the public in 1918 to elect a Democratic Congress as a means of demonstrating a vote of confidence in his position. That appeal had proved a tactical error. This new proposal was equally unrealistic; one could not expect the general voting public to be able to decipher the subtle difference of meaning separating a reservation from an interpretation. Nor had Wilson successfully educated the potential voters to the issue, a fact that was apparent to Ray Stannard Baker even while in Paris. Baker believed there was "a benevolent sentiment for a league of nations, but an abysmal ignorance of real international conditions and problems."[263] Perhaps that belated acknowledgment was precisely what Wilson's swing through the West in September 1919 was all about, but by then, it was too little, too late. Yet even now Wilson clung to the unrealistic hope that a mandate from the people might rescue him from his plight.

Wilson outlined still another futile proposition in January 1920, when he challenged the fifty senators who opposed him to resign and to seek immediate reelection on the Treaty issue. Wilson offered to resign himself if a majority of them were reelected.[264] Fortunately, nothing came of this notion, as the proposal was never made public. But these two examples do serve to demonstrate Wilson's increasingly unrealistic way of approaching the issue, and they stand in stark contrast to the reasonable position House had implored the President to take.

The significance of the House offer to Wilson is at least twofold. First, from that point on, after receiving no response to his suggestions, the Colonel finally admitted to himself that his advice was no longer welcome. He noted in his diary that he once believed Lodge to be the Treaty's worst enemy; now he had to admit that Wilson had preempted that role.[265] Second, Wilson's fears of Allied rejection of *any* Treaty reservations are simply not substantiated by the record. Sir Edward Grey, the former British Foreign Secretary, after waiting unsuccessfully for four months to meet with Wilson on the subject, finally published an open letter in the *Times* of London imploring Wilson to have the Treaty with reservations ratified, rather than forfeit United States participation in the League altogether. This position was echoed by French Ambassador Jean-Jules Jusserand, who assured Wilson that Britain and France would accept the reservations as proposed.[266]

So Wilson's alleged reason for allowing the Treaty to die proved to be unfounded after all. Rather than accept this recognition constructively, the President became more obstinate still. Now he could see such assurances only as a boost to Lodge's position. Indeed, at this juncture, his primary motivation was to defeat his nemesis. To the Georges' way of thinking Wilson "was acting out his personal conflicts in a public matter of the highest importance," and in a self-destructive way.[267] The medical clinician might be more inclined to weigh the anatomic consequences of previously suspected lacunar infarcts with new loss of cerebral cortical tissue as a result of his massive stroke. Drs. Chapman and Wolff, in an elegant study, correlated the amount of cerebral tissue lost by a selected group of patients with the degree of dementia present. Defects of orientation, memory, and judgment were not found to be conspicuous unless the extent of focal damage to the hemispheres was relatively extensive. Nor was the underlying cause of Wilson's restricted cognition and behavioral aberrations an unusual condition. Chapman and Wolff noted that "multi-infarct dementia" was found in 75 percent of their patients. [268] This is precisely the disease process that afflicted Woodrow Wilson. A dramatic change would, therefore, have been expected to occur in the President's capabilities after the September 1919 stroke, given the degree of cortical loss suffered in combination with his multi-infarct, or lacunar, state.

On April 13, 1920, for the first time in nearly seven months, the President was able to meet with his Cabinet. Secretary of Agriculture David F. Houston observed that one of Wilson's arms was useless, his jaw dropped, and his voice was weak and strained. [269] Wilson himself admitted to Grayson: "I feel so weak and useless. I feel that I would like to go back to bed and stay there until I either get well or die. I cannot make a move to do my work except by making a definite resolve to do so." [270] Walworth cited evidence that on issues prior to the cerebral thrombosis Wilson's mind was reasonably clear, but he was unable to follow new issues arising since that time. [271] A description of Wilson at the first Cabinet meeting as recorded by Secretary Houston illustrated this: "It appeared that [Wilson] would not take the initiative. Someone brought up the railroad situation for discussion. The President seemed at first to have some difficulty in fixing his mind on what we were discussing." Hoover asserted in his memoirs that it was "clear from Houston's statement that the President had not recovered his full mental and physical vigor." [272]

*Woodrow Wilson, 1914 and 1921*

1914                    1921                    FREE LANCE
                                               PHOTO GUILD

This inability to synthesize new information is characteristic of victims of stroke, who are often victimized by profound recent memory loss. This prevents the afflicted individual from learning new material. The fact that this was true of Wilson nearly seven months after the cerebrovascular accident testifies to the severe disability he suffered—but which was still never fully admitted to the American people. Grayson's bulletins emphasized only progress; no clear definition of the problem or its governmental implications was ever fully disclosed in his lifetime.

Wilson seemed to be unaware to the very end of the negative impact of his disability on events. Shortly after this first Cabinet meeting, he told Grayson: "If I become convinced that the country is suffering any ill effects from my sickness I shall summon Congress . . . [and] have my address of resignation prepared." Grayson rationalized the situation by observing that "as he never broached this topic again, it is evident that he believed what was true, that he had the strength to administer the office capably."[273] Both were blind to the harm the President's condition had, in large measure, already wrought. By then America's participation in the League was dead, the seeds of vengeance and retribution had been sown in the shortsighted agreements of the postwar settlement, and the viability of the Democratic party had been drastically compromised.

Much criticism has been directed toward Woodrow Wilson's decision to attend the Paris Peace Conference and the negative actions that resulted. The Georges spoke for diplomats and historians alike when they observed that had Wilson "been free of his painful personal involvement in the proceedings he might have been better able . . . to perceive the possible alternatives at hand, and to consider them flexibly in terms of the ultimate fate of his idealistic goals."[274] In view of the fact that his weakness was often visible to those with whom he was negotiating, and in view of his isolation, caused first by design and later by illness, this observation certainly rings true.

Nonetheless, the record has indicated that even far removed from the proceedings, the President's progressive illness would in any case have prevented him from exercising that breadth of interest, flexibility of goals, and depth of detail required to bring a successful postwar settlement to fruition.[275] That his extreme limitations were not made known to the public, in dangerous disregard for the nation's welfare, remains the responsibility of his personal physician, who violated the highest sense of professional integrity and national, if not international, interests.

## NOTES

1. Blum, *Wilson and the Politics of Morality*; Walworth, *Woodrow Wilson*, Bk. 2, p. 294.
2. George and George, *Wilson and House*; Post, "Woodrow Wilson Re-Examined."

3. Smith, *When the Cheering Stopped;* Walworth, *Woodrow Wilson.*

4. Weinstein, "Woodrow Wilson's Neurological Illness."

5. Weinstein, *Woodrow Wilson: A Medical and Psychological Biography.*

6. Wilson, *The Papers of Woodrow Wilson.*

7. The reader is referred to the following publications: Weinstein, "Wilson's Neurological Illness"; idem, *Woodrow Wilson;* Wilson, *Papers of Woodrow Wilson* (in which there are thirty references to Wilson's "strokes"); Link, Weinstein, et al., "Communication to the Editor"; and Ross, "Case for Psychohistory."

8. Michael F. Marmor, "Wilson, Strokes, and Zebras"; George, Marmor, and George, "Issues in Wilson Scholarship"; Monroe, "Comments on 'Woodrow Wilson's Neurological Illness'"; and Post, "Woodrow Wilson Re-examinined."

9. George, Marmor, and George, "Wilson Scholarship"; and Link, Weinstein, et al., "Communication to the Editor."

10. Long, "Aging in the Nervous System," p. 351.

11. See "Dementia" in American Psychiatric Association, *A Psychiatric Glossary.*

12. Busse, "Aging and Psychiatric Diseases," p. 78.

13. Lipowski, "Organic Mental Disorders," pp. 1375–76. The relationship of arteriosclerosis and hypertension to the development of dementia was recognized even in Wilson's time; see Osler, *Modern Medicine,* 4:439, printed in 1908.

14. Weinstein, *Woodrow Wilson,* p. 149.

15. Ibid., p. 159.

16. Ibid., p. 161.

17. Ibid., p. 165. Arthur Link confirmed that the disability involving Wilson's right arm was noticeable for years thereafter; personal communication to the author, September 25, 1985.

18. Ibid., p. 216.

19. Grayson, *Intimate Memoir,* p. 81.

20. Ibid. According to Grayson, "In the first attack he suffered from neuritis, of which he was not entirely cured until he became President of the United States. In the second attack he was operated upon for hemorrhoids. . . . In the third . . . there was a retinal hemorrhage in his left eye" (p. 81).

21. Ibid., p. 2.

22. One must assume that the discontinued medications included sodium nitrate and sodium iodide, which had been initiated for treatment of Wilson's hypertension and arteriosclerosis in 1906; see Link, Weinstein, et al., "Communication to Editor," p. 950. The use of these two drugs was supported by the leading authority in internal medicine of that day, Dr. William Osler; see *Modern Medicine,* 4:445–46.

23. Tumulty, *Wilson I Know,* p. 343.

24. Wilson, *Papers,* 32:67; cited in Weinstein, *Woodrow Wilson,* pp. 295, 296, 297.

25. Harrison, *Principles of Internal Medicine,* p. 710. Dr. de Schweinitz had told Wilson that he had serious changes of the arteries of the eyes, indicating that he had severe hypertension; Marmor, "Eyes of Woodrow Wilson," p. 463. The retina is the only tissue in which the arteries can be examined directly.

26. Osler, *Modern Medicine,* 4:443. Grayson's complacency cannot be justified, then, on the basis of unavailable data.

27. Weinstein, *Woodrow Wilson,* p. 251.

28. Ibid., p. 252.

29. "Reversible ischemic neurologic deficit"; a term signifying an episode compatible with stroke symptomatology that takes longer than twenty-four hours to clear completely.

30. Transient ischemic attack; identical to an RIND, but which clears in less than twenty-four hours.

31. Weinstein, *Woodrow Wilson*, p. 252. These pages contain no reference to weakness, numbness, or incoordination that would suggest an ischemic event, as opposed to that described in 1896–1897. Nor is the 1913 illness alluded to in Grayson's memoirs.

32. Weinstein argues to the contrary. See *Woodrow Wilson*, p. 252.

33. George and George, *Wilson and House*, p. 137.

34. Ibid., p. 142.

35. Corwin, *The President*, p. 267.

36. Link, *Wilson and the Progressive Era*, pp. 224–30.

37. Diary of Edward M. House, October 14, 1913, Library of Yale University; cited in Weinstein, *Woodrow Wilson*, p. 252.

38. Stockton Axson, Memoir of Woodrow Wilson, in the possession of Arthur S. Link; cited in Weinstein, *Woodrow Wilson*, p. 254.

39. Tumulty, *Wilson I Know*, p. 343.

40. Weinstein, *Woodrow Wilson*, p. 250.

41. Walworth, *Woodrow Wilson*, Bk. 2, p. 296.

42. Ray Stannard Baker, *Wilson and World Settlement*, 2:43.

43. Weinstein, *Woodrow Wilson*, p. 149. Another physician agreed; see L'Etang, *Pathology*, p. 48.

44. Loeser and Chin, "Hemifacial Spasm," p. 141.

45. House Diary, November 6, 1914, Wilson, *Papers*, 31:274; cited in Weinstein, *Woodrow Wilson*, p. 259.

46. Ibid., p. 258.

47. Ibid., p. 256. There is some conflict in the record on this point. Grayson asserted in his memoirs that he did in fact notify Wilson of the bad news. Grayson, *Intimate Memoir*, pp. 33–34.

48. Lansing, *Peace Negotiations*, p. 11.

49. House diary, April 2, 1916; cited in Weinstein, *Woodrow Wilson*, p. 303. Weinstein adds (n. 9, p. 303) that he doubts the normally discreet Grayson would have said this to House.

50. Lawrence Kolb, *Clinical Psychiatry*, p. 253.

51. Ibid., p. 253.

52. Weinstein, *Woodrow Wilson*, p. 328.

53. Baker and Dodd, *Public Papers of Wilson*, 4:435.

54. Weinstein, *Woodrow Wilson*, p. 313.

55. Busse, "Aging and Psychiatric Diseases," p. 78.

56. Katzman and Karasu, "Differential Diagnosis in Dementia," pp. 113–114.

57. Edwin Weinstein cited letters to Wilson's wife during this period with reference to episodes of transient weakness of the right hand. Wilson wrote: "At this point on the sheet this hand of mine went back on me and I had to let it off from further struggles with the pen. It's all right this morning." Weinstein, *Woodrow Wilson*, p. 295. This is a suggestive description of a transient ischemic attack (TIA). As a possible example of cervical nerve root compression, such intermittency of symptoms is inconsistent with that disease process; see Appendix 1, note 11.

58. Ibid., p. 313. This was the period during which Grayson discovered that Wilson's kidneys were not functioning adequately (see p. 8 in text). It is important to recall that the "same disease process [hypertension] which affects the vessels of the brain and retina may also involve the kidneys." Weinstein, *Woodrow Wilson*, p. 295.

59. Link, *Wilson*, 5:419–21; cited in Weinstein, *Woodrow Wilson*, p. 313.

60. George and George, *Wilson and House*, p. 176.

61. *New York Times*, February 17, 1918.

62. George and George, *Wilson and House*, p. 178.

63. Tumulty, *Wilson I Know*, p. 265.

64. Herbert Hoover, *Ordeal of Wilson*, p. 16 n. 2. Arthur Link is convinced that a definite change for the worse in Wilson's behavior had occurred by the summer and fall of 1918 (personal communication, September 25, 1985).

65. Weinstein, "Woodrow Wilson's Neurological Illness," p. 338.

66. Daniels, *Wilson Era*, p. 306.

67. Ibid., p. 307.

68. Lipowski, "Organic Mental Disorders," p. 1378.

69. Weinstein, *Woodrow Wilson*, p. 321.

70. George and George, *Wilson and House*, p. 213.

71. Ibid., p. 213; Seymour, *Intimate Papers*, 4:255.

72. Baker, *Life and Letters*, 8:481.

73. George and George, *Wilson and House*, p. 214.

74. Baker, *Life and Letters*, 8:539.

75. Lansing, *Peace Negotiations*, p. 22.

76. Baker, *Woodrow Wilson*, p. xxiv.

77. Herbert Hoover, *Ordeal of Wilson*, p. 77.

78. Ibid., pp. 72, 76.

79. Kinsbourne, "Cognitive Decline," p. 232.

80. Herbert Hoover, *Ordeal of Wilson*, p. 75.

81. Daniels, *Wilson Era*, p. 353. There were also some very personal, self-serving motives for Wilson's refusal to appoint Republican senators; see Link, *Wilson: Revolution, War, and Peace*, p. 105.

82. Daniels, *Wilson Era*, pp. 353, 355.

83. Baker, *Wilson and World Settlement*, 1:114.

84. Ibid., 1:112.

85. Link, *Wilson: Revolution, War, and Peace*, pp. 81, 82, 101. The original study detailing the impact of The Inquiry on the Paris Peace Conference is Gelfand's work *The Inquiry: America's Preparations for Peace, 1917–1919*.

86. Baker, *Wilson and World Settlement*, 1:193, 198.

87. Lansing, *Peace Negotiations*, pp. 215, 46, 24, 43. It should be acknowledged that Lansing had not been on good terms with Wilson since 1916; Link, *Wilson: Revolution, War, and Peace*, p. 16.

88. Baker, *Wilson and World Settlement*, 1:83, 104, 201.

89. Ibid., p. 261.

90. George and George, *Wilson and House*, pp. 216, 217.

91. Baker, *Wilson and World Settlement*, 2:275–76; Walworth, *Woodrow Wilson*, p. 293. For an overview of Wilson's economic thought, see William Diamond's analysis *The Economic Thought of Woodrow Wilson*.

92. Lipowski, "Organic Mental Disorders," p. 1378; Long, "Aging in the Nervous System" p. 349.

93. Baker, *Wilson and World Settlement*, 2:334, 272, 275.

94. George and George, *Wilson and House*, p. 226.

95. Ibid., pp. 214–15.

96. Lansing, *Peace Negotiations*, pp. 211–12.

97. Kurt Goldstein, "Functional Disorders in Brain Damage," p. 186. Some elements of the Goldstein hypothesis have undergone modification with time. Nevertheless, the overall implication for the individual with brain injury as it relates to his inability to employ abstract thinking is accepted by most neurologists and psychiatrists today.

98. George and George, *Wilson and House*, p. 218.

99. Personal communication, September 25, 1985.

100. Wilson to Richard Hooker, November 29, 1918, Wilson Papers, Library of Congress; cited in Weinstein, *Woodrow Wilson*, p. 331.

101. Weinstein, *Woodrow Wilson*, p. 323.

102. Lipowski, "Organic Mental Disorders," p. 1376.

103. Walworth, *Woodrow Wilson*, Bk. 2, pp. 236, 234.

104. George and George, *Wilson and House*, p. 215.

105. Ibid., p. 215. Statement attributed to the Australian Prime Minister.

106. Walworth, *Woodrow Wilson*, Bk. 2, p. 253.

107. George and George, *Wilson and House*, p. 258.

108. Wilson himself collaborated on this authorized biography. This is the only record in English currently available of the actual negotiations during the first month of the conference. Arthur Link is in the process of editing volumes of the *Wilson Papers* dealing with this period.

109. Ibid., 1:177.

110. Ibid., 1:178.

111. Ibid., 1:235.

112. Ibid., 2:20.

113. Ibid., 2:6.

114. Ibid., 2:292, 25–6.

115. Ibid., 1:292.

116. Ibid., pp. 292–93.

117. Wilson had temporarily returned to the United States on February 15, 1919.

118. Baker, *Wilson and World Settlement*, 1:309.

119. Walworth, *Woodrow Wilson*, Bk. 2, p. 257.

120. Goldstein, "Functional Disorders in Brain Damage," p. 186.

121. Walworth, *Woodrow Wilson*, Bk. 2, p. 259.

122. Ibid., Bk. 2, p. 279. House suffered from both gallbladder disease and kidney stones; see Walworth, *Woodrow Wilson*, Bk. 2, pp. 255, 384.

123. Herbert Hoover, *Ordeal of Wilson*, p. 3.

124. Walworth, *Woodrow Wilson*, Bk. 2, p. 281. Link took the argument one step further, declaring that House betrayed Wilson by agreeing to a preliminary peace treaty; *Wilson: Revolution, War, and Peace*, p. 88.

125. Walworth, *Woodrow Wilson*, Bk. 2, pp. 320–21.

126. Feerick, *Twenty-Fifth Amendment*, p. 14.

127. George and George, *Wilson and House*, p. 243.

128. Ibid., p. 245.

129. Baker, *Wilson and World Settlement*, 1:307, 306, 306–7.

130. Ibid., 2:48.

131. Ibid., 1:317.

132. Ibid., p. xxxiv. Link asserted that it was the European leaders who forbade direct press coverage and that Wilson gave briefings to Baker, his "liaison with the press"; *Wilson: Revolution, War, and Peace*, p. 102. The latter obviously was not satisfied with the amount of information he received, nor with what he could reveal to the press— which was very little. Baker, *Wilson and World Settlement*, 1:151.

133. Goldstein, "Functional Disorders in Brain Damage," p. 186.

134. Baker, *Wilson and World Settlement*, 1:152.

135. Ibid., 1:132.

136. Walworth, *Woodrow Wilson*, Bk. 2, p. 241.

137. Ibid., p. 256.

138. Lansing, *Peace Negotiations*, p. 217. In Wilson's defense, the President himself insisted that the phrase "open covenants, openly arrived at" was never intended to exclude private discussions between the participants on certain sensitive matters; see Baker, *Wilson and World Settlement*, 1:46; and Link, *Wilson: Revolution, War, and Peace*, p. 102. This is true. Yet his inability to acknowledge that the intent of his words

might be misconstrued again conjures up visions of a compromised abstract attitude. Goldstein described the failure to "perform concepts or symbols, to understand them." "Functional Disorders in Brain Damage," p. 186. This roughly correlates with what Weinstein interpreted in Wilson as a failure in "symbolic behavior in relation to speech." *Woodrow Wilson*, p. 342.

139. Walworth, *Woodrow Wilson*, Bk. 2, p. 309, n. 5.

140. Ibid., n. 8; George and George, *Wilson and House*, p. 248.

141. Lipowski, "Organic Mental Disorders," 2:1376.

142. Brill, "Postencephalitic States or Conditions," 4:158.

143. Heller and Kornfeld, "Delirium and Related Problems," 4:47. If not an overt infection by a virus within the brain (i.e., true encephalitis), a parameningeal inflammatory process from a systemic virus can still induce identical symptoms.

144. Ewald Busse speaks for most neurologists when he asserts that "there is now increasing evidence that prolonged marginal blood flow can produce degenerative changes in the brain which can lead to behavioral and intellectual impairment." Busse, "Aging and Psychiatric Diseases," p. 81.

145. L'Etang, *Pathology*, pp. 48–50.

146. Walworth, *Woodrow Wilson*, Bk. 2, p. 297 n. 13. Weinstein later felt the cause to have been either viral influenza or the virus of encephalitis lethargica. *Woodrow Wilson*, p. 338. These diagnoses have recently been questioned (personal communication, Arthur Link).

147. In a letter to Tumulty of April 10, 1919, Grayson wrote: "The President was taken violently sick last Thursday. . . . At six he was seized with violent paroxysms of coughing, which were so severe and frequent that it interfered with his breathing. He had a fever of 103 and a profuse diarrhœa." Tumulty, *Wilson I Know*, p. 350.

148. Weinstein, *Woodrow Wilson*, pp. 249–50.

149. Ibid., p. 250.

150. Ibid., p. 360.

151. Ibid., p. 297.

152. Lipowski, "Organic Mental Disorders," p. 1377.

153. Brill, "Postencephalitic States." 4:157, 158.

154. Kolb, *Clinical Psychiatry*, p. 253. Emphasis added.

155. Michael O'Brien, "Vascular Disease and Dementia," p. 88. "Ischemia" signifies lack of blood supply.

156. L. Sokoloff, "Effects of Aging on Cerebral Circulation," p. 370.

157. Lipowski, "Organic Mental Disorders," p. 1377.

158. Irwin Hoover, *Forty-Two Years*, pp. 98–99.

159. Grayson, *Intimate Memoir*, p. 85.

160. April 21, 1919, Edith Benham Helm Papers, Library of Congress; cited in Weinstein, *Woodrow Wilson*, p. 341.

161. Walworth, *Woodrow Wilson*, Bk. 2, p. 252.

162. Wilson's valet later recalled that "When he got back on the job, his peculiar ideas were even more pronounced." Irwin Hoover, *Forty-Two Years*, p. 98.

163. Walworth, *Woodrow Wilson*, p. 297; Starling, *White House*, p. 138.

164. Walworth, *Woodrow Wilson*, Bk. 2, p. 296.

165. Weinstein, "Woodrow Wilson's Neurological Illness," p. 324.

166. Baker, *Wilson and World Settlement*, 1:296; 2:64, 65, 67. Arthur Link agreed; *Wilson: Revolution, War, and Peace*, p. 90. Nevertheless, Link admits that the President's disease-induced state of mind may have influenced some of the compromises made. (p. 89). Whether he had true encephalitis is arguable—and probably immaterial—to the argument. Parameningeal infections can induce lasting behavioral changes in the aged.

167. Walworth, *Woodrow Wilson*, Bk. 2, pp. 297–98.

168. Weinstein, *Woodrow Wilson*, p. 339.

169. Walworth, *Woodrow Wilson*, Bk. 2, p. 294.

170. Ibid., pp. 293, 299, 300.

171. Weinstein, *Woodrow Wilson*, pp. 339, 344. Certainly there is agreement among physicians regarding the impact of this brief illness. Hugh L'Etang worded his verdict in the following manner: Wilson "fought on alone and must carry the responsibility for some serious mistakes. . . . He had unwittingly sowed the seeds for other tyrants to reap and use for their own destructive purposes." L'Etang, *Pathology*, p. 50.

172. Baker, *Wilson and World Settlement*, 2:67.

173. Ibid., 2:81.

174. Ibid.

175. Ibid., 2:82. Alexander and Juliette George comment that "Clemenceau and Lloyd George succeeded in defining the negotiating situation for Wilson in terms of the bargains they wished to drive. . . . *It does not seem to have occurred to Wilson* [italics mine] that he need not accept this definition . . . that his negotiating position . . . was not necessarily unfavorable, and that the situation could be structured differently and to his own advantage." George and George, *Wilson and House*, p. 257. In essence, Wilson was failing once again to utilize the abstract attitude in not recognizing this. See also Bailey, *Wilson and the Great Betrayal*, p. 190.

176. Link, *Higher Realism*, pp. 138–39.

177. Baker, *Wilson and World Settlement*, 2:78.

178. Ibid., 2:105, 104.

179. Weinstein, *Woodrow Wilson*, pp. 344–45, 352.

180. Baker, *Wilson and World Settlement*, 1:33. "A note made by [Wilson] upon a cablegram from Colonel House, dated November 15, 1918, shows that he knew something of these treaties at least." Wilson may have perjured himself at a later White House conference on August 19, 1919, when he stated that "the whole series of undertakings were disclosed to me for the first time [after reaching Paris]." For a full discussion of this controversial issue see ibid., 1:33–36 and Link, *Wilson: Revolution, War, and Peace*, p. 78.

181. Baker, *Wilson and World Settlement*, 1:39.

182. Walworth, *Woodrow Wilson*, Bk. 2, p. 309 n. 5.

183. Baker, *Wilson and World Settlement*, 2:131. Wilson had promised Orlando the Brenner Pass boundary in the Trentino, an area that contained some 250,000 Tyrolese Germans; see Walworth, *Woodrow Wilson*, Bk. 2, p. 256.

184. Baker, *Wilson and World Settlement*, 2:168.

185. Goldstein, "Functional Disorders in Brain Damage," p. 186.

186. Ibid.

187. Herbert Hoover, *The Memoirs of Herbert Hoover* (New York, 1951–57), 1:468; cited in Weinstein, *Woodrow Wilson*, p. 344.

188. Lipowski, "Organic Mental Disorders," p. 1388.

189. George and George, *Wilson and House*, pp. 264–65. Wilson feared new reservations would require renegotiation of the Treaty. He misread the forecast from the beginning, believing the Treaty would be accepted without change; Link, *Wilson: Revolution, War, and Peace*, p. 107. This proved to be a critical error in judgment.

190. Lipowski, "Organic Mental Disorders," p. 1376.

191. Weinstein, *Woodrow Wilson*, p. 344.

192. Walworth, *Woodrow Wilson*, Bk. 2, p. 345. Link considered Wilson's new attitude toward the Senate a noteworthy change in his behavior; Link, *Wilson: Revolution, War, and Peace*, p. 107.

193. Walworth, *Woodrow Wilson*, Bk. 2, pp. 291, 362.

194. Edith Wilson, *My Memoir*, pp. 280, 283.

195. Grayson, *Intimate Memoir*, p. 97.

196. Tumulty, *Wilson I Know*, p. 434.

197. Daniels, *Wilson Era*, p. 479.

198. George and George, *Wilson and House*, p. 311. Arthur Link agreed; *Wilson: Revolution, War, and Peace*, p. 106. See also Fleming, *League of Nations*, p. 336.

199. Grayson, *Intimate Memoir*, p. 97.

200. Smith, *When the Cheering Stopped*, p. 75; Edith Wilson, *My Memoir*, p. 283.

201. Smith, *When the Cheering Stopped*, p. 81. Edmund Starling described the speech in this manner: "He mouthed certain words as if he had never spoken them before. . . . He had difficulty following the trend of his thought." Starling, *White House*, p. 152.

202. Edith Wilson, *My Memoir*, p. 284.

203. Grayson, *Intimate Memoir*, p. 99.

204. Smith, *When the Cheering Stopped*, pp. 84, 85. Starling corroborated this description: "The left side of his face seemed to have fallen a little. . . . Only the right side . . . responded to his command." Starling, *White House*, p. 153.

205. Smith, *When the Cheering Stopped*, p. 90.

206. Ibid.

207. In a technical sense, it is possible that the middle cerebral artery alone was involved. Involvement of the leg as well might implicate occlusion of the lateral lenticulostriate branches of the middle cerebral artery, which supply both the arm and the leg in the internal capsule.

208. To be more precise, the "pure motor hemiplegic syndrome." See Fisher and Curry, "Pure Motor Hemiplegia of Vascular Origin."

209. George and George, *Wilson and House*, p. 293.

210. Ibid., p. 295.

211. *New York Times*, October 10, 1919. Link agreed that Wilson may have made conflict inevitable by the "partisan coloration" he gave to the process of peacemaking; *Wilson: Revolution, War, and Peace*, p. 105.

212. Smith, *When the Cheering Stopped*, p. 93. Other unconfirmed rumors persist to the present day. According to one confidential source, Wilson had been treated as a young man for syphilis by Dr. Louis A. Duhring, a dermatologist at the University of Pennsylvania. This was neither confirmed nor denied in the author's conversation with a relative of that physician, Dr. William Baltzell. Moreover, it has been alleged that a syphlitic gumma was removed from Wilson's brain at autopsy, accounting for his stroke (personal communication, Dr. Clifford Ameduri). All official sources deny that Wilson ever had an autopsy.

213. Ibid., pp. 89, 91.

214. Herbert Hoover, *Ordeal of Wilson*, p. 271.

215. Smith, *When the Cheering Stopped*, p. 99.

216. Ibid., p. 86; Walworth, *Woodrow Wilson*, p. 375.

217. Herbert Hoover, *Ordeal of Wilson*, pp. 271, 272.

218. Walworth, *Woodrow Wilson*, Bk. 2, p. 374; Weinstein, *Woodrow Wilson*, p. 357. This is readily explained on an anatomic basis. An infarct involving the right parietal-occipital lobe, such as would be involved with an occlusion of the right internal carotid artery, destroys the cortical visual centers on the left side of the peripheral visual fields of each eye. This, in conjunction with Wilson's longstanding limited vision of the entire left eye, would have left him with effective vision only in the right temporal field. Reading therefore would have been difficult, owing to the fact that one reads from left to right on a page.

219. Walworth, *Woodrow Wilson*, p. 375. Compromise of the muscles of phonation, involving the larynx and control of tongue movements, would account for his weakened, dysarthric speech.

220. Weinstein, *Woodrow Wilson*, p. 357.

221. Ibid., p. 359. The Goldstein hypothesis would cite this as another example of the impaired abstract attitude.

222. Walworth, *Woodrow Wilson*, Bk. 2, p. 375. He was aware enough, however, to convince those around him to conceal his infirmities (p. 375).

223. Ibid.

224. Edith Wilson, *My Memoir*, p. 289.

225. U.S. Constitution, Article 2, Section 1.

226. Tumulty, *Wilson I Know*, pp. 443–44. Grayson and Tumulty portrayed Lansing's efforts as an isolated vendetta by an ungrateful subordinate. Yet, among the legislative branch there were others of Wilson's own party who shared Lansing's concern. See Smith, *When the Cheering Stopped*, p. 112.

227. Weinstein, *Woodrow Wilson*, p. 367.

228. For an examination of this specious argument the reader is referred to Tumulty, *Wilson I Know*, p. 446, and Daniels, *Wilson Era*, p. 524.

229. Tumulty, *Wilson I Know*, p. 445. A few other supporters of Wilson, woefully uninformed, backed Tumulty and Grayson's successful attempt to blackball Lansing. Josephus Daniels asserted that "Wilson's restoration to ability to carry on, even though never strong again, justified [the Cabinet's] refusal to accept Lansing's point of view." Daniels, *Wilson Era*, p. 524. This is a hollow assertion. It is obvious that Daniels had no precise knowledge of Wilson's real disability, certainly not enough to consider the merits of Lansing's proposal. Nor did the issue ever come to a vote in the cabinet; it was nipped in the bud by Tumulty's peremptory actions.

230. Tumulty, *Wilson I Know*, pp. 441, 442.

231. Herbert Hoover, *Ordeal of Wilson*, p. 276.

232. Walworth, *Woodrow Wilson*, Bk. 2, pp. 320–21.

233. Herbert Hoover, *Ordeal of Wilson*, pp. 277–78.

234. Tumulty, *Wilson I Know*, p. 438.

235. Ibid.

236. Grayson, *Intimate Memoir*, p. 53. In Grayson's entire chapter on the subject he never once considers the implication of restricted accessibility to the President.

237. Herbert Hoover, *Ordeal of Wilson*, pp. 287, 293.

238. Ibid., p. 287.

239. Edith Wilson, *My Memoir*, p. 289. Mrs. Wilson's claim is belied somewhat by Gene Smith's assertion that she had been responsible for filling certain Cabinet vacancies during her husband's illness. Smith, *When the Cheering Stopped*, p. 143.

240. Edith Wilson, *My Memoir*, p. 290.

241. Bennett, "Social Isolation."

242. Kolb, *Clinical Psychiatry*, p. 271; Anthony Storr, "The Man," p. 243.

243. Weinstein, *Woodrow Wilson*, pp. 357–58.

244. Ibid., p. 365.

245. Tumulty, *Wilson I Know*, p. 454.

246. Weinstein, *Woodrow Wilson*, p. 369. Axson was Wilson's brother-in-law.

247. Tumulty, *Wilson I Know*, p. 455. Tumulty was guilty of inconsistency. He had earlier volunteered in these same memoirs that Wilson held the senators opposing him to be contemptible, narrow, selfish, and "poor little minds that never get anywhere, but run around in a circle." (pp. 378–79)

248. Smith, *When the Cheering Stopped*, p. 119. Subsequent research by Ralph Stone suggests this is an oversimplification, yet there is enough merit in it to warrant the

simpler distinction. See Stone, *Irreconcilables*, pp. 178–82, for a more precise distinction of the forces aligned against Wilson.

249. George and George, *Wilson and House*, p. 287.

250. Ibid., p. 292.

251. Goldstein, "Functional Disorders in Brain Damage," p. 187; see also Fleming, *League of Nations*, p. 493.

252. Smith, *When the Cheering Stopped*, p. 119.

253. Herbert Hoover, *Ordeal of Wilson*, p. 284.

254. Ibid., p. 281.

255. Daniels, *Wilson Era*, p. 473.

256. Edith Wilson, *My Memoir*, p. 297.

257. George and George, *Wilson and House*, p. 293.

258. Ibid., p. 300.

259. Hitchcock Papers, Library of Congress; cited in Smith, *When the Cheering Stopped*, p. 114.

260. George and George, *Wilson and House*, p. 301. These included Fleming, Taft, Hoover, Bliss, White, Miller, and Bailey; n. 29, p. 351. Mrs. Wilson had a different view of the question: "Mr. Lodge dropped the word amendment and began the gradual introduction of 'reservations.' . . . The difference between these reservations . . . and the original Lodge-Fall amendments was the difference between Tweedledum and Tweedledee." Edith Wilson, *My Memoir*, p. 290. This opinion, it appears, carried the day in the executive branch.

261. George and George, *Wilson and House*, p. 301. Link himself observed that Wilson's condition after the stroke "aggravated all his more unfortunate personal traits." *Wilson: Revolution, War, and Peace*, p. 121. This is precisely what the psychiatrist means when he speaks of "an accentuation of the premorbid personality" in early dementia states.

262. George and George, *Wilson and House*, pp. 305–6.

263. Baker, *Wilson and World Settlement*, 1:315.

264. George and George, *Wilson and House*, p. 307.

265. Ibid., pp. 306; taken from House diary entry, February 18, 1920.

266. Ibid., pp. 310–11; Stone, *Irreconcilables*, p. 161.

267. George and George, *Wilson and House*, p. 311.

268. Chapman and H. Wolff, "Diseases of the Neopallium," 42:677. With respect to an evolving dementia, Wilson's medical history may therefore be divided into two periods. The first was roughly a twenty-year interval characterized by untreated hypertension and a few episodes suggestive of lacunar strokes, ending with a severe febrile viral infection in April 1919. Following his devastating stroke in September 1919, Wilson entered the second phase of his illness, after which few observers denied that his mental faculties were compromised. The first period parallels what Wolff and Chapman define as phases I and II of impaired functional capacity antedating phases III and IV, during which obvious dementia is manifest. Recalling the examples of Wilson's changing behavior described in this review, it might be instructive to briefly recount those aspects of impaired adaptation that Wolff and Chapman believe typify phases I and II of this continuum of disease. The earliest change in phase I of dementia is a reduction in adaptive versatility. The affected individual's capacity to endure frustration declines. He may make unrestrained comments or criticisms. He complains of tiring easily after sustained effort in a given task. Accordingly, he concentrates on one issue at a time. Goals are pursued less effectively. "Diseases of the Neopallium," p. 681. These features correlate rather strikingly with Wilson's behavior during the year antedating his viral illness in Paris. As the process accelerates into phase II, the afflicted individual becomes increasingly self-absorbed with his own interests. There is less attention to detail. He becomes insensitive

to the reactions of others, recall is delayed, and frustration thresholds are even more evidently lowered (pp. 681–82). The record suggests that these qualities characterized Wilson from his April illness until his stroke in September 1919. Only with phase III do associates come to realize that there is something definitely abnormal about the person's behavior, which in Wilson's case would apply to his conduct after his stroke in September 1919. These phases evolve in conjunction with the increasing amount of cerebral tissue lost (p. 678). Yet in addition to the extent of tissue destroyed, a major determinant of impairment is the adequacy of adaptation as defined by the underlying premorbid personality. Those with rigid adaptive patterns before illness strikes demonstrate greater impairment as a rule. This last observation, of course, would have important implications, given Wilson's personality profile before the onset of his hypertension and cerebrovascular insufficiency.

269. Herbert Hoover, *Ordeal of Wilson*, pp. 276–77.
270. Grayson, *Intimate Memoir*, pp. 106–7.
271. Walworth, *Woodrow Wilson*, Bk. 2, p. 395.
272. Herbert Hoover, *Ordeal of Wilson*, p. 277.
273. Grayson, *Intimate Memoir*, p. 114.
274. George and George, *Wilson and House*, p. 266.
275. Despite his sympathetic view of Wilson, Arthur Link acknowledges the role of illness as events transpired, concluding that "his illness gravely impaired his perceptions of political reality and was probably the *principal cause* of his strategic errors." Italics mine. *Wilson: Revolution, War, and Peace*, p. 127.

# REFERENCES

**MEDICAL**

American Psychiatric Association. *A Psychiatric Glossary*. 3d ed. Washington, D.C.: The Association, 1969.
Arieti, Sylvano, ed. *American Handbook of Psychiatry*. 2d ed. 6 vols. New York: Basic Books, 1975.
Bennett, R. "Social Isolation and Isolation-Reducing Programs." *Bulletin of the New York Academy of Medicine* 49 (1973): 1142–45.
Brill, Henry. "Postencephalitic States or Conditions." In *American Handbook of Psychiatry*, 2d ed., edited by Sylvano Arieti, 4:152–65. New York: Basic Books, 1975.
Busse, Ewald. "Aging and Psychiatric Diseases of Late Life." In *American Handbook of Psychiatry*, 2d ed., edited by Sylvano Arieti, 4:67–89. New York: Basic Books, 1975.
Chapman, Loring, and Harold Wolff. "Diseases of the Neopallium." *Medical Clinics of North America* 42(1958): 677–89.
Fisher, C. Miller, and H. B. Curry. "Pure Motor Hemiplegia of Vascular Origin." *Archives of Neurology* 13(1965): 30–44.
Goldstein, Kurt. "Functional Disorders in Brain Damage." In *American Handbook of Psychiatry*, 2d ed., edited by Sylvano Arieti, 4:182–207. New York: Basic Books, 1975.
Harrison, T. R., ed. *Principles of Internal Medicine*. 5th ed. New York: McGraw-Hill Book Co., 1966.
Heller, Stanley, and Donald Kornfeld. "Delirium and Related Problems." In *American Handbook of Psychiatry*, 2d ed., edited by Sylvano Arieti, 4:43–66. New York: Basic Books, 1975.

Kaplan, Harold I., ed. *Comprehensive Textbook of Psychiatry.* 3d ed. 3 vols. Baltimore and London: Williams and Wilkins, 1980.

Katzman, R. and T. B. Karasu. "Differential Diagnosis of Dementia." In *Neurological and Sensory Disorders in the Elderly,* edited by W. S. Fields, pp. 103–39. New York: Stratton Intercontinental Medical Books Co., 1975.

Kinsbourne, Marcel. "Cognitive Decline with Advancing Age." In *Aging and Dementia,* edited by W. Lynn Smith and Marcel Kinsbourne, 217–35. New York: Spectrum Publications, 1977.

Kolb, Lawrence. *Modern Clinical Psychiatry.* 9th edition. Philadelphia: W. B. Saunders Co., 1977.

L'Etang, Hugh. *The Pathology of Leadership.* New York: Hawthorn Books, 1970.

Lipowski, Zbigniew J. "Organic Mental Disorders." In *Comprehensive Textbook of Psychiatry,* 3d ed., edited by Harold I. Kaplan, 2:1359–1469. Baltimore and London: Williams and Wilkins, 1980.

Loeser, John, and James Chin. "Hemifacial Spasm: Treatment by Microsurgical Facial Nerve Decompression." *Neurosurgery* 13(1983): 141–46.

Marmor, Michael F., "Wilson, Strokes, and Zebras." *New England Journal of Medicine* 307(1982): 528–35.

———. "The Eyes of Woodrow Wilson." *Ophthalmology* 92(1985): 454–65.

Monroe, Robert T. "Comments on 'Woodrow Wilson's Neurological Illness' by Dr. E. A. Weinstein," 1971. Arthur Walworth Papers. Yale University Library, New Haven, Connecticut.

O'Brien, Michael D. "Vascular Disease and Dementia in the Elderly." In *Aging and Dementia,* edited by W. Lynn Smith and Marcel Kinsbourne, pp. 77–90. New York: Spectrum Publications, 1977.

Osler, William. *Modern Medicine: Its Theory and Practice.* Vol. 4. Philadelphia and New York: Lea and Febiger, 1909.

Post, Jerrold M. "Woodrow Wilson Re-examined: The Mind-Body Controversy Redux and Other Disputations." *Political Psychology* 4(1983): 289–306.

Ross, Dorothy. "Woodrow Wilson and the Case for Psychohistory." *Journal of American History* 69(1982): 659–68.

Sokoloff, L. "Effects of Normal Aging on Cerebral Circulation and Energy Metabolism." In *Brain Function of Old Age,* edited by F. Hoffmeister and F. Müller, pp. 367–80. Berlin: Springer-Verlag, 1979.

Weinstein, Edwin A. "Woodrow Wilson's Neurological Illness." *Journal of American History* 57(1970): 324–51.

———. *Woodrow Wilson: A Medical and Psychological Biography.* Princeton, N.J.: Princeton University Press, 1981.


PRIMARY

Baker, Ray Stannard. *Woodrow Wilson: Life and Letters.* 8 vols. Garden City, N.Y.: Doubleday, 1927–1939.

———. *Woodrow Wilson and World Settlement.* 3 vols. Garden City, N.Y.: Doubleday, Page, and Co., 1922.

———. *Woodrow Wilson: Life and Letters.* 8 vols. Westport, Conn.: Greenwood Press, 1968.

Baker, Ray Stannard, and William E. Dodd, eds. *The Public Papers of Woodrow Wilson.* 6 vols. New York: Harper and Brothers, 1925–1927.

Daniels, Josephus. *The Wilson Era: Years of War and After.* Chapel Hill: University of North Carolina Press, 1946.

Grayson, Cary T. *Woodrow Wilson: An Intimate Memoir.* New York: Holt, Rinehart and Winston, 1960.

Helm, Edith Benham. Papers. Library of Congress, Washington, D.C.

Hoover, Herbert. *The Ordeal of Woodrow Wilson.* New York: McGraw-Hill Book Co., 1958.

Hoover, Irwin Hood. *Forty-Two Years in the White House.* Boston: Houghton Mifflin Co., 1934.

————. "The Facts about President Wilson's Illness." I. H. Hoover Papers. Library of Congress, Washington, D.C.

Lansing, Robert. *The Peace Negotiations: A Personal Narrative.* Boston and New York: Houghton Mifflin Co., 1921.

Seymour, Charles, ed. *The Intimate Papers of Colonel House.* 4 vols. Boston: Houghton Mifflin, 1926–1928.

Starling, Edmund W. *Starling of the White House.* New York: Simon and Schuster, 1946.

Tumulty, Joseph P. *Woodrow Wilson As I Know Him.* Garden City, N.Y.: Doubleday, Page, and Co., 1921.

Wilson, Edith Bolling. *My Memoir.* Indianapolis and New York: Bobbs-Merrill Co., 1939.

Wilson, Woodrow. *The Papers of Woodrow Wilson.* 49 Vols. to date. Edited by Arthur Link. Princeton, N.J.: Princeton University Press, 1966–.

NEWSPAPERS AND PERIODICALS

*New York Times*, October 10, 1919.

SECONDARY

Bailey, Thomas A. *Woodrow Wilson and the Great Betrayal.* New York: Macmillan, Co., 1945.

Blum, John Morton. *Woodrow Wilson and the Politics of Morality.* Boston: Little, Brown and Co., 1956.

Corwin, Edward S. *The President: Office and Powers, 1787–1948: History and Analysis of Practice and Opinion.* 3d ed., rev. New York: New York University Press, 1948.

Diamond, William. *The Economic Thought of Woodrow Wilson.* The Johns Hopkins University Studies in Historical and Political Science, vol. 61, no. 4. Baltimore: The Johns Hopkins Press, 1943.

Feerick, John D. *The Twenty-fifth Amendment: Its Complete History and Earliest Applications.* New York: Fordham University Press, 1976.

Fleming, Denna Frank. *The United States and the League of Nations.* New York: G. P. Putnam's Sons, 1932.

Gelfand, Lawrence E. *The Inquiry: American Preparations for Peace, 1917–1919.* New Haven: Yale University Press, 1963.

George, Alexander, and Juliette George. *Woodrow Wilson and Colonel House.* New York: Dover Publications, 1965. Copyright © 1956 by A. L. and J. L. George; renewed 1984.

George, Juliette L., Michael F. Marmor, and Alexander L. George. "Issues in Wilson Scholarship: References to Early 'Strokes' in The *Papers of Woodrow Wilson.*" *Journal of American History* 70(1984): 845–53.

Link, Arthur S. *Woodrow Wilson and the Progressive Era, 1910–1917.* New York: Harper, 1954.

————. *The Higher Realism of Woodrow Wilson, and Other Essays.* Nashville: Vanderbilt University Press, 1971.

————. *Woodrow Wilson: Revolution, War, and Peace.* Arlington Heights, Ill.: Harlan Davidson, 1979.

Link, Arthur, Edwin A. Weinstein, et al. "Communication to the Editor." *Journal of American History* 70(1984): 945–55.

Smith, Gene. *When the Cheering Stopped: The Last Years of Woodrow Wilson.* New York: William Morrow and Co., 1964.

Stone, Ralph. *The Irreconcilables.* Lexington: University of Kentucky Press, 1970.

Storr, Anthony. "The Man." In *Churchill Revised: A Critical Assessment.* Edited by A. J. P. Taylor, pp. 229–74. New York: Dial Press, 1969.

Walworth, Arthur. *Woodrow Wilson.* 2d ed., rev. New York: Houghton Mifflin Co., 1965.

*Whatever poet, orator, or sage*
*May say of it, old age is still old age.*

*Longfellow*

# Hindenburg, MacDonald, and Piłsudski: The Interwar Years

Europe had many ills during the interwar years. These included its aging leadership. Three of the dominant protagonists of that era—Paul von Hindenburg of Germany, Ramsay MacDonald of Great Britain, and Józef Piłsudski of Poland—suffered from varying degrees of senility during the critical period in which Adolf Hitler assumed the chancellorship of Germany. Yet the prevalence of compromised leadership at this time epitomized a far graver condition affecting the Old World. A virulent cancer ate away at its governing institutions, devouring the continent with alarming rapidity. Central Europe had attempted representative government and found it wanting; Germany itself was virtually ungovernable. Critical mutations had occurred. In both Poland and Germany dictatorship by emergency decree supplanted democracy. And in Britain recourse to a bipartisan national government ineffectively camouflaged the unhealthy state of traditional party rule.

Each of these institutional mutations reflected the effect of aging on the political process, and each indirectly contributed to the fascist malignancy that transformed the European landscape during the thirties. Medical dictum has long suggested that cancer is an unfortunate by-product of aging. Perhaps it was only fitting, then, that these aged leaders were among those who failed to effect a cure for the malaise triggered by the post—World War I settlement. Indeed, the increasing debility of Old World leadership only magnified the inadequacies of the Treaty of Versailles. The Hitlerian cancer fed upon the body of the Versailles text, and the dilatory efforts of the aging politicians called upon during the early thirties to exorcise the malady paradoxically hastened its spread. The Nazi malignancy could not have flourished in the early stages of its growth without other agents to trigger the fatal mutation. Both a fertile substrate and a breakdown of the host organism's defenses is required for cancer to gain a foothold. Neither were in short supply in Europe during the thirties. The substrate of Germany was in a perpetual crisis under the influence of the aging giant von Hindenburg, and the very heart of *corpus Europa*'s potential defense was cut out by British knives of appeasement and disarmament wielded by the unsteady hand of Prime Minister MacDonald.

These are harsh indictments indeed against the leadership of the Old World, and they necessarily call to mind two questions. First, were these three leaders truly senile, by the medical definition of the word? Second, did their respective medical conditions affect their actions as leaders and contribute to the ease with which Hitler overran Central Europe? Certainly there are intriguing parallels among the three. Each died either during or immediately after his tenure in office, attesting to the severity of the medical conditions that afflicted them. Each governed during the critical period of Hitler's ascent, roughly encompassing the years 1931 to 1935. Each relied upon traditional diplomacy to deal with an adversary who epitomized cynical duplicity. Each was increasingly isolated in office as the years passed and was forced to rely upon subordinate advisors as his eyes and ears on the world. And each, without question, clung to the trappings of power far too long, past his physiologic prime.

To examine the merits of the above argument, one must begin with definitions. The reader has already been introduced to one form of dementia in the last chapter. Perhaps the most authoritative textbook in its field today, Baker's *Clinical Neurology*, outlines the salient features of the disorder in general:

1. Memory is invariably restricted. The failure of memory is relatively greater for recent and impersonal events as compared to remote events and those which have more personal content.

2. The afflicted individual's perceptions of the immediate environment are distorted, and his actions may be inappropriate for the stimulus he receives.

3. Willed action is markedly reduced, often to the point of profound apathy.

4. The ability to solve problems reflects a diminished capacity to comprehend a situation. Judgment is impaired and decision making is left to others. This characterizes what neurologists term a "failure of the abstract attitude." [1]

Physicians are aware that observations by reliable witnesses are indispensable in making the diagnosis in a given patient. [2] This legitimizes the methodology used in the present study. The properly trained medical historian may use memoirs, testimonials, and other primary source materials to build a case, retrospectively, about a historical figure. Knowing that the diagnosis of dementia implies an interference with occupational function as well, even some secondary sources are of value in describing an afflicted leader's impact on his political or diplomatic environment. If the investigator knows what to look for, such historical data may be every bit as precise as a clinical history obtained by a physician. As 80 percent of diagnosis in medical practice relies on the medical history, and only 20 percent on physical examination, the latter is relatively unimportant in such medico-historical analysis. This is particularly true in assessing intellectual performance; obvious physical alterations occur only in the end stage of senility or dementia.

The aged final President of the Weimar Republic, Paul von Hindenburg, serves as an introductory illustration before embarking upon a study of the more perplexing cases of Ramsay MacDonald and Józef Piłsudski. For neither historians nor his own contemporaries have doubted that the decrepit octogenarian was senile during those last, dark years before Hitler assumed the chancellorship of Germany. Hindenburg compromised the viability of the Republic through his inexplicable dismissal of one chancellor after another during the early thirties; the government thereafter remained in a perpetual succession crisis.

The historian A. J. Ryder marked the year 1930 as the obvious turning point in Hindenburg's command over events—perhaps over himself as well:

> So long as the system worked, as it did until March 1930, Hindenburg could rely on the rules of the constitution and his own common sense to keep out of trouble. But by then he was in his eighty-third year, physically and mentally exhausted, hardly able to grasp, still less to solve a political crisis for which he had neither training nor aptitude. He leaned increasingly on his advisors. . . . To most Germans Hindenburg with his square head and massive frame was the incarnation of steadfastness. . . . Yet his solidity had for some time been hardly distinguishable from inertia; the inertia now became a senile torpor. [3]

In that same month Hindenburg appointed Heinrich Brüning as Chancellor, and asked him to form a government independent of the parlia-

*Paul von Hindenburg elected President, 1925*

mentary majority. The German scholar Rudolf Morsey asserted that Brüning's appointment marked the beginning of an era of presidential governments, "based on confidence in the Reich President and on his extraordinary constitutional powers. . . . There was to be no turning back to a parliamentary democracy in the spirit of Weimar."[4] Unfortunately, Hindenburg's intellect did not match the strong governing powers accorded him. Brüning later recalled how much the aged President had deteriorated. On one occasion Hindenburg had arrived at a railway station in Berlin to meet his chancellor, only to fail to recognize him![5] Here, then, are critical references to specific criteria required to establish a diagnosis of dementia: the inability to grasp, much less solve, problems;

an increasing dependency on others for decision making; a pervasive apathy; and last, disorders of perception and loss of memory.

Hindenburg's reliance upon others fostered the breakdown of Germany's parliamentary system as the increasingly incapacitated President was perversely forced to play a more active role. This proved to be one major factor leading to a striking degree of turmoil, confusion, and intrigue during the last years of the Weimar Republic. Hindenburg's obvious weakness allowed divisiveness among his subordinates to flourish. This brought out self-serving intriguers from the political woodwork. Chief among these was General Kurt von Schleicher, who fancied himself the army spokesman for political affairs. Probably no one individual exercised more influence over Hindenburg, and consequently over the course of German politics, than did this German Rasputin. He was the critical link between the succession of chancellors who passed through the door of the Weimar Republic and down the darkening corridor of the Nazi movement to Adolf Hitler's chamber beyond. Nothing speaks more to the depths of cynicism and intrigue in these years (and by inference to Hindenburg's increasing compromise) than the ease with which Schleicher manipulated his aged superior. Through Hindenburg's son, Oskar, who was serving as personal adjutant to his father, Schleicher easily gained admittance to the presidential palace at a moment's notice. This resulted in what the historian William Halperin called a "palace camarilla" that eventually took Hindenburg completely in tow.[6] Three chancellors and numerous subordinates were axed indirectly by Schleicher's hand under the myopic eye of the malleable President. This cynical manipulator adeptly cleared the cobwebs from the aging President's mind regarding actions, appointments, and resignations. He used those same cobwebs to weave threads that bound Hindenburg to a process that paradoxically unraveled any hope of orderly government function. Ultimately, Schleicher became so entangled in these webs of intrigue as to be a prisoner of them himself—but not before Germany had become essentially ungovernable.

But what of Hindenburg himself? It has already been observed that old age accentuates certain features of character developed in earlier years. The elderly often become caricatures of themselves. Qualities that were only mildly apparent at a younger age become magnified with the passage of years. In Hindenburg's case, certain disturbing qualities had already been evident for some time by the thirties. For one thing, he had demonstrated increasing distaste for responsibility and accountability since World War I. At Hindenburg's request, a trusted confidant, General Wilhelm Groener, had been made the sacrificial lamb for German acceptance of the Versailles Treaty. On June 23, 1919, the Supreme Army Command at Kolberg received a call from President Friedrich

Ebert requesting their recommendation for rejection or acceptance of the proposed Treaty. The Field Marshal's behavior at the time was telling, as Erich Eyck describes it:

> At the critical moment Hindenburg absented himself from the room. Groener was thus left to give President Ebert the advice that both the field marshal and Ludendorff knew was inevitable and urgent. . . . As soon as the conversation was over he reentered the room and told Groener, "You have assumed a heavy responsibility. Once more you will have to play the scapegoat."[7]

Groener would later bear similar burdens as Hindenburg's Minister of Defense, only to be dismissed unexpectedly in the end despite his loyalty. Heinrich Brüning suffered a similar fate as Chancellor in 1932. In his memoirs, Brüning described the same negative attributes of avoiding responsibility and relative inertia in the President's behavior. By 1930 this inertia had become indistinguishable from a senile stupor.[8]

These were not isolated observations; rather, they represented a continuum of behavior to that year. The President was eighty-three and behaved accordingly. This had been apparent to all for the previous five years. His decisions had become less independent judgments than reactions to suggestion.[9] To be more precise, his behavior bore the stamp of overt senility: his penchant for avoiding responsibility was augmented; his inability to make decisions on his own became more obvious.

The historian John Wheeler-Bennett observed that the petty jealousies and complexities of political intrigue swirling about Hindenburg remained incomprehensible to his limited abstractive capacities. He could not comprehend the perpetual problem his chancellors faced in obtaining a Reichstag majority, and he could never understand his role in either directly or indirectly forcing their resignations. "Why did he go?" the Marshal once asked his close confidant, Otto Meissner. "He was quite a nice man." "Yes," Meissner replied, "but he couldn't find a majority!" "Oh, well," Hindenburg concluded. "He suited me very well, but if they want a new one I don't mind."[10]

Hindenburg dismissed his first Chancellor, Hermann Müller, in 1930. The decision may not have been his own. His Foreign Minister, Julius Curtius, suspected that most of the Field Marshal's old comrades had exercised their influence over him in the matter to unhealthy degrees.[11] He did the same to Heinrich Brüning in 1932, and again that decision reflected others' input more than his own initiative. Certainly prior to Brüning's dismissal in Erich Eyck's words, "the old weathercock [had been] veering from point to point,"[12] unable to assimilate the contradictory arguments his subordinates presented. Any rigid thinking such dementia suspects exhibit is reserved for old familiar themes; with new or unfamiliar ones, they lose their way. Those who perceive this readily employ solicitous methods to gain their ends, and Ryder indicted Hindenburg on precisely this point: "Hindenburg's toleration of Schleicher's intrigues against the Chancellor also shows him in an unfavourable light. . . . Brüning was well aware of the extent to which Hindenburg's mental faculties had declined and realized that he had become the unconscious tool of irresponsible men."[13]

One might legitimately question why the President of a threatened republic should deal with the resignation of his Chancellor, Brüning, in such a cavalier manner. The answer rested with his relative lack of interest in the matter. From Hindenburg's limited perspective, the issue seemed somewhat removed from those matters concerning the army and foreign affairs that did occasionally stir his interest, however fleetingly. Not only do those afflicted with dementia lose their ability to abstract (in this case, failing to appreciate an association between Brüning and the credible implementation of a foreign policy beneficial to Germany), but they also simply have limited interests. What initiatives they take are reserved for matters that occupy them to the exclusion of all others. Political intrigue and a series of succession crises simply were not among them for the aged warrior. After all, Hindenburg's own position was not directly affected, and he was at least dimly aware that any future Chancellor would still be answerable to him—particularly one such as Franz von Papen, who waited patiently in the wings at the suggestion of the ubiquitous Schleicher. The implications for Germany's future were negative in the extreme, as the historian Erich Eyck made clear: "The guilt for [this disaster] must be placed primarily upon Hindenburg. The dagger thrust with which he felled Bruning . . . murdered not only the German Republic, but also the peace of all Europe."[14] This is what Germany had gained in choosing to depend upon an aging figurehead who lacked any abstractive capacity to appreciate the significance of his actions.

If some find it easy to influence the dementia sufferer in matters foreign to him, others quickly learn the value of ingratiating themselves with him. Franz von Papen, Brüning's successor, was but one example. "None so much enjoyed Hindenburg's confidence," according to Wheeler-Bennett, "as did this strange little man who flattered him as Brüning had never done."[15] He was a man of second-rate ability, but by this point Hindenburg was placing more importance on loyalty and ingratiating affection than political skill. This is typical of an individual suffering from an organic brain syndrome. Comfort and self-assurance are sought from those with whom he is familiar and in whom he trusts, for they soften criticism. Their sycophancy becomes a security blanket.

The mutual support Hindenburg and Papen required (the one psychological, the other political) shielded each from criticism. Under this aegis, mutual deception flourished. The sheer madness of the resulting confusion in executive affairs was underscored in 1932 by Sir Horace Rumbold, the British Ambassador to Berlin: "The present Cabinet is a Cabinet of mutual deception. Herr von Papen thinks he has scored off General von Schleicher and Hitler, General Schleicher thinks he has scored off Hitler, and Hitler . . . believes he has scored off both."[16] The score at any given moment was not the criticial issue. If Hitler proved the ultimate victor in this contest of wits, Hindenburg (who certainly lacked the mental capacity even to compete) was the immediate loser.

The German province of Prussia also lost in the exchange. Accepting Papen's suggestion that the previous ban on Nazi SA and SS activity should be rescinded, Hindenburg embraced the dubious belief in 1932 that "the conflict of public opinion will henceforth assure more orderly form, and acts of violence will cease."[17] Nothing could be further from the truth. He had once again failed to appreciate the significance of his actions; in the medical vernacular, he had failed in utilizing the abstract attitude. The result was the rape of Prussia. Papen had charged that Prussia was too weak to control its own affairs. When a domestic disturbance in mid-July 1932 occurred there, the Chancellor had already secured a decree from the perplexed President appointing Papen national commissioner for Prussia, with the power to dismiss its government. The aging weathercock had once again been blown in the direction of least resistance, readily won over by an ingratiating subordinate simply because he was unable to make up his own mind. As one historian ruefully observed: "Papen's coup d'etat remained a coup d'etat into which an irresponsible adventurer had lured a tired old man."[18]

The Prussian premier, Otto Braun, was unsuccessful in alerting the apathetic Hindenburg to the implications of his actions. Braun recognized the futility of attempting to influence a compromised President whose perception of events was so effectively screened by scheming subordinates. "The President," Braun concluded,

> probably did not at all comprehend what was at stake. . . . I had not seen [him] for quite some time. . . . Hindenburg seemed so terribly senile that my anger at his decree was outweighed by my sympathy for the old man who . . . was by now being misused by unscrupulous men in such an infamous way.[19]

Nothing seemed to have been learned from the past lessons of excessive deference to, and dependency on, the aging President. The quality of both government leadership and Cabinet membership had become inversely proportional to the degree that Hindenburg's subordinates manipulated him, and his abstract attitude became more fallible still.

Above all, he failed to assess Adolf Hitler's potential power realistically. "That man for a Chancellor?" he exclaimed in mid-1932. "I'll make him a postmaster and he can lick the stamps with my head on them."[20] Within six short months the tables had turned. Hitler had become the Grand Master and the head of the President would be used as a stamp of approval legitimizing Hitler's rule.

Hindenburg's compromised ability to abstract reached new levels when he backed an order to dissolve the Reichstag that in effect signified his intent to make the temporary encroachments on the legislative domain by emergency executive decree a permanent fixture. The irony of this pronouncement was not lost on Erich Eyck, who concluded that "the President wished to change his role from that of the limited legislator envisioned by the Constitution to one of unrestricted power. But how could he do this and still claim to be loyal to the Constitution?"[21] The fact is he could not do both. More to the point, the medical cynic might ask: How could a restricted man exercise unrestricted power effectively?

Under Hindenburg's uncertain hand, the Republic careened toward its final, and darkest, crisis. Through the veil of senility that obscured the obvious from view, he was vaguely aware that Schleicher had successively nominated Müller and Brüning, then orchestrated their dismissal. Now it was Papen's turn, and Hindenburg lacked the capacity or the will to oppose Schleicher's latest power play. His own unprincipled methods, bereft of self-analysis in recent years, had severely restricted his options. The piper of intrigue had to be paid. By November 1932 Weimar had its newest, and last, Chancellor in Schleicher himself.

Within two months Hindenburg would see his way clear to emasculating Schleicher as well and appointing Hitler as Chancellor. Again the decision bore the imprint of a trusted but duplicitous subordinate. The aging President was beguiled by Papen into accepting as his new Chancellor a former "Bohemian corporal" whom he had never trusted.[22] Characteristically, Hindenburg accommodated his increasing senility by both abrogating responsibility for negotiating with his adversary, Hitler, and unquestioningly trusting a loyal, if not prescient, subordinate, Papen. The groundwork thus laid, and the decision taken, were difficult to follow—too difficult in fact for an aged victim of dementia who longed only for the peace of retirement.

The major stumbling block to complete agreement was the Enabling Bill, which transferred the power of legislation from the Reichstag to the Government, allowing the latter to change the Constitution as it saw fit. Hindenburg, to be sure, wanted to be let off the executive hook. He no longer had a taste for power, nor the capacity to exercise it effectively. Under the circumstances, the bill became less a stumbling block and more a stepping stone. For Papen perceived, and Hindenburg accepted without demur, that the Enabling Bill would relieve the President of his burden while effecting the necessary compromise with the Nazis. Hitler verbally agreed not to use the extraordinary powers the bill accorded him if Hindenburg objected. But, of course, Papen was to exercise this veto in the President's name.

From Hindenburg's limited perspective, then, the bill represented little more than a matter of convenience. With its passage, he "offhandedly" gave up his dominant role in German politics, as the historian Andreas Dorpalen described it. [23] For Hindenburg perceived its impact largely at the personal level, and nothing is quite so typical of demented individuals as their increasing preoccupation with self as the disease progresses. They turn inward, and all environmental stimuli become mere accessories to that preoccupation. Concerns for bodily function and comfort become paramount. The aged President was no exception, as Dorpalen surmised: "It was not only old age and Hindenburg's natural lethargy that account for this ready surrender of all his powers; his health was beginning to fail and preoccupied him more than ever." [24] Such concrete thinking represents the endstage of the dementia sufferer's inability to abstract. Erich Eyck described this circumstance in Hindenburg's case succinctly enough:

> One had only to slip into the Presidential palace and gain the ear of the Old Gentleman. . . . No matter how difficult the old field marshal found the task of mastering intricate problems . . . he always found it easy to arrive at a firm position on questions . . . which affected his personal interests. [25]

Never in Germany's modern history had the perceptions and abstractive capabilities of her chief executive been so limited. The tragedy is compounded by the realization that Papen, the weakest of the lot of individuals who had held the title of Chancellor under the Republic, now commanded the President's ear, and Hitler was fully prepared to reap the harvest they had sown. This situation points up the major flaw in the concept of the presidential cabinet that had evolved to this time:

> A German government [Eyck points out] which was responsible only to the President and which rejected any form of party ties would have been conceivable only if a large number of German votes had been ready to support this President with complete loyalty and [without consideration for party]. But such, of course, was not the case at all. The first requirement for such a situation would have been the nation's confidence in the President's nonpartisan objectivity; yet Hindenburg had destroyed his claim to such trust when he deserted Brüning. . . . The impossibility of this so called "system" was heightened even further by the fact that it was supposed to be directed by an eighty-five-year-old man whose intellectual powers were now even less able

*Changing of the guard: Hitler and Hindenburg in Pots-*
*dam, March 1933*

than before to grasp the difficult . . . problems which his successive governments had to face. [26]

If one accepts the medical axiom that with increasing senility afflicted individuals magnify their most characteristic traits in their actions, then a fuller understanding of the remainder of Eyck's indictment
of the Hindenburg method is gained: "Hindenburg had clearly reverted
so completely to his old military habits of tolerance that he regarded the
head of 'his' presidential cabinet as a subordinated officer whom he was
free to detach as he pleased." [27] The Old Gentleman, then, during the
final days of the Weimar Republic, clearly became a pathetic caricature
of himself. This is one of the hallmarks of dementia, and Germany's

democratic institutions were not only captive to it, they were victimized by it.

In effect, all of the safeguards negotiated by the aging President's advisors to hold Hitler in check proved worthless, and by this point Hindenburg was too befuddled to appreciate the fact. His actions just prior to Hitler's succession demonstrated as much. According to A. J. Ryder, "The President . . . was now intercepted by periods of blankness, had failed to preserve the rule of law, or even the decencies of civilised life."[28] Instead, he was wedded by necessity to the opinions of his advisors, as such compromised individuals are wont to do in order to fill the voids in their own understanding of events. This was a fatal dependency for the future of German democratic institutions. "It seems that little or nothing was done," Ryder concluded, "to alert the old man—lethargic by nature, and now with his faculties failing—to the dangers inherent in Hitler's assumption of unprecedented power."[29]

Hermann Göring was guilty of self-serving hyperbole when he observed: "How gloriously had the aged Field Marshal been used as an instrument in the hand of God." One might respond: How tragically had this victim of senility been used by his advisors. Wheeler-Bennett's assessment struck to the heart of the matter: "No father of his people had so genuinely enjoyed the trust of his electors as did Hindenburg . . . and [yet] it is certain [he] had no conception of how terribly he had betrayed his trusteeship. . . . He had undoubtedly done his duty *as it had been indicated to him.* [Italics mine]"[30] This last observation speaks to the tragic flaw that characterized the man's final three years as President. Hindenburg was too easily swayed by brighter, self-serving, duplicitous advisors. He knew little of what was really going on within his own government, trapped as he was by total dependence on others for his view of the political world.

By now evidence of Hindenburg's overt disorders of perception was commonplace—and common knowledge. Wheeler-Bennett recorded a telling vignette about the night of Hitler's ascension. Hindenburg was watching the enthusiastic marchers in the street below his window. What he evidently failed to appreciate was that they were cheering Hitler and not himself. Those in the room witnessed the peculiar spectacle of the Old Gentleman beckoning over his shoulder. "Ludendorff," he said, "how well your men are marching, and what a lot of prisoners they've taken." Other more apocryphal stories abounded in those days: "They say the Old Man signs anything now. The other day Meissner left his sandwich bag on the table and when he came back the President had signed it."[31]

Hindenburg's level of awareness and ability to abstract were now compromised to such a degree that even his nemesis Hitler manipulated him with ease. He also catered to the Old Man's emotions in cleverly tying him to the new order. At a dedication ceremony on March 21, 1933, Hitler honored Hindenburg as the leader of World War I in an attempt to divorce him from his connection with the Weimar Republic in his own mind. Hindenburg's emotions were fragile, in contradistinction to the petrifaction that characterized his otherwise rigid preoccupation with self. With tears flowing down his cheeks, he was taken in by the spectacle and became a new figurehead of sorts—yet this time as a symbol of the National Socialist revolution.[32] It proved to be a tragic leap into obscurity.

Over the next two months, most of the verbal promises made to Papen or the President were broken. In March the Enabling Bill was finally brought to a vote in the Reichstag and passed, but without the promised written agreement by Hitler to uphold the presidential prerogative of the veto he had agreed to in January. Wheeler-Bennett was moved to ask the rhetorical question: "Why," under the now rapidly changing circumstances, "did Hindenburg not more energetically defend his oath?" The answer was obvious. He was "a weary Old Gentleman of 86, of rigid mind and slow reasoning, anxious to avoid responsibility, and surrounded by a pack of watch-dogs." He was no match for Hitler. "With the signing of the Enabling Bill, the President simply faded from the picture and from the public mind."[33]

*Hindenburg being honored by Hitler at Tannenberg, 1933*

He retreated in asylum to Neudeck, where the reality of the terror that was engulfing Germany was studiously hidden from him. The old flair for intrigue in the German ministerial character raised its head once more. Hindenburg could not be told the truth: Papen had erred in believing he could control the Nazi menace. Otto Meissner correctly perceived that his job as secretary to Hindenburg depended upon the old man's ignorance, which—never in short supply—was now nurtured to a numbing degree. His compromised health assured a more willing receptivity to these new informational whitewashes. Every visitor was carefully screened to assure him all was well.

On the few occasions when he was exposed to the outside world, it was at the behest of Hitler and was permitted only for the new Chancellor's benefit. In October 1933, Wheeler-Bennett recounted, Hindenburg "was haled forth in some bewilderment to summon the German people, incongruously enough, to subscribe to Hitler's policy of peace in withdrawing from the Disarmament Conference and from the League of Nations."[34] Hindenburg simply no longer appreciated the implications of his own words.

Surely there would be a limit to this, and by year's end Papen had begun to realize the extent of his error. Alarmed by news of a planned bloody purge in the party ranks to be orchestrated by Joseph Goebbels, Papen resolved to inform his master, who remained awash in his senile torpor at Neudeck. But his revelations of still more Nazi excesses elicited no reaction. Papen thereafter openly confronted Goebbels in a speech on June 17, 1934, and both German and world opinion reacted favorably. Yet, inexplicably, Hindenburg did not react at all. His apathy, a by-product of dementia, perversely accommodated his adversary. He gave no sign of support for Papen, and the Nazis recouped their psychological losses. Wheeler-Bennett was forced to ask: "Did Hindenburg betray [his advisor]? Had he ever really understood the full meaning of what Papen had told him. . . ?" He answered his own question: "It was difficult at eighty-six suddenly to reverse his ideas and be told that what he had been led to believe for the last eighteen months . . . had been false."[35] Senility had scored yet another victory for the Nazis. Hindenburg's rigid mindset precluded his reassessing the situation in this new light. The intriguers and protectors had done their job too well.

And so thereafter did the Nazis. Ernst Röhm was assassinated, as were many of his best officers, at the hands of the SS. Papen was placed under house arrest; Schleicher was murdered. Another opportunity to prevent the violence that wracked Germany had been squandered. Sensing that Hindenburg would not survive the news of this latest misfortune, his advisors told him very little of this. The pathos of it all was underscored when Hindenburg actually congratulated Hitler for having "nipped treason in the bud."[36] Within a month he was dead.

LOYAL SUPPORT.

*Punch cartoon, June 30, 1934: "Loyal Support"*

*Death of Hindenburg, August 2, 1934*

Yet even in death the Old Gentleman served Hitler's purposes. In his last will and testament, written on May 11, 1934, Hindenburg bequeathed all his support to the Hitler regime. Although some dispute exists as to the authenticity of this document, most historians are of the opinion that it represented the President's true sentiments at the time it was written.[37] Given his limited knowledge of what was really transpiring in his homeland outside the walls of Neudeck, he had no reason to renounce the legitimacy of the new government he had personally escorted into power.

During the first two months of 1934, the outside world viewed with some alarm the consolidation of fascism in Europe in general and of Nazi power in Germany in particular. One of the most interested spectators was Ramsay MacDonald, at that time the Prime Minister of Great Britain. His efforts represented the heart of the Disarmament Conference, which Hitler deserted—an action that substantiated the troubling vision MacDonald had confided to his son Malcolm a year earlier when Hitler had assumed the Chancellorship: "I shall not see peace again in my lifetime. . . . I hope you will see it in yours."[38] Nor had he been assuaged thereafter by the transparency of the German-Polish Nonaggression Pact of 1934, negotiated with the aging Polish President Józef Piłsudski, which Hitler's propagandists waved before a gullible Europe as proof of Germany's peaceful intentions. He took the Dollfuss *putsch* in Austria in February 1934 to be a further sign that fascism's tyranny was sweeping uncontrollably over Europe.[39] Ominously enough, the Nazis would shortly be indicted for influencing, if not controlling, such fascist movements outside the borders of Germany. For Chancellor Englebert Dollfuss was soon assassinated, and Hitler's fingerprints were found at the scene of the crime.

These were the events in Europe, then, that captivated the attention of its leadership during the first half of 1934. Significantly, the three most important protagonists in the events just outlined were the same three leaders who are the subjects of the present study as they related to the rise of Hitler. Paul von Hindenburg's accountability has already been detailed; indeed his death, occurring precisely at the time the Nazis were under fire for their involvement in the Dollfuss affair, rescued Hitler from his amoral plight. With Hindenburg gone, Nazi power was not only consolidated but legitimized as a result of the senile figurehead's last will and testament. And what of the German-Polish Nonaggression Pact? Its principles had been authored by the aging Marshal Józef Piłsudski, whose last years as the Father of Poland bore a striking similarity to Hindenburg's last years as president of the Weimar Republic. There remains the Disarmament Conference, and who had been its most faithful advocate but the troubled and rapidly failing Ramsay MacDonald?

At this fateful point in world history, when Adolf Hitler consolidated his position by combining the offices of Chancellor, Commander in Chief of the Armed Forces, and President, the careers of these three aging leaders dovetailed in a poignant exposure of the Old World to the new forces of extremism. It began with perhaps the most pervasive theme that characterized Europe's approach to Hitler in the thirties—the doctrine of appeasement. No understanding of the British policy of pacification, disarmament, and appeasement can be had without recognizing the profound impact MacDonald's Labour party had in its formulation and propagation. The historian Laurence Lafore has summarized that influence:

> Although Labour was in office only a few months in the postwar decade, its programs and pressures had a decided effect in shaping public opinion and, in a negative way, in shaping conservative policies. The Labour party . . . was dominated . . . by a series of impulses toward pacifism, internationalism, support for the League, and a general belief that Frenchmen were untrustworthy. [40]

MacDonald was the critical link that carried this influence into the thirties. For years he had been the champion of Labour's cause and the acknowledged head of his party as Prime Minister at the turn of the decade. Yet the impact of the Depression in 1930 played a peculiar trick on MacDonald, compelling him to abandon his friends in Labour in order to retain the prime ministership by forming a new bipartisan National Government in 1931. [41] Forced now to cooperate with the Conservatives, and often dominated by them, he remained unable to divest himself in good conscience of the principles he had believed in for so many years. His background was a legacy he could not leave behind in the thirties, yet the results of this personal conflict were to destroy him both personally and politically while fatally compromising Britain's position vis-à-vis the Hitler menace.

As head of the Conservative-dominated National Government, MacDonald perceived the devaluation of the pound as his only viable option to combat the Depression. If the policy enjoyed some limited success in Great Britain, it nonetheless exported hardships to less economically viable neighbors, making the National Government in one historian's view "the most important symptom and symbol of the final ruin of the European system." [42] Yet it became this for more than economic reasons. Neither MacDonald nor any of his Cabinet had any proven expertise in foreign affairs; indeed, the Government had no realistic understanding of what was transpiring outside Britain's national boundaries. This circumstance deprived London of much of its capacity for positive action in world affairs. [43]

Many subsequent critics have suggested that the Prime Minister's limited perspective had much deeper roots, manifested the year before. They noted an ominous parallel between Britain's declining political influence and the decline of MacDonald's health and his command of his own government. Significantly, he had abandoned Labour and lost his effectiveness at precisely the time his physical and mental compromise became apparent. "In 1930," according to Lafore, "when the Depression began to affect Britain . . . a Labour Government . . . led by the impressive but inadequate and already senile Ramsay MacDonald, was in office." [44] The rigors of the Depression only brought his failing leadership into clearer perspective. In order to borrow abroad, MacDonald had to assure his creditors that he was running a tight ship; a reduction of expenditures was required in conjunction with a modest reduction in the gold content of the pound. This also entailed a planned 10 percent reduction in unemployment benefits, which of course ran counter to Labour's vested interests.

A showdown was not long in coming. On September 8, 1931, venomous debates in Parliament led to a vote of confidence over the economic policies the new Government was following. It narrowly passed. A second reading of the National Economy Bill was then presented on September 11. It included £70 million in cuts, £13 million of which were to be taken from unemployment benefits. MacDonald gave a fighting speech in defence of the measure, and he got a fighting response in return. The Prime Minister was heckled unmercifully, not only by the Opposition but by many of his former friends in the Labour party. Ten days later the decision was made to devalue the pound by abandoning the gold standard. The debate was exceedingly acrimonious, and MacDonald was again roundly criticized. Both physically and emotionally the turmoil caused by the transition of government in general and by these debates in particular had taken a heavy toll on MacDonald. At the close of these proceedings he suffered his second physical collapse in two weeks.

These encounters with alleged illness in 1931 date the onset of his supposed physical decline as some of his contemporaries perceived it. [45] Yet from the medical perspective, the suggestion that he was afflicted by any organic disease—much less senility—is somewhat premature. [46] To develop this argument further, it is necessary to know something more— not only of the alleged "collapses" themselves, but of MacDonald's character and personality, which probably had a great deal more to do with the collapses than even he realized.

In his diary entry of September 9, 1931, MacDonald confided: "Morning of collapse, suddenly going as mist with the sun." On September 13 he noted: "Not well. . . . My body warns me to behave better." [47] Passage of the Gold Standard Bill followed on September 21, and MacDonald was faced with the decision of whether to call new elections. During the night of September 21, not surprisingly, "he was kept awake by a violent head-ache." The next morning "he broke down" and was bundled off for a four-day respite to recover his composure and assess his options. [48]

MacDonald's most recent biographer, David Marquand, describes the episode on September 9 as having been a "mild seizure of some sort." The September 21 episode may have been a political illness, as Marquand acknowledged that he was playing for time. [49] Little more is known of the two episodes; they were not even alluded to in the *Times* of London during September. There are two reasons why the alleged illness of someone as important as the Prime Minister might have gone un-noticed: either MacDonald and his physician did not want the news di-vulged, or the "collapses" were so trivial that no notice was taken of them. Taking into account some other peculiar features of MacDonald's personality, the latter interpretation seems correct. Sir Maurice Hankey had this important observation to make on September 11: "The Prime Minister has been very seedy. When under severe nervous strain he is apt to vomit, and this leaves him terribly weak. I fear he is feeling the break with the rest of the Labour Party very badly." [50]

These two statements are more significant than Hankey intended or realized. For what he is suggesting here is the strong probability of an hysterical or psychosomatic illness. First, the reference to vomiting

*MacDonald (center) with his Cabinet, 1931*

under the stress of nervous anxiety is a typical vasovagal response to pain or discomfort. In such a circumstance an emotionally triggered physiologic reaction involving increased neural stimulus through the vagus nerve may elicit various symptoms. Vomiting and fainting are the two most frequently observed. It is significant that a recurring pattern of vomiting while under nervous strain was revealed in this account of an observer who spent a great deal of time with MacDonald during these trying days. More significant still is the recognition that both "seizure" episodes occurred immediately after a period of intense psychological stress. And of the utmost significance is the realization that most such vasovagal attacks occur in high-strung individuals prone to hypochondria and depression. Neither were foreign to Ramsay MacDonald's character, as the voluminous references to poor health and depression in his diaries demonstrate. To cite but one example in his own words:

> The depression has been one of the blackest & has affected everything. . . . The strain is at last telling on me, & I am feeling as though [in the] last few weeks I have crossed the frontiers of age. I walk as an old man, & my head works like an old man's. . . . How long can I go on? [51]

MacDonald's private parliamentary secretary, L. MacNeill Weir, thought his employer was a hypochondriac. His testimony is invaluable as a portrait of those features of MacDonald's character that best explain the man: "Self-love with MacDonald was a psychological neurasthenia . . . His fear of ill-health was constant from his childhood, and at times tended to make him hypochondriac." [52] September 1931 was one such time. This trait would become increasingly evident as the months passed and the psychological burdens of MacDonald's office grew, for his sensitivity knew no bounds. In the words of Harold J. Laski, "He can become almost feminine in his sensitiveness. He feels criticism acutely, and he has a curious power of retaining the memory of attack long after its consequences have completely disappeared." [53] Weir was certain that many such character traits were a logical extension of MacDonald's childhood. He believed that MacDonald's fawning, adoring mother wanted him to remain a child, and that emotionally he had never grown up. [54] Many of the reflections MacDonald later recorded in his diary also suggest this.

By nature a shy man who preferred books to the camaraderie of other men, [55] MacDonald was portrayed by his secretary as aloof to the point of being inaccessible. He was also vain, which in itself accentuated his distance from others. "MacDonald's vanity complex," Weir said, "was such that he could never imagine himself on the stage of life in any but the star rôle." He played this role to the hilt in political life and often overdramatized the rigors of his office to promote his self-image as Great Britain's suffering servant. He often assumed such predictable poses at the end of the day that some Members of Parliament took to mimicking his acts in jest: Weir described one MP's mimicry: "His whole body would droop, his head would fall forward, his arms hang listless. . . . In a voice of the utmost weariness, he would say: 'Ah! my friends, I am so very tired.'" From Weir's perspective, all these traits were a product of his childhood. [56]

Yet genuine tragedies in midlife accentuated these character traits and molded the man he would become in his years as Prime Minister. Such shy, retiring individuals frequently turn to their wives both for the companionship they miss in other relationships and for the enhancement of their self-esteem that the insensitive world withholds from them. MacDonald was no exception. With his wife's unexpected death from septicemia in 1910, MacDonald experienced a depression that he never fully conquered in his lifetime. His son Malcolm recounted this poignant recollection of his father: "[At] the time of my mother's death . . . my father's grief was absolutely horrifying to see. . . . [T]his continued right down the years and over and over again not only during the next years but the next decades." [57] Years later MacDonald was asked why he had never remarried. "My heart is in the grave," he said. [58]

MacDonald's biographer suggested that in fact there had never been a healthy catharsis. Marquand concluded that "more than most public figures, he needed the trust and support of others. . . . Margaret had given him what he needed." Marquand returned to this theme late in the account of his subject's checkered career. In so doing, he found some answers to the perplexing MacDonald character: "The memory of his bereavements had been part of MacDonald's life for more than twenty years. There is no reason to believe that it was any weaker in the 1930s than it had been before." [59]

This is why MacDonald's estrangement from the Labour party, described earlier, is so important in understanding his persisting psychological duress. The party had been his last remaining personal support group. Much more than legitimate illness, then, his self-centeredness and depression were mutually reinforcing influences that were given vent in the form of hypochondriacal concerns and imaginary illnesses. This behavior was compelled by what Marquand termed "the desolation of loneliness" in his life. [60] MacDonald was made acutely conscious of this immediately after his break with Labour in 1931, because he had assumed that the newly formed National Government would not last, and that when it came to an end, so would his political career. [61] Given his personality, it is not coincidental that a series of mysterious and ill-defined collapses occurred in concert with this sobering thought. Labour had been his home, his source of strength, a substitute for the support of a wife he lacked.

Some illnesses were not imaginary, most notably his struggle with failing vision brought on by glaucoma, which began, ominously enough, in 1932. For a man whose solace and relaxation were inextricably bound up with reading, such an affront by disease further augmented his depression, which was partly endogenous (personality based) and partly reactive (responsive to environmental stimuli). Not surprisingly, his convalescence from both operations he underwent to correct the malady far exceeded the length of time normally anticipated for such procedures, even in those days. [62]

This is the necessary background of character development that explains MacDonald's behavior and alleged failing health in 1931 and 1932. Take an individual predisposed by upbringing to a strongly egocentric view of the world; add several key reversals of fortune within the context of his life's work (including the loss of a very supportive wife and estrangement from equally supportive political colleagues, with whom he had always identified); compromise him further by threatening blindness—and healthy defense mechanisms devolve into paroxysms of self-pity, manifested by further depression and psychosomatic illness.

Which leads us in a circuitous fashion to the argument for senility. Some believe that as early as 1930 or 1931 Ramsay MacDonald showed signs of mental deterioration suggesting presenile dementia (that occurring roughly before age sixty-five and also known as Alzheimer's disease). Indeed, they believe that he was never the same after his brush with death in 1927 during a severe upper respiratory tract infection. [63] It is well known among neurologists and psychiatrists that unexplained depression may be one of the first signs of senility. [64] Only with progression of the overall condition does deterioration in other intellectual spheres define the nature of the process. Whether presenile dementia may have affected MacDonald will be considered later. The question here is whether the depressive equivalents (symptoms of depression), which were evident by 1930 and were accentuated by the events of 1931, might have been a harbinger of that condition.

Certainly most of MacDonald's depression during the years 1931 and 1932 was reactive rather than endogenous. Events snowballed thereafter, compounding his discomfiture. As Marquand observed, his dwindling stock in the mind of the British voter centered upon the fateful formation of the National Government. In the end, he did more than lose his political allies; he made many enemies. He had convinced the Labour and Liberal voters that the country needed a nonpartisan government and that he could be trusted to provide it. These voters were now his only constituency; when they came to believe, as they did, that the National Government was merely a front for the Conservatives who were really in power, it was he and not the Conservatives who became the target for their displeasure. [65]

Marquand also argues that MacDonald's intellectual powers were not failing in this period and that the failure that did occur was both later and more slowly progressive than some historians have believed.[66] Yet the depression may have been the tip of the iceberg of the real disease, which appeared in 1933. For the moment, however, this depression alone was a more formidable adversary for MacDonald than overt senility.

From 1931 on MacDonald was plagued by the difficulty of reconciling Conservative protectionism with Liberal belief in free trade, not to mention preventing the Conservatives from dominating or humiliating their Labour allies.[67] Such recurring conflicts ate away at his psyche and eventually destroyed him. He complained, "It is all too terrible. . . . The people I care for most in my heart suspect me & are confused. Will the old relations & affections return?"[68]

They did not. Almost diabolically, he was required on October 28, 1931, to lead an anti-Labour alliance of Conservatives and Liberals into a new election. With their victory he mused: "It has turned out all too well. How tragically the Labour Party has been let down. . . . No honest man should trust . . . the Conservative wirepullers."[69] This was an exercise in self-flagellation, if not self-indictment. MacDonald's depression was augmented by this sobering realization. On November 1 he noted: "Worn out and work impossible. . . . But really head would not work. So depressing."[70] Inability to concentrate is a hallmark of depression and not, as some historians have supposed, in this instance a result of senility. As a current medical authority, Dr. Donlin M. Long, emphasizes: "It is extremely important to differentiate the demented patient from the elderly patient who is simply depressed."[71]

Remaining Prime Minister under such psychological duress was also an exercise in the illusion of indispensability—not so much that MacDonald's continuing as Prime Minister was indispensable to Britain's well being, but that retaining the office was indispensable to his own self-esteem. It provided an escape from loneliness and a means of assuaging his self-doubt over the decision to form the National Government. "If he had managed to cap his successes . . . with some great stroke of pacificatory diplomacy," Marquand concluded, "he might have been happy to leave Downing Street in the knowledge that he had achieved something worthwhile. But . . . the times were against him."[72]

This is not to suggest MacDonald did not have the chance. The times were at least propitious in one respect: the long-awaited Disarmament Conference at Geneva opened in February 1932. Yet genuine illness tragically compromised his best intentions. He was forced to miss its opening session because of his first eye operation. When the conference resumed in mid-April, ironically enough, his other eye began to give him trouble—enough to require a second operation in early May at precisely

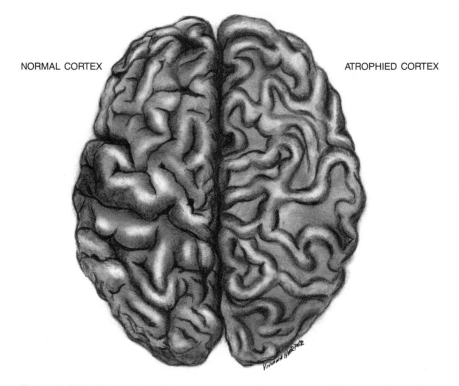

NORMAL CORTEX                              ATROPHIED CORTEX

*Fig. 2.1  This illustration offers a comparison between normal brain and atrophic brain such as seen in Alzheimer's disease or generalized cortical atrophy.*

the time critical negotiations were underway at Geneva. MacDonald's convalescence, probably extended by depression as a result of having to acknowledge his missed opportunity, was unexpectedly prolonged, despite what was declared to have been a successful operative result. [73] That depression undoubtedly was a factor in his convalescence was underscored by the notation that he required "a tonic for 'brain fag'" from his physician, Sir Thomas Horder. [74]

By the beginning of 1933 genuine manifestations of incipient dementia began to reveal themselves. MacDonald was now sixty-five years old. To understand the case, the reader should have some understanding of the symptoms and physical signs seen in presenile dementia, or Alzheimer's disease, which is caused by a progressive loss of neurons in the cortical layers of the brain, leading to generalized cerebral atrophy. (See Fig. 2.1.) Robert Katzman outlines the essential features of the malady:

Alzheimer's disease presents as a progressive dementia with increasing loss of memory, intellectual functions and disturbances in speech. In the initial stages there is a slight dulling of the intellectual faculties. Thought processes are slowed and memory is defective. *Disturbances in the functions of speech are commonly early symptoms.* [Italics mine.] [75]

This reference to speech is axiomatic to the consideration of dementia in MacDonald's case. Marquand observed that as early as 1933

> deterioration showed in his speeches. He had always been a prolix speaker, relying for his effects on dramatic gestures, lofty flights of language and long, elaborate periods in which subordinate clauses were piled remorselessly on top of one another. It was a powerful style, but it was also a dangerous one. It needed a speaker in full command of himself and his audience to use it effectively; used ineffectively, it could easily topple over into absurdity. Increasingly, this happened to MacDonald. The dramatic gestures began to seem forced and histrionic; the lofty flight of language disappeared more and more frequently into clouds of mixed metaphors; the elaborate periods lost their way in confusion and anticlimax.
>
> Occasionally the results were comic. . . . More often, they were merely embarrassing. [76]

MacDonald's Parliamentary Secretary alluded to the same problem as increasingly obvious to all: "It was as much this increasing indolence and dereliction of duty as any deterioration of his mental powers, that made MacDonald's speeches in the House such ludicrous travesties." [77] If Weir was guilty of ignoring that MacDonald's deteriorating mental powers may have been more a cause for, rather than an effect of, indolence and dereliction, his observation is nonetheless telling enough.

The effect was devastating on MacDonald's impact as a speaker in the House. In one reply to a vote of censure of the National Government for its treatment of the unemployed, his speech was said to have "amazed the House. It was a long and confused rigmarole of incoherent irrelevancies, which left his hearers in all parts of the House quite unable to follow him." MacDonald welcomed an interruption in the speech "as a 'punch drunk' boxer welcomes the bell. He sank, dazed, into his seat." No one was listening any longer. [78]

A new idiom of expression found its way into the British vocabulary: the "MacDonaldism," defined as "a confusion of thought," or a "lack of clearness and definition." [79] Verbosity had characterized MacDonald's speeches as early as 1932. Winston Churchill deftly summarized this peculiar habit in the following manner: "The Prime Minister has the gift of compressing the largest number of words into the smallest amount of thought." [80] Weir believed the deterioration in MacDonald's speeches and his habit of getting lost in his words after 1931 was a product of his having to use the unfamiliar idioms of the Conservative vocabulary after abandoning Labour. [81] The neurologist would be inclined, on the other hand, to consider this the early effects of an incipient dementia on his speech pattern.

One other frequent consequence of senile or presenile dementia is an unwarranted paranoia, often coupled with hallucinations or other disorders of perception. Hugh L'Etang recounted one such episode in the middle of a speech MacDonald delivered in Parliament early in 1933. He interrupted his speech and looked nervously over his shoulder. His audience was perplexed as to the cause of his behavior. Later he explained that he had had a sudden fear that someone was about to shoot him. [82] Toward the end of the Prime Minister's increasingly desultory, if not embarrassing, tenure Major-General A. C. Temperley recalled yet another startling MacDonald performance. While speaking to the House, he suddenly seemed to lose his train of thought. Suddenly "I saw him reel backwards," Temperley recalled, "exhorting his audience to 'be men, not mannequins'." He rambled on in a completely irrelevant fashion. MacDonald admitted afterwards "that for a half-minute he had completely lost consciousness and did not know what he was saying." [83] It was left to another contemporary politician to assess the impact of the failing Prime Minister's oratory: "His speeches became increasingly incoherent and for the last years of his life he was only a melancholy passenger in the Conservative ship." [84] Drs. John Gilroy and Sterling Meyer illustrate the real significance of these vignettes with the following observation taken from the textbook *Medical Neurology:* "As Alzheimer's disease progresses . . . paranoid ideas frequently develop and some patients assault or harangue members of their family and those attending them." [85] MacDonald's behavior certainly fit this characterization of presenile dementia.

MacNeill Weir made a very significant allusion to the language tool known as the "Latin period" in discussing MacDonald's deterioration in his speeches, and his allusion has important implications for the consideration of progressive dementia. The Latin period is a very complex style of sentence structure that the former Prime Minister William Gladstone popularized at one time in his own oratory. To use it effectively, Weir explained, requires "above all, a retentive memory," because it enlists complex sentence structures with several subordinate clauses. Bear in mind that loss of recent memory is the most obvious symptom that impacts upon the Alzheimer's victim. The observations Weir made in comparing MacDonald's moving and effective speeches from 1924 with those debacles a decade later, therefore, take on new meaning for the medically trained historian. Due to MacDonald's increasingly unreliable memory, Weir now noted that his habit was to pile "with increasing ir-relevance subordinate clause upon subordinate clause, los[ing] sight en-tirely of the subject. . . . Thus it happens that a sentence ressembles those roads that, in the pioneer days used to be built in Canada by am-bitious optimists. They begin well, diminish as they proceed, dwindle down to a squirrel track, and finally run up a tree."[86]

Having already acknowledged the pervasive depression that haunted the aging Prime Minister, and adding to that the evidence for recent mem-ory loss, disorders of perception, and increasingly ineffective speech patterns, there remains only to document a progression of symptoms to solidify the case for presenile dementia, for this is a steadily progressive disease, eclipsing the sufferer completely within five to ten years.[87] Mac-Donald's depressive symptoms were in fact magnified in the years after 1932. One well-known sign of depression is insomnia, and this was no stranger to MacDonald, as Marquand makes clear: "The insomnia which had plagued him for years, particularly at moments of crisis, grew even worse."[88] This would be an expected accompaniment of anxiety in the depressed. In January 1933 MacDonald recorded in his diary: "Weary night, sleepless and worried," and a few weeks later, "At night my mind [is] like a pool which seeks to be quiet but which is stirred by springs at the bottom." In August he wrote, "Cannot shut eyes to fact that am un-usually depressed and no wish to talk. . . . Decidedly older and of di-minished vigor." His anxiety accelerated: "I surely cannot be well or I have got old suddenly." By January 1934 he was being advised to take sleeping aids.[89]

MacDonald's recognition of his deterioration compounded his depres-sion to almost pathetic degrees, as so many Alzheimer's sufferers dis-cover in the early stages of the disease. In later months he dreaded the prospect of speaking before the House of Commons. As Marquand noted, "The night before making a speech, he would lie awake worrying; after a bad performance, he would torture himself with the memory."[90] In March 1933 MacDonald recorded: "Trying to get something clear into my head for the H. of C. tomorrow. . . . Cannot be done. Like man flying in mist."[91] By early 1934 he acknowledged that all too frequently: "I am a little depressed about my own tired head. . . . To speak now is a great effort . . . and [in] the development of the argument I get more & more confused."[92] By 1935 he was openly scorned for his oratorical gaffes. Ernest Hunter, a London Parliamentary journalist, spoke for all observ-ers when he wrote: "His recent speeches in the country have quite defi-nitely lowered his political stature."[93]

That Ramsay MacDonald suffered from dementia, and that he was a drastically changed entity in his last years in office due to its irresistible progression, make David Marquand's empathetic assessment of the impact of disease fairly accurate, but still somewhat wide of the mark:

> It seems to me that the psychological element can be accounted for quite easily by his rupture with the Labour Party and the "desolation of loneliness" which followed it, and by the slow collapse of his hopes for peace and disarmament. It is also necessary to remember that . . . some people age more quickly than others. . . . For much of the time he was in pain and for some of it he was unable to see properly. [94]

There now appears to be a more plausible explanation for MacDonald's conduct than merely the psychological element. True, much of his depression was an intrinsic part of his personality, and much was the product of tragedies, both political and personal, that befell him. Yet it can now be argued that his depression was in part the incipient phase of the dread disease of dementia. It is not enough to observe that some individuals age more readily than others. The key question in Ramsay MacDonald's case is why. The argument for Alzheimer's disease now affords an answer. There was more than chronic pain and the threat of blindness to account for his deterioration. Moreover the failure of disarmament undeniably affected him profoundly. Yet the most important historical question remains to be answered: What impact did MacDonald have on that failure? Might it not also be argued that MacDonald's condition was a factor in his inability to restrain Adolf Hitler? We turn now to this final question.

Marquand again sets the stage for the argument:

> Once the fiscal question was out of the way, he intervened only intermittently in home affairs, often to scant effect, but on the foreign-policy questions . . . his influence was usually considerable and often decisive. . . . Yet when all is said, there can be no doubt that he stayed on as prime minister for at least two and perhaps three years more than he should have done. . . . When he left Downing Street at last, his reputation was in ruins. [95]

But if his influence was "considerable and often decisive," was it also constructive? Did it merely postpone the inevitable, or even aid and abet the rising Nazi menace? How far down the road of appeasement did the old Labour principles that were so engrained in his character carry Great Britain, and Europe with it?

In his epilogue, Weir drew a parallel between the formation of the National Government in Britain and the Nazi regime in Germany, insofar as both were disasters for their respective countries. Citing opinions of such opponents of MacDonald as A. C. Temperley (who was head of the

War Office delegation at Geneva), Weir proposed that the National Government must "bear a major responsibility" for the rise of Hitler.[96]

Temperley indicted the National Government, and Ramsay MacDonald either directly or indirectly, for the following:

1. The National Government discredited the League.

2. It rejected the modest proposal of Chancellor Brüning to end compulsory unilateral disarmament as a prelude to the establishment of a respectable government in Germany that would assure stability in Europe, thus creating conditions leading to the rise of Hitler.

3. It failed to halt Japanese incursions in Manchuria.

4. It rejected the American proposals for disarmament.

5. It missed a golden opportunity to obtain an agreement between France and Germany on April 22, 1932, that would have meant peace.

Taking a Labour view of the entire issue, Weir asserted in his final analysis that "the 'National' Government has lost the moral leadership of the world which Britain had won during the years the Labour Government held office."[97] Many of these indictments are false and bear the stain of partisan sour grapes. The task remains to examine those instances in which the National Government's actions, as exercised by an intellectually compromised Prime Minister, did in fact exert a negative impact on the quest for peace.

In contrast to the Labour spokesmen who saw Conservative influence behind every distasteful action, Marquand argued that MacDonald ran foreign affairs virtually without Conservative input. As such, what transpired in foreign policy was largely the product of the Prime Minister alone—at least in the early going. Yet this certainly had its negative side. MacDonald feebly addressed the Japanese Shanghai-Manchurian crisis of 1931–32. He "dithered and prevaricated" over the use of force and used the seemingly ubiquitous excuse of illness to absolve himself from responsibility for not backing an American plan for more forceful intervention. To Marquand's way of thinking, MacDonald's inability to make up his mind here foreshadowed a recurring pattern of behavior over the next few years.[98] If it might be argued, as Weir did, that MacDonald failed to act because of his "ideological affiliation" with Germany and Italy,[99] the medical historian would be inclined to address the well-known propensity for individuals with compromised abstractive capabilities to be unable to make up their minds.

With regard to the second of Temperley's charges, Marquand enlisted the same dilemma to explain MacDonald's course of action. Here we find one of the old Labour principles—prejudices, to be more precise—

which was a part of the legacy MacDonald could not ignore. What had really mattered at Geneva in February 1932 was an agreement between Germany and France concerning reparations, disarmament, and the establishment of an international peace-keeping force. If MacDonald was not entirely responsible for the British delegation's refusal to acknowledge this, or their tendency to empathize with Germany, he nonetheless agreed with their stand on both points. As he had observed more than once: "The diplomacy of France is an ever active influence for evil in Europe."[100]

This deeply engrained perception of the French within MacDonald's Labour psyche is enough to account for his action there. It is doubtful that the ravages of the process of dementia were exerting strong enough effects to make him blind to the issue in February 1932. How can this assertion be defended, given the aforementioned evidence that depression and an increasing lack of felicity of expression signified some degree of compromise at this early date? Simply because he *learned* from his mistake. Failure of the abstract attitude effectively precludes the severely demented individual from changing his course or assessing alternative forms of action. MacDonald's illness had not progresssed this far by early 1932.

The initial failures at Geneva compelled MacDonald to realize he had erred; he had to work with France after all. For one thing, the urgency of events compelled him to do so. Heinrich Brüning was replaced as Chancellor by the inadequate Franz von Papen. Europe now appeared more unstable than ever, and an agreement on the reparations issue was even more critical at this juncture. This led to a second meeting at Lausanne during the summer of 1932. By most accounts, MacDonald's tireless efforts finally forced through what appeared to be a rational settlement of the emotionally charged issue of reparations. In exchange for French guarantees of a consultative pact with Great Britain regarding any future German demands against the Versailles Treaty, the Germans agreed to pay a lump sum into a fund for the reconstruction of Europe. This gave the appearance of not being a required reparation. For its part, Germany was to receive a proclamation that the reparations issue was at an end.

This was considered a well-deserved victory for MacDonald, his obvious physical compromise at the conference notwithstanding. Just prior to the conference, MacDonald was described as "a man with jaundice." By the time it ended, he was "prostrate with exhaustion."[101] Nevertheless, he had failed to take the German public's response to the agreement into account, though he was not alone in this failure. The news of the settlement at Geneva was received with outright indignation. Germany still demanded the "equality of status" she had sought all along. If Mac-

Donald's failure to foresee this reaction suggested some compromise in his abstract thinking, his conduct in 1932 still should not be construed as being based solely on compromised mentation. With the coming of the new year, however, his command over affairs both at home and abroad began to bear the imprint of his progressive disease.

Three qualities characterized MacDonald's last three desultory years in office: his loss of authority among his peers, his increasing attention to foreign affairs at the expense of the home front, and his deteriorating health. The Prime Minister's political clout first waned on the domestic scene. Some of this was by default alone, as he was absent from Downing Street a good part of the time, either because of illness or international conferences abroad. Some was induced by swings against the Government in the by-elections of 1933 and 1934. Whether MacDonald's increasing divorce from the domestic political scene or his occasionally inept public appearances contributed to these election setbacks is a moot point; what is certain is that his own authority suffered as a result. This only added to his increasing insecurity. He often contemplated resigning, but his illusion of indispensability kept him from doing so. "More than once," Marquand observed, "he told himself that he would have to resign unless things changed; when they failed to change there was always some new reason for staying on."[102]

MacDonald's increasing frustration was enhanced by two humiliating defeats in his Cabinet, plus a major Cabinet reshuffle necessitated by resignations over his economic policy. Not surprisingly, his paranoia increased and some of it was warranted. "As time went on," Marquand noted, his colleagues "increasingly came to see him as an incubus rather than as an asset."[103] MacDonald's old friend Arthur Salter concluded that by June 1933 he "was already no longer in a mental and physical condition to be capable of the continuous and exacting responsibilities of high office."[104]

On occasion the rapidly aging Prime Minister attempted to reassert his waning authority. Yet his clarion calls became hollow valedictories. "Our domestic programme will require to be infused with a bold energy . . ." he declared, "with some definite objectives worth fighting for."[105] But the energy was no longer there. In contrast to his years as Labour's Prime Minister, he was now content to remain largely on the sidelines; consequently, what few initiatives he proposed were never translated into action. "One reason was his declining health," Marquand was forced to admit. "Another was his continuing concentration on foreign affairs."[106]

To be sure, at least through mid-1934 MacDonald's influence in international affairs remained substantial, perhaps too much so in the view of some historians. Laurence Lafore, for example, has concluded that "in the end the foreign policy of Great Britain was being secretively conducted by the Prime Minister and a clique of friends not only without the professionals but actually against them." More injurious still, Lafore believes, he depended upon the precepts of traditional diplomacy in negotiating the various German demands, determined "to build a fortress out of paper" with individuals he innocently believed were dealing in good faith. [107] MacDonald also failed to perceive the slow erosion of the principles upon which his foreign policy was based. These included the beliefs he had carried with him from the Labour party: that Germany's intentions were good, that she had been mistreated, that her claims for equal status should be honored, and finally, that this could all be assured on faith alone in what her leaders said.

Why, then, this perseverance with Labour principles even when events continued to demonstrate their bankruptcy? It was a vicious cycle. Labour doctrine embraced the belief that, in Marquand's words, "reliance on force . . . bred war; to abandon disarmament was to admit that war had become inevitable." [108] In a frantic attempt during the autumn of 1933, MacDonald tried to bring the Germans back to the negotiating table. Yet he and his Foreign Secretary John Simon swam alone against the allied tide. For they surrendered the concept of equal status to the Germans in exchange for their return to Geneva. The concept of equal status included, ominously enough, that no arms should be denied to Germany that were allowed to others. The *Daily Express* later expressed the fears of its countrymen, while indicting the man it held responsible for the country's weakness by 1935:

> Mr. MacDonald is Prime Minister and bears prime responsibility. . . . He let the Nazis build an air force, raise an army, lay down the keels of a navy. He has exposed Britain to Hitler's threats. Can the people trust him to restore to them the power of defence? [109]

Once the reality of having to scuttle the policy of disarmament became obvious (as was apparent when MacDonald agreed in late 1933 to German rearmament as the price for resuming negotiations), this should have triggered British rearmament in kind to balance the ledger. Yet to avoid having to make that distasteful commitment, the Labour ethos compelled MacDonald to continue to negotiate with Hitler as if he could be trusted; hence, he made even more concessions to Hitler even while Germany was rearming. This was the beginning of the policy historians have identified as appeasement, which blighted the career of Neville Chamberlain. Ironic indeed that a Conservative would be crucified on the cross constructed five years before by Labour pacifist policies!

MacDonald should have known better than to persist with such a policy long after its intrinsic weakness had been exposed. Tragically enough, the evidence suggests that he may in fact have known better, yet his emotions overrode his intellect. Certainly he passed the signposts of danger along the way. He had seen enough of Hitler already in two short months to record in his diary entry for March 2, 1933 that he was beginning to fear "the dissolution of Europe through a Germany ruled by tyranny."[110] In September 1933 he was forced to witness Germany's withdrawal from the Disarmament Conference and the League of Nations. He also saw through the transparent veneer of Germany's cynical agreement with Poland of January 1934, describing it as another of Hitler's "temporary peace arrangements [combined] with effective nationalist aggressive propaganda."[111]

Why, then, did MacDonald follow so doggedly the course he chose? The answer rested in large measure with the characteristic tendency of dementia sufferers to cater to their emotions when their intellect muddles facts that they have haphazardly assimilated. In MacDonald's case, as Marquand noted, "even when he had become convinced intellectually that force might have to be answered by force, his emotions rebelled against the idea."[112] The distasteful alternatives his compromised intellect perceived were simply no match for the deep-seated beliefs of a political lifetime. Not that he alone held to the cherished Labour assumptions. British public opinion still embraced the appeals of internationalism, disarmament, and idealistic rules of law. Yet the guilt lies with a failing Prime Minister who, quite unlike his adversary Winston Churchill during this time, refused to swim against the tide of public opinion. After all, MacDonald had tried that once before with his unpopular economic policies and acquiescence to Conservative hegemony disguised under the banner of a so-called National Government. This experiment had only increased his discomfiture, isolated him further, and ushered in the "desolation of loneliness." Little wonder, then, that— three years further into a progressive dementia—he would take an easier route this time.

MacDonald's emotional allegiance to the old Labour principles simply ran counter to the conditions of the hour. In Marquand's words,

> Even when it was clear that there was no longer any hope for disarmament, the prospect of a large-scale rearmament programme filled him with alarm. So did the prospect of new or more precise military commitments—partly because of his old suspicion of the French, . . . but even more because of his deep-seated belief that true security and military alliances were inherently incompatible. Thus, he found himself in an intellectual and emotional *impasse*—an exhausted old man, searching despairingly for a way to meet the Nazi threat without doing violence to the assumptions of a lifetime, and subject to savage criticisms from his old followers for betraying the values

which he was trying vainly to uphold in the face of political disappointment and physical decline. [113]

Hitler's price for returning to the negotiating table at Geneva in December 1933 had included the acceptance of German rearmament as a fait accompli. Yet MacDonald's own assessment of the situation was restricted enough by this time that, while already having recognized that Britain might have to rearm, he failed to appreciate that now was the time. He clung instead to a dangerously pacific position. To his way of thinking, if disarmament was no longer a viable consideration, then at least security must not be linked to the vagaries of further military alliances. He later presented such a proposal to the Defence Requirements Committee in April 1934, only to find to his dismay that he was totally out of step with those he was addressing.

Clearly he had reached the end of the road now, physically spent and politically emasculated. Both conditions had been evident for some time. Indeed, while at the Geneva conference his obvious decline had been painfully obvious to even the most casual observer. He was, as Marquand notes, "a tired and failing old man, straining for rhetorical effects which he could no longer achieve, and in places unable to hold the thread of what he was trying to say." [114] Now, with his political estrangement at the hands of the disarmament committee complete, he excused himself from its proceedings and left for a needed respite in Canada. In doing so, he surrendered any residual political influence he had had. His own personal acceptance of that reality was long overdue. [115] Yet he had remained just long enough to imbue the British reaction to Hitler with a peculiar, schizoid character; in essence the British continued to appease Hitler, yet saw no need to rearm to a degree that was prudent. This would prove Britain's greatest failing during the thirties, and it was authored, sadly enough, by an increasingly compromised Prime Minister who had already lost political support in his own party and public confidence at home.

One would have thought this was the time to step down. Even MacDonald recognized the depths to which his intellectual deterioration had plunged. When he set out on his return trip from Canada he noted in his diary that his head was "still clogged & dull." During the voyage he wrote: "Last night my memory went badly. I could remember nothing for some time like my dog's name, certain incidents of my holiday . . . & such trifling things." [116] Marquand recounted that his diary entries toward the end of that year were "full of confessions of 'stupidity', 'tiredness' and lapses of memory, and it seems clear that his performance in Cabinet was beginning to deteriorate as well." [117] The Conservative J. C. C. Davidson noted in his memoirs, "I knew that his rambling incoherence frequently shocked those who heard him."[118] MacDonald himself closed the volume of his 1934 diary with one of the last accurate assessments of his failing mental powers he was to make: "And so this volume ends. . . . I end rather worn out & the worse for wear; my head slowing up & sometimes hardly working at all."[119] Beyond that point his diary entries reflected only his perception of the intractable depressive phase of his illness; he was now relatively unaware of his intellectual shortcomings, which were so obvious to others. Certainly his physician attempted to apprise him of his compromised mentation; MacDonald noted in his diary in January 1935 that Horder "thinks [I] should not let my brain tiredness go too far."[120]

Yet MacDonald was immune to such warnings, and he took his "tired brain" as far into 1935 as political circumstances allowed. Tragically, he took his country farther still—down the road of appeasement, while the Government floundered about in a form of chronic succession crisis. Attacks came from both Right and Left. It was the personal attacks from the Right that struck MacDonald most deeply. Ironically enough, his own limited perceptions served almost as a psychological buffer during that final year while discontent swirled about him:

> Discontent with him and discontent with the Government fed on each other. Conservatives came to feel that the Government could not recapture the ground which it had lost while MacDonald remained at its head. . . . He was [only] half-aware that they were right in thinking that he was no longer able to carry on. [121]

Much as Winston Churchill would do during the last years of his second term in office, MacDonald kept his government in limbo regarding the date of his resignation. Yet there was a greater sense of urgency now than Churchill would face after World War II, when Great Britain had already surrendered its role as a major mover and shaker in world affairs. By March 1935 plans for Stanley Baldwin's succession were already in motion, but they would not take effect before MacDonald played a part in some final critical activities on the international stage.

For one thing, a debate over the Defence Requirements Committee's proposed program was reopened in the spring of 1935. Up to this time, MacDonald had backed Neville Chamberlain in his attempt to reduce the expenditures for rearmament recommended by the Committee. In early March, however, a controversy arose over a rather militant white paper on defense that Maurice Hankey had encouraged the Prime Minister to initial. Nothing more completely exemplified MacDonald's loss of control over happenings within his own government than this controversy. Indeed, MacDonald was originally unaware that he was even implicated in the matter. He may not have read the report prior to initialing it—or if he did, he certainly did not digest it. As he recorded in his diary, "When I got to the H. of C. I found unfortunately . . . that it appeared over my initials as well as announced a date for the debate—the 11th—before the House knew.—Most annoying blunders. It is rather odd that I cannot be protected . . . against such mistakes." [122]

A still graver blunder followed. In essence a call for increased expenditures for defense that others now recognized as essential, the white paper ran counter to MacDonald's long-held position in favor of disarmament. When the predictable outcry arose from the Left, the embattled Prime Minister waffled again under the strain of criticism. As Marquand observed: "If [the white paper] was not an 'armaments document, marking the beginning of a new policy,' it was a waste of time: if it was, MacDonald's defensiveness boded ill for the success of the operation." MacDonald backpedaled: "I have been fixed on as the chief of culprits because by accident my initials . . . were printed. . . . [Still,] I am of opinion that Hitler will cool down like a sensible man." [123]

Again he had misread Adolf Hitler. When Hitler reacted menacingly to the white paper by reintroducing conscription and increasing the number of German army divisions to thirty-six on March 16, MacDonald again attempted to appease him. On March 18 the Prime Minister and his Cabinet sent a cable to Hitler, ostensibly protesting Germany's action, yet assuring him nonetheless that Britain still wished to replace the detested Versailles Treaty with a freely negotiated settlement! It was yet another in a long string of typically mixed signals from the spineless democracies, which Hitler perceived he could manipulate. The pattern of behavior that would later foster such lasting images of Allied irresolution in the late thirties had as its model the actions of a senile Prime Minister, trapped between the pretensions of a Labourite and the will of the Conservatives who dominated him. In Marquand's assessment,

> [MacDonald's] colleagues, and still more his opponents, floundered at least as badly as he did. But it could hardly be claimed that he had given them a positive lead. . . . In principle, at any rate, he now accepted the notion that Hitler's Germany could be dealt with only on the basis of older and harsher assumptions, which he had always rejected in the past. But he was too ill, too tired and, above all, too unsure of his bearings in the illiberal world in which he now had to operate to translate that theoretical acceptance into a coherent policy. When others led, as Hankey had done over the white paper, he was prepared to follow. When no lead came from elsewhere, he was content to mirror the prevailing Cabinet consensus. [124]

One may argue, however, that MacDonald's "unsure bearings" were now much more a product of bonafide organic disease than merely an unfamiliar political environment. This was three months before his resignation. The *Times* of London addressed the obvious needs of the hour for its countrymen, rather than MacDonald's true intent, when it later acknowledged in his obituary that the white paper was his last great state paper. [125]

If it was to be his last great act, nonetheless MacDonald still had three more months to promulgate others. Evidence indicates he made the worst of it. In mid-April he journeyed to Stresa in northern Italy for discussions with the British and Italians over the latest German affronts. True to form, though an agreement was reached in principle to oppose further repudiations, there was no agreement on substance, as MacDonald still refused to accept potentially risky military commitments to the Continent. Again, these were mixed signals to Hitler: a strong statement of intent but no application of its principles.

While at Stresa an even graver sin was committed against the efforts to preserve peace, and it was one for which the deteriorating Prime Minister bore personal responsibility. In February 1935 Mussolini mobilized Italy for an incursion into Ethiopia. Before MacDonald left for Stresa, Anthony Eden had briefed him on the situation, imploring him to raise the issue with Mussolini. But, though fully aware of the potentially disastrous implications of the Ethiopean crisis, MacDonald chose to say nothing about it. Marquand struggled to understand why:

> It may be that he . . . quailed at the prospect of a difficult encounter with Mussolini. It may be that Vansittart . . . persuaded him to say nothing. It may be that he decided that there was no point in saying anything; it may be that . . . he forgot. But, whatever the reason, it was a bad lapse. [126]

Many historians have perceived the negative implications of the lapse. Laurence Lafore observed that "the British held the ultimate power of decision at Geneva, and they supported compromises, arbitration, evasion, which did not strengthen the League or relieve Ethiopia but did mislead Mussolini." [127] This was Italy's green light; it tacitly sanctioned the Duce's action. Weir believed MacDonald's silence on the issue appeared to show that Abyssinia "was no immediate concern of ours. . . . We seemed inclined to allow Mussolini to carry out his policy of aggression unmolested." [128] This, in the final analysis, is what he did.

The Stresa conference had other negative implications for the future. The so-called Stresa Front, an anti-German coalition, was more apparent than real. Certainly it offended the French. Their general policy at the time was one of containment of Germany, whereas MacDonald was working at cross purposes with his potential allies by proposing a general security system to include Germany. This envisioned extending the system to every frontier in Europe, including Poland, the existence of which would be "guaranteed" by everybody. [129]

This last proposal was unacceptable to at least one European state, for Poland, to be sure, wanted no guarantees from anyone, in particular Germany or Russia. [130] Germany, after all, was seeking to alter the very frontiers the allies were attempting to persuade Hitler to accept. If this isolated concept was disruptive of the French policy of containment in the first place, the entire conference exposed the tragic flaw of dealing with Hitler along traditional diplomatic lines: Whereas the British and French perceived treaties as inviolable agreements, Hitler used them much more cynically and self-servingly, casting them aside when the need arose.

Foreign Secretary John Simon may have been directing the diplomatic play at Stresa, but it was MacDonald who was on the stage, and the strain of three days of negotiation was simply too much for him. It was apparent to all that MacDonald was no longer in command either of his delegation or of himself. "He found it difficult to read his papers," Marquand noted, "and often rambled badly in discussion; on one occasion, the interpreter could make no sense of what he had said and had to be told to invent a speech for him." [131] He could not even dress appropriately, much less be responsible for any potentially damaging comments he might make, so he had to be shielded from the press. Despite these drawbacks, he still managed to leave his mark on the proceedings—however negative it proved to be. Marquand concluded that "Thanks largely to MacDonald's refusal to budge . . . [the] declarations [deploring Germany's repudiation of the peace] had no practical content. The Stresa front . . . was broken before it was established." Within the month, Hitler repudiated the remaining disarmament clauses of Versailles, and the collective security system was left for dead. It had taken him less than two years to shake off the restrictions on German rearmament. [132]

MacDonald returned to England exhausted and disillusioned. There was no longer any justifiable pretense for his staying on; in May he tendered his resignation. It had been long overdue. Not the last man who would attempt to cling to power after he had lost it, MacDonald accepted the figurehead position of Lord President, perhaps to assuage his flagging self-esteem. As Marquand observed, he "feared the emptiness of retirement. But although his decision to stay in office is easy to forgive, and easier still to understand, there can be no doubt that it was mistaken. He had [already] paid a high enough price for staying in Downing Street longer than he should have done." [133]

Great Britain had paid an even higher price for that miscalculation. To be sure, MacDonald's inability to deal with the Hitler menace was shared by almost everyone, particularly before 1934, and his illness

*At time of resignation,
June 1935*

*Last public photograph
of Macdonald, 1937*

probably had not progressed to such an extent before that time to cause him to act any more discreditably than other statesmen of that era. Yet after that date there is just cause for indictment on a very personal level. MacDonald had surrendered the principle of equality of status to bring the Germans back to the negotiating table in 1933. If this was a necessary requirement in the give and take of diplomacy, his insistence in carrying that principle into the negotiations of 1934 and 1935 had much less justification. For now, both at home and abroad, MacDonald's rigid stance cultivated a policy of appeasement upon which Hitler's ravenous appetite fed. Similarly, the Prime Minister had been largely responsible for the apparent impotency of the League's response, or lack of it, to the Ethiopian crisis. From that point on, Hitler's suspicions were confirmed; such a flaccid international organization could not possibly stand in his way. In the end, the entire Stresa accord was rendered powerless by MacDonald's persevering with themes that ran counter to French policy. If there were no pious assurances of "peace in our time" in 1934–35, the principles underlying these later expressions of impotence were still a large part of the compromised repertoire of alternatives with which MacDonald forged the mistaken popular opinion of his countrymen.

Great Britain was not the only country that was misled in the mid-thirties. Other nations had their own problems in dealing with the rising star of Adolf Hitler. They were a logical extension of the notion that Germany was peacefully participating in Europe's rebuilding. Such a false belief contributed to many unresolved issues in Europe. One problem was Poland, which signified the preoccupation of Hitler with the space required for German growth. The Polish Question serves as an example of how the new German Chancellor dealt duplicitly with Europe in the mid-thirties, before his aggressive instincts turned toward the more explicit instrument of war.

Poland had been recreated by the post–World War I settlement. One of the most intolerable aspects of that settlement to the Germans was the loss of a portion of West Prussia known as the Polish Corridor. This area divided eastern Prussia from the rest of Germany. Historically, Poland had always suffered from having stronger neighbors on its borders. Its peculiar geographic position alone exemplified the pervasive instability that characterized central and eastern Europe.

Admittedly, some modicum of internal stability for Poland had been gained in 1926 by the consolidation of power under the Grand Marshal of the army, Józef Piłsudski. His ascension in that year as a military dictator had been Poland's response to its floundering democratic experiment. During the last half of the twenties a personality cult developed around the Marshal, who was often required to govern by decree. Like

*Marshal Jósef Piłsudski, World War I*

*In his office at Belvedere, 1930*

his contemporaries Hindenburg and MacDonald, he was an old man, subject to the whims and opinions of his subordinates and retaining all the while an unrealistic appraisal of Poland's strength. As age increasingly took its toll during the early thirties, two characteristics of his regime became increasingly obvious: his dependency upon fewer advisors and his unrealistic perception of Poland's military and diplomatic strength.

Yet this should not obscure the overriding fact that Poland was caught between two aggressive powers, and between the two, the Russians' actions had always made the Poles fear them more than the Germans. More important still, if they feared Germany at all, it was really the Prussians they feared—and Adolf Hitler was not a Prussian. These facts in large measure may have governed Piłsudski's response to the German threat that arose during his last four years in office, and Hitler used them to his distinct advantage.

What sort of man was Piłsudski, and what role did he play, directly or indirectly, in Germany's rise to preeminence in European affairs by 1935? Laurence Lafore outlined one troubling perception of the man when he stated: "Marshal Piłsudski had been an able and patriotic if not very adventurous statesman, but by 1934 his mind had failed."[134] Viewed in such a perspective, it might be postulated (as some historians have) that Piłsudski's rigid frame of mind, his lack of interest in domestic politics, and his fitful intervention in military and foreign affairs left Poland in a vulnerable position during the years immediately preceding and following Hitler's ascension to the German chancellorship. A review of his last years in power reveals that several ominous features characterized Polish affairs. They include:

1. An increasing infiltration of the military into government affairs, which had significant repercussions for Poland's experiment with democratic institutions;

2. A progressive deterioration in the preparedness of its army;

3. A perceptible repression of minorities and dissidents on the domestic front;

4. A gradual disintegration of constitutional democratic institutions as the government became more dependent on presidential decree in order to function; and

5. An underestimation of Hitler's intentions and potential power, which in large measure played into his hand.

Why had Poland, like so many other nations of that period, chosen to entrust its future to an aging, perhaps senile, figurehead? If one is to implicate a "failing mind" in Piłsudski's case, what early influences may have molded his perceptions before the impact of his alleged senility?

Three early and totally unrelated events had proved to have a distinct influence on Piłsudski's beliefs.

The first occurred in 1897. In that year Piłsudski was sentenced to five years in Siberia for his role in a conspiracy against the life of Alexander III. By all accounts it was a sobering experience for the young revolutionary. From that period on he embraced a belief that influenced his thinking on the relative threat to Polish identity posed by Germany and Russia. "He quickly came to the conclusion," Antony Polonski has noted, "that Tsarist Russia, 'that Asiatic monster covered with European veneer,' was Poland's principal enemy."[135] This opinion reflected what has largely remained a feature of the Polish psyche—the belief that Russia was to be feared second to none in matters related to maintaining Poland's political autonomy. Such a perception would later influence Piłsudski's acceptance of the German-Polish Nonaggression Pact of 1934.

A second event played a major role in his perceived need to repress dissident behavior once it became injurious to the orderly functioning of government. Gabriel Narutowicz became the first President of the new republic in 1922. Elected with the support of a broad center-left alliance, the right felt that Narutowicz had been forced upon it by a conspiracy of national minorities including, significantly enough, Jews and Germans.[136] The political situation at once became tense and violent, resulting in the assassination of the newly elected President on December 16, 1922, by a nationalist fanatic. Piłsudski was appalled by the crime, and it left a lasting impression upon him, as Wieslau Domaniewski, who later served in his government as the Director of the Department of Movement of Funds and assistant under-secretary for Monetary Affairs, recounted in an interview: "After the assassination Piłsudski changed completely. From then on he spoke vilely and profanely of all of his political opponents. He used every vulgar expression to denounce them and resolved to deal firmly with dissident behavior forcibly in the future if necessary."[137] This event may have persuaded him to seek higher office as a means of redressing any such grievances in the future. Just after Narutowicz's assassination, Piłsudski confided to Maciej Rataj: "I cannot give up power at a time when a band of gangsters is disturbing the peace, insulting the President, and the Government does nothing. Give me power, and I will quiet the streets."[138] To his way of thinking, the strong hand of executive action was required if governmental institutions were threatened. This would have significant implications for the future.

The third event was more a phenomenon than an isolated happening: Piłsudski inspired intense loyalty among his subordinates. Indeed, even before the coup in 1926 that brought him to power, a personality cult had evolved around him. Among this inner group of advisors, absolute allegiance was the rule. As president, Piłsudski's decisions were not questioned, even though after taking office he demonstrated little interest in government, attending only thirty-four of ninety-two Cabinet meetings from 1926 to 1929.[139] Once Piłsudski's health began to decline, by 1930, the inordinate influence of this inner circle of advisors became instrumental in turning the government down the road to increasing authoritarianism. One of the most obvious reasons for this was the growing prominence of military men in all spheres of government after 1930. As Antony Polonsky noted, "A qualitative change seems to be evident in the years 1929–30. . . . As the Marshal's health declined former P.O.W. [Polish Military Organization] officers in the inner circle of Piłsudski-ites came to take more initiative, and they largely favoured dependence on military men. . . . This military take-over assumed vast proportions in the period after 1930." Polonsky concluded that this movement of military officers into the civil government "was certainly one of the most significant reasons for increasing inadequacy and incompetence of the Piłsudski régime in the 1930s."[140]

These three events, then, were the source of much of what was wrong with Poland in the early thirties: the pervasive tendency to view Germany with relative equanimity compared to Russia; an increasing authoritarianism both in dealing with dissident behavior and in directing government affairs, which Piłsudski increasingly neglected; and the collective influence of the Piłsudski-ites, whose allegiance to their hero never wavered, despite increasing signs of compromise in his behavior. That government administration was in a chronic state of disarray was suggested by a member of the General Staff during this period, who referred to the influx of military men into the system as "an attack of bandits on a lunatic asylum."[141]

Essential to an understanding of Poland's inability to govern itself effectively at this time is the realization that Piłsudski's increasing isolation and divorce from governmental affairs left no legitimate successor waiting in the wings. One of the peculiarities of his group of inner advisors was the absence of any single individual who could emerge to take the lead as Piłsudski's interest in domestic affairs waned. On the home front, at least, little of the palace intrigue that characterized interwar Germany was apparent in Poland during the thirties.

This was not the case in foreign affairs. Although Piłsudski divided his fitful interest between military matters and the formulation of foreign policy, it was Colonel Józef Beck whose influence became paramount at approximately the same time the military was infiltrating the government. Beck became Under Secretary at the Foreign Office in 1930 and single-handedly molded Piłsudski's perception that Poland required a dramatic departure from its prior dependence on both French power and

League assurances. She must now learn to live by her wits and play one neighboring power off against the other. Though Beck personally disliked the Germans, it was his belief that Poland must attempt to buy time for military preparedness by playing Germany's cynical diplomatic game. This led to his suggestion to Piłsudski in 1933 that it was "time to try something new." The result was the German-Polish Nonaggression Pact of 1934, with all of the good and ill it would come to imply for Poland's future. [142]

The new policy sought to buy time for Polish military preparedness. Yet there remained one fatal flaw, which historians later acknowledged: the negative effect of Piłsudski's influence on the state of the military from 1930 through 1934. In Polonsky's assessment, a "fundamental reason for the technical backwardness of the Army was the increasing paralysis resulting from the lack of any clear directives from the Marshal." [143] What directives he gave betrayed his increasing failure to grasp how much modern warfare had changed since World War I. Modernization of the elite sapper battalions was neglected due to Piłsudski's failure to recognize the need for more technical training, and their number reduced, not to mention, in Polonsky's words, "his rather confused views that since any future war would be a 'war of movement' . . . trenches would not be needed, and therefore neither would sappers." This shortage became painfully obvious during the 1939 German blitzkreig that overran Poland. [144]

More disturbing still was his misplaced pride in the Polish cavalry. Piłsudski liked to describe his cavalry as the best in Europe. The statement rings true—but only insofar as it ignored the salient fact that it was the *only* cavalry left in Europe. [145] According to Waclau Jedrzejewicz, who served as minister of education under Piłsudski, funding for the military was adequate enough; by 1935, 45 percent of the annual budget was appropriated for defense. [146] Yet many of the funds may have been misdirected, for there is no doubt that between 1930 and 1935 the failure to modernize the army or develop new weaponry became even more exaggerated. Supply and transport still relied on horses. Acceptance of modern artillery and motorized armor units proved to be extremely slow. Communications remained primitive.

Nor did Polish industry meet the challenge of the thirties. In truth an attempt was made, most notably with nationalization of the war industries under General Felicjan Sławoj-Składkowski, Chief of Army Administration from 1931 through 1936. But, as with the influx of the military into government administrative affairs, the penetration of the military into the economy left its negative mark. "The industries concerned," according to Polonsky, were not so much nationalized as militarized. Their administration was handed over to officers, generally closely connected with Składkowski, and generally without any real technical competence. Little control was exercised over their activity and these positions thus became for the most part extremely lucrative sinecures, while the efficiency of military industries correspondingly suffered. [147]

If Piłsudski-ites such as Jedrzejewicz were later to argue that it was the French failure to continue their advance during the 1939 campaign that sealed Poland's fate, [148] statistics from the first half of the thirties nevertheless offer evidence to support at least a negative drift in the area of military preparedness long before. In 1932 Poland had a respectable army of 266,000 men, a number that compares favorably with Germany's restricted army of 100,000 and Russia's of 562,000. But by the autumn of 1935 a radical transformation in the numerical balance had occurred. Germany now had 450,000 men and Russia nearly 1 million, whereas the size of Poland's forces had remained static. Polonsky offered a harsh indictment of those years: "The discrepancy in numbers remained shattering and it proved a slow and difficult task to overcome the negative effects of Piłsudski's last years on the organization of the fighting forces." [149]

Marian Romeyko, a member of the Army General Staff during this critical period, concurred with the verdict that the old Marshal had progressively lost his touch and was unable to adjust to the changing conditions of the new decade. This same observer witnessed an acceleration in the downgrading of his own General Staff, detected a resistance on the part of Piłsudski to technical changes, and encountered favoritism in officer appointments. All of this was augmented by the Marshal's increasing inaccessibility. Romeyko's overall assessment of Piłsudski's limitations summarized much of what proved to be Poland's Achilles' heel in the thirties:

> Piłsudski not only exercised total power in the military field, but became at the same time the center of power for the country as a whole. As an old, tired man, sick, nervous [and] burdened with a whole range of complexes, he was simply unable to penetrate deeply matters which required decision and arbitration as a result of the uncoordinated activity of his subordinates. He certainly was not able to follow the rapid development of military thought in Europe, to create his own conception of the war of the future, or, finally, to give detailed directives, both military and political, which could form the basis of an effective system of national defense. . . . [He epitomized the] tired and passive dictator, who devotes himself to a number of problems by fits and starts from occasion to occasion, who cannot inspire ideals and who does not wish to give up his privileged position. [150]

Romeyko was describing many features underscoring the argument that senility may have overtaken the old Marshal during the early thirties. The reference to Piłsudski being unable to "penetrate deeply matters which required decision and arbitration" certainly speaks to the compromise of the abstract attitude so characteristic of individuals harboring an organic brain syndrome. [151] His alleged inability to "follow the rapid development of military thought" and "to create his own conception" of future wars speaks to the senile individual's inability both to learn new material and to appreciate the essentials of a given whole. [152] Then, too, such afflicted sufferers characteristically address issues only in "fits and starts," because their attention span is limited. Finally, the reference to Piłsudski's insistence on not giving up his privileged position exemplifies his inflexible mind-set. Such individuals react defensively when confronted and become more rigid in the belief that they are indispensable.

Perhaps as a result of progressive illness, Piłsudski exercised even less control over government affairs by 1933 than previously. Most of his inner circle found it increasingly difficult to ascertain his intentions—except on those rare occasions when he chose to call his confidants together in order to speak ex cathedra on a particular subject. For example, up until a week before Ignacy Mościcki's term as president expired in 1933, no one knew whether Piłsudski wanted him to remain in office. As events transpired, he did; yet Piłsudski's endorsement (which was as important to an officeholder in Poland under Piłsudski as it had been to an official in Germany under Hindenburg) might have served better had it been made earlier than six days before the election. [153]

Piłsudski did, however, arbitrarily force Aleksander Prystor to resign as Prime Minister in May 1933, largely on the spurious charge that he "relies on his 'own men.'" [154] None of Piłsudski's immediate subordinates believed there was anything to substantiate this allegation. The incident merely heightened their awareness that his actions were being dictated by whim as much as by rational appraisal, and were often arbitrary in the extreme. Kazimierz Świtalski believed the decision to be a product of his increasing isolation from anyone outside his immediate circle of advisors. "My impression," he said, "is that the Commander is a solitary individual. He cuts himself off from people and is thus the prisoner of the opinions . . . of those . . . who give him a distorted picture of the internal political situation." [155] These vignettes only add to the argument for progressive intellectual and behavioral compromise. Such restricted individuals' actions are characterized by just such arbitrariness, which betrays a rigid mind. Furthermore, these individuals increasingly isolate themselves, becoming dependent on fewer advisors when the alternatives for action become too difficult to extrapolate, and the isolation they seek protects them from any psychologically distressing reactions to the few decisions they do make.

As discussed earlier, dementia sufferers in old age become caricatures of themselves, often magnifying earlier personality traits or beliefs. We have seen that as early as 1922 Piłsudski reacted strongly and defensively to dissident behavior perceived as threatening to the state. It is not surprising, therefore, that before the election of 1930 he arrested leaders of the opposition and confined them in the Brześć military fortress, contrary to provisions of the existing penal code. This was correctly viewed by the opposition as an abuse of power and an exercise in police brutality. Strong public protests resulted. An open letter from professors at Jagielloniau University following the incident outlined what was perceived as an increasingly repressive pattern of government activity: "Many occurrences in the past few years are undermining the moral basis of social and political life in Poland and . . . threaten . . . the existence of the Polish State. Among these matters, the most alarming is the question of the prisoners in Brześć. [156]

An increasing authoritarianism in all areas characterized Piłsudski's government over the next five years. Parliament's role during this period remained small. It diminished further in March 1932 when a law was passed giving the President (in reality Piłsudski, as Mościcki remained his rubber stamp) the right to issue decrees between parliamentary sessions. Events subsequently proved that the government intended to take considerable advantage of the increasingly authoritarian power vested in it. As an extension of this, censorship was maintained and minority groups on the troubled periphery of Poland were increasingly oppressed. Even progovernment sources like the newspaper *Kurjer Poranny* were alarmed by this drift toward authoritarianism: "Our Parliament has become a machine which receives on a conveyor belt projects emanating from the Government. . . . This is not a parliament . . . it is an automaton. The Deputies talk, but they might just as well go home." [157]

Greater power did not necessarily assure greater efficiency. This was most obvious in the government's inability to deal effectively with the Depression. None of the ministers entrusted with economic affairs demonstrated more than a superficial understanding of the problem. The prescribed treatment was harsh indeed for a country with such a restricted economy: deflation, a balanced budget, and adherence to the gold standard. Naturally, no guidance in these matters was forthcoming from the highest quarter—demented or not, Piłsudski had neither the awareness nor the interest to pursue economic issues. Accordingly, the government continued to flounder in the harsh economic realities of the day.

Did Piłsudski's leadership mirror this circumstance? Or was it, as some have argued, one of its causes? Sławoj-Składkowski alleged that the Marshal's deteriorating health was a major factor in Poland's regression during this period. Subsequent writers have accepted this view, and used his evidence to build a case for compromised cognition on the part of Piłsudski. Antony Polonsky cited Sławoj-Składkowski's discussion of the Marshal's health to suggest that after 1931 "his health deteriorated still further . . . and his severe bronchitis necessitated long absences from Poland. . . . In addition he was suffering from arteriosclerosis and, unknown to his entourage, from cancer of the liver." [158] Piłsudski himself acknowledged that by 1931 "he cast too big a shadow on Polish life, . . . which was not a healthy situation." [159] Polonsky saw the negative implications in all of this: "Since there was no one among his associates who could easily take the lead, his withdrawal did not stimulate . . . any greater political capacity on the part of his 'boys', but, on the contrary meant that more and more the Government lacked direction and failed to take any decisive initiative." [160]

It is one thing to document that disease existed; it is quite another to propose that it adversely affected Piłsudski's judgment and consequently his ability to govern. More evidence directed toward those illnesses that may have restricted his cognitive powers is needed before a verdict can be handed down. But the illnesses that Polonsky advanced to support the thesis play *no* significant role in this consideration. If that writer exercised the literary license to extrapolate from Składkowski's memoirs, it would be appropriate to examine the references made in the primary source itself in some detail. [161]

According to Składkowski, on December 27, 1932, Piłsudski experienced paroxysms of coughing while playing solitaire in Składkowski's presence. After one such paroxysm, he "suddenly became very flushed in the face and his eyes glassed over. 'You are seeing me have an attack of atypical influenza,' he said. 'I have been experiencing shaking chills over the last few days.'" [162] This was an obvious reference to the chronic bronchitis from which he suffered. The shaking chills at least raise the possibility of a viral pneumonitis or bacterial pneumonia superimposing itself on that condition.

If bronchitis with superimposed infection was the probable cause of this isolated episode in 1932, there still remains the possibility that much of the chronic cough his associates ascribed to bronchitis may have been secondary to recurrent bouts of pulmonary edema (fluid build-up on the lungs) related to congestive heart failure. The evidence for this is only suggestive and includes the following observations. First, before World War I, Piłsudski experienced frequent palpitations (or arrhythmias) of the heart that remained undiagnosed, as the Marshal even at that time had a morbid distrust of doctors and never allowed a physician to perform a physical examination upon him. [163] Recurrent palpitations may suggest the possibility of a cardiac arrhythmia, such as atrial fibrillation; indeed Piłsudski's history of a stroke in April 1928 may even suggest that an embolus from the heart associated with atrial fibrillation later occurred. [164]

Secondly, Wieslau Domaniewski described a 1933 episode recounted to him by one of the Marshal's aides. This suggests a symptom, discussed in Chapter 1, that is frequently associated with congestive heart failure and is termed "paroxysmal nocturnal dyspnea"—a sudden shortness of breath occurring in the night when the patient is recumbent. [165] As Domaniewski described the episode,

> The Marshal was sleeping in a room in the General Staff building and I had been assigned to guard duty on the night shift. His door was ajar, and I suddenly heard heavy moaning and deeply labored breathing. Though strictly forbidden to enter the room, I became alarmed with the increasing struggle of a man trying to get his breath. It became so accentuated that I entered, and found him sitting up in bed, heavily panting. "Should I call a physician?" I asked. "Sit down, my child," he said. "You realize why I am moaning. It is because the tragic circumstance of our country lying between Germany and Russia weighs heavily on my mind." [166]

A third episode occurred in that same year. Piłsudski experienced another three-week seige of illness during which consultants from Warsaw and Wilno were requested. Significantly enough, the doctors concluded that "his heart was weakening"; nonetheless, the old Marshal refused to take the medication his physician prescribed. [167]

These isolated symptoms of cardiac palpitations, a chronic cough, and extreme shortness of breath occurring at night, when taken in combination, may suggest a consideration of congestive heart failure in this aging leader. Why might this be important? Simply because one of the known causes of clouding of consciousness, or encephalopathy, is severe congestive heart failure. [168] The body of available evidence as a whole, however, does not support the supposition that this condition—if indeed he had it at all—was sufficiently severe to have altered his mentation significantly. Encephalopathy occurs only in serious cases, usually of long standing. The strongest evidence militating against this is simply that no further progression of such symptoms was noted by any observer at any time during Piłsudski's last three years in office. Jedrzejewicz stated categorically that the mysterious palpitations later disappeared and that no signs of cardiac compromise were noted at all during the last decade of Piłsudski's life. [169]

Returning to Polonsky's assertions regarding possible adverse effects of liver cancer and arteriosclerosis, the first consideration can be dismissed out of hand as being irrelevant, if not inaccurate, for his statement implied that liver cancer was present in 1931. In fact, the lesion was not discovered until three weeks before Piłsudski's death in 1935 and most likely had spread from an undiscovered cancer in the gastrointestinal tract. That the gastrointestinal tract may have been implicated is suggested by the fact that he ultimately died of a massive gastrointestinal hemorrhage; that his liver involvement was a late occurrence in this disease process is suggested by the medical axiom that nearly all patients with spread of cancer to the liver die within six months of that discovery. Moreover, physicians know that only massive liver involvement of long standing can cause significant enough chemical alterations to induce encephalopathy on the basis of liver disease. [170]

Polonsky's reference to arteriosclerosis, on the other hand, is important and deserves further consideration. He inferred this from Składkowski's account of a stroke the Marshal experienced in 1928. On January 24, 1934, Składkowski stated: "What concerned me was the hardening of the arteries which Piłsudski has. We are all afraid of a repeat of the stroke he had a few years before, which fortunately had been very mild." [171] It was left to Waclau Jedrzejewicz to clarify the nature of this nebulous reference, which most historians have ignored. On the night of April 17, 1928, Piłsudski suffered an apoplectic attack that affected the use of his right hand. He had trouble writing intermittently for a few days thereafter in conjunction with hand incoordination. Yet his speech was not affected, and he experienced no sensory compromise. No other extremity was involved, and he improved significantly by the fifth day. Thereafter he experienced only intermittent difficulty with his right hand, manifested occasionally by a slight tremor. [172]

The precision of Jedrzejewicz's account allows the physician to establish not only the location of the stroke, but its probable cause. The area controlling hand function within the motor cortex of the brain (where strokes occur on the basis of large-blood-vessel occlusion or embolism) is juxtaposed to the cortical areas related to speech and sensory input (see Fig. 2.2). Strokes in this area of the left side of the brain (where the speech center for right-handed individuals is located) usually affect speech and sensation together, unless only an extremely small vessel is affected. This area, which is supplied by the left middle cerebral artery, might appear at first glance to have some relevance to Piłsudski's case, as emboli (blood clots) from the heart most frequently lodge in this vessel. What is required, then, is anatomic evidence to clarify this issue. Fortuitously, it exists.

The Piłsudski Institute in New York possesses thirty-six extraordinarily detailed enlargements of photographs of Józef Piłsudski's brain taken at the autopsy. They were the subject of an anatomic study of "elite

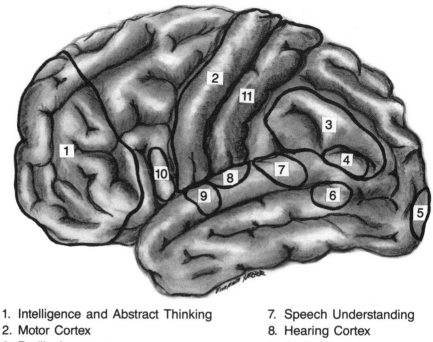

1. Intelligence and Abstract Thinking
2. Motor Cortex
3. Bodily Awareness
4. Writing
5. Visual Cortex
6. Reading

7. Speech Understanding
8. Hearing Cortex
9. Audito-Psychic
10 Speech Cortex
11. Sensory Cortex

*Fig. 2.2 This side view of a normal brain outlines various cortical areas controlling different brain functions.*

brains" by Maximilian Rose. [173] Using magnification, it is possible to examine those areas in question with relation to the stroke of 1928. Given the facts of the case as presented thus far, it is not surprising that structural evidence for a stroke in the superficial cortex of the left parietal region of the brain accounting for hand dysfunction is *absent*. More significant still, Fig. 1.2 (a view of the brain from below, including its largest vessels) fails to reveal evidence of significant arteriosclerosis for a man Piłsudski's age, with the exception of some obvious arteriosclerotic plaques in the right vertebral artery. Nor do the carotid arteries cut in cross section at this particular level show the characteristic thickening of arteriosclerosis usually found there. The suggestion by Polonsky that Piłsudski suffered from arteriosclerosis, which by inference was accepted to be the cause of the stroke in 1928, is therefore not substantiated.

This leaves the only other area of the brain that might account for a stroke involving hand dysfunction: the internal capsule, a structure that transmits motor signals and coursing deeply through the brain (see Fig. 1.1). It is a frequent location of transient or small strokes in individuals with hypertension. [174] This cannot be confirmed anatomically here, because photographs of the sectioned brain are not available. Nor can the presence of hypertension—a necessary antecedent for strokes of this type—be confirmed in Piłsudski's case, as he always refused to have his blood pressure taken. [175] By the documented exclusion of other possibilities, however, a strong inferential case can be made for this to have been the site, and hypertension the probable cause, of the stroke in 1928.

Most significant of all, however, was the finding of no greater amount (and probably a lesser degree) of arteriosclerosis in the major vessels supplying the brain, [176] than would be expected in a man of Piłsudski's age. This effectively eliminates the consideration that any organic brain syndrome from which he may have suffered was on the basis of diffuse arteriosclerosis—itself a frequent cause of dementia in the elderly. What is intriguing, however, is the finding of very prominent sulci, or grooves, in the frontal lobes of the brain. This was noted as well by Professor Maximilian Rose. [177] Such a finding signifies a degree of cortical atrophy, as the gyri of the cortex separated by the sulci (grooves) become smaller with age, thereby accentuating the grooves. It is just such atrophy in the frontal lobes of aging individuals that is the morphologic correlate of the physiologic effect of aging on the brain. One may therefore conclude that Piłsudski's failing mental powers were secondary to by far the most common cause of senility in the aged: forebrain atrophy (see Fig. 2.3). The reader should not infer that the changes described were severe. An examination of numerous brains of the same age group might be expected to yield variable degrees of similar cortical atrophy. The finding of this rather common condition in Piłsudski's case, however, does serve to legitimize the old medical axiom of diagnosis: "When one hears hoofbeats, one should not think of zebras"—such as bronchitis, arteriosclerosis, or cancer.

Having suggested that Marshal Piłsudski was affected by some degree of senility during his last years in power, [178] and having identified a probable cause for it, the important question remains: What role might this have played in contributing to Hitler's domination of Europe in general, and Poland in particular, during the thirties? Can the following harsh indictment of the aging Marshal by Polonsky be defended?

For the most part, [Piłsudski] left the implementation of foreign policy to Józef Beck. . . . But he was more than anyone else responsible for the underestimation of the dynamic and aggressive character of Nazism which marked Polish foreign policy throughout the 1930s. [179]

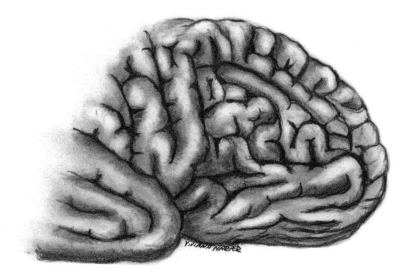

Normal Brain

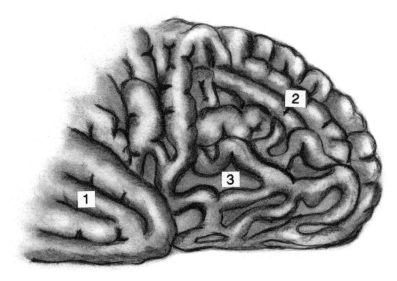

1. Normal Temporal Lobe
2. Normal Frontal Lobe
3. Frontal Lobe Atrophy

*Fig. 2.3 A comparison of normal temporal and frontal lobe cortex with that seen in milder degrees of dementia than the whole-brain atrophy depicted in Figure 2.1.*

If this can be substantiated, a second and more perplexing question arises: Was this underestimation a product of the European viewpoint of the time, or was it the individualized shortcoming of an aged figurehead victimized by dementia? Indeed, many have found it significant that at precisely the time Piłsudski's ill health became apparent he chose to embark on a more active foreign policy turned in a new direction. In November 1932 he picked Józef Beck as the spokesman for that policy, and together they made a dramatic break with Beck's predecessor as Foreign Minister, August Zaleski. Prior to that time, Zaleski had emphasized the preeminence of the alliance with France and the fulfillment of Polish obligations to the League. Yet Piłsudski had always harbored suspicions of French reliability, [180] and pressure on Poland's eastern frontier had lessened dramatically with the initiation of the first Soviet Five-Year Plan in 1928 and the Japanese invasion of Manchuria in 1931. Having ostensibly settled his own internal political conflict for the moment, Piłsudski perceived that the times were auspicious for a new beginning in Polish foreign affairs. [181]

This should not be construed, however, as a blind, vainglorious leap compelled merely by the fantasies of a diseased brain. Poland had cogent reasons to be fearful of her present circumstance: the League had declined in prestige; Germany had become more aggressive in her claims for equal status; the domestic scene in France appeared more unstable by the hour; and most significant of all, MacDonald had carried his policy of appeasement far enough to be considering altering the eastern German border at Polish expense. The perception arose that the previous instruments safeguarding Poland's future were breaking down. She must look out for herself—to set a "new course," in Polonsky's words. [182]

New guidelines were therefore promulgated, largely at Piłsudski's insistence. From this point forward, Polish foreign policy was to be based on two approaches: a reliance on Poland's own military strength and the improvement of relations with both Germany and Russia. [183] During a meeting in 1931, Beck and Piłsudski agreed to the following tenets: the traditional safeguards of Europe were becoming increasingly unreliable; Poland should rely less on the League of Nations and collective security; and finally, by increasing her independence of action she might be able to resolve many unsolved problems. [184]

In retrospect there is nothing that smacks of senility in such an assessment. If Piłsudski's appraisal was unrealistic at this point, it may have been more an underestimation of Germany's potential rather than an overestimation of Poland's strength and ability to stand alone. Yet even this caveat is tempered by the realization that Poland's weakness vis-à-vis its immediate neighbors was not nearly as obvious in 1931 as it would be by 1935.

The first concrete manifestation of a changing Polish foreign policy occurred on January 25, 1932, with the signing of a nonaggression treaty with Russia. A genuine improvement in relations resulted, though Piłsudski did not surrender his belief that Russia still constituted the major threat to Polish independence. [185] Most historians contend that the Russians gave more in the exchange, as the pact represented a significant movement away from the Soviet policy of cooperating with Germany against Poland established at Rapallo. [186] Certainly compromised mentation played no role in this chosen course of action.

The ascension of Hitler to the chancellorship in January 1933, however, necessitated an increasing preoccupation by Piłsudski with German intentions. The Germans insisted on a revision of Poland's western frontier, and tension over Polish rights in the port of Danzig reached new heights. Whether Piłsudski ultimately sought an accommodation with Hitler on the basis of the alleged French refusal to become involved in a "preventive war" against Germany, or whether this accommodation instead squared more readily with Piłsudski's belief that Russia was the true enemy, is beyond the scope of this examination. What is unassailable, however, is that he underestimated Hitler's intentions and his power to implement them. Referring to the Nazis as late as 1933 as "nothing but windbags," [187] Piłsudski still held to the apparently contradictory view that such blowhards should somehow be accommodated. If he was by that time still rational enough to recognize that Poland was too weak to risk war, his lack of any great prescience is demonstrated by his unfounded belief that Hitler would be unable to circumvent the disarmament clauses of the Versailles Treaty. [188]

Józef Beck—who was many things, but certainly not demented—showed a similar lack of prescience at this juncture. In September 1933 he submitted a memorandum to Piłsudski outlining in broad strokes a Polish policy toward Hitler. In it he asserted that Hitler would require a period of calm in foreign affairs in order to consolidate his position at home. Piłsudski agreed. [189] If this view was correct, as Hitler's signing of the German-Polish Pact of 1934 would imply, it nonetheless ignored the fact that such a modus vivendi served the ambitious Nazis' purposes all too well. In buying time for Poland's own military preparedness, the respite was poorly utilized. The aging Marshal ignored the fact that a unified, consolidated Germany was a genuine threat to Poland's independence. History had already underlined that fact all too clearly. Yet he willingly accommodated the German requirement of the moment, while attaching some misplaced significance to the fact that Hitler was, after all, not a Prussian.

Significantly enough, the German-Polish Pact had first been proposed by the Germans—highlighting in bold relief the importance of this temporary rapprochement for Hitler's plans. Beck and Piłsudski's limited assessment of the implications of the accord was further epitomized by their ignoring the effect it had on the Russian psyche—despite Beck's belated assurances to the Soviets. [190] Not surprisingly, a perceptible deterioration in Polish-Soviet relations resulted. Moreover, the French were even further estranged, as they had not been informed of the agreement in advance and persisted in believing that there was more to the declaration than had been disclosed. As Polonsky pointed out: "The main beneficiary of these developments was Germany. . . . Poland in the long run could only lose by any modification of the Versailles settlement which, far more than her own strength, was the main guarantee of her continued existence within the 1921 frontiers." [191] Lafore reached the same conclusion regarding the German-Polish Pact: "Its real importance was to give Hitler a diplomatic success that allowed him to consolidate his domestic position and prepare for rearmament." [192]

Accommodating Hitler's diplomatic needs on the one hand while estranging Poland's own allies on the other—this was the ultimate impact of Piłsudski's attempt to "try something new" in 1934. If the former had short-term usefulness for Hitler, the latter had more fatal long-term consequences for the collective security system of Europe. Many Frenchmen perceived the German-Polish Pact as a betrayal of that system. Indeed, Poland was the second ally to reject the French attempts to preserve the old order. [193] The Poles may have thought of the measure simply as a safety device; they nevertheless ignored its effect on the collective security system, which would have better suited their ends. To fully understand how this had evolved, something in the way of background information regarding the French perspective is in order.

By 1934 the chronic instability of French politics had compelled the government to present a more responsible appearance in foreign policy, and much as other such troubled European states had done, the French turned to a respectable and aged figurehead, in this case Gaston Doumergue. In Lafore's words: "His choice [as Premier] was another example of the singular tendency of constitutional regimes in interwar years to try to shore themselves up by confiding their destinies to national figures of advanced age and doubtful intellectual vigor." [194] Unlike those of Hindenburg and Piłsudski, however, Doumergue's tenure was brief, even for French premiers of that era. Yet he brought Jean-Louis Barthou into his government as Foreign Minister, and (despite his assassination shortly thereafter) it was Barthou's policy of containment that dominated French diplomatic efforts during the interwar years.

The need to create an eastern bloc within that security system was axiomatic to French policy. The French received little in the way of assistance from MacDonald and the British; the Poles proved equally obstreperous. This would prove critical to its failure. Up to that point, the French had been successful in enlisting support for their policy in every European country except Poland (which by now was content to rely on the Nonaggression Pact and unwilling to make further commitments to France or associations with Russia). [195] By the very nature of the German-Polish Pact, Poland had become Germany's only ally in Europe, running against the mainstream of diplomatic efforts and ultimately against its own best interests. More sinister still, after Barthou was assassinated responsibility for pursuing the policy of containment fell to Pierre Laval, who chose to woo Italy in secret. By January 1935 these changes had essentially destroyed the anti-German alliance, which might have reached full effectiveness the year before had Poland not chosen to stand alone.

Piłsudski and Beck ultimately refused to cooperate with Hitler in his plans to partition Russia (which had been part of Hitler's goal in suggesting the German-Polish alliance in the first place), yet the damage had already been done. An effective anti-German front had been surrendered in what would prove to be Europe's last chance to stand together before Germany's strength and aggressive intentions became all too obvious after 1935. By fatefully overestimating Poland's strength in 1934 to stand alone and "restore her own position in the European equilibrium," her leaders had collectively demonstrated a revealing degree of compromised abstract attitudes—the inability to identify separate parts from the whole. [196] European security was the whole, and Polish aspirations should have been but a part. In failing to perceive this, they had ignored the dangers inherent in standing apart rather than hanging together. In like manner, they had tended to place too much reliance on Hitler's promises, much as they had exaggerated the role of horses in twentieth century war. [197]

Antony Polonsky suggested in his analysis a more reasonable path Poland might have followed, which now seems to be vindicated: "A policy less determined to assert Polish independence and more bent on cooperation with France, Czechoslovakia, and Russia to maintain the frontiers and disarmament provisions of the Versailles settlement would therefore seem . . . to have been more to Poland's advantage." [198] If Józef Beck was the author of the policy Poland actually followed, still it could not have been implemented without the sanction of his aging superior. On this indictment, therefore, Piłsudski is found guilty, and the inroads of a compromised abstract attitude become accessories to that crime. This verdict epitomizes a recurring scenario in interwar leadership and its implementation. If foreign policy often bore the imprint of a Schleicher, a Simon, or a Beck, it nonetheless gained legitimacy from its acceptance by their respective superiors—all three of whom were compromised to varying degrees by senility.

*In Warsaw with French Foreign Minister Louis Barthou (center) and Józef Beck (right), 1934*

*Near the end, 1935*

Each of the subordinates often carried his superior along as an unwitting accomplice in his schemes. If Schleicher's machinations were duplicitous and self-serving, at least Simon and Beck were motivated by more defensible considerations. In the case of Poland, it may be argued that in 1933 German rearmament posed no real threat, but by 1934, when it had gained substantial momentum, diplomacy between France and Poland had been so poisoned with suspicion as to preclude any effective cooperation against it. With Piłsudski compromised, there simply was no longer a rational basis by which to assess the merits of the policy Poland was following. As Polonsky concluded, "Piłsudski, dying of cancer, was in no position to take bold initiatives, while Beck was prepared to go much further than the Marshal to maintain good relations with Germany and to attribute benevolent intentions to Hitler." [199]

Certainly the vagaries of the aging process contributed more to Piłsudski's restrictions than did the cancer that was present, and in the Marshal's defense, Polonsky's indictment of Beck would suggest substantially less guilt on the part of Piłsudski for the course Poland followed after 1934. Yet that year was a watershed in Europe's ability to organize a collective defense. True, Piłsudski's intellectual deterioration was less than that of his counterparts in Great Britain and Germany. But this should not obscure the fact that the *perception* of his compromise was perhaps more important to his subordinates—and to Hitler—than its reality. As this perception became pervasive, other protagonists saw the opportunity to take a more active, untethered role in what transpired. After Piłsudski's death in May 1935, the restraints became almost nonexistent, as no forceful leadership emerged to fill the void.

If Piłsudski's death from a sudden gastrointestinal hemorrhage had come as a surprise to some, his perceived debility prior to that time had at least emphasized the need to enact a new constitution that might ensure the permanency of his life's work. [200] As with Hindenburg, decisions made before the Marshal's passing were later exploited by his successors. The President had been given the power to dissolve Parliament, to represent the state in its foreign affairs, and to hold the highest military authority. More significant still, he could not be held personally responsible for his acts. From 1935 on, Piłsudski's successors used the wide powers the constitution had accorded the government to keep themselves in power. [201] Yet, just as in Germany, those who remained in Poland were woefully inadequate.

If 1934 represented a watershed for collective security, 1935 represented a turning point for Poland's safety. By that year a perceptible transformation had occurred in the military balance. As has been shown, it proved nearly impossible to overcome the negative effect of Piłsudski's influence on the preparedness of the fighting forces. Yet despite his obvious compromise, Piłsudski's presence had been a unifying factor. After his passing, deep divisions occurred in the ranks of those entrusted with preserving his legacy. "It remained to be seen" Polonsky noted, "how far he had schooled his 'boys' to take over from him, and how far he had, as he believed, laid the foundations for the secure political evolution of Poland." [202] It appears he had not gone very far. With Piłsudski's death, Lord Kennet concluded, "the nation had to pay the price . . . for confiding national destinies to the authority of a single person; it had to face the doubt and danger involved in finding an heir to an authority which does not provide for its own succession." [203]

Thereafter events ran a predictable course. By 1937, rapprochement with Poland was no longer as important to the Germans. They were gaining new friends as Europe divided between fascist and nonfascist camps. Apparently this shift in Nazi emphasis was lost on the Poles. Even the later blows to Austria and Czechoslovakia failed to trigger a reassessment. Poland was now surrounded. It would only be a matter of time before she was consumed in like manner, and 1939 was not that far away.

From the medical perspective, it would be inappropriate to attribute too much to Piłsudski's age in assessing the Polish role in Europe's tragedy. Being the same age as MacDonald, and nearly twenty years younger than the decrepit Hindenburg, Piłsudski's cognitive limitations were probably compatible with his age—restricted to be sure, but not to the same degree as his two contemporaries. Indeed, he had been rational enough to recognize that the 1934 accord with Germany was a temporizing measure at best; he had confided to Waclau Jedrzejewicz at the time that such a respite "would not last long. It was good for four to five years at the most." [204]

Yet the restrictions that did exist were telling enough. After 1930, Piłsudski's interest in government affairs was fitful at best. Domestically, Poland drifted from crisis to crisis over the next five years under Piłsudski's aging guidance. In those areas of foreign relations and military affairs that did pique his interest, his incursions proved on balance to be negative. If the 1934 German-Polish Pact afforded Poland time for military preparedness, the time was not spent wisely. Nor was Piłsudski correct in his assessment that Poland could stand apart from the possible safeguards that the Versailles Treaty and the French afforded. Equally significant, he left little in the way of constructive appointments to carry the Polish banner into the final explosion that threatened to destroy traditional Europe. By retaining an unrealistic view of Polish strength, Piłsudski's foreign policy merely underscored the instability that typified Central Europe. Adolf Hitler became the ultimate beneficiary of this aging statesman's pretentions.

To be sure, Józef Piłsudski was but one unwitting accomplice contributing to the rise of Nazi Germany during the thirties, and Europe's aging leadership was but one factor in that disaster. In relation to this isolated issue, perhaps the historian Laurence Lafore perceived its implications more clearly than most:

> Poland shared with Great Britain and Germany on the eve of Hitler's rise the curious distinction of having a senile chief executive. It was significant of the kind of helplessness of European nations then . . . that they found it convenient to be governed by mindless national heroes. The substitution of figureheads for leaders argued a desperate effort to put national unity and stability above all other considerations and led, of course, to disaster. [205]

For the second time in twenty years, the lights were going out all over Europe.

## NOTES

1. Baker and Baker, *Clinical Neurology*, 2:27, p. 2.
2. Lipowski, "Organic Mental Disorders," 2:1376.
3. Ryder, *Twentieth-Century Germany*, p. 262.
4. Morsey, "The Center Party," p. 68.
5. Brüning, *Memoiren*, p. 183.
6. Halperin, *Germany Tried Democracy*, p. 409. From the summer of 1931, Schleicher was secretly dealing with the Nazis to a degree unsuspected by Brüning or Hindenburg, the latter being described by John W. Wheeler-Bennett as "rapidly degenerating into that state of senility into which he was prey to the advice of whomsoever had last spoken with him." *Nemesis of Power*, p. 232.
7. Eyck, *Weimar Republic*, 2:47.
8. Brüning, *Memoiren*, p. 183.
9. Ryder, *Twentieth-Century Germany*, p. 262.
10. Wheeler-Bennett, *Wooden Titan*, p. 304.
11. Curtius, *Young-Plan*, p. 110.
12. Eyck, *Weimar Republic*, 2:384. Regardless of how senile Hindenburg might be, Brüning, Groener, and Schleicher had agreed that the best chance of defeating Hitler in 1932 was keeping the aged figurehead in office; see Wheeler-Bennett, *Nemesis of Power*, p. 232. Brüning was rewarded by Hindenburg with his dismissal. Morsey, "The Center Party," p. 73.
13. Ryder, *Twentieth-Century Germany*, pp. 268, 270.
14. Eyck, *Weimar Republic*, 2:392. Illness, as much as intrigue, played a major role in Hindenburg's unpardonable action according to Wheeler-Bennett. In September 1931 "the Marshal suffered a complete mental breakdown for some ten days—a fact which had to be kept a deathly secret—during which time he developed an almost violent antipathy" to Brüning. *Nemesis of Power*, pp. 232–33.
15. Wheeler-Bennett, *Wooden Titan*, p. 397. Karl D. Bracher spoke for most observers in asserting: "No German Chancellor was ever chosen more frivolously." Bracher, *Auflösung*, p. 519.
16. Woodward and Baker, *Documents*, 3:186; Eyck, *Weimar Republic*, p. 400.
17. Eyck, *Weimar Republic*, 2:401.

18. Ibid., p. 424.

19. Braun, *Von Weimar zu Hitler*, p. 417.

20. Meissner, *Staatssekretar*, p. 2.

21. Eyck, *Weimar Republic*, 2:432–33.

22. Wheeler-Bennett, *Wooden Titan*, pp. 425–26. While admitting that Hindenburg was "aging fast and gradually ceased to impose his personal authority in day to day political developments," Papen argued that the President was lucid until the latter part of 1933; see Papen, *Memoirs*, pp. 258, 328. Considering the benefits the situation afforded to himself, his assertion comes as no surprise.

23. Dorpalen, *Hindenburg*, p. 463.

24. Ibid., p. 464.

25. Eyck, *Weimar Republic*, 2:461–62.

26. Ibid., 2:461–62. Ignoring Hindenburg's obvious infirmities, Karl Bracher highlighted the problem in constitutional terms: "The dictatorial powers of the Presidency under . . . Article 48 of the Weimar Constitution, which was originally designed to safeguard the democratic order . . . , under a differently disposed President had the opposite effect. . . . The ever-present resort to emergency powers . . . accustomed the public to authoritarian concepts of government." Bracher, "National Socialist," p. 118.

27. Eyck, *Weimar Republic*, pp. 474–75, 469.

28. Ryder, *Twentieth-Century Germany*, p. 308.

29. Ibid. Hindenburg was unable to perceive what was clear to Karl Bracher: Among the many factors that led to Hitler's consolidation of power, the most important was Hitler's basic demand that "he, too, as Chancellor, must have the emergency powers of Article 48." Bracher, "National Socialist," p. 118.

30. Wheeler-Bennett, *Wooden Titan*, pp. 433, 437.

31. Ibid., pp. 435, 432.

32. As the historian Helmut Krausnick observed: "The President seemed to be turning back into the Imperial Field Marshal, and Hitler deliberately played on his anti-republican sentiments. This was enough to give the President's clouded vision a reassuring picture of events." Krausnick, "Stages of 'Coordination,'" p. 146. Moreover, poorly controlled emotion is yet another characteristic of the dementia sufferer. This relates to frontal and temporal lobe atrophy, where emotions and their response to environmental stimuli are initiated.

33. Wheeler-Bennett, *Wooden Titan*, pp. 433, 437, 448.

34. Ibid., p. 450.

35. Ibid., p. 460.

36. Ibid., p. 464. During the last months of his life, Hindenburg's health and mental faculties deteriorated precipitously. Dorpalen noted that "most of the time he kept reminiscing about the wars of 1866 and 1870." Dorpalen, *Hindenburg*, p. 479.

37. Wheeler-Bennett, *Wooden Titan*, pp. 468, 470, 474; *Nemesis of Power*, p. 314.

38. Malcolm MacDonald, interview with David Marquand; quoted in Marquand, *MacDonald*, p. 749.

39. Ibid., p. 750.

40. Lafore, *End of Glory*, p. 53.

41. Prior to 1931 the swelling unemployment rolls had placed an increasing burden on the treasury. The Labour government had resigned over the issue, and MacDonald had solicited Conservative help to keep himself prime minister in the new coalition government. That his tenure proved to be largely a failure is inferred by the extraordinarily brief treatment his most sympathetic biographer, Benjamen Sacks, afforded it. See *J. Ramsay MacDonald*.

42. Lafore, *End of Glory*, p. 90.

43. This was highlighted early on by the National Government's response to the Japanese invasion of Manchuria in 1931. The League of Nations failed to take a firm stance, partly because Great Britain lent no active support to the organization against the aggressive action. Lafore, *End of Glory*, pp. 92–93.

44. Ibid., p. 86.

45. Lord Swinton recalled: "When I sat in MacDonald's cabinet after 1931, I found him rather woolly. . . . His physical and mental powers weakened all too rapidly." Swinton, *Sixty Years*, p. 94.

46. A contemporary, Harold Nicolson, believed MacDonald was already failing by 1930. "In October, 1930," Nicolson recalled, "he forgot the name of the Canadian Prime Minister . . . and exclaimed 'My brain is going!'" Nicolson, *Diaries and Letters*, 1:56.

47. Diary entries, September 9, 13, 1931; quoted in Marquand, *MacDonald*, p. 657. Due to inaccessibility of the diaries, Marquand's biography remains the main source for them.

48. Diary entry, September 25, 1931; cited in Marquand, *MacDonald*, p. 661.

49. Ibid., pp. 657, 661.

50. Berkely, *Myth*, p. 112.

51. Diary entry, January 19, 1933; quoted in Marquand, *MacDonald*, p. 695.

52. Weir, *Tragedy*, p. 552.

53. Quoted in Weir, *Tragedy*, pp. 551–52.

54. Ibid., p. 551.

55. The significance of this will become apparent later in explaining the impact of MacDonald's failing vision on his emotional health.

56. Weir, *Tragedy*, pp. 553, 556, xii.

57. Marquand, *MacDonald*, p. 134.

58. Ibid., p. 135.

59. Ibid., pp. 134, 693.

60. Ibid,, p. 693.

61. Ibid., p. 655.

62. Ibid., p. 694.

63. Ibid., p. 693.

64. Dr. Robert Katzman described, in Houston Merritt's esteemed *Textbook of Neurology*, some of the earliest symptoms of presenile dementia observed: "If the patient has insight into his deterioration [as one would expect to be the case in its incipient stages] he may become depressed; signs of depression are seen in about one-quarter of these patients." Katzman, "Degenerative Diseases," pp. 486–87.

65. Marquand, *MacDonald*, p. 702. The theses of Weir and Berkeley substantiate this claim.

66. Ibid., p. 495. Many of MacDonald's political opponents believed otherwise. After MacDonald dismissed Countess Snowden from the BBC Board of Governors in 1931, her husband, Viscount Philip Snowden, alluded to the mental deterioration of the Prime Minister in vicious terms. Weir, *Tragedy*, p. 460

67. Marquand, *MacDonald*, p. 663.

68. Diary entry, October 7, 1931; quoted in Marquand, *MacDonald*, p. 666.

69. Diary entry, October 29, 1931; quoted in ibid., p. 671.

70. Diary entry, November 1, 1931; quoted in ibid., p. 693.

71. Long, "Aging in the Nervous System," p. 352.

72. Marquand, *MacDonald*, p. 696.

73. Ibid., p. 694.

74. Ibid., p. 695.

75. Katzman, "Degenerative Diseases," p. 486. Alzheimer's is an exceedingly common condition in MacDonald's age group. According to Katzman, "Community surveys

in Northern Europe . . . indicate that about 47% of persons age sixty-five are incapacitated by an organic dementia, and about 10% have progressive mental deterioration. . . . "Degenerative Diseases," pp. 484–85. For a fuller understanding of the disease and its increasing prevalence, the reader is referred to Long, "Aging in the Nervous System," pp. 349–50.

76. Marquand, *MacDonald*, p. 697.

77. Weir, *Tragedy*, p. 477. This pitiful impression endured in the public conscience. As one detractor noted: "Did he ever say anything worthwhile?" See Sacks, *J. Ramsay MacDonald*, p. xvii.

78. Weir, *Tragedy*, pp. 473–74.

79. Ibid., p. 479.

80. Ibid., p. 480.

81. Ibid., p. 486.

82. L'Etang, *Pathology*, p. 71.

83. Temperley, *Whispering Gallery*, p. 240. One might postulate here an episode of transient global amnesia caused by a temporary decrease of blood flow to the base of the temporal lobes on the basis of atherosclerosis. Yet this would be postulating two separate disease processes affecting MacDonald—an unnecessary consideration if one acknowledges the progressive difficulties with speech that affect the Alzheimer's sufferer.

84. Attlee, *As It Happened*, p. 87.

85. Gilroy and Meyer, "Degenerative Diseases," p. 158.

86. Weir, *Tragedy*, p. 487.

87. Katzman, "Degenerative Diseases," p. 486. MacDonald died in 1937, six years into the progressive spiral of physical and mental deterioration.

88. Marquand, *MacDonald*, p. 696.

89. Diary entries, January 19, March 29, August 9, 28, 1933, and January 27, 1934; quoted in Marquand, *MacDonald*, p. 696.

90. Ibid., p. 698.

91. Diary entry, March 23, 1933; quoted in Marquand, *MacDonald*, p. 698.

92. Notebook, January 5, 1934; quoted in Marquand, *MacDonald*, p. 699.

93. Weir, *Tragedy*, p. 473.

94. Marquand, *MacDonald*, p. 700.

95. Ibid., p. 700.

96. Weir, *Tragedy*, p. 565.

97. Ibid., pp. 566, 569.

98. Marquand, *MacDonald*, pp. 714–15.

99. Weir, *Tragedy*, p. 567.

100. Diary entry, April 7, 1932; quoted in ibid., p. 717.

101. From notebook of Maurice Hankey, July 6, 1932; quoted in Roskill, *Hankey*, 3:45.

102. Marquand, *MacDonald*, pp. 735–37.

103. Ibid., p. 737.

104. Salter, *Personality*, p. 64.

105. Marquand, *MacDonald*, p. 734.

106. Ibid., p. 735.

107. Lafore, *End of Glory*, pp. 114, 115. As the historian A. J. P. Taylor cryptically commented: "The British went on sympathizing with Germany's claims . . . and MacDonald still set the course for both government and opposition"; see *Origins of Second World War*, p. 106.

108. Marquand, *MacDonald*, p. 749.

109. *Daily Express*, April 3, 1935; cited in Gilbert, *Britain and Germany*, p. 62.

110. Quoted in Marquand, *MacDonald*, p. 749.

111. Diary entry, February 4, 1934; quoted in Marquand, *MacDonald*, p. 750.

112. Ibid., p. 751.

113. Ibid. This is not to suggest that MacDonald was so compromised as to fail to recognize the severity of the Hitler threat. This was everyone's dilemma; MacDonald merely addressed the problem more ineffectually than most. As Winston Churchill charged in a speech to the House of Commons on May 22, 1935: "I have been told that the reason for the Government not having acted before was that public opinion was not ripe for rearmament. I hope that we shall never accept such a reason as that. . . . There is no vote that [the Government] could not have proposed for the national defence which would not have been accepted with overwhelming strength." *Hansard;* cited in Gilbert, *Britain and Germany,* p. 62.

114. Marquand, *MacDonald*, p. 754.

115. The depth to which MacDonald's political abilities had fallen is shown by his failure to propose any realistic alternatives to the Conservatives in his own government once it became clear that they had never accepted liberal pacifism.

116. Diary entries, September 29, October 1, 1934; quoted in Marquand, *MacDonald*, pp. 761–62.

117. Ibid., p. 762.

118. James, *Memoirs of Davidson*, p. 402.

119. Diary entry, February 23, 1935; quoted in Marquand, *MacDonald*, p. 763.

120. Diary entry, January 29, 1935; quoted in ibid., p. 762.

121. Ibid., p. 764.

122. Diary entry, March 4, 1935; quoted in ibid., p. 770.

123. Ibid., pp. 770–71.

124. Ibid., p. 772.

125. London *Times*, November 10, 1937. Perhaps recognizing that there had been little else during MacDonald's last four years in office to excite positive comment, it is significant that his obituary, through default, was forced to focus on an item for which he had not really been responsible. In that same obituary, a polite reference was made to his waning powers: "There had been signs that the peak of his powers had been reached in 1931, and he could never quite shake off the undermining influence of bitter detractors. His health had suffered under the strain." In truth, it had suffered under much more than just a hostile political climate, as has been shown.

126. Marquand, *MacDonald*, pp. 773–74.

127. Lafore, *End of Glory*, p. 144.

128. Weir, *Tragedy*, p. 495.

129. Lafore, *End of Glory*, p. 116. This concept was largely the brainchild of Sir John Simon. Though MacDonald and Piłsudski paid lip service to the French, little of substance resulted, as their foreign ministers usually overrode them; see ibid., p. 140.

130. Langer and Gleason, *Challenge to Isolation;* cited in Snell, *Outbreak of the Second World War: Design or Blunder?* "Cold War Era Revision: Stalin's 'Blank Check' of 1939," (Boston, 1962), p. 16.

131. Lord Vansittart, *The Mist Procession* (1958), p. 519; cited in Marquand, *MacDonald*, p. 772.

132. Marquand, *MacDonald*, p. 773; Taylor, *Origins of Second World War*, p. 117.

133. Marquand, *MacDonald*, p. 778. MacDonald's views were never seriously considered thereafter, and not simply because his position now was that of a figurehead. In July 1935 he despaired over his failure to guide the Cabinet on foreign policy: "I am not able; though my views, perfectly clear & definite, my brain will not express in effective speech." Ibid. The curse of Alzheimer's disease would haunt him to the end.

134. Lafore, *End of Glory*, p. 118.

135. Polonsky, *Independent Poland*, p. 61.

136. *Gazeta Poranna*, December 19, 1922.

137. Interview with author, September 27, 1984.

138. Rataj, *Pamietnike*, p. 126. Rataj served as Marshal of the Sejm (Parliament) during the twenties.

139. Polonsky, *Independent Poland*, pp. 187–88. Piłsudski's lack of interest in government was confirmed in an interview with one member of the inner group, Waclau Jedrzejewicz; interview with author, October 3, 1984.

140. Polonsky, *Independent Poland*, pp. 332, 333.

141. Romeyko, *Przed i po Maju*, 2:298.

142. Waclau Jedrzejewicz, interview with author, October 3, 1984. The reader should not infer that the Pact was solely Beck's initiative. According to Lord Kennet, Piłsudski "kept foreign affairs under his special supervision; and his foreign ministers . . . were his agents only. . . . Later he gave his policy a new direction, turning . . . to an effort to find a basis for stable relations with Germany." Lord Kennet, "Pilsudski," p. 606.

143. Polonsky, *Independent Poland*, p. 337.

144. Ibid., pp. 336–37.

145. Lafore, *End of Glory*, p. 118.

146. Interview with author, October 3, 1984.

147. Polonsky, *Independent Poland*, p. 333.

148. Jedrzejewicz, interview with author, October 3, 1984.

149. Polonsky, *Independent Poland*, pp. 337, 391, 392.

150. Romeyko, *Przed i po Maju*, 2:77–78.

151. Goldstein, "Functional Disorders in Brain Damage," p. 186.

152. Ibid.

153. Polonsky, *Independent Poland*, p. 335.

154. Ibid., p. 335.

155. Quoted in Polonsky, *Independent Poland*, p. 335. Świtalski was himself one of Piłsudski's inner group of advisors. He had served as Director of the Political Department of the Ministry of Internal Affairs.

156. *Robotnik*, December 18, 1930.

157. *Kurjer Poranny*, October 17, 1931; see Debicki, *Foreign Policy of Poland*, p. 67.

158. Polonsky, *Independent Poland*, p. 334.

159. Ibid.

160. Ibid.

161. I am indebted to Wieslau Domaniewski for translating portions of Składkowski's work *Strzepy Mildenkow* from Polish to English.

162. Domaniewski translation of Składkowski text, *Strzepy Mildenkow*, p. 369.

163. Jedrzejewicz, interview with author, October 3, 1984.

164. Emboli frequently occur with atrial fibrillation. These are small blood clots that form on the heart valve of that chamber due to stagnant flow. They occasionally break off, to be propelled to distant parts of the circulation, where blockage of a vessel ensues. This is an occasional cause of stroke in patients afflicted wih this condition.

165. Lying flat allows fluid to back up into the lung due to compromised pumping action of the heart, leading to sudden shortness of breath during periods of decompensation.

166. Domaniewski, interview with author, September 27, 1984.

167. Jedrzejewicz, "Chronicles of Joseph Pilsudski." Manuscript in possession of author.

168. Plum and Posner, *Stupor and Coma*, p. 170.

169. Jedrzejewicz, interview with author, October 3, 1984.

170. This occurs almost invariably after jaundice is noted, and it rapidly induces coma. Piłsudski was never observed to have jaundice, nor did he have any symptoms remotely compatible with hepatic (liver-related) encephalopathy.

171. Domaniewski translation of Składkowski text, *Strzepy Mildenkow*, p. 477.

172. Jedrzejewicz, interview with author, October 3, 1984.

173. Rose, *Cerveau de Pilsudski*. Piłsudski willed his brain to the University of Wilno for medical study.

174. Some residual incoordination and occasional tremor would likewise be expected by a small-vessel occlusion in this area. For a medical description of this entity, see Fisher, "Pure Motor Hemiplegia."

175. Jedrzejewicz, interview with author, October 3, 1984.

176. This excludes the internal carotid arteries in the neck, which were not photographed.

177. Translation of M. Minkowski's book review of Rose's work, *Le Cerveau de Pilsudski*, in *Sonderdruck aus Schweizer Archiv fur Neurologic und Psychiatric*, Band. XLIV, Heft 2 (1939). I am indebted—and heavily so—to Dr. Gisela Kopp for this translation.

178. Members of Piłsudski's inner circle, understandably loyal to the image of the man to this day, would take exception to this claim. Shortly before he died, Piłsudski had a long conversation with Beck, during which his memory was described as excellent. According to Jedrzejewicz, "His mind worked as in the best of times." Jedrzejewicz, *Pilsudski*, p. 358. One of the perplexing characteristics of the modest dementia victim is the ability to demonstrate interludes of cogent, rational behavior. Only in the progressive condition do the bad days begin to outnumber the good.

179. Polonsky, *Independent Poland*, p. 336. In foreign policy, as ever, according to Roman Debicki, "it was Pilsudski who set the course. Beck had referred to him all questions of importance." Debicki, *Foreign Policy of Poland*, p. 98.

180. This does not suggest, as some historians have concluded, that Piłsudski wrote off the French entirely. As Jedrzejewicz pointed out: "The French army *was* weak, but Pilsudski clearly perceived the need to keep relations with the French intact at all costs." Interview with author, October 3, 1984.

181. Polonsky, *Independent Poland*, p. 379.

182. Ibid.

183. Ibid., p. 380.

184. Beck, *Dernier rapport*, pp. 8–10; cited in Polonsky, *Independent Poland*, p. 380.

185. Jedrzejewicz, "Pilsudski i Kemal."

186. Polonsky, *Independent Poland*, p. 381.

187. Laroche, *Pologne de Pilsudski*, p. 113.

188. Polonsky, *Independent Poland*, p. 383.

189. Beck, *Dernier rapport*, pp. 28–29.

190. Waclau Jedrzejewicz defended the German-Polish Pact because "it bought valuable time for Poland militarily." Interview with author, October 3, 1984.

191. Polonsky, *Independent Poland*, p. 385. Bohdan Budurowycz placed more emphasis on the potential protection of the French eastern Locarno scheme: "It must be admitted, of course, that the fatal years 1932–34 and their aftermath had prejudiced very strongly the possibility of bringing the developing crisis to a halt. . . . The nations of East Central Europe had a unique opportunity to create and consolidate a bloc . . . able to resist the encroachments of both Berlin and Moscow. . . . It seems reasonably certain . . . that it would have considerably reduced the possibilities of Germany's territorial expansion." Budurowycz, *Relations*, pp. 196–97.

192. Lafore, *End of Glory*, p. 119.

193. Ibid., p. 118. The reader may recall Britain's attempt at Stresa to torpedo the French policy of containment originally espoused by Louis Bartou; see p. 179.
194. Ibid., p. 126.
195. Ibid., p. 132.
196. Goldstein, "Functional Disorders in Brain Damage," p. 186.
197. Lafore, *End of Glory*, pp. 118–19. According to Lafore, "They did not fully understand Hitler's attitude toward the first Polish initiative, which was to seize the opportunity to . . . disarm their suspicions and therefore their hostility." (p. 119)
198. Polonsky, *Independent Poland*, p. 386.
199. Ibid.
200. Ibid., p. 387.
201. Kennet, "Pilsudski," pp. 613–14.
202. Polonsky, *Independent Poland*, p. 390.
203. Kennet, "Pilsudski," p. 614.
204. Jedrzejewicz, interview with author, October 3, 1984.
205. Lafore, *End of Glory*, p. 118.

# REFERENCES

## MEDICAL

American Psychiatric Association. *A Psychiatric Glossary.* 3d ed. Washington, D.C.: The Association, 1969.

Baker, A. B., and L. H. Baker, eds. *Clinical Neurology.* 3 vols. Hagerstown, Md.: Harper and Row, 1975.

Busse, Ewald. "Aging and Psychiatric Diseases of Late Life." In *American Handbook of Psychiatry*, 2d ed., edited by Sylvano Arieti, 4:67–89. New York: Basic Books, 1975.

Fisher, C. Miller, and H. B. Curry. "Pure Motor Hemiplegia of Vascular Origin." *Archives of Neurology* 13(1965): 30–44.

Gilroy, John, and John S. Meyer, eds. "Degenerative Diseases of the Nervous System." In *Medical Neurology*, 157–211. London: Macmillan Co., 1969.

Katzman, Robert. "Degenerative Diseases." In *A Textbook of Neurology*, edited by Houston Merritt, 453–641. Philadelphia: Lea and Febiger, 1978.

L'Etang, Hugh. *The Pathology of Leadership.* New York: Hawthorn Books 1970.

Lipowski, Zibigniew J. "Organic Mental Disorders." In *Comprehensive Textbook of Psychiatry*. 3d ed., edited by Harold I. Kaplan, 2:1359–1469. Baltimore and London: Williams and Wilkins, 1980.

Minkowski, M. *Sonderdruck aus Schweizer Archiv fur Neurologic und Psychiatric.* Band XLIV. Heft. 2. 1939.

Plum, Frederick, and Jerome Posner. *Diagnosis of Stupor and Coma.* 2d ed. Philadelphia: F. A. Davis Co., 1972.

Rose, Maximilian. *Le Cerveau de Pilsudski.* Wilno: 1938.

Weinstein, Edwin A. *Woodrow Wilson: A Medical and Psychological Biography.* Princeton, N.J.: Princeton University Press, 1981.

## PRIMARY

Attlee, Clement R. *As It Happened.* London: Heineman Press, 1961.

Beck, Józef. *Dernier rapport: politique polonaise 1926–1939.* Neuchatel: Editions de la Baconnière, 1959.

Bracher, Karl Dietrich. *Die Auflösung der Weimarer Republik: Eine Studie zum Problem des Machtverfalls in der Demokratie.* Stuttgart and Düsseldorf: Ring-Verlag, 1957.

Braun, Otto. *Von Weimar zu Hitler.* New York: Europa Verlag, 1940.

Brüning, Heinrich. *Memoiren, 1918–1934.* Stuttgart: Deutsche Verlags-Anstalt, 1970.

Curtius, Julius. *Der Young-Plan: Entstellung und Wahrheit.* Stuttgart: Franz Mittelbach Verlag, 1950.

Domaniewski, Wieslau. Interview with author. Piłsudski Institute, New York, September 27, 1984.

James, Robert Rhodes. *Memoirs of a Conservative: J. C. C. Davidson's Memoirs and Papers, 1910–37.* London: Macmillan Co., 1969.

Jędrzejewicz, Wacław. Interview with author. Piłsudski Institute, New York, October 3, 1984.

———. *Piłsudski: A Life for Poland.* New York: Hippocrene Books, 1982.

———. "Pilsudski i Kemal." *Wiadomosci,* May 23, 1954.

Laroche, Jules. *La Pologne de Pilsudski: souvenirs d'une ambassade, 1926–1935.* Paris: Flammarion, 1953.

Meissner, Otto. *Staatssekretär unter Ebert-Hindenburg-Hitler.* Hamburg: Hoffmann und Campe Verlag, 1950.

Nicolson, Harold. *Diaries and Letters, 1930–39.* 3 vols. London: Weidenfeld and Nicolson, 1967.

Rataj, Maciej. *Pamietnike.* Warsaw: Ludowa Spoldzielnia Wydawnicza, 1965.

Romeyko, Marian. "Przed i po Maju." Warsaw: Wydawnicza Ministerstwa Obrony Narodwej, 1967.

Simon, John. *Retrospect: The Memoirs of the Rt. Hon. Viscount Simon, G.C.S.I., G.C.V.O.* London: Hutchinson, 1952.

Swinton, Earl of, with James D. Margach. *Sixty Years of Power: Some Memories of the Men who Wielded It.* London: Hutchinson, 1966.

Sławoj-Składkowski, F. *Strzepy Meldunków.* Warsaw: Instytut Badania Najnowszej Historji Polski, 1938.

Temperley, A. C. *The Whispering Gallery of Europe.* London: Collins, 1938.

Weir, L. MacNeill. *The Tragedy of Ramsay MacDonald.* London: Secker and Warburg, 1938.

Woodward, E. L., and Butler, Rohan, eds. *Documents on Foreign Policy: 1919–1939.* Vol. 6. London. HMSO, 1946.

PERIODICALS AND NEWSPAPERS

*Gazeta Polska.* August 6, 1934.
*Gazeta Poranna.* December 19, 1922.
*Kurjer Poranny.* October 17, 1931.
*The Times* (London). September 1931 and November 1937.
*Robotnik.* December 18, 1930.

SECONDARY

Berkeley, Humphry. *The Myth That Will Not Die: The Formation of the National Government, 1931.* London: Croom Helm, 1978.

Bracher, Karl Dietrich. "The Technique of the National Socialist Seizure of Power." In *The Path to Dictatorship, 1918–1933,* pp. 113–32. New York: Frederick A. Praeger, 1967.

Budurowycz, Bohdan B. *Polish-Soviet Relations 1931–1939.* New York: Columbia University Press, 1963.

Debicki, Roman. *Foreign Policy of Poland, 1919–39.* New York: Frederick A. Praeger, 1962.

Dorpalen, Andreas. *Hindenburg and the Weimar Republic.* Princeton, N.J.: Princeton University Press, 1964.

Eyck, Erich. *A History of the Weimar Republic.* Vol. 2, *From the Locarno Conference to Hitler's Seizure of Power.* Translated by Harlan P. Hanson and Robert G. L. Waite. Cambridge, Mass.: Harvard University Press, 1967.

Gasiorowski, Zygmunt J. "The German-Polish Nonaggression Pact of 1934." *Journal of Central European Affairs* 1 (1955): 3–29.

Gilbert, Martin. *Britain and Germany Between the Wars.* London: Longmans, Green and Co., 1964.

Halperin, S. William. *Germany Tried Democracy.* Hamden, Conn. and London: Archon Books, 1963.

Holborn, Hajo. *The Political Collapse of Europe.* New York: Alfred A. Knopf, 1954.

Kennet, Lord. "Pilsudski." In *The Cambridge History of Poland,* pp. 589–615. 1697–1935, 2d ed. Edited by W. F. Reddaway, J. H. Penson, O. Haleski, and R. Dyboski. New York: Octagon Books, 1941.

Krausnick, Helmut. "Stages of Coordination." In *The Path to Dictatorship, 1918–1933,* pp. 133–52. New York: Frederick A. Praeger, 1967.

Lafore, Laurence. *The End of Glory: An Interpretation of the Origins of World War II.* New York: J. B. Lippincott, 1970.

Langer, William L., and S. Everett Gleason. *The Challenge to Isolation, 1937–1940.* New York: Harper and Brothers, 1952.

Lukasiewicz, J. *Polska jest mocarstwem.* Warsaw: Ludowa Spoldzielnia Wydawnicza, 1939.

Marquand, David. *Ramsay MacDonald.* London: Jonathan Cape, 1977.

Morsey, Rudolf. "The Center Party Between the Fronts. In *The Path to Dictatorship, 1918–1933,* pp. 68–88. New York: Frederick A. Praeger, 1967.

Palmer, R. R., and Joel Colton. *A History of the Modern World.* 3d ed. New York: Alfred A. Knopf, 1965.

Peele, Gillian, and Chris Cook. *The Politics of Reappraisal, 1918–1939.* New York: St. Martin's Press, 1975.

Polonsky, Antony. *Politics in Independent Poland, 1921–1939.* London: Oxford University Press, 1972.

Roskill, Stephen. *Hankey: Man of Secrets.* London: Collins, 1972.

Ryder, A. J. *Twentieth-Century Germany: From Bismarck to Brandt.* New York: Columbia University Press, 1973.

Sacks, Benjamen. *J. Ramsay MacDonald in Thought and Action.* Albuquerque, N.M.: University of New Mexico Press, 1952.

Salter, Arthur. *Personality in Politics.* London: Faber, 1938.

Taylor, A. J. P. *The Origins of the Second World War.* Harmondsworth: Penguin Books, 1963.

Wheeler-Bennett, John W. *Hindenburg: The Wooden Titan.* New York: St. Martin's Press, 1969.

Wheeler-Bennett, John W. *The Nemesis of Power: The German Army in Politics, 1918–1945.* London: Macmillan and Co., 1964.

# 3

# *Hitler: Into the Abyss*

Historians have often ignored the impact of ill health upon national leaders. They assume that such men deal with crises late in their careers with the same skills that had propelled them to positions of leadership at a younger age. It is as if leadership capabilities exist in a vacuum, remain unchanged, and are impervious to the influences of stress and aging. Such thinking simplifies historical analysis, but ignores the essential observation that men in power are often required to make decisions at an age when their faculties have been compromised by advanced years and disease.

From this perspective, the case of Adolf Hitler represents a most intriguing medical history. In clinical practice the physician is taught early in his training to enlist only one diagnosis to explain a given set of symptoms, simply because at any given time only one disease is usually affecting the patient. In Hitler's case, extraordinarily enough, the record suggests that *four* very different but interrelated conditions plagued him, while being caught in a deadly spiral of physical deterioration that paralleled his policies and actions during the last four years of the Third Reich.

*The emerging leader, 1930*

The evidence indicates not only that Hitler suffered from Parkinson's disease, but that the mysterious abdominal pains that afflicted him from 1929 onward, incorrectly described by many as psychosomatic in origin, were a manifestation of chronic cholecystitis (inflammation of the gallbladder, usually accompanied by gallstones) with acute exacerbations. These two illnesses seem to be the least of the four evils to have compromised his leadership significantly, even though they were detrimental enough. Parkinson's disease in its later stages often causes depression. When coupled with periods of pain and abdominal discomfort associated with cholecystitis, decision making would have been difficult. In relation to cholecystitis, moreover, the questionable treatments used by Hitler's physician, Dr. Theodor Morell, certainly had an adverse effect on his thought processes. Given the myriad of other medications Hitler was taking, an identifiable clinical syndrome of "polypharmacy" evolved. [1] This represents the third diagnosis. Finally, a fourth and previously unrecognized disease process may shed new light on Hitler's abnormal personality: He probably suffered from temporal lobe epilepsy. Indeed, he demonstrated all of the enduring interictal (between seizures) personality defects accompanying that phenomenon.

Historians have not properly understood, much less emphasized, the available medical data, yet no definitive study of Hitler is complete without a detailed understanding of the diseases that plagued this demonic figure during his meteoric rise and fall. Years ago, Percy Schramm addressed the need for a biomedical analysis of Hitler when he stated: "New developments in medical science might well lead to new conclu-

*Adolf Hitler, March 1933*

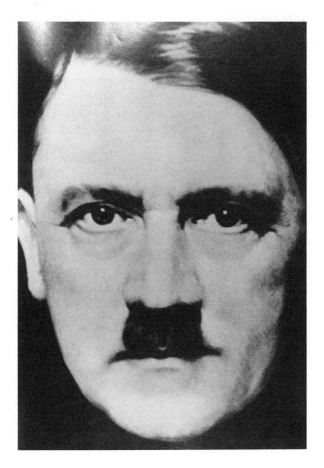

sions on the basis of critical re-evaluation of the data."[2] This becomes even more compelling when one recognizes that these diseases were progressive and that parallels existed between their progression and the deterioration in Hitler's leadership between 1941 and 1945. (See Appendix 2.)

To begin with, there is simply not much doubt that Adolf Hitler suffered from Parkinson's disease. Dr. Maximilian de Crinis, an SS physician specializing in neurology, first suggested that Hitler had the ailment after viewing newsreels of the Fuehrer.[3] This has been discounted by a few subsequent writers,[4] but de Crinis's original suspicion can readily be defended. One of the characteristic features of Parkinson's disease is the appearance of premature aging. Afflicted individuals are seen to become progressively more stooped in their posture, to walk with a shuffling gait, to experience exacerbations of muscle rigidity and tremors of the extremities, and to show facial features suggesting dullness, apathy, and listlessness. Hitler's contemporaries observed these symptoms without realizing their significance. Albert Speer, who devoted but six pages of his lengthy memoirs to Hitler's ill health, made the incriminating observation that he appeared to have become senile during the last weeks of his life.[5]

This view was corroborated by Hans Karl von Hasselbach, one of Hitler's doctors: "Up till 1940, Hitler appeared to be much younger than he actually was. From that date he aged rapidly. From 1940 to 1943 he looked his age. After 1943 he appeared to have grown old."[6] Hugh Trevor-Roper attributed Hitler's premature aging to "his manner of life . . . and his doctors."[7] Certainly these were contributing factors; they probably had more effect on Hitler's leadership capabilities than Parkinson's disease per se. Still, Hitler's rapid aging itself was probably related as much to Parkinson's disease as to any other factor.

There are several salient features in the typical case of Parkinson's disease, or syndrome. A tremor, initially one-sided, is usually the first symptom noted. Eventually this gives way to increasing tremors of all the extremities, but generally not before other symptoms of Parkinson's disease have become manifest.[8] These include bradykinesia (generalized slowness of movement and poverty of spontaneously initiated motor actions, which makes such movements as sitting or changing direction in walking more difficult); rigidity (an increased tension of the muscles accounting for a stooping posture and inflexibility in carrying out coordinated motor tasks that require dexterity); and "masked facies" (a peculiar countenance characterized by a fixed, staring gaze devoid of animation). Other associated symptoms include excessive salivation and difficulty with balance. These are the physical changes that occur with this tragic disease.

Less obvious but equally incapacitating are the emotional and intellectual changes that occur. Medical neurologists originally believed that, except in unusual cases, intellectual deterioration was not manifest in patients suffering from Parkinson's disease. Recent evidence, however, has altered this misconception. In the words of two prominent neurologists: "Careful testing has shown some evidence of dementia in over half of these patients."[9] Furthermore, as long as the patient retains his ability to perceive his own physical degeneration, he suffers from frequent bouts of depression. Depression occurs much more frequently in Parkinsonism than in the normal population—and depression itself may have a very damaging effect upon an individual's ability to make decisions with clarity.

Significant, too, is the observation of Dr. Houston Merritt, who suggests that intellectual deterioration may be even more prevalent in cases of nondominant hemisphere involvement.[10] (The left side of the brain is dominant in virtually all right-handed individuals, as this hemisphere controls the function of speech.) In Hitler's case, predominantly right-sided, or nondominant, hemisphere compromise was suggested on the basis of his originally left-sided tremor. Merritt's hypothesis, then, might support a greater predilection for intellectual deterioration in Adolf Hitler as a Parkinsonian suspect.

There is a strong possibility, therefore, that the disease had sinister effects on Hitler by 1944, in terms of both depression and intellectual compromise, as his Parkinsonism appeared to be well advanced by this time. As Dr. Ernst Gunther Schenck, who has studied Hitler's medical history in great detail, concluded: "I believe that in the end the Parkinsonism was affecting his mind too."[11] This fact notwithstanding, the effects of Parkinson's disease in Hitler's case pale in comparison to other medical factors of far greater significance. In the final analysis, the importance of the disease rests primarily with its responsibility for his apparent rapid aging.

Suffice it to say that available descriptions of Hitler during the period after 1943 abound with what the neurologist would term "classical stigmata" of Parkinson's. Hitler's tremor occurred as early as 1923, when it was confined to the left arm and leg.[12] By 1943, moreover, his physical impairment had become obvious to all. Citing Morell's testimony, Maser noted that "as in November, 1923 . . . he now suffered from a tremor of the left arm and leg and when walking he dragged his left foot. His movements were abrupt and jerky." He also developed a stoop.[13] Heinz Guderian's description of Hitler in 1943 corroborated these details in his statement that "not only his left hand but the entire left side of his body shook. In sitting he had to hold his right hand over his left, his right leg crossed over his left in order to make the constant shaking less noticeable. His gait became shuffling, and his posture bent, his movements slow as in a slow-motion film. He had to have a chair placed under him when he wanted to seat himself." [14]

Erwin Giesing had the rare privilege in October 1944 of examining Hitler when he was bedridden from other causes. Although this physician was not examining Hitler with Parkinson's disease in mind, his findings are compatible with that diagnosis. He noted increased rigidity of the arms. There were no abnormalities in the examination of the cerebellum (the hindbrain involved with coordination and balance, among other functions) or the corticospinal tracts (pathways that control motor activity and connect the cerebral cortex with the spinal cord), such as would have been found in other neurologic diseases aside from Parkinson's. He also noticed an absence of body perspiration. [15] The finding of decreased perspiration might suggest generalized sympathetic-system dysfunction occasionally seen in a variant of Parkinson's disease called the "Shy-Drager syndrome." [16] Impotence and postural hypotension (giddiness, or lightheadedness occurring in the upright position due to a drop in blood pressure) accompany this disorder. The former was repeatedly suggested in Hitler's case; and the latter was suggested both by Giesing and Joseph Goebbels. [17]

By 1945 Hitler's symptoms had worsened. Giesing was shocked by the rapid change: "He seemed to me to have aged, and to stoop much more than before. . . . I was immediately struck by a marked tremor . . . which invariably increased when his hand was unsupported. . . . He was somewhat absent-minded and no longer able to concentrate." [18] Captain Gerhard Boldt later recalled: "There was an indescribable flickering stare in his eyes. . . . He shuffles slowly forward . . . his movements are those of a very sick old man." [19]

At least two later investigators were only partially correct in their assessment of Hitler's Parkinsonism. That is, they acknowledged the disease, but imparted too much significance to its impact on his decisions and policies. Anton Braunmuehl asserted that the remarkable personality changes engendered by the disease "explained the atrocities and the political and military failures after 1942." [20] An American physician, John Walters, also indicted Parkinson's to account for the tragedies and horrors of the Third Reich, postulating that the disease caused "personality alterations" amounting to "moral insanity." [21] Although modest intellectual changes do occur in half of those afflicted and, much less frequently, paranoia may be observed, there is little in the record to substantiate these extravagant claims—particularly in light of other factors of far greater significance to account for Hitler's behavioral aberrations.

This is not to discount the possibility that the disease may have had a negative impact on Hitler's decisions. Both a modest dementia and depression can dull the perceptions of these victims. The term "subcortical dementia" has been associated with alterations in the basal ganglia (structures deep within the brain) such as occur with Parkinsonism. Dr. Martin Albert et al. assert:

> Subcortical dementia differs sharply from cortical dementia; in subcortical dementia the verbal and perceptual motor abilities may be largely preserved. A striking feature of the subcortical dementia is the marked slowing of thought processes, associated with personality change, memory deficits, and the impaired capacity for abstraction. [22]

This description is strikingly consistent with Hitler's behavior. He certainly preserved verbal and perceptual motor abilities—most notably in his lengthy, repetitive monologues—to the very end. However, his inability to assimilate new facts, his disease-induced inflexibility of mind that was evident by 1944, [23] and his inability to make resolute decisions on a rational basis fit the second half of the description outlined by these investigators. As we have seen, Hitler's contemporaries noted these changes from 1943 onward. They probably did have a negative impact on his leadership abilities; but to make the sweeping assertion that they accounted for all the tragedies, horrors, and failures of Nazi Germany is to carry the argument too far.

The depression accompanying Parkinsonism can occur at any stage of the disease and bears no direct relation to the degree of the disability. [24] Disturbances of mood closely resembling those observed in either a depressive or a manic episode are the predominant and essential clinical features. This is termed an "organic affective syndrome." [25] It is significant that the *Comprehensive Textbook of Psychiatry* presents this specific disorder as a warning to the psychiatrist: "The main practical purpose of introducing the concept of the "organic affective syndrome" is to encourage clinicians to screen every patient exhibiting a manic or depressive disorder for a possible physical illness or exposure to a drug." [26] Such subtleties of diagnosis were understandably missed by Hitler's physicians, in spite of the peculiar alternation between manic and depressive states that characterized his behavior.

Parenthetically, it has been asserted by many scholars that Morell did not suspect Parkinson's disease, both because he dismissed it on several occasions and because he did not prescribe the appropriate drug available for the disease (see Appendix 2). Data available in Morell's recently edited diary, however, now establish that he ultimately gave it some consideration in the last month of Hitler's life. By April 15, 1945, he was suspicious enough to record in his diary: "As the tremor is a variety of paralysis agitans [Parkinson's disease], I am making an attempt at temporarily influencing it by subcutaneous injections of Harmin and administering Homburg 680." [27]

By way of summary, the reader is asked to compare Hitler's condition, as it has been described, to a synopsis of Parkinson's disease taken from one of today's most authoritative textbooks of neurology:

> Usually the feature that first calls the patient's attention to his disorder is the appearance of tremor. As the disorder progresses, the tremor worsens and usually spreads from one extremity to the other on the same side, but it may cross to the opposite side and involve both upper and lower extremities. The tremor is made conspicuously worse . . . by a stressful situation. As patients develop increasing rigidity, tremor may be dampened. . . . With bradykinesia and rigidity patients report slower and more difficult walking, difficulty arising from and getting into chairs. As rigidity becomes more prominent, postural changes become apparent. Patients develop a simian posture with slight flexion at all joints. . . . The loss of facial expression results in a mask-like face, and the staring look is due to infrequent eye blinking. [28]

Parkinson's disease usually occurs without a recognizable antecedent cause. Thousands of cases, however, are known to have occurred years after the outbreaks of encephalitis so prevalent during 1918 and 1919. [29] Uncommonly, it may result immediately following any viral inflammation of the brain. [30] Theodor Morell believed (as did Werner Maser) that Hitler was affected by encephalitis at Vinnitsa in 1942. [31] One might therefore suppose that this illness triggered Hitler's Parkinson's disease. That supposition ignores the presence of other more defensible causes for its development. Furthermore, the illness at Vinnitsa was probably not encephalitis at all, a point which will be argued below (see p. 345).

Parkinsonism is also know to develop after carbon monoxide poisoning and other exposures to inhalants. [32] Hitler had been exposed to mustard gas in 1918 as a soldier on the front lines at Ypres, after which he remained blind and mute for two weeks (allegedly on a psychosomatic, or hysterical, basis). The substance was clearly mustard gas since this was the only gas the French used at Ypres. A noted authority on gas warfare recorded that its use there produced "feelings allied to panic in the [exposed] German ranks."[33] This may account in part for the assertion by others that Hitler's blindness was caused by hysteria,[34] but in fact the delayed onset of transient blindness was one of the specific symptoms found in mustard gas victims. In the words of a survivor: "I was gassed by diclor-diethyl sulphide, commonly known as mustard stuff. . . . It had no immediate effect on the eyes or the throat. The next morning, myself and all the eighty men we had up there were absolutely blind."[35] There was, then, characteristically a delayed action on the eyes causing temporary blindness. This symptom, coupled with the insidious skin lesions resulting from burns, were the two most prominent clinical features associated with mustard gas exposure. This effect is substantiated in a modern pharmacology textbook edited by J. R. De Palma: "Eye irritation does not appear until a substantial latent period. . . . Exposures to a more concentrated solution cause significant eye damage and slow down recovery to two to six weeks."[36] That Hitler was exposed at Ypres and suffered the eye injuries seen in this class of vesicant (blistering) compounds[37] is evidence enough to establish, first, that mustard gas was the offending agent; second, that his blindness was not hysterical; and third, that his exposure was significant.[38] The question remains: Was it significant enough to have caused Hitler's Parkinson's disease?

It is well known that carbon monoxide or carbon disulfide exposure may lead years later to a clinical syndrome indistinguishable from Parkinson's disease termed "toxic Parkinsonism."[39] Drs. Kubic and Anders found that a close halogenated hydrocarbon analogue of diclor-diethyl sulfide (mustard gas), dichloromethane (chloroform) could exert additional toxic effects because it is metabolized to carbon monoxide by cytochrome P-450.[40] The significant corollary to this in Hitler's case is that this same enzyme by the same oxidative process metabolizes diclor-diethyl sulfide to carbon disulfide, one of the agents known to induce Parkinson's disease. Perhaps this adds up to a plausible argument that an incident assumed by historians to have been representative of an hysterical conversion reaction was in fact due to physical causes, and may well explain the onset of Parkinsonism in Hitler's case.

Interesting indeed—yet the critical reader may not be so readily swayed. Cases of Parkinson's that occur as a result of carbon disulfide intoxication generally do so after chronic exposure such as occurs among workers in the rayon and rubber industries. That a single exposure could do so is unproved. Moreover, a much more defensible cause for Hitler's Parkinsonism can be related to the impure opiates the Fuehrer received intravenously after 1942 (see p. 187).

Hitler had other ailments that have frequently been referred to as psychosomatic or hysterical: the abdominal pains and flatulence that plagued him from the late 1920s to the end of his life. After studying Morell's diary, for example, the historian David Irving surmised that "the epigastric disturbances were certainly a product of his growing frustration."[41] But it is necessary to differentiate what is known as "spastic colon" on a functional basis from other genuine disease processes of an organic cause.[42] Clinical evidence in previous accounts and recent data in Morell's diary suggest that Hitler suffered from chronic cholecystitis, which is, as mentioned earlier, an inflammation of the gallbladder, with or without gallstones.[43] Several facts support this conclusion. First, from 1932 onward Hitler was a confirmed vegetarian, and several episodes of abdominal distress followed a meal of vegetables.[44] It is well known that certain vegetables are often poorly tolerated by gallbladder sufferers.

Second, jaundice occurred on at least three occasions during particularly severe exacerbations of his gastrointestinal disturbances. [45] Transient obstructions of any segment of the biliary system (in which the gallbladder plays a significant role) are known to increase bilirubin in the blood stream. If levels become sufficiently high, overt jaundice results. Third, right upper quadrant abdominal pain and tenderness were a constant feature accompanying the spasms. [46] Tenderness in the gallbladder, which is located in the right upper quadrant, is characteristically noted when the gallbladder becomes inflamed or enlarged due to transient obstruction of the cystic duct from edema or gallstones. As Drs. Sleisenger and Fordtran have observed:

> Chronic cholecystitis is associated with discrete attacks of epigastric or right upper quadrant pain, either steady or intermittent, and is associated with tenderness to palpation [in that region] of the abdomen. Since cholecystitis is a common disease, the sudden onset of pain and tenderness in the right subcostal region should always suggest that diagnosis. [47]

These fragmentary facts, when taken collectively, point to a consideration of this rather common malady in the differential diagnosis of Hitler's abdominal pain. [48]

Perhaps Hitler's most serious encounter with gastrointestinal-related disease occurred in September 1944. The Fuehrer suffered from severe abdominal colic and became jaundiced. Some have argued that this was caused by viral hepatitis. [49] During the course of his treatment, Morell made recommendations for radiographic examination of the gastrointestinal tract and gallbladder—an indication that he at least considered gallstones. Interestingly enough, Morell may have stumbled onto the origins of the jaundice that afflicted Hitler for three days during this episode of alleged hepatitis. According to Irving, "Morell maintained that Hitler's 'hepatitis' had been brought about by nothing more sinister than a retention of bile caused by a nervous cramp at the gallbladder exit [the cystic duct]." [50] Contemporaries of Morell ignored this opinion, as other investigators have been prone to do.

Significantly, Morell never noted in any of his examinations of Hitler that the liver was palpably enlarged. This would argue against a disease such as hepatitis, in which the organ is usually enlarged but is generally not particularly tender. Prompt relief of Hitler's symptoms was gained by intravenous injections of Eukodal (a synthetic opiate analogue) and Eupaverin (or Eupaverinum, an antispasmodic and anticonvulsant). Whereas the effects of these medications taken in combination might be expected to ameliorate acute exacerbations of gallbladder distention or inflammation, [51] such rapid relief would not be anticipated with hepatitis. Nor do individuals with hepatitis have any appetite for food over an extended period of time. Although Hitler ate sparingly as a rule, there is no mention during these episodes of total cessation of dietary intake (termed anorexia) such as is characteristic of patients who have hepatitis.

Dr. Ernst Gunther Schenck, nevertheless, postulated that "most probably Hitler had contracted infectious hepatitis, which is not infrequent among troops living under crowded conditions." [52] Assuming that Hitler ever had the disease, he was hardly living under such crowded, unsanitary conditions in September 1944. A much more likely cause of such an infection—if he contracted it—would be the less than aseptic conditions under which his physician gave Hitler intravenous medications. Morell was observed on several occasions to reuse needles after merely wiping the end of them with a cloth he carried with him before giving an injection! Indeed, he volunteered in his diary on November 1, 1944 (one month after this illness) that

> The Fuehrer thought I was not massaging the place [for injections] long enough with alcohol first—said I always did it too little—and suggested this was why he kept getting little red pimples lately where I had made the injections. . . . [He] thinks it is perhaps the injections themselves which were responsible for the bacteria getting into his blood. [53]

It could just as easily have been the hepatitis virus! Such exposure is a leading cause of hepatitis in individuals such as drug addicts, who share the use of contaminated needles.

This observation notwithstanding, it seems doubtful that the ailment Hitler had in September 1944 was in fact hepatitis. Severe pain and cramping, as well as right upper quadrant tenderness on examination, are unusual findings with hepatitis, except of the most severe nature. Nor was the duration of the illness compatible with that disease. Jaundice is rarely seen to clear over such a short period of time as three days, and overall recovery takes a period of weeks, not days. [54] On the other hand, all of Hitler's symptoms, physical findings, and laboratory data are consistent with acute cholecystitis, which had plagued him intermittently for years. Only by ignoring the previous medical record could one indulge in the folly of postulating two separate disease entities, particularly when all symptoms are compatible with the one far more common malady. It is instructive to note that by November 21, 1944, seven weeks after the above episode, and frequently thereafter, Morell would again observe tenderness in the area of the gallbladder, accompanied by frequent exacerbations of painful abdominal spasms. [55] Recurrent cholecystitis, then, was to plague Adolf Hitler until the very end.

What effect did this recurring illness have on Hitler's leadership? One must not make the error of attributing too much of his aberrant behavior to cholecystitis. Nevertheless, the reader need only ask any individual who in the past has suffered from the excruciating pain of either renal or biliary colic to learn how severe it can be. It is a well-substantiated medical precept that no pain of any illness rivals that associated with colic. In Hitler's case, we know how pervasive this pain must have been; there are no less than thirty references to it in Morell's diary. During these periods, it must have been very difficult for Hitler to attend to affairs of state and to direct the war. More important, however, the deleterious impact of medications Morell used to treat this and other perceived illnesses became increasingly manifest from 1941 onward, the full significance of which will be brought out at a later point in this review.

The literature on Adolf Hitler is replete with speculative, largely psychoanalytical, accounts concerning the personality of this enigmatic, unpredictable, and increasingly volatile leader. Both his contemporaries and later historians noted how his character changed for the worse after 1942. The cause for the deterioration has never been adequately explained, although there have been many explanations offered: a psychoneurosis related to a Freudian-style Oedipal complex, including fear that his family's bloodlines were contaminated; the secondary effects of tertiary syphilis; an isolated lifestyle, increasingly divorced from reality, that fostered delusions; the stress of administering a losing war effort; and the deleterious impact of various pharmacologic poisons (most notably amphetamines) administered by his unprincipled physician. On the other hand, a few historians do not believe Hitler's personality significantly changed. They maintain that his behavior was consistent from beginning to end, and that he either had a "borderline personality" disorder or was a "psychopath."

With regard to the question of a personality disorder, the evidence afforded by both primary and secondary sources suggests that Hitler may have suffered from an insidious condition that has not previously been considered: psychomotor epilepsy emanating from the temporal lobe, a form of seizure disturbance that is often difficult to recognize. Drs. Benson and Geschwind present the following significant fact in the authoritative six-volume textbook *American Handbook of Psychiatry:* "It is generally accepted that the temporal lobe contains the most epileptogenic tissue in the brain, but only in recent years has the full implication of temporal lobe seizures been realized."[56] Epilepsy originating from this location produces typical behavioral changes that develop over a period of months or years. These changes are not episodic, but become enduring "interictal" features of the personality, meaning that they persist between brief periods of overt psychomotor seizure activity. Doctors Bear and Arana have described these changes:

1. Deepening emotions and attribution of significance by the subject to small details and intra- or extrapersonal events. This accounts for a characteristic worsening of temper and well-executed aggression, including a strong tendency toward paranoia.

2. Alterations in sexual interest, ranging from loss of sexual drive to fetishism, transvestism, and hypersexuality.

3. The syndrome of hypergraphia, the tendency to compose autobiographical texts illustrating moral or religious themes.

4. A sense of personal destiny and megalomaniacal delusions. [57]

Equally important, many investigators have established that psychomotor epilepsy produces behavioral changes that are clinically indistinguishable from pure psychiatric disorders. [58] Taken in combination, then, there is deepening emotionality, evangelistic and messianic zeal, a sense of personal destiny, altered sexual interest, aggressiveness, and periods of poorly controlled rage alternating with overt paranoia. Is there a more inclusive description of the personality traits of Adolf Hitler?

The diagnosis of psychomotor seizures is often difficult to make, even by the trained physician, unless the observer exercises a high index of suspicion to recognize the patterns that characterize this disease. [59] These seizures are rarely accompanied by overt manifestations of major-motor seizure activity (the grand mal seizure), which the layman can readily recognize: tonic-clonic convulsions, frothing at the mouth, tongue biting, loss of bladder control, etc. Rather, such seizures are manifested by transient periods of loss of awareness called "absence" or "fugue states," repetitive motor activity as subtle as smacking of the lips or even more complicated but stereotyped acts, hallucinations or perceptual disorders, or perseveration with certain themes, with or without phraseology of speech and forced thinking. [60] During the seizure itself, the motor manifestations of temporal lobe discharges may be extremely limited, often consisting of only a few seconds of absence, and are easily mistaken for the thought-blocking of a schizophrenic or a neurotic. According to Benson and Geschwind: "Often the patient resumes activity or conversation immediately after the short episode, and continues as though nothing had happened. Thus even an experienced observer may be unaware that he has witnessed an epileptic seizure." [61] These seizures are categorized according to the initial symptoms, termed a "prodrome" or "aura." The seizure may consist of this initial phase only, or it may develop into a more complex seizure pattern involving other temporal lobe phenomena. Electroencephalographic (EEG) studies have shown that the overwhelming majority of psychomotor seizures arise from the temporal lobe. [62]

The diversity of seizures in this category is legion, and numerous patterns of behavior have been described. Of singular importance is the observation that sometimes the pattern of behavior differs from seizure to seizure in the same patient, making diagnosis more difficult still. [63] Many individuals have undoubtedly gone undiagnosed, their aberrations being dismissed as caused by stress, psychiatric disease, or extreme variations of normal behavior. Adolf Hitler may have been one such individual.

This is not to say that it can be documented unequivocally that Hitler was a psychomotor seizure victim. This diagnosis can be made with certainty only in those suspect individuals who demonstrate suggestive repetitive, stereotyped activity, who have documented electroencephalographic abnormalities referable to the temporal lobe, and who respond to seizure medication. For the majority of patients, even today, a tentative diagnosis is made based upon transient stereotypical patterns of behavior, with or without the characteristic interictal features of the personality disorder associated with this disease, as outlined above. If both conditions are met, a presumptive diagnosis is virtually assured. A favorable response to anticonvulsants is then relied upon as a therapeutic trial to complete the diagnosis after an EEG is obtained that shows a seizure focus in the temporal lobe. The absence of either an EEG or a therapeutic trial of anticonvulsant medication precludes the use of these diagnostic criteria in Hitler's case. [64] Nonetheless, his personality profile is consistent with that found in most psychomotor seizure victims. It remains, therefore, to document transient behavioral aberrations suggesting such seizure activity from the available record and to compare them with those seen in patients harboring this disease.

To begin with, unexplained fear is the most common emotional experience during a psychomotor seizure. One reference textbook of neurology estimates this to occur in as many as 80 percent of these patients, though most large series studied would estimate the number to be closer to one-half. [65] *The American Handbook of Psychiatry* corroborates this view: "Fear is reported most often . . . and a report of paroxysmal, unexplained feelings of fear should suggest the possibility of psychomotor seizures. [66] Hermann Rauschning's portrayal of Hitler during one episode in 1944 at least invokes suspicion of this:

Hitler wakes at night with convulsive shrieks. . . . He shakes with fear . . . he shouts confused, unintelligible phrases. He gasps, as if imagining himself to be suffocating. . . . [He] stood swaying in his room, looking wildly about him. "He! He! He's been here!" he gasped. . . . Suddenly he began to

reel off figures, and odd words and broken phrases, entirely devoid of sense.
. . . He used strangely composed and entirely un-German word formations.
. . . "There! There! In the corner! Who's that?" He stamped and shrieked in
the familiar way. [67]

Not only is the phenomenon of irrational fear evident in this vignette, but
the description of phraseology and forced thinking devoid of sense is
likewise a common form of motor behavior observed in many types of
psychomotor seizures. Individuals compulsively repeat certain stock
phrases during an attack. It is the absence of meaningful content that
may bring them to others' attention even if overt disorders of perception
are not immediately apparent. Albert Speer recalled that Hitler's speech
on many occasions "became an overflowing torrent. . . . In his talk Hitler
seemed to me to be in the grip of an obsession. . . . He talked in a kind
of waking dream, his eyes expressionless, and frequently—in keeping
with his artistic nature—confounding fantasy with reality." [68] A glassy-
eyed stare and dreamlike states are also often seen during these seizures.
In retrospect, physiologic compromise rather than an artistic temperament may have accounted for the bizarre behavior Speer observed.

The reference to delusions and hallucinations in Rauschning's description is equally exemplary. As Drs. Gilroy and Meyer have observed,
"more complex hallucinations of familiar scenes and of human figures or
animals, sometimes of a bizarre appearance, are described. The epileptic focus in this case lay in the posterior part of the temporal lobe which
adjoins the visual association areas." [69] (See Fig. 2.2.) This is an important distinction to make, as schizophrenic patients are also plagued by
delusions, paranoid ideation, and overt hallucinations. According to
Benson and Geschwind:

> There are also frequent delusions—both primary and secondary—[in the
> condition of psychomotor epilepsy] and hallucinations. . . . Paranoid states
> are common as well as repetitive, stereotyped, ritualistic activities. Affec-
> tive responses [ability to interact with one's environment] are usually pre-
> served; this preservation of affect and the ability to establish rapport are the
> major clinical points which differentiate the "schizophrenia-like" states [of
> epilepsy] from the true schizophrenic. [70]

Other observers of Hitler besides Rauschning and Speer reported incidents similar to the ones described above, emphasizing the pervasiveness of such singular behavior. [71] These two descriptions alone, however,
are representative of several features consistent with psychomotor seizure activity, including irrational fear, forced thinking, speech automatisms, dreamlike states, and hallucinations.

Temporal lobe epilepsy obviously has many implications for psychiatric illness, and it is important to consider the possibility of this disorder in determining the cause of either a supposed "psychosis" or "neurosis." Drs. Guerrant, Anderson, and Fischer reviewed the literature comparing the behavior of psychomotor and other seizure patients and found that "psychotic" abnormalities (disorders of perception, hallucinations, etc.) were more common in the temporal lobe group.[72] Dr. J. R. Stevens performed studies of psychiatric abnormalities in psychomotor and grand mal seizure patients and found prevalent psychiatric disturbances in the psychomotor group to include "schizophrenia, mood disturbance, anxiety and withdrawal, while the 'grand mal' group showed apathy and mental slowing."[73] That Adolf Hitler suffered both disorders of perception and hallucinations on some occasions, and mood disturbance, anxiety, and withdrawal on others, should not be surprising in light of this information.

Fugue states (transient periods of unawareness, even though the victim preserves his ability to carry out simple motor tasks) are also quite common in temporal lobe epilepsy. A brief vignette recounted by Alan Bullock illustrates one possible occurrence of an absence attack in isolation. Having received yet another round of advice contrary to his expectations and desires, a peculiar change suddenly overcame Hitler at the close of a session with his advisors. Bullock recorded that "when Guderian finished a long silence followed. Hitler slowly stood up, staring into space, and took a few shuffling steps forward. Without a word he signalled them to go. . . . This was Hitler at his clumsiest: unable to answer Guderian, he fell back on the oldest of his tricks. . . ." If Bullock believed the Fuehrer's behavior was governed by "calculation" and "conviction,"[74] a neurologist might see parallels between it and an absence attack or fugue state of psychomotor epilepsy. In such a state, there are feelings of incongruity, in which the patient has the sensation of being detached from what is going on around him.[75]

H. R. Trevor-Roper and Robert Waite have dealt at length with one recurrent theme in Hitler's thinking—that of an unbridled, obsessive preoccupation with blood. He lived in constant fear of "blood poisoning," literally and figuratively. Whether in writing, public speaking, or idle conversation, Hitler was captivated by the theme. "Alone the loss of purity of the blood destroys the inner happiness forever," he declared. When he observed his associates eating meat he jeered: "I will have blood sausages made from my excess blood as a special culinary treat for you. Why not? You like meat so much." He saw the history of the world as a spectacle of one people making war on another, saying, "one creature *drinks the blood* of another. The death of one nourishes the other." One chant was said to have contained particularly gruesome phrases which Hitler found so appealing: "The blood of the Jew will squirt from our knives." Most noteworthy of all, Hitler's behavior would change abruptly with the very mention of the word blood. [76] This topic was often included in the increasingly prevalent monologues that dominated such disparate events as social conversations at night in the bunker and highly charged meetings with his group of military advisors during the day.

Inflexibility was another theme Hitler repeatedly extolled as a virtue in his monologues. He reminisced by the hour upon past political decisions or victories, by which he intended to demonstrate that inflexibility was the source of his strength. Rather than a source of strength, this inflexibility may have been yet another pathologic fixation with certain ideas and phrases, termed a perseveration, which is characteristically seen in the psychomotor seizure victim. As Gilroy and Meyer have stated: "Complex hallucinations with recall of scenes from the past, often including great detail . . . can be a manifestation of psychomotor seizures. This invokes controlled activity of memory patterns and is too complex to be regarded as hallucinations alone." [77] The preoccupation with the theme of blood in particular, and inflexibility in general, may have represented two of the most primitive of these fixations for Hitler.

Such disease-induced fixations may have accounted for Hitler's often bizarre and inappropriate preoccupation with bloodshed and destruction beyond what was necessary to accomplish the objective. For example, on one occasion General Franz Halder and he were discussing the storming of Warsaw by German troops. Halder volunteered the opinion that such action would not be necessary, as the Polish army no longer existed and the city would fall of its own accord. Hitler countered with a description of what he wanted, and in doing so, included the triggering phrase "the people drowned in blood." With that utterance, Halder said, "his eyes popped out of his head, and he became quite a different person. He was suddenly seized by a lust for blood." [78]

Robert Waite devotes several pages to the importance of the word blood for Hitler: "He used the word often in describing his rise to power . . . he spoke of the sacred "Blood Flag" of 9 November 1923; he established a special "Blood Order" for those who had marched on that day. He also introduced the idea of *Blutkitt* (blood cement) in training his elite guard, the SS." [79] At a later date, after receiving rather gruesome descriptions of the decimation of his personal SS division in Russia, those in attendance were startled by Hitler's spirited response that "losses can never be too high! They sow the seeds of future greatness." [80] What was originally received despondently as devastating news was suddenly transformed by the blood bath being described as nearly a stroke of good fortune!

That the "blood lust" theme played an important role in his thinking, then, is unassailable. But was there more significance to the word than a mere fascination with it would suggest? Patients with temporal lobe epilepsy are often propelled by a specific sound, smell, word, or activity into rather stereotyped behavior that produces evidence of abnormalities in the temporal lobe on an EEG tracing. Cursive (or running) epilepsy, musicogenic epilepsy, and reading epilepsy are all examples of this phenomenon. [81] Was the word "blood" itself a trigger for reflex psychomotor seizure activity? Trevor-Roper's revelations suggest as much. On numerous occasions, "the mere mention of the great Blood Purge of 1934 set him off into one of his famous tantrums. Satisfaction never abated this terrible appetite for blood." [82] These were recurrent stereotyped outbursts, and the pattern of his outrage became an entirely predictable matter each time the memory of 1934 was envoked. A scene was described by Eugen Dollmann, Heinrich Himmler's highest officer and Police Leader for Italy:

> All this time Hitler . . . sat quiet and reserved. . . . Then, quite suddenly, someone mentioned . . . the Roehm plot of 30th June 1934, and the bloody purge which followed it. Immediately Hitler leapt up in a fit of frenzy, with foam on his lips . . . and he ranted wildly about terrible punishments. . . . [He] raged for a full half hour; the visitors thought he must be mad. . . . [After finishing] he sat still; in his hand he held a tube of coloured pastilles which he continually sucked; only at intervals, like a still sputtering volcano, would he utter some savage phrase . . . about blood, and Providence, and concentration camps. [83]

This episode illustrates several important points. First, the description of "foam on his lips" at the beginning of the tirade may have represented autonomic system hyperactivity (such as increased sweating and salivation) often seen during such seizures. Second, what was to become stereotyped behavior was triggered by the phrase "blood purge." Third, the description of Hitler sitting quietly sucking on a tube of coloured pastilles afterward suggests the compulsion of oral exploration occasionally seen in psychomotor seizure victims. Fourth, the period of calm after the storm during which he sat placidly and seemed unaware of his environment suggests a postictal (after seizure) state following the temporal lobe seizure activity. During the height of any epileptic seizure, the EEG demonstrates voluminous, repetitive spikes of brain wave activity, following which periods of near-electrical silence emerge, correlating with a period of total unresponsiveness in the typical grand mal seizure or of relative unawareness in a psychomotor seizure.

Albert Speer recounted another vignette that has particular relevance to the observations above:

In the past Hitler had had a fine sense of discrimination. He had been able
to adapt his language to the people around him. Now he was unrestrained
and reckless. He would lose his temper, flush deeply. . . . After such an
outburst Hitler would have to pace the room furiously for a long time, word-
lessly snapping his fingers, until his agitation somewhat subsided. Then
again he would go back to the table to sit . . . looking up . . . like a stranger
among them. Truly he came from a different world. [84]

His "world" on this particular occasion may have been restricted to the
domain of the temporal lobe epilepsy victim. The wordless pacing and
snapping of fingers Speer alluded to are examples of characteristic motor
automatisms seen during such attacks, and the postictal period of unawareness afterward that Speer described correlates with a relative
absence of neuronal activity in brain cells that is typically seen immediately after their exhausting activation to seizure thresholds. The victim
remains unaware of his surroundings during this period and then re-
covers; yet he is oblivious to the event that just occurred. Gilroy and
Meyer describe psychomotor seizures with disturbances in thinking as
"the experience of sudden compulsive thoughts, usually of an unpleasant nature, or of compulsive ideas that force themselves into the patient's
mind to the exclusion of all others." [85] Could there be any more explicit
examples of just such a phenomenon than the descriptions of Adolf
Hitler's behavior in response to the word blood?

Trevor-Roper assumed that Hitler's preoccupation with blood represented merely a perseveration with a subject that fascinated him in a
negative, repulsive sense: "Though he was physically afraid of the sight
of blood, the thought of it excited and intoxicated him." [86] The examples
given above, however, suggest more than just a peculiar fascination. The
theme of destruction in general, and blood in particular, may have triggered episodes of psychomotor seizures—just as other external sensory
stimuli (such as music, reading, and bright colors) have been observed
to be catalysts for seizure activity in other temporal lobe epilepsy victims.
These come under the heading of "reflex epilepsy," a phenomenon that
Dr. Houston Merritt describes with clarity in his *Textbook of Neurology:*

> The attacks may be always related to some specific stimulus, and in many
> others, an occasional attack may be attributed to some precipitating factor.
> This is not surprising when it is remembered that abnormalities in the ac-
> tivity of the cerebral cortex of epileptics can be activated by a wide variety
> of stimuli. [87]

The phenomenon of musicogenic epilepsy may suggest another triggering mechanism in Hitler's behavior. Wagner's operas had a very profound
effect on Hitler, even as a young man. Certain strains of music are known

to elicit classic psychomotor seizure activity in susceptible subjects,[88] and one illustrative vignette at least suggests that possibility in young Adolf Hitler's case, as described by his childhood companion, August Kubizek. At age seventeen Hitler had sat enthralled listening to Wagner's opera *Rienzi*. After the performance, he was uncharacteristically subdued, walking in silence to the top of the hill. His friend Kubizek recounted:

> Never before and never again have I heard Adolf Hitler speak as he did in that hour. . . . There was something strange about Hitler that night. It was as if another being spoke out of his body, and moved him as much as it did me. It wasn't at all a case of a speaker being carried away by his own words. On the contrary, I rather felt as though he himself listened with astonishment and emotion to what burst forth from him with elementary force. I will not attempt to interpret this phenomenon, but it was a state of complete ecstasy and rapture. . . . The impact of the opera was rather a sheer external impulse which compelled him to speak.[89]

Did this episode merely presage the haunting effectiveness of the future orator? Or is it conceivable that Hitler was subject to a musical stimulus that propelled him toward oratorical frenzy? Was there more than meets the eye in the fact that Hitler was later to order the playing of the opening overture to Wagner's *Rienzi* at the beginning of all of the enormous party rallies of the Third Reich? During certain of his speeches, was Hitler captive to the covert impact of psychomotor epilepsy? Langer's description of Hitler's speeches suggests this:

> The mouth that can never utter a fragment of profanity off the speaker's platform now pours forth a veritable stream of curses, foul names, vilification, and hatred. Hanfstaengl compares the development of a Hitlerian speech with the development of a Wagnerian theme, which may account for Hitler's love for Wagnerian music and the inspiration he derives from it. . . .[90]

Did he derive more—a triggering sensory stimulus? With respect to the Wagnerian connection, it is known that "in patients responsive to specific sensory stimuli such as in musicogenic epilepsy, the most common seizure is psychomotor. . . . Rarely these patients have their seizures in response to a particular note or chord, but more often the evoking stimulus is subtle and lies in the theme of the music.[91] Taking into consideration the theme of the opera *Rienzi*, a curse of destruction against the "un-German rabble" of humanity, this intriguing hypothesis, though it cannot be defended with certainty, should not be dismissed out of hand.[92]

One of the peculiar assets Hitler possessed was the ability to stage outbursts of rage to influence those he felt would be susceptible to the

*The orator, Nuremberg, September 1938*

tactic. He used this to great advantage on several occasions. Nonetheless, not all of his fury was staged, even as a young man. Kubizek frequently alluded to Hitler's volubility that was triggered by the most inexplicable impulses: "It only needed the slightest touch—as when one flicks on the electric light and everything becomes brilliantly clear—for his self-accusation to become an accusation against the times, against the whole world; choking with his catalogue of hates, he would pour his fury over everything."[93] Birger Dahlerus described another episode in 1939 that suggested a spontaneous outburst rather than a contrived display. What originally began as a response by Hitler to the prediction that England would oppose German aggression against the Poles ended in a startling transformation of character:

> Hitler jumped up and became very agitated. He nervously paced up and down and declared, as if he were talking to himself, that Germany was invincible. . . . Suddenly he stopped in the middle of the room and stared straight ahead. His speech became more and more garbled, his whole be-

havior gave the impression of a person who was not at all himself. Sentences tumbled after one another. . . . "If there is a war," he said, "I build U-boats, U-boats, U-boats, U-boats!" His voice became increasingly indistinct and gradually one could no longer understand him. . . . At this moment he acted more like a demon in bad fiction than a human being. I looked at him in amazement. [94]

This vignette again suggests several features compatible with psycho-motor seizure activity. Most significant, agitation or distress lowers epileptogenic thresholds, predisposing the individual to begin or continue seizure activity. According to Houston Merritt, "During the seizure itself . . . there is repetitive, usually stereotyped automatisms of varying complexity which involve either partially purposeful or inappropriate behavior associated in interplay with the environment and occasionally determined by psychological factors."[95] Once Hitler became upset, he experienced the characteristic aura manifested by a transient period of unawareness of his surroundings, followed by a typical outburst of automatisms of speech and forced thinking. In such instances, the rush of thoughts and phrases characteristically results in "sentences tumbling one after another," to the point that, at the climax of dissociated, repetitive neuronal impulses, comprehensible speech is lost. Given what is now known of speech disorders associated with psychomotor seizures, one might further propose that the right temporal lobe was the focus of Hitler's disturbance. Drs. Serafetinides and Falconer found that speech automatisms (recurrent utterances) occurred most often in cases with right temporal lobe abnormalities. Patients producing speech automatisms were *always unaware*, while those with dysphasia (inability to produce or comprehend speech, associated with left temporal lesions) were usually aware of language difficulties.[96]

The same pattern of events occurs time and again in Hitler's behavior. First there is the period of agitation or other sensory stimuli, which may act as a triggering mechanism, followed by the aura, or period of unawareness. The seizure may end here as a typical absence attack, as occurred in the conversation with Guderian, or it may evolve into full-blown hyperactivity manifested by forced thinking, speech automatisms, perseveration, and autonomic hyperactivity—as exemplified in the diatribe triggered by the "blood purge" stimulus, as described by Eugen Dollman. During such a phase, of course, observers would recognize a true metamorphosis of the afflicted sufferer; his actions and statements would bear no resemblance to reality—even though by the nature of the disorder he was still able to interact with his environment. The tragedy is compounded, however, by the realization that this was still the Fuehrer, and his word was law. The consequences of this recurring scenario Germany was to endure can only be imagined.

Returning to the typical interictal features of the personality disorder frequently seen with longstanding psychomotor seizure activity, a few examples will suffice to reinforce the claim that Hitler's character reconstruction exemplifies all of these features. Certainly there exists no more classic example of the hypergraphic syndrome, manifested by the tendency to compose autobiographical texts, than the publication of *Mein Kampf.* The title alone (*My Struggle,* in translation) demonstrates the work's preoccupation with autobiographical themes, but other themes exist within it as well—such themes as the Jewish Question and Hitler's belief that Divine Providence had chosen him to lead Germany to greatness. These preoccupations are consistent with a temporal lobe seizure victim's compulsion to emphasize moral and religious themes in both word and action. By way of example, in May 1943 Hitler declared that "the antisemitism which formerly animated the Party must again become the focal point of our spiritual struggle."[97] This was a clarion call for reestablishing a spirit of evangelism concerning what Hitler perceived as a religious matter, but it came at a time when circumstances cried out for Germany's energies to be directed toward more important matters, such as administering the war effort. Alan Bullock has concluded that "it is all too easy to dismiss such a conception as the fantasy of a diseased brain."[98] Albert Speer disagreed. By the summer of 1942 he noted in Hitler "a peculiar state of petrifaction and rigidity, apathetic uncertainty, agonized indecisiveness, . . . and a permanent state of caustic irritability. . . . He often gave the impression of being mentally impaired."[99] This is but one example of how a personality disorder caused by illness may have pathologically overridden rational thought. The promulgation of the Final Solution and the concurrent medical experiments undertaken in the concentration camps may therefore take on even more sinister implications than have been acknowledged to date.

One writer, Sebastian Haffner, constructed a thesis based upon the belief that after the first year of the Russian campaign Hitler took virtually no interest in the war effort, attempting to delay the obvious outcome of defeat only long enough to complete the work of the Final Solution. In *The Meaning of Hitler* Haffner asserted that after 1941 Hitler surrendered his political interests to his aggressive instincts. In essence, he abandoned his hopes for German domination of Europe and concentrated upon extermination of the Jews.[100] If Haffner and Speer were correct in underscoring a significant change in Hitler's behavior by 1942, the evidence suggests that the transition was an unconscious process. It may have signified a subconscious surrender by Hitler to the impulses of a personality disorder spawned by epilepsy as the deleterious effects of the many pharmacologic poisons, discussed below, began to take hold.[101]

Other historians have expressed puzzlement in attempting to understand the depths of Hitler's anti-Semitism. Percy Schramm asserted: "We must be satisfied with the realization that there is about Hitler's anti-Semitism an unknown factor." This same writer could only despairingly acknowledge nameless "demons" that must have plagued him. [102] In like manner, the preeminent German scholar of the Third Reich, Karl Dietrich Bracher, was unable to explain Hitler's fanatical conviction in rational terms. [103]

Perhaps the psychomotor epilepsy hypothesis offers an explanation for understanding this fanatical conviction. The personality disorder associated with temporal lobe seizures encompasses a preoccupation with religious matters in a perverted sense. Hitler's fanaticism in handling the Jewish Question is consistent with this behavior. Since Hitler saw himself, in Robert Waite's words, as a "Messiah with a divine mission to save Germany from the incarnate evil of 'International Jewry,' it is not surprising that he likened himself to Jesus. . . . 'Just like Christ, [Hitler declared,] I have a duty to my own people.'" . . . 'What Christ began,' he observed, he, Hitler, 'would complete.'" In a speech on February 10, 1933, Waite notes, "he parodied the Lord's Prayer in promising that under him a new kingdom would come on earth, and that his would be 'the power and the glory, Amen.' He added that if he did not fulfill his mission, 'you should then crucify me.'" [104]

The critical event in the development of Hitler's messianism came in 1918 when, he claimed, he had received a supernatural vision that commanded him to save Germany—while lying mute and blind in a hospital bed after having been exposed to mustard gas. This view of himself remained as an enduring interictal feature of his character. "God has created this people," Hitler declared in 1937, "and it has grown according to his will. And according to *our* will it shall remain and never shall it pass away." In 1938 he proclaimed that "I believe that it was God's will that from [Austria] a boy was sent into the Reich and that he grew up to become the leader of the nation." Even his miraculous escape from the assassination attempt of July 1944 was to reaffirm his delusions. He concluded that it was "new proof that I have been selected from among other men by Providence to lead Germany to victory." [105]

Perhaps as a result of his personality disorder, Hitler's whole conception of history bore the stamp of religious mythology. Waite concluded that "he believed that a pure German people had lived in an early Garden of Eden," and in fact Hitler declared that "The mixture of the races is the original sin [*Erdsünde*] of this world." [106] Accordingly, he viewed the Party and the Reich as no mere secular organization. Hitler said: "I consider those who establish or destroy a religion much greater than those who establish a State." Years later he proclaimed: "We are not a movement, rather we are a religion." [107] That he believed himself ordained by the Almighty is beyond question: "I hereby set forth for myself and my successors . . . the claim of political infallibility." He predicted, "I'm going to become a religious figure. Soon I'll be the chief of the Tartars. Already Arabs and Moroccans are mingling my name with their prayers." He often referred to the "inseparable Trinity": the state, the movement, and the *Volk.* "As the sign and symbol of his movement," Waite notes, "Hitler chose a special type of cross, and personally modified the design." [108]

Much of the fanaticism Hitler employed toward the Jewish Question can therefore be ascribed both to a twisted conception of the Christian ethic and to a messianic fervor bordering on the delusional—both of which are consistent with the personality features associated with long-standing psychomotor epilepsy. [109] If further evidence is required, one need only review the text of *Mein Kampf* from the perspective of its being written by a victim afflicted with this disorder.

One tragic result of Hitler's unrecognized personality disorder was his assimilation of messianic zeal and perseveration with blood as means of legitimizing unlimited obedience to his cause. He proclaimed that "whoever has sworn his oath of allegiance to Hitler has pledged himself unto death," and warned, "Woe to them who do not believe. These people have sinned . . . *sinned* against all of life." [110] Referring to the "disciples" who had fallen during the Beer Hall Putsch, he concluded that "their death would bring forth a true belief in the resurrection of their people. . . . The blood that they shed becomes the baptismal water of the Third Reich." [111] This metaphorical twist of turning, not water into wine, but blood into baptismal water, brings to mind one of the megalomaniacal delusions of Hitler's personality disorder—that he could change the unchangeable. This would have serious repercussions for the war effort.

As already implied, oral fixation is a peculiar characteristic of some temporal lobe epilepsy victims. Waite described Hitler as "an infallible dictator who anxiously sucked his little finger." [112] In speaking to the Hitler Youth in 1932, he charged them to be "either hot or cold, but lukewarm should be damned and spewed from your mouth." As Waite suggested: "The phrasing is too close to the New Testament to be coincidental." [113] The Book of Revelation reads: "Thou are neither cold nor hot. I would thou wert cold or hot. So then because thou art lukewarm, and neither cold nor hot, I will spew thee out of my mouth." [114] The neurologist might add that the inference to an orally related metaphor is also too close to the psychomotor-seizure characterization to be coincidental. [115]

The criteria of hypergraphia, messianism, and religiosity are therefore readily fulfilled in Hitler's case. Another typical feature in these cases is a worsening of temper and a well-executed aggression, often grounded in paranoia, which may result in the individual's estrangement from others. Gilroy and Meyer note that "Some patients exhibit antisocial behavior. This may take the form of moodiness, irritability, and outbursts of anger on slight provocation."[116] Even as a boy Hitler's temper knew no bounds, perhaps indicating the longevity of the disease. "In those early days in Vienna," August Kubizek observed, "I had the impression that Adolf had become unbalanced. He would fly into a temper at the slightest thing."[117] Certainly Hitler's retreat into isolation during the last years of the war—first at the *Wolfsschanze* in East Prussia and later at the bunker in Berlin, surrounded only by a few trusted confidants—is example enough of his increasingly antisocial behavior. His press secretary described the rigid limitations of what little social interaction he permitted himself during the last years of the war: "He remained perpetually in the same company, among the same faces, in the same atmosphere and . . . in the same state of monotony and boredom, producing eternally the same speeches and declarations." More than one observer noted that his ability to adjust to people in general was very poor. At social gatherings he was often "ill at ease, awkward, and moody."[118]

Descriptions of Hitler after 1941 abound with references to his outbursts of temper at the slightest provocation. A single example will serve to illustrate the point and to emphasize how destructive such behavior often was to his administration of the war effort. During a discussion of the Stalingrad campaign with his military advisors, who were attempting to bring some rational alternatives into consideration, Hitler refused to accept their pleas regarding troop deployment. His irrational response was both typical and illuminating as Chief of the Army General Staff Franz Halder recalled: "Hitler flew at the man who was reading, with clenched fists and foam in the corners of his mouth, and forbade him to read such idiotic twaddle."[119] This led Halder to conclude that Hitler's decisions regarding the conduct of the war with Russia "had ceased to have anything in common with the principles of strategy and operations as they had been recognized for generations past. They were the product of a violent nature." The Fuehrer dismissed his Chief of Staff on this occasion with a revealing epitaph. "You and I have been suffering from nerves," he told Halder. "Half of my nervous exhaustion is due to you. It is not worth it to go on. We need National Socialist ardour now, not professional ability."[120] From that point on, Hitler no longer ate with his staff officers.[121]

This vignette exemplifies several points. First, and most important, was the deleterious effect of an evolving personality disorder resulting, in part, from Hitler's suspected seizure disorder. Second, rather than even consider his top military advisors' rational appraisal of the situation, Hitler defensively reverted to a theme of spiritual resolve and messianic zeal. He substituted emotion for reason, attempting to change the unchangeable. This theme would be invoked time and again in his orders not to give any ground in any tactical military situation whatsoever. Third, unbridled paranoia triggered retreat into isolation, far removed from the advice of his most skilled subordinates and confidants.

With regard to any aberrant sexual behavior, still another criterion used to identify the psychomotor seizure personality, both Waite's and Langer's accounts document that aberrations existed in Hitler's case. Waite surmised that his sexual gratification may have been attained by the perversely masochistic practice of having the opposite sex defecate or urinate over his exposed head. [122] If such a claim stretches the limits of even the most fertile imagination, there remain still other equally telling examples of sexual aberrations in the available record. *Mein Kampf* is filled with sexual imagery. "Every chapter," according to Waite, "bespeaks a mind that is inordinately excited by rape, prostitution, syphilis, and the most disgusting sexual practices." [123] Depraved sexual practices were also among Hitler's favorite topics of conversation as a young man. [124] Any idea that his sexual views and practices may have been ordinary ones is dispelled by a reading of both Robert Waite and Walter Langer on the subject.

It may be significant that as early as 1920 Hitler appeared to require foster-mother relationships with older women. Indeed, many temporal lobe seizure victims develop a clinging dependency in their relations with parents or siblings. Frau Carola Hofman, a sixty-one-year-old widow was the first parental substitute, to be followed by Frau Helena Bechstein. Walter Langer noted that "Hitler would often sit at her feet and lay his head against her bosom while she stroked his hair tenderly and murmured, 'Mein Woelfchen'" (my little wolf). [125] By 1924, moreover, he had developed a strong sexual relationship with his niece, Geli, the daughter of his half sister. It was in fact Geli's description of the acts of defecation and urination that Langer cited in his work. After her death by suicide, Hitler went into profound depression for months.

Thereafter he began to cultivate an attraction to theater types. Aside from Eva Braun, there were two other actresses with whom Hitler kept company during the early 1930s, one of whom also took her own life. Indeed, six of the seven women with whom Hitler is believed to have had intimate relations attempted or succeeded in committing suicide. This and other data were sufficient enough for some investigators to suggest that Hitler had a "masochistic coprophilic perversion." [126] Langer probably understated the case by claiming that "Hitler's associates know that in respect to women Hitler is far from the ascetic he and the Propaganda Bureau would like to have the German public believe." [127]

On the other hand, some suspected him of being overtly homosexual. According to Langer, "Many of the inner circle were well-known homosexuals." Ernst Röhm, and possibly Rudolf Hess, were included among this group. There were others, and it is supposed that Hitler may have been guilty by association. One of Hitler's hobbies that appears to refute this assertion was his love for pornography. Hitler had a large collection of nudes and enjoyed viewing lewd movies in his private theater." [128] Paradoxically, his longstanding affair with Eva Braun was suspected to be largely asexual. Perhaps this is why it has been alleged that Hitler was impotent in his later years. [129] Possibly he was, for impotence is a frequent sequela known to occur in Parkinsonism.

The duality of Hitler's view of women is seen in the way he frequently linked aggression and fear with his sexual imagery. Hitler, according to Waite, "compared sexual intercourse to the trauma a soldier faces in battle." [130] He was fascinated by situations that placed women in danger. Circus acts and wild-animal acts held no interest for him unless they included beautiful women. "Then he watched avidly," Waite recorded, "his face flushed, and his breath came quickly in little whistling sounds as his lips worked violently." [131] Waite also noted that "Hitler was fond of quoting . . . Nietzsche: 'Thou goest to women? Do not forget thy whip!' Whips, of course, are the traditional symbol and sign of sadomasochistic impulses." [132] The psychoanalysts have used such information to explain Hitler's sexual conduct in terms of an unresolved Oedipal complex. Yet the paucity of available data on Hitler's infancy and early childhood compromises the highly readable, but largely theoretical, works of Walter Langer and Robert Waite. How can one build a case for an unresolved Oedipal complex when documented evidence related to Hitler's early life is so meager? On the other hand, all of these qualities—duality, fear, aggression, sexuality—are also semantic references neurologists apply to the psychomotor-seizure-induced personality disorder.

There is, then, substantial evidence to support the assertion that Adolf Hitler suffered from longstanding psychomotor epilepsy, with all the deleterious consequences that assertion implies. Hugh Trevor-Roper vividly summarized Hitler's personality, although he was unaware of the medical implications of what he was describing. He extracted a quote from *Mein Kampf* to highlight the delusions of grandeur that were so typical of Hitler. Yet knowledge of the characteristics of the personality disorder associated with temporal lobe epilepsy aids in assessing the real significance of Trevor-Roper's chosen extract:

> At long intervals in human history, it may occasionally happen that the practical politician and the political philosopher are one. . . . Such a man does not labour to satisfy the demands that are obvious to every philistine; he

reaches out toward ends that are comprehensible only to the few. . . . The protest of the present generation, which does not understand him, wrestles with the recognition of posterity, for whom he also works. [133]

Trevor-Roper further asserted that Hitler's own firm belief in his messianic mission was perhaps the most important element in the extraordinary power of his personality."[134] This is undoubtedly true, yet what has not been recognized to date is that Hitler's compelling power, ironically enough, may have been the product of an underlying personality disorder caused by a clandestine disease process, the ultimate effects of which were to trap Hitler into a growing web of self-destructive, uncontrollable impulses. The Final Solution and the approval of euthanasia and other "medical experiments" might be considered in part as negative results of that illness. As one German physician who has studied Hitler intensively suggested: "Knowing the punishment he inflicted tells us that probably he had at least some kind of personality disorder. . . . [Yet] Hitler was not insane. He had a political obsession that led him to attempt insane things."[135] Robert Waite summarized this aspect of the case succinctly when he stated that some political leaders "may find it both personally therapeutic and politically profitable to 'externalize' their internal conflicts."[136] The medical record would now suggest that in Hitler this may have been an uncontrolled process linked to organic disease.

One would suppose that the pain associated with cholecystitis; the depression, intellectual deterioration, and physical infirmities due to Parkinson's disease; and the negative aspects of a personality disorder secondary to undetected psychomotor seizures would be enough to indict Adolf Hitler's behavior on medical grounds alone. But there is more! It is now clear that Hitler suffered adversely from the administration of over *seventy* different medications at varying intervals between 1941 and 1945. The case for this was originally documented in 1965 by a German physician, Dr. H. D. Röhrs, and was subsequently brought to the American reader's attention by Werner Maser. Recently, it has been highlighted in the publication of Dr. Theodor Morell's diaries, edited by Dr. David Irving. These three investigators have presented the evidence but have not fully digested its significance. They may have made a few errors in interpretation and emphasis that need to be corrected.

For example, neurologists are now aware that some of the medications prescribed for Hitler would have accentuated an underlying seizure disturbance. One such controversial remedy given in large quantities was Doctor Koester's Anti-Gas Pills which contained strychnine and belladonna alkaloid (atropine). Hitler consumed an incredible number of these "little charcoal tablets" (up to 150 per week)[137] at his own discretion for his chronic gastrointestinal ailment. Strychnine was at one time employed for constipation on the assumption that it stimulated the gastrointestinal tract. Experiments have now shown this to be false. Today the poisonous drug has no place in this type of therapy. [138] It would have been of no benefit for Hitler's intestinal problems and would have had very deleterious side effects (both of which proved to be true).

Strychnine is known to induce seizures, probably because it interferes with the inhibition of impulse transmission between neurons. [139] The loss of physiologic inhibition predisposes toward uncontrolled transmission of electrical impulses, leading to seizures if the dose is significant. Strychnine, therefore, enhances neuron activity, and responses to sensory stimuli are exaggerated. It is a powerful convulsant. [140] Equally important, even if overt seizures do not occur, several notable researchers have documented that even with very low doses, toxic symptoms are manifested by a sense of excitement and marked irritability. [141]

Since Hitler is known to have taken at least sixteen tablets per day, and perhaps more, one would anticipate their having ominous effects on his behavior. Yet Irving states that, "As Morell's papers show, this was a completely harmless medicine." [142] There is certainly room for argument about this. Irving, an historian, bases his claim on the opinion of the German physician and nutritionist Ernst Gunther Schenck, who has said this about Dr. Koester's anti-gas pills:

> In one hundred twenty pills there would have been . . . 0.035 grams of strychnine [thirty-five milligrams]. So if Hitler had taken a dozen pills he would still have consumed one-tenth of these amounts. But the maximal permissible dose of strychnine was far more—one hundred milligrams per day. [143]

This last statement is misleading. Although different individuals will have varying levels of tolerance, Goodman, Goodman, and Gilman report that "the fatal adult dose of strychnine is about fifty milligrams . . . but thirty milligrams has been lethal." [144] Other investigators, in fact, have reported deaths with as little as 20 milligrams. [145]

Schenck's argument also ignores the cumulative effect of the poison. Eighty percent of the drug is metabolized in the liver. In Hitler's case, the periodic increase of urobilinogen and bilirubin in his urine (signifying altered biliary transport and conjugation) may imply that his ability to metabolize the drug had been compromised. It is known that Hitler took at least 120 tablets per week—and perhaps more, as his valet dispensed them at his request. Over a week's time this quantity at least equaled the possibly lethal thirty-five—milligram dose! Considering that he had intermittent liver and bile conjugation dysfunction during his last years, retarded metabolism of the drug by the liver might accentuate its toxicity on a cumulative basis. Indeed, E. Poulsson's German *Handbook of Pharmacology* warned contemporary physicians about the possibility of cumulative toxicity: "If small doses were taken over a long period, a sudden cumulative poisoning might result."[146] At the very least, then, Hitler was well within the range in which toxic effects would be expected, even if one ignores the problem of cumulative toxicity.

Erwin Giesing, however, calculated that but ten tablets per day would contain more than the permissible maximum dose of strychnine.[147] This is an opinion more in keeping with the views of most pharmacologists today. Equally important to the issue, and ignored by others, is the synergistic interaction of other drugs in the class of central nervous system stimulants Hitler was known to have used—among them Cardiazol (pentamethylenetetrazol), Pervitin (an analogue of amphetamine), Coramin (diethylnicotinamide) and cocaine—any of which, in conjunction with the simultaneous administration of strychnine, would augment the latter's effects.[148]

In 1941, Morell prescribed Cardiazol, which Maser notes was for "stimulation of the circulatory centre in the brain," and which Irving concludes was "to overcome the circulatory disorder evident from the edema observed [in Hitler's legs]."[149] Since there is no such defined anatomic "center" in the brain, this therapeutic use is questionable at best. There is, however, no doubt concerning the drug's action as a central nervous system stimulant. Its mode of action is different from strychnine, but its convulsive effects are well known. In fact, its therapeutic use today, when given intravenously, is to activate the EEG as a diagnostic aid in epilepsy! As Goodman, Goodman, and Gilman note, "Subconvulsive doses of the drug . . . will often activate *latent epileptogenic foci* [emphasis mine]. In addition, pentamethylenetetrazol-induced convulsions are of value in characterizing underlying cerebral disorders in patients with proven epilepsy."[150] It is interesting indeed that Hitler would be taking a drug from 1941 onward whose specific use today is to *elicit* seizure activity for the purpose of diagnosis! More interesting still, Morell allowed Hitler unlimited use of Cardiazol.[151] Even if the amount taken may have been small, this drug is known to be "readily absorbed from all sites of administration, and is rapidly and equally distributed throughout the tissues."[152] Its provocative effect alone on Hitler's underlying seizure disorder therefore cannot be discounted.[153]

Morell used Coramin for the same purposes as Cardiazol. This class of drugs also stimulates the central nervous system: Appropriate doses produce tremors in both men and laboratory animals; with somewhat larger doses, the tremor is followed by convulsions.[154] This drug would have not only lowered the seizure threshold like the other drugs discussed; in Hitler's case its action may have had an additive impact upon his tremor from Parkinson's disease. It too is primarily metabolized by the liver: "Toxicity may be manifested by nausea, abdominal pain, . . . headaches, disturbed vision, mental confusion and marked weakness."[155] Its effects must again be considered additive and detrimental to Hitler's behavior aberrations, and as implied by the last description, it may have played some additional role in his gastrointestinal disturbances.

Hitler was also the willing recipient of daily doses of Morell's own manufactured product, the golden Vitamultin tablets. These contained Pervitin and caffeine.[156] Captain Heinz Assmann, who observed Hitler daily as his adjutant until April 23, 1945, maintained "that there were always grounds to believe that the shots Adolf Hitler got were beefed up with stimulants such as Pervitin."[157] Irving thought that it was unlikely Pervitin was administered, "as Morell knew of its dangers."[158] It is puzzling that Irving accepted Ernst-Günther Schenck's arguments in relation to strychnine but ignored his testimony in regard to Vitamultin:

> One day in 1942 or 1943 I received from a reliable quarter some small 'golden' tablets. . . . I was told that these 'golden' Vitamultins were provided exclusively for the Führer by Morell. . . . [After having them analyzed] I learnt that the powder contained caffeine and Pervitin in what seemed to me a truly horrifying concentration.[159]

Moreover, on November 17, 1944, Morell wrote a prescription for Eupaverinum plus Pervitin,[160] indicating that he was not immune to using it when he felt it necessary. Indeed Irving did admit that "a mysterious special version of Morell's patented Vitamultin product appears [eight months before the above prescription was written], denoted only as 'Vitamultin-forte'—evidently it contained a special additive not used in the others."[161] The dramatic effect on Hitler with the first injection of Vitamultin-forte makes it clear that this was yet another central nervous system stimulant. "Before the injection he was very limp and tired, . . . after it he came to life at once . . . and stayed wide awake a long time tonight."[162] Pervitin, as an amphetamine analogue, is one of a class of drug known to be a very potent stimulator of the central nervous system. For the purpose of discussing Hitler's case, the following pharmacologic actions should be underscored: (1) certain adverse effects of amphetamine toxicity can be elicited in any individual if sufficient quantities are ingested for a prolonged period; (2) these include restlessness, tremor, talkativeness, tenseness, irritability, insomnia, confusion, assaultiveness, increased libido, anxiety, paranoid hallucinations, and panic states; (3) the psychic effects depend on the mental status and personality of the individual—in effect accentuating premorbid personality traits; (4) amphetamines accelerate and desynchronize the EEG.[163]

As the first point above indicates, in order to judge the toxic effects, one must know the dosage and frequency of administration. This information is difficult to cull from the data in Morell's diary, due to the variable composition of the Vitamultin tablets. It may be, as Irving asserts, that the standard variety of Vitamultin preparations contained no Pervitin at all. Nonetheless, after March 1944 Morell increasingly utilized intravenous doses of a new preparation, the mysterious Vitamultin-forte, and on occasion his diary also refers to its analogue in a tablet form. From Morell's own description of Hitler's response, the evidence is strong that these fortified preparations contained Pervitin. They were a mainstay in Morell's pharmacologic armamentarium after that date. Ingestion (let alone the more-powerful intravenous administration) of any amphetamine over a period as short as three months is regularly observed to induce a paranoid psychosis nearly indistinguishable from paranoid schizophrenia. [164] And Morell did deal in large quantities. He placed one order on February 20, 1943, for "ten packets of two hundred Vitamultin tablets for headquarters." His diary entries over just the two weeks following the initial March 14 injection of Vitamultin-forte contain references to at least six different administrations of the fortified drug. [165] This is enough to dispel any question of insufficient quantity or infrequent exposure over time.

Concerning the second point, the adverse toxic manifestations of amphetamines listed by both the American Medical Association and Kaplan's *Comprehensive Textbook of Psychiatry* read like a comprehensive description of Hitler's daily behavior. "Larger doses," according to the AMA, "cause apprehension, volubility, and excitement. Other prominent effects include impulsiveness, aggressiveness, and poor judgment." [166] In Drs. Freedman and Sadock's words, "There are delusions of persecution and ideas of reference. The paranoid state is often preceded by restlessness, increased irritability, and increased perceptual sensitivity. The patient often experiences . . . visual hallucinations, frequently of a bizarre nature." [167]

With regard to the third observation, the psychic effects on Hitler would have been serious. Indeed, the hallucinogenic syndrome of chronic amphetamine abuse bears a close resemblance to that seen in the personality disorder of temporal lobe epilepsy. [168] An accentuation of Hitler's personality disorder might therefore be expected with the addition of amphetamines. That is to say, this medication would be anticipated to have a more profound effect on an individual of Hitler's temperament and character.

Finally, the fact that the drug desynchronizes the EEG is important because seizure activity is, simply stated, nothing more than a barrage of abnormally activated cortical neuronal impulses. That being the case, the drug's effect in activating neuronal excitability (which is what most central nervous system stimulants do) would lower the seizure threshold in various epilepsy states—including that from Adolf Hitler's temporal lobe.

Morell's Vitamultin also contained caffeine, another central nervous system stimulant whose effects are well known to the general public and require no further discussion except to acknowledge that excessive amounts cause reflex excitability, with chronic symptoms that include insomnia, restlessness, and irritability,[169] all of which Hitler suffered from on an almost daily basis. Its synergistic effect in combination with the amphetamine contained in the same compound would further serve to augment the hyperexcitable state that characterized the unstable Fuehrer—if not to precipitate psychomotor seizures in concert.

After July 1944—when Hitler barely escaped being assassinated by a bomb blast—his ear, nose, and throat physician, Dr. Erwin Giesing, began to prescribe twice-daily inhalations of cocaine and frequent swabbing of the nostrils with the same drug in 10 percent concentrations to combat Hitler's acute and chronic suppurative sinusitis. Still another associate recalled Hitler faithfully crouching for hours each morning and evening over an inhalator containing cocaine.[170] This is also documented in Morell's diary. Hitler in fact began to look forward to his twice-daily treatments with cocaine—not surprising, considering the amount administered.[171]

Ear, nose, and throat specialists today would recognize that 10 percent cocaine inhaled or applied to mucous membranes twice daily for long periods represents a cumulative dose far above the permissible range. Indeed, on three separate occasions after cocaine treatments Hitler complained of dizziness and giddiness,[172] and he actually overdosed on one occasion, to the horrified dismay of Giesing, who was the physician-in-attendance administering the drug. This occurred on October 1, 1944. Giesing had just administered 10 percent cocaine to Hitler's left nostril with the patient lying down.

> A few moments later [he recorded] I noted that Hitler's eyes were closed and that . . . his face, previously rather flushed, had turned pale. I took his pulse which was . . . rapid and weak. . . . I asked Hitler how he felt and I received no reply. He had obviously suffered a slight collapse . . . and was not responsive. . . . Just then Hitler's face grew even paler and for a moment his features twitched convulsively.[173]

Giesing had apparently witnessed an abbreviated "major motor" (as opposed to psychomotor) seizure as a result of an acute overdose of cocaine. Neurologists are aware that cocaine is a convulsant in large doses—and the drug has little margin of safety. Rather than developing tolerance, as is often seen with narcotics, the cocaine abuser is frequently sensitized and may experience toxic effects from doses he previously tolerated. [174]

The drug's mechanisms of actions and toxic symptoms are well known: "Cocaine stimulates the central nervous system generally. . . . As the dose is increased, tremors and eventually tonic-clonic convulsions may result from stimulation of lower motor centers and enhancement of cord reflexes." [175] Absorption of cocaine through mucous membranes is also enhanced if these are inflamed (and Hitler's were, chronically), so the systemic effects of his nasal swabbings may therefore have been markedly increased. Solutions employed clinically for surface anesthesia vary from 1 to 10 percent. Hitler was therefore receiving the maximum dose twice daily. More troubling still is the realization that during this period he was also taking frequent doses of Sympathol (a catecholamine), which has the potential for interacting dangerously with cocaine. [176] If that is not enough to capture the attention of the skeptic consider the fact that cocaine and amphetamines, when taken together, are known to be a "potentially lethal drug combination"! [177]

Although tolerance to the convulsant and cardiorespiratory effects of cocaine has been reported in isolated cases, the preponderant medical view today suggests that the central nervous system will show increased sensitivity to toxic levels when the drug is administered repeatedly. [178] The fully developed toxic syndrome includes vivid visual, auditory, and sometimes tactile hallucinations, and there is also paranoid ideation, loosening of associations, and changes in affect occurring in association with a clear sensorium (awareness of the immediate environment). [179] The latter is an important observation in Hitler's case, as his enigmatic behavior may not have been recognized as secondary to drug effect—as would have been more easily recognized in other forms of narcotic addiction in which sensorium is clearly altered.

To this group of central nervous system stimulants one may add belladonna, another ingredient of Dr. Koester's anti-gas pills. Belladonna is a pharmacologic agent almost as deleterious as strychnine if taken in large enough doses. Hitler's own physicians knew this, and a controversy between them developed over its use in combination with strychnine. According to Irving, "an analysis of the actual composition of the antigas pills [by Dr. Schenck] suggests that Brandt, Giesing, and Hasselbach had willingly exaggerated their toxicity in an attempt to dislodge Morell." [180] Yet Morell himself was horrified by the amount Hitler was taking, judging from the entry in his diary of October 3, 1944, at the height of the physicians' dispute over the pills:

> I declared that I had never prescribed this intense consumption of the anti-gas pills and that I had heard of it these last few days with horror. . . . [Hitler] said he had been taking them for about two years, and for the last few months at a rate of about sixteen pills per day, . . . that he had been taking them on his own initiative. [181]

Hitler certainly seems then to have been taking larger quantities than Schenck assumed when he made his calculations.

Giesing surmised that the pills had a great deal to do with Hitler's poor health, and eventually told him so. His revelation, tragically enough, caused himself and other physicians far more reputable than Morell to fall into disfavor with Hitler, as the Fuehrer ultimately sided with his accused doctor. This was to have ominous implications for the future medical management of Hitler's rapidly deteriorating health. He had been overdosing himself with two poisons—atropine (belladonna) and strychnine. Giesing postulated (probably incorrectly) that all of his intestinal problems, including jaundice, were due to the pills. He was, however, correct in relating them to other symptoms Hitler was experiencing after taking some of the "suspect black pills" himself. Immediately thereafter, Giesing noted the same symptoms: "extreme sensitivity, photophobia, acuteness of taste, and increased thirst." [182] According to Toland, Giesing postulated that "perhaps that explained [Hitler's] attacks, his growing debility; his irritability and aversion to light; his hoarse, dry throat, and the strange reddish tinge of his skin." [183] Evidently without realizing it, Giesing was describing many features of belladonna toxicity. In the words of one of the best current neurological textbooks: "Early restlessness and irritability may resemble an acute psychosis. . . . Frequent giddiness and muscle tremors develop. The pupils are dilated and respond poorly to light; consequently blurred vision and photophobia may be constant and annoying." [184] This description is supported by Drs. Goodman, Goodman, and Gilman:

> The mouth becomes dry and burns [Hitler's lips were noted to be dry and cracked]. There is marked thirst [a frequent complaint of Hitler's]. Vision is blurred and photophobia is prominent [a persistent complaint]. The skin is hot, dry and flushed ["strange reddish tinge of his skin"]. The patient is restless, excitable and confused and exhibits weakness and giddiness. [Joseph Goebbels frequently noted Hitler's complaint of "giddiness"]. Memory is disturbed [a side effect of his bad health was deterioration of his remarkable memory], orientation is faulty, and hallucinations, especially visual, are common. The syndrome may be punctuated by convulsions. [185]

Not only are the belladonna alkaloids, like all other central nervous system stimulants discussed thus far, capable of causing seizures; most of the manifestations consistent with toxicity from this medication in particular were documented in Hitler's case.

A further word about Schenck's calculations, on which Irving relied: In 120 pills, he calculated that there were 75 milligrams of the toxic alkaloid atropine.[186] Using the same quantity of twelve pills per day he had applied to the strychnine calculations (a conservative figure, since it was acknowledged in Morell's edited diary that Hitler took at least sixteen tablets per day), 7.5 milligrams of atropine would have represented the approximate minimal daily dose Hitler was taking. Goodman, Goodman, and Gilman have eloquently tabulated reproducible toxic effects of atropine analogues in specific doses. At two milligrams, palpitations, dryness of mouth, dilated pupils and blurring of near vision is noted. At five milligrams all of the above symptoms are marked, plus disturbance of speech, difficulty swallowing, restlessness and fatigue, headache, and dry hot skin. By the time ten milligram dosages are reached, vision is very blurred, the skin is flushed and scarlet, there is an unsteady gait, restlessness and excitement are pronounced, and hallucinations and delirium may result.[187] This would correlate roughly with Giesing's calculations that just ten of the pills contained the maximum daily dose of extract from belladonna.[188] Clearly, then, Hitler showed deleterious side effects of the medication, both by calculation and by observed symptomatology. Once one accepts that Giesing was essentially correct in his calculations regarding atropine, one is even more prepared to believe what he had calculated in regard to strychnine (see p. 179). At the very least, Hitler showed detrimental side effects from both medications—not to mention the provocative effects of these drugs on his suspected seizure disorder.

This discussion of a handful of central nervous system stimulants, chosen from among the seventy-odd medications Morell gave Hitler, is enough to establish the case for a polypharmacy syndrome that affected Hitler's conduct in a most significant and sinister way. Those interested in the often-dangerous drug interactions that may have resulted from various combinations of such a formidable list of medications should consult Eric Martin's exhaustive work *The Hazards of Medication,* which cannot be recommended too highly. Suffice it to say that such an exercise would extend far beyond the scope of this review—not to mention the reader's patience.

There remain only two final items of significance in this pharmacologic dissertation: the subject of narcotic addiction, in which the medication Eukodal played a part, and the antibiotic Ultraseptyl, which is the only medication that David Irving seems willing to indict Theodor Morell for prescribing. In Irving's opinion, Dr. Morell's diary dispels any notion that Hitler may have been addicted to narcotics. Yet, some of Hitler's own physicians were worried about that possibility. Erwin Giesing was later to testify:

> Not that Hitler was your common drug addict, but his neuropathic constitution led to his finding certain drugs, like strychnine and atropine . . . and the cocaine in the sinus treatments I gave him, particularly pleasurable; and there was a clear inclination toward becoming an habitual user of such medications as he himself admitted to be. [189]

Admittedly, Giesing was not referring to narcotics; yet any of the central nervous system stimulants previously discussed are capable of fostering drug dependency.

One medication not given sufficient emphasis in Irving's account was the pain-killer Eukodal, frequently used intravenously to treat Hitler's abdominal pains. In Appendix II of his work, Irving acknowledges that the medication was listed as a controlled substance in the Narcotics Act, as it was a "synthetic morphium derivative." [190] Its nonproprietary name is dihydrohydroxycodeinon hydrochloride, but its precise analogue in present-day medicine has the tradename Percodan [191] and is one of the most dangerously addicting, and hence abused, *oral* pain medications on the market. Hitler was receiving this medication at frequent intervals *intravenously*. The usual dose is ten to fifteen milligrams orally. [192] The intravenous dosage prescribed by Morell was twenty milligrams [193]— nearly double the recommended dose, and injected directly into the bloodstream.

At least one of Hitler's physicians, Hans Karl von Hasselbach, was bothered by the fact that "none of his other doctors knew what was in those jabs of his." His suspicions may have been allayed, however, by a conversation with Morell; the latter claimed to "never have injected morphine, but only hormones, vitamins, and glucose." [194] Morell's extant diary entries contradict his own statement, showing that Eukodal was injected on no less than sixteen occasions beginning on July 18, 1943. How many more times the drug was given can only be surmised, as in almost every entry Morell simply recorded "injections as always." [195]

Oxycodone (Percodan) is almost as potent as morphine, and is ten to twelve times more potent than codeine. [196] Is it any surprise that the abdominal colic from which Hitler suffered was invariably and almost instantaneously relieved by the injected cocktail containing this potent narcotic? Approximately two-thirds of these opiate analgesics leave the blood and accumulate in the tissues. Enterohepatic circulation also occurs, prolonging their presence in the body, so that small amounts are routinely found in the urine for several days after a normal dosage of ten to fifteen milligrams. [197] One can well imagine the tissue accumulation that would have occurred by doubling the recommended dosage. Considering the tenuous condition of Hitler's hepatobiliary system, one might expect that the drug's breakdown would be still further reduced in his case. In fact, Goodman, Goodman, and Gilman warn that "all of the opioid analgesics are metabolized by the liver, and these drugs should be used with caution in patients with [biliary] disease."[198] Moreover, small doses of amphetamine substantially increase the effects of opioid analgesics—yet another perilous example of drug synergism.[199]

Was Hitler, then, addicted to opiates? Considering the infrequency with which such narcotics are used in clinical medicine, addiction as a complication of traditional medical treatment is uncommon. It is doubtful that Hitler was in fact addicted, as the administration *appears* from the record to have been intermittent. One cannot be sure. Nonetheless, the large dosages employed would probably have been sufficient to create an "abstinence syndrome" between injections. What would this have meant for Hitler? According to Goodman, Goodman, and Gilman,

> This syndrome is known to include loss of appetite, restlessness, irritability, insomnia and tremor. Weakness and depression may be pronounced. Abdominal cramps are also characteristic. Weight loss and dehydration may ensue. Most of the grossly observed symptoms disappear in seven to ten days, but it is uncertain how long it takes to restore physiologic equilibrium completely. In addition, there seems to be behavioral manifestations including incapacity to tolerate stress, and an over-concern about discomfort.[200]

It is noteworthy that Morell was to wrestle with every one of these characteristics from time to time after 1942. One may infer from such evidence as the following description recorded by Field Marshal Gerd von Rundstedt that Hitler experienced periods of anxiety during such abstinence: "Since September 1944, Hitler loses himself in details, and questions why this pillbox or that has not been fortified."[201] All too frequently today clinicians encounter this same drug dependency in Percodan users taking less of this medication orally than Hitler was taking intravenously.

One final very recent revelation concerning the effect of synthetic opioid derivatives is of particular interest in relation to Hitler's Parkinson's disease. In December 1983 physicians in San Francisco uncovered evidence linking bad batches of synthetic street heroin to the production of Parkinson's disease symptoms in more than twenty heroin addicts. Interestingly enough, this toxic drug was concocted in illicit laboratories, much as many of Morell's own remedies were manufactured in his own factories. Dr. J. William Langston, Chief of Neurology at the Santa Clara Valley Medical Center, reported that "the Parkinson symptoms could strike days, weeks, months, or even a year after injections of the bad substance."[202] This report naturally has intriguing implications for Hitler's medical history, above and beyond drug dependency alone. It probably was the cause of his Parkinson's disease.

One other medication manufactured in Morell's laboratories was his own brand of sulfonamides (sulfa drugs). Hitler was known to be subjected to large doses of Morell's patent variety of sulfanilamide, called Ultraseptyl. He received up to six grams per day, some by injection, others by tablet. This led David Irving to conclude:

> One thing is certain. Many of Morell's medicines were quite harmless, and he injected the others in such minute quantities that they would have been virtually useless. . . . The same charitable view cannot be taken of his lavish use of inferior proprietary sulfanilamines like Ultraseptyl, long after they had been publicly exposed as toxic by experts. [203]

The drug was known by 1942 occasionally to crystallize out in the renal tubules, thereafter obstructing them, and yet Morell used the antibiotic for every conceivable malady. Irving was right to condemn Morell in this matter, but he overemphasized the drug's dangers. Physicians even today prescribe any number of antibiotics almost as a panacea for a variety of viral illnesses (including the common cold) with no real therapeutic effect, since antibiotics do not affect viruses. Furthermore, the "shock treatments" described by Irving of five to seven courses of up to six grams per day totaled little more than the standard doses of the drug used today. Current pharmacologic texts report that less than 5 percent of those treated with sulfa drugs will experience untoward reactions. [204] Goodman, Goodman, and Gilman acknowledge that with the older sulfonamides, crystallization in the kidney tubules was an occasional problem, but Hitler neither suffered from overt renal (kidney) disease, nor did his frequent urine analyses reveal significant renal damage.

Among the reported list of miscellaneous reactions to sulfonamides, effects upon the nervous system are described by Goodman, Goodman, and Gilman as very uncommon, with neuropsychiatric disturbances occurring less than 1 percent of the time. [205] Any legitimate concern with the "neurotoxicity" of the drug, then, is unfounded. Although Irving asserted that the "unfortunate role of the sulfonamide drug Ultraseptyl on Hitler's health becomes apparent from these diaries,"[206] it is neither apparent nor of justifiable concern. In truth, among the formidable armamentarium of deleterious drugs to which Hitler was subjected, Ultraseptyl must surely have been one of the *least* significant of the lot. Within the forest of polypharmacy, Irving focused on a sapling and ignored the numerous, and far larger, trees of central nervous system stimulants.

In like manner, the Hestons have not placed enough emphasis on the overriding consideration of polypharmacy, given their enthusiasm for building a legitimate case for amphetamine and cocaine abuse. In the introduction to their work, they state: "We will make diagnoses that we think are so highly probable that in the light of the evidence, few will contend them." True enough—given the diagnoses they make and the evidence they present to support them. Taking the forest analogy one step farther: Not only have the shadows of the largest trees of amphetamines obscured the recognition of other elements, such as Parkinson's disease, they have camouflaged the grounds of a personality disorder consistent with temporal lobe epilepsy as it was affected by the forest of other central nervous system stimulants. Ernst Gunther Schenck, for one, did not ignore the polypharmacy issue, as he alluded to 92 drugs in all to which Hitler was exposed. He concluded: "Hitler's basic treatment was pharmacological, and by today's standards, the amounts are incredible."[207]

One cannot really understand how Hitler came to suffer from polypharmacy without knowing something about Theodor Morell. Who was he? How did he establish his medical authority in Adolf Hitler's eyes, and how did he maintain it in spite of his methods and in the face of his colleagues' criticisms? In a word, what was the attraction between the neurotic national leader and this greedy, self-serving doctor of sorts? Trevor-Roper speaks for most historians and physicians in asserting:

> It is difficult to speak [of Morell] in the measured terms and discreet vocabulary proper to his profession. He was a quack. . . . But Hitler not only chose him . . . [he surrendered] his person . . . to the disastrous experiments of a charlatan. [208]

Morell's contemporaries apparently shared this opinion. Joseph Goebbels recorded in his diary that "orthodox medical circles considered him a phony."[209] Dr. Karl Brandt concurred: "He was a businessman, not a doctor, very greedy and very stingy."[210]

Some have hypothesized that the friendship that had evolved between Frau Morell and Eva Braun may have been reason enough for Hitler to choose Morell from among other doctors. David Irving delved more deeply. Morell had married a wealthy screen actress, which afforded him both a luxurious practice in Berlin and exposure to the elite of the city. He was probably introduced to Hitler through screen friends, as Hitler himself is known to have had a keen interest in movie stars. It also seems that Morell had cured Hitler's photographer, Heinrich Hoffmann, of gonorrhea, legitimizing his self-proclaimed expertise in venereal disease—at least in the eyes of the Fuehrer. In 1936 Hitler personally solicited the doctor to deal with his perplexing stomach problems and eczema, which up to that point had defied traditional medical treatment. Here, too, Morell was apparently dramatically successful. No other proof was necessary. [211] For the next eight years, he would be allowed to use his borderline medical skills on the leader of Germany's Third Reich.

Karl Brandt was one of Hitler's less-influential physicians, but he also owed his position as much to serendipity as to any other factor. Like Morell, his association with Hitler stemmed initially from a marital relationship, having betrothed one Anni Reyborn, whom Hitler had known through his one-time chauffeur. [212] Like Morell, Brandt's successful treatment of a Hitler associate propelled him into a highly visible position. In Brandt's case it was one of Hitler's adjutants, who had been injured in an automobile accident. [213]

The quality of his physicians' skills and training, then, held little interest for Hitler. Morell had advertised himself as a skin and venereal disease expert. He had no postgraduate training in these areas, yet his timely success with bold, if unfounded, techniques attracted Hitler, who characteristically disdained "experts" of whatever variety—be they in the field of military strategy or medical practice. "I know that Morell's new-fangled methods are still not recognized internationally," he said, "but isn't that how it has always been with innovations in medicine?" [214] This antipathy toward all experts may represent as satisfactory an explanation as any of why most top party officials also favored doctors of dubious repute. Heinrich Himmler and Rudolf Hess patronized non-medical practitioners and masseurs, and Joachim von Ribbentrop as well as Goebbels consulted Morell on a regular basis. [215]

Karl Brandt had been schooled in more traditional circles of German medicine and was much less impressed than his Fuehrer with Theodor Morell. He was concerned that Morell might literally have "ensnared Hitler by intravenous injections of morphine or hormones, or by playing upon his gratitude." [216] If morphine per se cannot be implicated in the record, perhaps the injections of Eukodal played a more significant part here in the later years than has been acknowledged. Undeniably, mutual gratitude also served to solidify the bonds of dependency between the two. As late as November 1944, Hitler was to salute his physician: "My dear doctor, I am pleased and happy that I have you." [217] The Fuehrer accepted ostensible cures for his ailments, fleeting though they were, in return for giving both financial and personal support to Morell's pot-pourri of research and drug manufactures. "The moment he needs financial support for his researches he'll get it from me," [218] Hitler once said.

Trevor-Roper concluded that Morell's position with Hitler depended upon his weaknesses, not his skill. [219] Having once established himself

*Morell receiving the Knight's Cross for services rendered*

as a "specialist," Morell thereafter found it financially profitable to manufacture patent remedies, and he needed buyers. Purchases of his products were sometimes made compulsory nationwide by the Fuehrer. With such formidable backing, Hitler's physician was able to monopolize the market for his own company's manufactured drugs. [220] Irving thought that this activity was harmless enough, but correctly indicted Morell's use of new drugs without sufficient testing of their side effects. [221] He also asserted that Morell was both cautious and methodical. In truth, Morell was to exercise caution in only one particular detail—that of covering his own tracks with a recorded account of his medical ministrations to Hitler. He needed to keep a diary, Irving surmised, "to provide the Gestapo with detailed records of his treatments and sessions with Hitler lest something befall his top patient." [222] Since the diary was a tool for self-preservation, it hardly appears that with its publication "the medical picture of the world's most infamous dictator is now complete," as Irving would have us believe. [223]

The case against Morell cannot, and must not, be dismissed. Several of the medications he prescribed, in concert with Hitler's Parkinson's disease and possible psychomotor epilepsy, deleteriously affected this leader's conduct in affairs of state and war. In the end, Werner Maser concluded, it was above all else "his deteriorating health that affected the course of the war."[224] The evidence shows that Maser's assertion can be generally substantiated.

Among other reasons for the transition in Hitler's health, and consequently his behavior, a statement by Joseph Goebbels adds to this list the effect of isolation on the Fuehrer by March 1942:

> I became especially conscious of this during a talk with Hitler's personal adjutant Julius Schaub. . . . The Fuehrer practically lives in a concentration camp. . . . The loneliness of General Headquarters and the whole method of working there naturally have at long last an extraordinarily depressing effect upon the Fuehrer. The solitude in which he is compelled to perform his duties must sooner or later affect him deeply and gnaw at his vitals. . . . The superficial impression is that he is in the very best physical shape. In reality this is not the case.[225]

Was this penchant for isolation compelled by the performance of his duties? Was it a manifestation of his documented antisocial behavior? Or was it a result of illness, perceived or real? The record would indicate the latter factor to be of great, perhaps preeminent, importance.

As early as 1938 Hitler volunteered to Albert Speer that anxiety about his health created in him a sense of temporal urgency. He felt he had not long to live. According to Trevor-Roper, he believed he had a weak heart, and after 1938 avoided all forms of exercise."[226] This, and his fear of adverse exposure to the elements, served to isolate him. Trevor-Roper believes that Hitler's heart disease was imaginary: "In [the] rarified atmosphere [of the Bavarian Alps,] he felt a tightening of his chest, which he ascribed to the weakness of his heart; but his doctors found no evidence of such a condition."[227] We now know that Morell diagnosed "rapidly progressing coronary sclerosis" on the basis of electrocardiograms made in 1941 and 1943, which was confirmed by an esteemed German cardiologist.[228] Partly as a response to his perceived cardiac condition, and perhaps as a gesture of self-defense to protect himself from the detrimental effects of bad news, Hitler remained cloistered away in his barren quarters at the *Wolfsschanze* from 1941 until 1944. The effect of this isolation on his conduct of the war, the consequent surrendering of his previous gift for mobilizing public opinion through the spoken word, and his increasing preoccupation with himself (most notably with his bodily functions) were all detrimental to effective leadership.

The timing of his self-imposed isolation was particularly critical in relation to the war and his relationship with the military. Already by 1941 a large segment of the General Staff had become critical of the direction of the war effort. [229] Following the disastrous Stalingrad campaign in 1942 and 1943, Hitler refused to allow any serious input from his leading military advisors. Yet he blamed them when things went wrong. It is a measure of his increasing paranoia and intransigence that only one of Hitler's seventeen field marshals served throughout the war. [230]

This peculiar behavior is in fact consistent with neurologically compromised individuals, who demonstrate increasing rigidity of thought and lash out defensively when their views are contested—largely because their mental infirmities prevent them from appraising alternatives rationally. Such individuals feel most comfortable when they avoid exposure to what is distasteful to them. Yet any chance for successful rehabilitation rests with maintaining them in a milieu of social interaction. Trevor-Roper suggested just such a well-recognized medical therapeutic rule-of-thumb in nonmedical terms: "It is the disappearance of criticism, not the inherent errors of his thought, which made Hitler's strategy in the end as calamitous as his politics."[231] One would therefore anticipate a deterioration between Hitler and his staff under the circumstances of isolation imposed by this dangerously ill man. His solitude pathologically enhanced the effects of his neurologic illness, and these effects adversely influenced his conduct of military affairs.

Other writers have chosen to highlight exclusively psychoanalytic causes for the decline in Hitler's military capabilities. Robert Waite postulated an "unconscious urge for self-destruction."[232] Indeed, this writer admitted to advancing "cautious guesses" when the recognition of organic disease would have sufficed. He suggested that Hitler's fateful military decisions were influenced by three things: "his lifelong difficulty with personal identification; his unconscious desire for defeat; and his irrational belief that ultimate triumph lay in total destruction."[233] The following criticism of these assertions is not intended to dismiss Waite's arguments out of hand. Many are compelling and thoughtfully presented. Waite held that most of Hitler's impulsive acts were the products of a "borderline personality disorder." He cited many credible examples. In declaring war inexplicably against the United States, Hitler may have chosen to attempt to defeat an even stronger opponent than Russia. In trying to resolve the question of who he was he may have provoked a crisis to affirm his own existence. In the end, Waite argues, "if he could not be creator, he would be destroyer"—a realization that may have come to him during the stalled offensive in Russia in 1941. The extent of Hitler's destructive impulses may also have spawned orders to massacre the Jews. In fact, Waite suggests that Hitler's whole conception of things may have stemmed from a preoccupation with *"how to achieve a catastrophic defeat worthy of his historic greatness."* [234]

This is heady stuff, and it contains elements of truth from a psychoanalytic perspective. But the argument is blunted by the author's complete absorption with Freudian hypotheses to the exclusion of any consideration of organic illness. [235] On the other hand, the borderline personality disorder Waite so graphically described is really quite consistent with similar but more specific behavior patterns that occur in temporal lobe epilepsy victims of long standing, augmented by the astounding combination of drugs Hitler was taking. Perhaps this conclusion fills the void of understanding alluded to by those physicians who knew Hitler. "I was never able to explain Hitler's personality to my own satisfaction," Morell admitted in a rare interview in 1945. [236] Forty years later, Schenck added that "I, too, am not satisfied." [237]

Waite was certainly correct in acknowledging that Hitler suffered from a personality disorder, and his argument is bolstered by testimony from many psychiatric experts. What this review is suggesting is not a refutation of that *description* but an organic cause for its *origins*, based on a less psychoanalytic analysis. If Waite accurately described the personality disorder, the psychomotor epilepsy thesis gives it medically based credibility. If that author emphasized Hitler's paranoid tendencies, his belief in magical omnipotence, his aggressive oral demands, his gross forms of sexual perversion, his infantile behavior, and his splitting of the ego, the same features are characteristic of the temporal lobe seizure victim. Further, there are other characteristics—hypergraphia, religiosity, and belief in his own destiny—that are also typical of this personality type and are not comfortably assimilated into the generalized "borderline personality disorder" thesis described by this investigator.

Waite also declared that "neurological findings may deepen and complement psychohistorical understanding; they cannot replace it." [238] A neurologist would assert the opposite—that, given the existence of a well-documented neurologic disability, one should not ignore the presence of organic disease in favor of psychoanalysis. In this respect, psychohistorical findings may deepen and complement our understanding of the secondary effects of bona fide neurologic illness, but they should not replace them.

From a psychological viewpoint, Waite saw a continuity of behavior in Hitler's life springing from early childhood experiences. This assertion has not been universally accepted, and understandably so. Most other writers correctly perceive that Hitler's behavior diverged from the norm after 1941. Percy Ernst Schramm, for example, took a rather traditional historical view of that transformation:

> Hitler changed during the war. The reverses on the battlefield had a profound effect upon him. He did not draw the obvious military conclusions from the grave crises [after 1941]. . . . He *did* react to them by becoming more obstinant, more unteachable, or, in Hitler's language, more fanatical. [239]

But even such a traditionalist as Schramm raised the question of whether illness may have affected Hitler's attitude: "To what degree this rigidity can be attributed to physiological factors remains unanswered. But Hitler continued, in the everyday sense of the word, to be more or less 'normal' to the very end." [240]

Others have been unable to believe that Hitler's behavior was "normal" in any way, nor could they ignore his physical infirmities. Werner Maser, for one, properly but insufficiently underscored the influences of Hitler's medications on his thought processes and observed that Hitler's behavior "could not be considered normal in the strictest sense of the word." [241] Maser considered a few of the central nervous system stimulants discussed earlier and concluded:

> As early as the autumn of 1940 and more especially when, in the spring of 1941, his medical adviser first began prescribing *Coramine, Cardiazol, Pervitin* and caffeine, it became clear that certain of his decisions and declarations were not subject to rational control. Under the influence of these drugs he would sometimes make fantastically exaggerated assertions. . . . Because such measures were sometimes included in memoranda that were otherwise unimpeachable, . . . his entourage, and more especially the military, remained almost wholly unaware that their author was not always *compos mentis*. [242]

Yet Maser was overstating the case when he said that the military may not have been aware of Hitler's unstable frame of mind. As early as 1941, General Heinz Guderian complained about the lack of clear strategic directives. [243] By 1942 others had declared Hitler to be nothing more than a second-rate military strategist, and even such a fawning sycophant as Field Marshall Wilhelm Keitel made note of his paranoid behavior. [244] Another Field Marshal, Erhard Milch, who observed Hitler at close quarters during 1941–42, later confirmed the testimony of others concerning the Fuehrer's behavior:

> The abnormality is not such that one could say "this man is out of his senses" or "this man is insane." It would not have to reach that stage. It often happens that abnormalities are such that they escape both the public

and the nearest associates. I believe that a doctor would be better able to give information on that subject. [245]

This review has attempted to provide the necessary information to which Milch referred, and it appears to confirm the essential truth of Maser's overall assessment: "Hitler's illnesses were neither transitory nor imaginary; they were permanent factors which exerted an increasingly negative influence." [246] As Percy Schramm put it: "The overall picture of that character change [after 1940] cannot be clarified without an understanding of the changes in Hitler's health. [247]

The record is hardly disputed on this point, even though some investigators noticed foreshadowings of disaster at an earlier date. For example, the overwhelmingly successful invasion of France in 1940 has traditionally been viewed as a masterstroke in the art of tactical armor mobility and air supremacy. Less appreciated is the fact that after his success in France in May, Hitler inexplicably imposed a two-day halt and removed Guderian from his command. [248] Military strategists of a later time recognized that had the French taken advantage of the hiatus the effect on the German advance could have been catastrophic. Again, in late May Hitler suddenly gave orders to "halt all tank movements on the Dunkirk salient," relinquishing inexplicably the opportunity to smash the entire British Expeditionary Force. B. H. Liddell Hart spoke for most military historians in observing that "it will never be possible to learn for certain why he came to his decision and what his motives were." [249]

Robert Waite would have the reader believe that not only can no rational explanation be given for either of Hitler's decisions but that "unconsciously he did not really want a victory." [250] This is a difficult proposition to accept. Rather, it would now appear more defensible to acknowledge the vagaries of an unstable personality subject to the influences of a probable seizure disorder, manifested by delusions and unwarranted fears. General Ritter von Thoma, referring to Hitler's attitude at the time, bitterly remarked: "You can never talk to a fool. Hitler spoilt the chance of victory." [251]

Fatefully, on May 14, 1941, Hitler issued a war directive assuring that thereafter the reins of power for strategic and even most tactical decisions were to be held exclusively in his own hands. Precisely at this time, however, several sources refer to an uncharacteristic anxiety and uncertainty that began to characterize the Fuehrer's actions. Fear may have played a more prominent role in the two tactical decisions in France than Hitler was willing to admit. With regard to the halting of the Panzer divisions, Alan Bullock advanced the view that Hitler's reticence was based on fear that the French would launch a counterattack from the south. Bearing in mind the earlier observations regarding psychomotor seizure victims often being consumed by irrepressible fears, this same author's revelations regarding the Fuehrer's behavior are telling. During the pause, Halder recorded in his diary on May 17 that the "Führer is terribly nervous. Frightened by his own success, he is afraid to take any chance." That Hitler's perceptions were bordering on the paranoid at this point was highlighted by Halder a day later in a second diary entry: the "Führer keeps worrying about south flank. He rages and screams that we are on the way to ruin the whole campaign. He won't have any part in continuing the operation in a westward direction."[252] On May 24 a similar scenario evolved with the halt of the advance on Dunkirk. In an angry interview with Halder and Walther von Brauchitsch, Bullock noted, "Hitler insisted on holding back the German tanks. Forty-eight hours later he reversed his decision. . . . But by then it was too late. The British had used the unexpected respite to strengthen their defences and were able to hold off the Germans long enough to complete their evacuation."[253]

That both these situations were anxiety-provoking interludes for the Fuehrer, punctuated by outbursts of rage, and that both were followed by rapid reversal of orders, suggests that the irrational impulses of a neurologically compromised individual may have been at work. Certainly Hitler's later explanation for the Dunkirk halt, that it had been made "on a mere whim . . . 'in a sporting spirit,'"[254] lacks credibility. His documented anxiety and rage hardly represent a frame of mind in which such benign considerations would surface.

Many military historians believe Hitler lost two other critical opportunities when he rejected a proposal some of his generals made in 1941 for a Mediterranean campaign and when he scrapped the planned cross-channel invasion of England. Considering that Hitler's overwhelming superiority would have given him a reasonable chance of success with either venture, he remained uncharacteristically passive. Was his reticence at this time also due to illness? Certainly Maser believed this to have been the case. As early as July 1940, Hitler

> evinced a sudden disinclination to take the risk which an offensive against Britain would necessarily entail. He vacillated and was apparently incapable of paying attention when addressed. . . . Sometimes his eyes would glitter in a way they had never done before and his habitual peremptoriness began to border on aggression.
>
> He was no longer the man he had been four years earlier, and this applied not only to his external appearance. He himself . . . was aware of the change and redoubled his calls upon his personal physician.[255]

As we now know, this was the period during which Morell accelerated the amount and variety of medications he gave Hitler. It would be tempting (and certainly consistent with this review's thesis) to support Maser's view without reservation. But the truth of the matter is that the invasion of England was probably scrapped because the Luftwaffe failed to gain control of the air over the English Channel, making the invasion an increasingly tenuous gamble.[256] Thereafter, Hitler was also too consumed with planning for the Russian campaign to consider any other major offensive. Only later, in the spring of 1942, was Admiral Erich Raeder finally successful in rousing Hitler's interest in expanding German operations in the Mediterranean, and then only because Raeder catered to Hitler's megalomaniacal delusions. He portrayed the objective of the offensive in grandiose terms as in Bullock's words, "a drive through the Middle East to join the Japanese in a vast encirclement of Britain's Asian Empire."[257]

The fatal gamble to open up the war on the Eastern Front in 1941, on the other hand, appears in part to have borne the stamp of neurologic illness. There may be no other way to explain it. Many explanations to date have proven inadequate, including Hitler's strange assertion that "he invaded Russia in order to defeat England."[258] Waite theorized that he had gone to war with the Soviet Union "because of a compulsion to punish himself and to fail."[259] Bullock's explanation followed the more traditional mold: "Hitler invaded Russia for the simple but sufficient reason that he had always meant to establish the foundations of his thousand-year Reich by the annexation of the territory lying between the Vistula and the Urals."[260]

The peculiar aspect was of course the *timing* of his decision to go ahead without first settling accounts with England, a provision which had previously been considered indispensable. He deluded himself into believing that Britain was already defeated and that the Russian offensive could be completed in a single campaign over a two- to three-month period. He was blind to the strength of Stalin's armies, which he believed would crumble in the face of the Wehrmacht onslaught. Yet, ironically, Russia was his most valued ally at the time.[261] Percy Schramm examined Hitler's decisions concerning the Russian campaign and posed the ultimate question: "What was going on in the head of this man?"[262] Something had clearly changed.[263]

Other inexplicable decisions followed in short order. Hitler failed to secure Japanese cooperation before launching the Russian invasion. Indeed, he kept it a secret from them.[264] The General Staff was dismayed to learn he had actually given orders to reduce the level of armaments production on the eve of the offensive and had not taken the precaution to equip the soldiers with winter clothing. Of even greater impact was his decision, against the advice of his closest military advisors, to divide his forces between Moscow (his strategic objective) and the Ukraine (which should have been a secondary front).[265] Halder commented cryptically that, in Bullock's words, "this was the turning-point of the campaign and that Hitler threw away the chance of inflicting a decisive defeat on the Russians for the sake of a prestige victory and the capture of the industrial region of the Ukraine."[266] The campaign was dominated by Hitler's indecisiveness from the beginning. According to Bullock, "Throughout the campaign of 1941 Hitler swung between a number of objectives, losing time in switching from one to another . . . fanning out his armies across a thousand-mile front, while always falling short of the decisive blow."[267] Thereafter, overt disorders of perception, rather than mere indecisiveness, colored Hitler's thinking: "After 1941," Maser concluded, "his assumptions were only partially based on real circumstances."[268]

In addition to the pervasive effects of medication abuse (most notably through amphetamines) and a personality disorder spawned by suspected temporal lobe epilepsy, a more mundane illness also appears to have played an important role in sealing the fate of the Russian campaign by delaying its starting date. Late in July, Hitler experienced a three-week bout of dysentery. Admiral Karl-Jesko von Puttkamer believed that his weakened condition left him incapable of countering the arguments of the remainder of the German staff. For Hitler had sought to divide the German thrust between Leningrad and the Baltic states on the north and the Ukraine on the south. The General Staff argued for a concerted effort first on Moscow alone. What eventually resulted was a division of forces in assaults on all three areas, but only after needless delays as the Fuehrer and his staff wrangled over the issue. Unable to silence his critics in his heretofore forceful manner, Hitler's weakness because of a gastrointestinal disturbance delayed the offensive unnecessarily. Puttkamer was convinced that Brauchitsch and Halder had taken advantage of his condition by sabotaging the Fuehrer's plan during this attack of dysentery.[269]

Yet another puzzling decision occurred in late 1941. Hitler's unnecessary declaration of war against the United States in December, amidst signs of possible defeat in both Russia and Africa, was an exercise in bad judgment and poor timing. He declared war when he least could afford the luxury of doing so. Hermann Göring, chief of the Luftwaffe, saw the error in this action and, according to Waite, concluded "his Führer must have acted 'impulsively.'"[270] Hitler was later to recognize the unexplained mistake himself. "War with the United States was a tragedy and illogical," he admitted.[271] Such an admission solidifies the impression that during this period many of Hitler's decisions were both impulsive and inexplicable. The expanded medical record may now offer some insight into motivations that have remained cloaked in mystery to the present day.

In regard to the expanded operations in the Mediterranean under-taken in the summer of 1942, still another peculiar reversal occurred, seemingly without regard for tactical considerations. In the face of General Erwin Rommel's advances, Hitler suddenly demonstrated a "curious reluctance" to complete the plan by embarking upon the assault on Malta. [272] He refused to consider what was obvious to other military advisors: without the capture of Malta, Rommel's supply lines would remain precarious and unprotected. The ultimate effect of this untimely reversal was to allow England to remain in a position to choke off Rommel's supplies, which subsequently meant German defeat in that theater. Alan Bullock asserted that in Hitler's view the Mediterranean forever remained secondary to a successful completion of the "real campaign" on the Eastern Front. "His interests in the Mediterranean and North Africa," Bullock said, were "never more than fitful." [273] It is one thing, however, to select from a list of available strategic alternatives a particular theater into which most energies are to be poured. It is quite another to halt a successful strategic offensive in midstream, when all available evidence argues to the contrary.

Werner Maser's summation of Hitler's military decisions from this point onward adds the element of paranoia to the behavioral aberrations that were already manifest: "From 1942 onwards Hitler avoided taking military risks and even began to intervene in matters that would more properly have been the concern of a regimental commander, so morbidly mistrustful he had grown." [274]

Hitler's remaining years in power witnessed a plethora of perplexing and destructive military decisions. In January 1943 he was so distraught with the Navy's failure to intercept Allied convoys bound for the ports in northern Russia that, in a furious outburst on New Year's Day, he ordered the German surface fleet to be scrapped. [275] Werner Maser drew attention to a later series of errors on Hitler's part: "Had he been in a more normal frame of mind, he would certainly have made dispositions to counter undertakings such as the Soviet Orel offensive in July 1943 or the attacks on the German positions in the region of Briansk in August, or again, the operations against the southern wing of the German Eastern Front in March 1944." [276] Moreover, after the assassination attempt in July 1944, Hitler nearly repeated the train of thought that had sealed the fate of the German surface navy. Demonstrating mounting anger and paranoia over the impotency of the Luftwaffe, he formulated a short-lived plan to dissolve his useless Air Force altogether. In a similar destructive vein, he chose to leave an entire German army behind in the Crimea, and he similarly left an army group to fend for itself in the Baltic long after the conflict had become a lost cause. [277]

The final exemplary blunder occurred with the specter of a Russian counteroffensive in January 1945 threatening to cut off the retreat of the German armies. Guderian had met with Hitler to recommend a tactical withdrawal in East Prussia in the face of the impending disaster. Scarcely acknowledging the information given him, Hitler labeled the maps spread before him "completely idiotic" and ordered the man who made them to be "shut up in a lunatic asylum."[278] Guderian knew Hitler was aware that any major Russian offensive could easily break through the unreinforced lines in the east. This view was dismissed. Three days later the Russians attacked and the demise of the Third Reich was in view.

By way of review, many historians have concluded that Hitler's basic fault as a commander lay in his inability to concentrate either sufficient forces or his own attention consistently upon a single objective. The Russian campaign represented the most revealing example of Hitler's increasingly characteristic dispersion of effort, both on a military and personal level. As Toland has stated:

> First had come his insistence on striking simultaneously at both Leningrad and the Ukraine, before belatedly pressing on to Moscow. All this was accompanied by a further diffusion of energy through waging political and ideological warfare while pushing his personal goal of exterminating Jews. Similarly in the present dilemma—Stalingrad or the Caucasus—he was insisting on taking both, at the risk of taking neither. The ancient Greeks would have called it hubris, the overweening pride that eventually overtakes all conquerors.[279]

Pride may well go before a fall, but the modern neurologist would term this behavior at least in part a reflection of Hitler's chronic neurologic illness. This was exacerbated by the pharmacologic poisons of a variety of central nervous system stimulants that prevented him from expending concentrated effort on a single subject for a sufficient duration of time to accomplish the objective.

There is a remarkably stark contrast between the way in which Hitler switched erratically from one objective to the next in all his military actions after 1941 and the extreme concentration of will and military force that characterized his earlier successful campaigns in Poland, Norway, and the Low Countries—during which time, it should be noted, he was taking none of the drugs discussed. Werner Maser concluded that after 1942 Hitler

> shunned risky undertakings and . . . would permit no flexibility where long-term objectives were concerned. He never voluntarily surrendered conquered territory, as circumstances after 1943 sometimes demanded, and he

refused to weaken secondary fronts and theatres of war in favour of more crucial ones. . . . Now he had become an overcautious, obstinate, intransigent old man. . . . [He] remained immune to the lessons of experience. [280]

Then there is Robert Waite, taking the psychoanalytic approach, maintaining that Hitler was subconsciously trying to fail. There is an element of truth in both arguments. What then, is the common denominator—that critical link unifying the whole? Perhaps it is the medical argument of organic disease, which encompasses all of the historiographical arguments proposed. Hitler's perseveration with certain themes, the fanatical zeal with which he pursued them, the rigidity of thought that brooked no opposition and that dissolved in rage when his ambitions were thwarted—all are features at least consistent with the interictal personality disorder associated with temporal lobe epilepsy and augmented by drug abuse.

Significant too were the disease-induced delusions and disorders of perceptions that plagued him. Hitler's frequent assertion that he would not act unless the "inner voice" of conviction spoke to guide him may be a sinister indication of one effect of that personality disorder. [281] The overt emergence of Parkinson's disease in concert with the behavioral and intellectual changes that accompany this disorder served to harden these tendencies into a rigid, dogmatic mind-set incapable of seeing alternatives or learning from experience. Trevor-Roper observed that "Hitler's repudiation of inconvenient facts would be incredible, were it not so well attested." But he added that "we must remember that they were the last days, and were different from the first." [287] Add to the cauldron of illness the destabilizing influence of the most powerful and ultimately disabling central nervous system stimulants medicine can concoct and the ease with which Hitler short-circuited into erratic bursts of behavior and inexplicable delusions is readily understood and assimilated into the whole.

One is left, then, with the following thesis: Whereas traditional historical reviews of the tragic Hitler phenomenon have emphasized various political, diplomatic, military, and even psychological conditions, there can be no well-balanced appreciation of Hitler's failings without a retrospective medical examination. Such an examination cannot replace the traditional approaches, but it can offer a balanced account, and it has been the intent of this review to meet that need by interpreting the medical aspects of the argument.

What has been documented is an extraordinary combination of illnesses that at least influenced Hitler's thinking on such matters as the Jewish Question, the increasingly perverse application of totalitarianism within the Third Reich, and the administration of a losing war effort. Mentally rigid and emotionally unstable due to a personality compro-

*Hitler in 1944, showing the stooped posture and masked facies of Parkinson's disease*

*Increasing physical deterioration, 1944*

mised by a suspected temporal lobe disorder, increasingly immobilized due to Parkinson's disease, and subject to Morell's pharmacologic poisons (some of which were directed toward a "psychosomatic gastrointestinal disorder" eventually suggested to be cholecystitis), Adolf Hitler was poorly equipped during his last four years to function as the Fuehrer of the Thousand-Year Reich.

It has been suggested by some that Hitler was less an aberration than a personification of the violent aspects of fascism. Another American physician, Frederic Wertham, in his compelling examination of violence in society, asserted that "Fascism, with its politics of physical force is not accidental, nor is it a symptom of individuals. It is an historical event . . . the outcome of socioeconomic processes. . . ."[283] Citing, among other factors, that one half of all German families were either unemployed or semiemployed during the last days of the Weimar Republic, he developed his argument that "suppressed people looking for a way out of their socioeconomic dilemma are prone to believe in two things: a false savior and a false scapegoat."[284] This premise is accurate enough in determining how Adolf Hitler acquired power, but is not sufficient to explain how he used power so poorly in his last years. There was a clear transition of behavior and decision making after 1940 that Wertham's argument does not address.

*Nearing the end, 1944*

On the other hand, Wertham does make a good point when he criticizes the psychohistorical approach. "Psychopathological diagnoses of Fascist leaders are mostly based on speculation and facile analogies. . . . [these] evaluations vary and change according to the times and the circumstances."[285] Organic disease states may also prompt the appearance of psychiatric disturbance, an important point that the psychohistorians have not dealt with successfully in Hitler's case.

This is the crux of the matter that has moved the present study out of the realm of speculation and facile analogies into an objective appraisal of Hitler's behavior from a present-day medical perspective. If such issues as cholecystitis, Parkinson's disease, temporal lobe epilepsy, and polypharmacy can be successfully established by objective data, then a place does in fact exist for examining Adolf Hitler as a case study within the larger context of fascism. This review has substantiated that at least in one regard Wertham is in error; individuals do make a difference in history. In the position of unrivaled authority that Hitler occupied, this individual's compromised health may have had more to do with the course of his career than the socioeconomic processes which gave rise to fascism.

Occasionally, a proper marshaling of objective data on medical grounds may allow for a more credible application of the psychoanalytical argument. Adolf Hitler is such a case. There was more than fascism in Hitler's Reich; there was also a touch of madness. Historians and psychologists have often argued as much. On objective medical grounds, this is now a defensible argument, and should serve to balance both traditional and psychohistorical assessments of this tragic man.

## NOTES

1. In medical terminology, "polypharmacy" implies drug intake administered or sanctioned by a physician in combinations that adversely affect the patient.

2. Schramm, *Hitler*, p. 132. If most historians have generally failed to give proper emphasis to the available medical data, at least two other sources have recognized their importance. These are Leonard L. Heston and Renate Heston's book, *The Medical Casebook of Adolf Hitler*, and an interview with Dr. Ernst Gunther Schenck, a German physician who knew Hitler, which appeared in *American Medical News* on October 5, 1985. Yet there are critical differences between our conclusions that justify further study and discussion.

3. Frischauer, *Himmler*, pp. 242–43. See also Waite, *The Psychopathic God*, p. 352; and Heston and Heston, *Medical Casebook*, p. 122.

4. The Hestons suggest that the chronic long-term administration of amphetamines "perhaps combined with some physiologic eccentricity of Hitler's led to a total syndrome that had Parkinsonian elements." (*Medical Casebook*, p. 123) They stress that the known actions of amphetamines involve the same brain chemical, dopamine, that is implicated in Parkinson's disease. This implies, however, the inverse of what really occurs to sup-

port their thesis. Parkinson's is caused by a depletion of dopamine in the brain, yet amphetamines increase the release and consequently the physiologic effects of dopamine in the brain (Goodman, Goodman, and Gilman, *Pharmacological Basis of Therapeutics*, p. 161). This is precisely the opposite of what occurs in Parkinson's disease. Aside from the tremor (which itself is distinctly different from that which occurs in Parkinson's), the symptoms of chronic amphetamine ingestion do not suggest (nor is there induced) other specific features of that disease.

5. Speer, *Inside the Third Reich*, p. 472; also cited in Trevor-Roper, *Last Days of Hitler*, p. 120. Speer was Minister of Armaments and War Production from 1942 to 1945.

6. Trevor-Roper, *Last Days of Hitler*, p. 120.

7. Ibid. In 1944 Dr. de Crinis saw Hitler in person. Not only did he regard his initial diagnosis of Parkinson's as confirmed, he also "became convinced that the disease had already reached an advanced stage." See Schramm, *Hitler*, p. 123.

8. The Hestons link Hitler's tremor to amphetamine toxicity. *Medical Casebook*, p. 123. This ignores the fact that a left-sided tremor had occurred long before his exposure to amphetamines. Furthermore, amphetamines would elicit a generalized tremor, as is seen in other toxic-metabolic states, not a selective one as occurred initially in Hitler's case; see Cohen and Flora, "Cerebral Intoxication," 2:20, p. 25.

9. McDowell and Lee, "Treatment of Parkinson's Syndrome," p. 29.

10. Houston Meritt, *A Textbook of Neurology*, p. 515. One should not make too much of this; intellectual impairment is still only modest in these patients; ibid., p. 515.

11. Schenck interview, *American Medical News*, p. 40.

12. Maser, *Legend, Myth and Reality*, pp. 231–32. Undeniably, this would be a young age for the development of Parkinson's disease. The idiopathic type begins in the fifth and sixth decades as a rule, yet Parkinsonism secondary to other causes may occur much earlier—the possible significance of which will be revealed in the text.

13. Ibid., p. 218.

14. Guderian, *Erinnerungen*, p. 402; quoted in Langer, *Mind of Adolf Hitler*, p. 235. Guderian later became Chief of Staff of the Army in 1944.

15. Deposition of Erwin Giesing, June 12, 1945; quoted in Maser, *Legend, Myth and Reality*, p. 224. Giesing was an army ear, nose, and throat specialist who ministered to Hitler after July 1944.

16. Shy and Drager. "Neurological Syndrome," p. 511. In passing, it should be acknowledged that the decreased perspiration may have related to the atropine Hitler was taking; see pp. 183–85.

17. Hanfstängl, *The Missing Years*, p. 22; Goebbels, p. 130. Joseph Goebbels was Chief of the Propaganda Ministry in the Third Reich.

18. Deposition of Erwin Giesing; June 12, 1945; quoted in Maser, *Legend, Myth and Reality*, p. 226.

19. Boldt, *Die letzten Tage*, pp. 15, 63–64; quoted in Langer, *Mind of Hitler*, p. 235. See also Boldt, *Hitler: The Last Ten Days*, pp. 14–15.

20. Braunmuehl, "War Hitler Krank?" pp. 88–89.

21. Walters, "Hitler's Encephalitis." Still another physician, Hugh L'Etang, erred in the opposite direction when he stated that Parkinsonism "is by no means associated with mental impairment." L'Etang, *Pathology*, pp. 198–99.

22. Albert, Feldman, and Willis, "Subcortical Dementia," p. 121.

23. Maser, *Legend, Myth and Reality*, pp. 279–80.

24. Robbins, "Depression in Parkinsonism," p. 141.

25. Kaplan, Freedman, and Sadock, *Comprehensive Textbook of Psychiatry*, 2:1387, 1388. Dr. Donald R. Bennett, a noted pharmacologic expert, also believed Hitler suffered from depression, particularly in view of some of the drugs Morell used to treat his patient's condition. See Schenck interview, *American Medical News*, p. 40.

26. Kaplan, Freedman, and Sadock, *Comprehensive Textbook of Psychiatry*, 2:1388.

27. Irving, *Diaries of Hitler's Doctor*, pp. 17, 270, 271.

28. McDowell and Lee, "Extrapyramidal Diseases," *Clinical Neurology*, 2:26, pp. 19–20.

29. Poskanzer and Schwab, "Parkinson's Syndrome," p. 961. Hugh L'Etang argues unconvincingly that this was the cause of Hitler's Parkinsonism. L'Etang is in error when he enlists unsubstantiated "oculogyral spasms" as evidence for postencephalitic Parkinson's disease. None of the descriptions of Hitler's eyes used as evidence are compatible with the oculogyric crises so familiar to practicing neurologists. See *Pathology*, pp. 198–99.

30. Gilroy and Meyer, *Medical Neurology*, p. 172.

31. Irving, *Diaries of Hitler's Doctor*, p. 98.

32. Merritt, *Textbook of Neurology*, p. 515.

33. Lefebure, *Riddle of the Rhine*, p. 81.

34. Langer, *Mind of Adolf Hitler*, p. 157; Waite, *Psychopathic God*, p. 235.

35. Lefebure, *Riddle of the Rhine*, p. 67.

36. DePalma, *Drill's Pharmacology*, p. 978. Therefore L'Etang's hypothesis that "Hitler's visual failure could conceivably have been due to the ocular disturbances associated with acute encephalitis" (*Pathology*, p. 199) does not withstand medical scrutiny.

37. Bullock, *Hitler*, p. 52. Author's note: The epithelium of the eyes is blistered by the gas.

38. The Hestons agree with this assessment; *Medical Casebook*, p. 60.

39. Gilroy and Meyer, *Medical Neurology*, p. 170.

40. Kubic and Anders, "Metabolism of Dihalomethanes."

41. Irving, *Diaries of Hitler's Doctor*, p. 103.

42. Dr. Ernst Gunther Schenck believes that Hitler's chronic gastrointestinal symptoms were compatible with an "irritable bowel syndrome," a term synonymous with "spastic colon"; see Schenck interview, *American Medical News*, p. 39. These diagnoses should be made only after all other possibilities are excluded.

43. The discussion found in Heston and Heston, *Medical Casebook*, pp. 105–13, further serves to substantiate this claim.

44. Irving, *Diaries of Hitler's Doctor*, pp. 25, 119, 247, 255; Heston, *Medical Casebook*, pp. 29, 31.

45. Irving, *Diaries of Hitler's Doctor*, pp. 190, 234, 252.

46. Ibid., pp. 235, 239, 249.

47. Sleisenger and Fordtran, *Gastrointestinal Disease*, p. 1116.

48. Disorders of the gallbladder are among the most common diseases of adult life. Gallstones occur in approximately 20 percent of people over the age of forty; Davis, *Christopher's Textbook of Surgery*, p. 787.

49. Irving, *Diaries of Hitler's Doctor*, p. 199.

50. Ibid., p. 198.

51. Ibid., pp. 247, 249. The addition of an antispasmodic is important, as opiate analogues are known to induce spasm of the gallbladder duct and its opening. Consequently, taking the opiate alone may, paradoxically, have made Hitler's symptoms of cholecystitis worse. Perhaps the Eupaverin vitiated this effect. As Morell noted in his diary three months after the alleged bout with hepatitis: "The Fuehrer has his spasms again. Injected intravenous Eukodal and Eupaverin. Checkup showed gall bladder [sic] region resistant, but during my examination it softened up." Ibid., p. 249.

52. Ibid., p. 199.

53. Ibid., p. 227. Hitler was a better diagnostician than Morell in this instance. The pimples probably represented small foci of staphylococcal infection, a strain of bacteria found on the skin.

54. "If abdominal pain is present in hepatitis, it is usually dull and aching; rarely is it severe. The jaundice [of hepatitis] reaches a maximum in three to fourteen days and then recedes at a somewhat slower rate, clearing up completely in one to six weeks. . . . Full clinical and *biochemical* recovery is to be expected in *four months*." Italics mine. Harrison, *Principles of Internal Medicine*, p. 1049. Hitler's jaundice had cleared in three days. Morell documented a normal urobilinogen in the urine *twelve days* after the onset of the illness. Irving, *Diaries of Hitler's Doctor*, p. 298.

55. Irving, *Diaries of Hitler's Doctor*, p. 239.

56. Benson and Geschwind, "Psychiatric Conditions," 4:229. Skeptics of this hypothesis are undoubtedly aware of the unfounded attribution of epilepsy in the past to the powerful and the wicked. See Karlen, *Napoleon's Glands*, p. 29. The following argument presented below is not intended as conclusive evidence regarding the presence of this disease process. The data is strongly supportive but not incontrovertible. It is but a beginning to an ongoing investigation.

57. Bear and Arana, "Nonfunctional Disorders," 1:12, p. 3. Even in the 1940's patients with psychomotor seizures were recognized to demonstrate abnormal traits, including "egotism, moodiness, perseveration, [all] elements of the so-called epileptic personality." *Cecil's Textbook of Medicine* (1944), p. 1477.

58. For a discussion of psychomotor seizure behavior masking as a psychiatric disturbance, see Gibbs, Bibbs, and Fuster, "Psychomotor Epilepsy," pp. 331, 339. These features are not specific for psychomotor seizure victims, but they are statistically more prevalent in that population. Critics who choose to discount this should not ignore that, today, earlier and more effective treatment has decreased their prevalence.

59. Benson and Geschwind, "Psychiatric Conditions," 4:229.

60. Gilroy and Meyer, *Medical Neurology*, p. 309. Any representative text in neurology contains the same information detailed in this review of psychomotor epilepsy.

61. Benson and Geschwind, "Psychiatric Conditions," 4:230.

62. Gilroy and Meyer, *Medical Neurology*, p. 309.

63. Ibid., p. 296.

64. EEGs were available by this time, as were drugs to treat the disease; *Cecil's Textbook of Medicine*, 1944, pp. 1477, 1479. Then, too, a family history of neurologic disorders may be helpful. There is a higher percentage of such cases in epilepsy suspects than in the normal population. Gestapo files reveal that three of the children of one Joseph Veit, a cousin of Hitler's father, "were mentally retarded, and one of them committed suicide in a mental institution. Other branches of the family seemed to have been similarly affected." Waite, *Psychopathic God*, p. 144.

65. Gilroy and Meyer, *Medical Neurology*, p. 310; D. MacRae, "Isolated Fear," p. 497.

66. Benson and Geschwind, "Psychiatric Conditions," 4:231.

67. Rauschning, *Voice of Destruction*, p. 256; also quoted in Langer, *Mind of Adolf Hitler*, p. 132. A sensation of suffocation is one of the vegetative signs of temporal lobe epilepsy described by Dr. H. Gastaut, an early investigator of these seizure patterns; see Arieti, *American Handbook of Psychiatry*, 4:230.

68. Introduction by Albert Speer in Heston and Heston, *Medical Casebook*, p. 13. See Birger Dahlerus' description of Hitler on page 169 for another example of compulsive speech phraseology.

69. Gilroy and Meyer, *Medical Neurology*, p. 311. "During some psychomotor seizures patients experience hallucinations, both visual and auditory." Merritt, *Textbook of Neurology*, p. 854.

70. Benson and Geschwind, "Psychiatric Conditions," 4:231. Whether this behavior is seizure-induced or a part of the interictal personality disorder is not agreed upon by investigators.

71. Interview with A. Zeissler, June 24, 1943; cited in Langer, *Mind of Adolf Hitler,* p. 132. One might argue that this behavior is also consistent with amphetamine toxicity, a drug that Hitler abused. This stimulant undoubtedly accounted for some of his behavior but this ignores the presence of interictal personality features in Hitler's case consistent with temporal lobe epilepsy.

72. Guerrant, Anderson and Fischer, *Personality in Epilepsy;* cited in Benson and Geschwind, "Psychiatric Conditions," p. 232.

73. J. R. Stevens, "Psychiatric Implications of Psychomotor Epilepsy," p. 466.

74. Bullock, *Study in Tyranny,* p. 768.

75. Gilroy and Meyer, *Medical Neurology,* p. 309.

76. Waite, *The Psychopathic God,* pp. 147, 25, 12.

77. Gilroy and Meyer, *Medical Neurology,* p. 309.

78. Trevor-Roper, *Last Days of Hitler,* p. 134. General Franz Halder was Chief of the Army General Staff from November 1941 to September 1942.

79. Waite, *The Psychopathic God,* p. 24.

80. Trevor-Roper, *Last Days of Hitler,* p. 134.

81. Gilroy and Meyer, *Medical Neurology,* p. 312; Baker and Baker, *Clinical Neurology* 2:24:20−21. These are termed "reflex" seizures.

82. Trevor-Roper, *Last Days of Hitler,* pp. 134−35.

83. Ibid., pp. 94−95.

84. Heston and Heston, *Medical Casebook,* p. 12. Perhaps the deep flush described was caused by anger, but it may also have represented one of the vasomotor changes that occur in such seizures; see H. Gastaut, "So called 'Psychomotor' and 'Temporal Epilepsy.'"

85. Gilroy and Meyer, *Medical Neurology,* p. 310.

86. Trevor-Roper, *Last Days of Hitler,* p. 133.

87. Merritt, *Textbook of Neurology,* p. 860. Baker and Baker's *Clinical Neurology* gives a more detailed account of these; see 2:24, pp. 20−22.

88. Gilroy and Meyer, *Medical Neurology,* p. 312. The EEG shows epileptic activity when the patient listens to recordings containing the musical stimulus.

89. Kubizek, *Young Hitler;* pp. 99−100.

90. Langer, *Mind of Adolf Hitler,* pp. 203.

91. Forster and Booker, "Epilepsies and Convulsive Disorders," 2:24, p. 21.

92. Gutman, *Wagner: Man and Music,* p. 80. The author wishes to emphasize that the argument for musicogenic epilepsy is far more speculative than other data supporting the psychomotor seizure hypothesis. It represents, however, one area which deserves further study.

93. Kubizek, *Young Hitler,* p. 155.

94. Quoted in Waite, *The Psychopathic God,* p. 10. Birger Dahlerus was described by Robert Waite as a Swedish visitor to Hitler in August, 1939. The observations of both Kubizek and Dahlerus are important examples of behavioral aberrations in Hitler long before his involvement with amphetamines (which loomed so large in the Hestons' analysis of his character disintegration). After 1941, amphetamine abuse was indeed a major factor in the changes that evolved, as the authors have skillfully argued. Yet such evidence as the above suggests there must be much more to the story than dependence on a single causative agent suggests. Even Albert Speer, who largely supported the Hestons' thesis, implied as much: "Hitler had already made some of his monstrous, evil errors, such as the creation of concentration camps, the persecution of the Jews, or the struggle against the Church, before he came under the sway of amphetamines." Speer concluded that "There is indeed a disclosure of the abnormal in the Hestons' revelations, but this abnormality is inseparable from the demonic aspects of Hitler's nature." Heston and Heston, *Medical Casebook,* pp. 19, 20. Indeed, it will be argued below that the "de-

monic aspects" to which Speer referred might have been integral parts of the personality disorder associated with temporal lobe epilepsy. The amphetamines certainly may have accentuated them.

95. Merritt, *Textbook of Neurology*, p. 854.

96. A. Serafetinides and D. Falconer, "Speech Disturbances in Temporal Lobe Seizures." Emphasis added.

97. Langer, *Mind of Hitler*, p. 33. Interestingly enough, this theme was a recapitulation of a second, and lesser known, example of Hitler's hypergraphia. Although having no training as an historian, Hitler embarked in 1919 on an ambitious (and unfinished) work dealing with the history of humanity entitled (in translation) "Monumental History of Humanity." *The Psychopathic God*, p. 64.

98. Bullock, *Study in Tyranny*, p. 703.

99. Heston and Heston, *Medical Casebook*, p. 13

100. Haffner, *Meaning of Hitler*, pp. 143–44.

101. The author wishes to emphasize, as in every other issue discussed in this review, that causation for any action or belief on Hitler's part was multifactorial. Illness was not the only factor, nor is that implied.

102. Percy E. Schramm, Introduction to Picker, *Hitler's Tischgespraeche*, pp. 51–52, 119.

103. Bracher, *German Dictatorship*, p. 63.

104. Waite, *The Psychopathic God*, p. 29.

105. The first two quotes are taken from Hitler's speeches in Breslau (1937) and Vienna (1938) respectively, and are cited in Waite, *The Psychopathic God*, p. 30. The last is taken from the observation of Heinz Assmann in "Some Personal Recollections of Adolf Hitler," p. 1290.

106. Waite, *The Psychopathic God*, p. 31.

107. Ibid.

108. Ibid.

109. It should be acknowledged, of course, that anti-Semitism was quite prevalent throughout Europe at this time.

110. Conway, *Nazi Persecution of the Churches*, p. 147, and Heer, *Der Glaube des Adolf Hitler*, p. 316; both quoted in Waite, *The Psychopathic God*, p. 32.

111. Hans Mueller, "Der pseudoreligiose Charakter," p. 349.

112. Waite, *The Psychopathic God*, p. 61.

113. Ibid., p. 35.

114. Rev. 3:15–16.

115. The Hestons have another explanation for Hitler's oral fixation. Noting that he chewed on his fingers incessantly—almost compulsively—they described this habit as a stereotype mannerism typical of the amphetamine abuser; *Medical Casebook*, pp. 113–14. Add to this the oral fixation occasionally seen in psychomotor seizure suspects and it can readily be appreciated how the two concurrent conditions may have accounted for this peculiar behavior in one so vain.

116. Gilroy and Meyer, *Medical Neurology*, p. 310.

117. Kubizek, *Young Hitler*, p. 111.

118. Waite, *The Psychopathic God*, p. 16; Langer, *Mind of Hitler*, pp. 83, 82.

119. Bullock, *Study in Tyranny*, p. 686.

120. Ibid.

121. Ibid., p. 687.

122. Waite, *The Psychopathic God*, pp. 60–61. Langer, *Mind of Adolf Hitler*, p. 134. The Hestons err in discounting Hitler's documented sexually aberrant behavior.

"Ignorance [about Hitler's sex life] has fostered blatant speculation," they assert; *Medical Casebook*, p. 118. In truth, some facts are known, which may take the content of the present study out of the realm of speculation.

123. Waite, *The Psychopathic God*, p. 270.

124. Ibid.

125. Langer, *Mind of Adolf Hitler*, p. 86.

126. Waite, *The Psychopathic God*, pp. 276–77; Langer, *Mind of Hitler*, pp. 168, 171. Coprophilia is a fascination with filth or feces.

127. Langer, *Mind of Adolf Hitler*, p. 91.

128. Ibid., p. 92.

129. Hanfstängl, *The Missing Years*, p. 22. The charge of homosexuality, like syphilis, has often been made against the tyrants of history.

130. Waite, *The Psychopathic God*, p. 57.

131. Ibid., p. 58.

132. Ibid., p. 60.

133. Hitler, *Mein Kampf*, 45th ed. (1938), p. 231; quoted in Trevor-Roper, *Last Days of Hitler*, pp. 103–4.

134. Trevor-Roper, *Last Days of Hitler*, p. 104.

135. Schenck interview, *American Medical News*, pp. 41, 43.

136. Waite, *The Psychopathic God*, p. 403. Even such a credible skeptic as Arno Karlen is willing to give epilepsy in history some consideration. Napoleon Bonaparte may also have been victimized by the excesses of what Karlen terms a *"form fruste* of epilepsy"; see Karlen, *Napoleon's Glands*, p. 29.

137. Toland, *Adolf Hitler*, p. 678.

138. Goodman, Goodman, and Gilman, *Pharmacological Basis of Therapeutics*, p. 586.

139. Bradley, Easton, and Eccles, "An Investigation of Primary or Direct Inhibition."

140. Goodman, Goodman, and Gilman, *Pharmacological Basis of Therapeutics*, p. 586. Chemical transmitters between nerve cells may be either facilitative or inhibitive and can be blocked by chemicals—in this case, strychnine.

141. Cohen and Flora, "Cerebral Intoxication," 2:20, p. 24.

142. Irving, *Diaries of Hitler's Doctor*, p. 307.

143. Ibid., p. 199.

144. Goodman, Goodman, and Gilman, *Pharmacological Basis of Therapeutics*, p. 586.

145. Cohen and Flora, "Cerebral Intoxication," 2:20, p. 24.

146. Cited in Irving, *Diaries of Hitler's Doctor*, p. 197. The Hestons assert that, due to its rapid inactivation in the body, cumulative excesses of strychnine "are thought not to occur." *Medical Casebook*, p. 74. This ignores the likelihood of significant accumulation if metabolism is delayed by hepatobiliary illness, as has been noted. More important, even acceptable therapeutic levels of the drug would augment the central nervous system stimulating effects of the numerous other convulsants Hitler was taking in combination.

147. Irving, *Diaries of Hitler's Doctor*, p. 198.

148. Schenck's calculations concerning the alleged amount of strychnine in the tablets also do not correspond to what was on the label of the tin that contained them: one hundred and twenty tablets contained 0.5 grams (five hundred milligrams) of extractum nucis vomic (strychnine)—not thirty five milligrams, as Schenck maintained; Irving, *Diaries of Hitler's Doctor*, p. 197. Taking this into account, twelve tablets, or 10 percent of the amount taken in a *single* day, would represent a potentially lethal dose, as already documented. Given the presence of synergistic effect (meaning an augmentation of the

actions of one drug when taken in combination with another), as well as a probable decreased ability to metabolize the strychnine, it is unlikely that Hitler could have been free of the drug's deleterious side effects.

149. Maser, *Legend, Myth and Reality*, p. 343; Irving, *Diaries of Hitler's Doctor*, p. 305.

150. Goodman, Goodman, and Gilman, *Pharmacological Basis of Therapeutics*, p. 589.

151. Maser, *Legend, Myth and Reality*, p. 221.

152. Goodman, Goodman, and Gilman, *Pharmacological Basis of Therapeutics*, p. 589.

153. The timing of the initiation of its administration is perhaps significant: at the height of the conflict with his commanders over conduct of the war in the East. See Toland, *Adolf Hitler*, p. 678.

154. Goodman, Goodman, and Gilman, *Pharmacological Basis of Therapeutics*, p. 213.

155. Ibid., p. 214.

156. Maser, *Legend, Myth and Reality*, p. 230. This was one major source of the large doses of amphetamines to which the Hestons attribute such significance. Caffeine is known to augment amphetamine effect.

157. Irving, *Diaries of Hitler's Doctor*, p. 13.

158. Ibid.

159. Hans-Dietrich Röhrs, *Hitler—die Zertörung einer Persönlichkeit* (Neckargemünd, pp. 110f; quoted in Maser, *Legend, Myth and Reality*, p. 230.)

160. Ibid.

161. Irving, *Diaries of Hitler's Doctor*, p. 140. Vitamultin-forte apparently came in both a tablet and an injectable form.

162. Ibid., p. 151. Albert Speer remarked: "It was obvious that Hitler was being revived and sustained by these constant doses of drugs. . . . I am now convinced . . . that this . . . was produced by the amphetamines he was being given." Hitler admitted to the same: "I was completely exhausted and after his injection I felt fresh again." Heston and Heston, *Medical Casebook*, pp. 16, 18.

163. Goodman, Goodman, and Gilman, *Pharmacological Basis of Therapeutics*, pp. 160–62.

164. Bear and Arana, "Nonfunctional Disorders," p. 4.

165. Irving, *Diaries of Hitler's Doctor*, p. 64. See diary entries from February 20 to March 5, 1943.

166. American Medical Association, Council Report, "Aspects of Amphetamine Abuse," p. 2317.

167. Kaplan, Freedman, and Sadock, *Comprehensive Textbook of Psychiatry*, 2:1620.

168. Bear and Arana, "Nonfunctional Disorders," p. 4.

169. Cohen and Flora, "Cerebral Intoxication," 2:20, p. 26.

170. Toland, *Adolf Hitler*, p. 821.

171. Irving, *Diaries of Hitler's Doctor*, p. 177.

172. Toland, *Adolf Hitler*, p. 822. Schenck admits that the dosages of cocaine were excessive; see Schenck interview, *American Medical News*, p. 39.

173. Maser, *Legend, Myth and Reality*, pp. 224–25.

174. Cohen and Flora, "Cerebral Intoxication," 2:20, p. 17.

175. Goodman, Goodman, and Gilman, *Pharmacological Basis of Therapeutics*, p. 307.

176. Ibid., p. 308.

177. Martin, *Hazards of Medication*, p. 415.

178. Costellani, Ellingwood, and Kilby, "Behavioral Analysis of Chronic Cocaine Intoxication."

179. Goodman, Goodman, and Gilman, *Pharmacological Basis of Therapeutics*, p. 557.

180. Irving, *Diaries of Hitler's Doctor*, p. 199.

181. Ibid., p. 204.

182. Ibid., p. 198. Toland, *Adolf Hitler*, p. 824.

183. Toland, *Adolf Hitler*, p. 824.

184. Cohen and Flora, "Cerebral Intoxication," 2:20, p. 29. The term "photophobia," as implied, means an aversion to bright light. If the pupils are widely dilated (as occurs in belladonna toxicity), excess light is allowed to reach the retina.

185. Goodman, Goodman, and Gilman, *Pharmacological Basis of Therapeutics*, p. 127.

186. Irving, *Diaries of Hitler's Doctor*, p. 199. As with the calculations for strychnine, there is some dispute regarding the precise amount in milligrams of atropine. The Hestons' calculations give a different result—all of which remains a moot point, as the precise number of pills Hitler took in a given day is unknown.

187. Goodman, Goodman, and Gilman, *Pharmacological Basis of Therapeutics*, p. 199, Table 7-2.

188. Irving, *Diaries of Hitler's Doctor*, p. 197.

189. Ibid., pp. 17, 12.

190. Ibid., p. 305.

191. Goodman, Goodman, and Gilman, *Pharmacological Basis of Therapeutics*, p. 507.

192. Ibid.

193. Irving, *Diaries of Hitler's Doctor*, p. 306; Heston and Heston, *Medical Casebook*, p. 76.

194. Irving, *Diaries of Hitler's Doctor*, p. 13. Hans Karl von Hasselbach was Brandt's assistant as surgeon-in-attendance to Hitler from 1936 until 1944.

195. Ibid., pp. 130–39.

196. Goodman, Goodman, and Gilman, *Pharmacological Basis of Therapeutics*, p. 507.

197. Ibid. Enterohepatic circulation, simply stated, implies a recycling of the drug from bowel to liver and back again, prolonging drug effect.

198. Ibid., p. 508.

199. Forrest, Brown, et al., "Dextroamphetamine with Morphine."

200. Goodman, Goodman, and Gilman, *Pharmacological Basis of Therapeutics*, p. 548.

201. Irving, *Diaries of Hitler's Doctor*, p. 214.

202. *Springfield (Missouri) News and Leader*, December 10, 1983. Detailed studies of this have recently been reported in the medical and scientific literature. In the March 1985 issue of *Science* a few implications for the present day are disclosed that have tragic relevance for Nazi Germany. "These drugs . . . had been synthesized in clandestine laboratories. Furthermore, the drugs were completely legal." (p. 60) Precisely the same conditions existed in Germany: Morell manufactured many of his own drugs and often tried them out for the first time on his gullible patient, Hitler.

203. Irving, *Diaries of Hitler's Doctor*, pp. 17–18.

204. Goodman, Goodman, and Gilman, *Pharmacological Basis of Therapeutics*, p. 1113.

205. Ibid., p. 1114.

206. Irving, *Diaries of Hitler's Doctor*, p. 140.

207. Schenck, *American Medical News*, p. 39.

208. Trevor-Roper, *Last Days of Hitler*, pp. 122–23.

209. Goebbels, *Diaries*, p. 314.

210. Irving, *Diaries of Hitler's Doctor*, p. 42.

211. Ibid., p. 23.

212. Ibid., p. 26.

213. By such curious circumstances, then, are physicians of individuals in high positions of leadership often chosen—a fortuitous marriage here, treatment of a close associate there. These relationships epitomize a critical recurring problem in the quality of selection of these uniquely positioned medical men.

214. Ibid., p. 14. The Hestons asserted that "when Morell first examined Hitler, he had probably not practiced serious medicine for twenty years." *Medical Casebook*, p. 35.

215. Heston and Heston, *Medical Casebook*, p. 77.

216. Irving, *Diaries of Hitler's Doctor*, p. 17.

217. Ibid., p. 231.

218. Ibid., pp. 15, 14.

219. Trevor-Roper, *Last Days of Hitler*, p. 123.

220. Ibid.

221. Irving, *Diaries of Hitler's Doctor*, p. 61.

222. Ibid., p. 5.

223. Ibid., p. 8.

224. Maser, *Legend, Myth and Reality*, p. 277.

225. Goebbels, *Diaries*, p. 130.

226. Speer, *Inside the Third Reich*, p. 103; Trevor-Roper, *Last Days of Hitler*, p. 121.

227. Trevor-Roper, *Last Days of Hitler*, p. 121.

228. Irving, *Diaries of Hitler's Doctor*, p. 50. Professor A. Weber, the physician consulted, was director of a cardiology institute at Bad Nauheim.

229. Trevor-Roper, *Last Days of Hitler*, pp. 71–74.

230. Bullock, *Study in Tyranny*, p. 733.

231. Trevor-Roper, *Last Days of Hitler*, p. 297.

232. Waite, *The Psychopathic God*, p. 475.

233. Ibid., p. 474.

234. Ibid., pp. 477, 475–76.

235. Ibid.; Langer also depended heavily on Freud; see *Mind of Hitler*, p. 17.

236. *New York Times*, May 15, 1945.

237. Schenck interview, *American Medical News*, p. 43.

238. Waite, *The Psychopathic God*, pp. 413–14.

239. Schramm, *Hitler*, p. 135.

240. Ibid.

241. Maser, *Legend, Myth and Reality*, pp. 298–99. According to the Fuehrer Principle, Hitler's word was law no matter the consequences, and indeed the consequences were to prove disastrous time and again after 1941.

242. Ibid. Perhaps Schramm stated it best, while hedging his bet that Hitler remained more or less "normal" to the end: "Although it was apparently possible . . . to crank Hitler up to an abnormally high level of physiologic activity [with numerous stimulants] . . . the concomitant overstimulation of his brain . . . might well have . . . adversely affected his judgment." Schramm, *Hitler*, p. 121.

243. Heinz Guderian, "Erfahrungen im Russlandkrieg," *Bilanz des Zweiten Weltkrieges* (Oldenburg, 1953), p. 87; cited in Maser, *Legend, Myth and Reality*, p. 294. Guderian was at that time Hitler's premier tank commander.

244. Keitel, *Memoirs*, p. 184.

245. *Proceedings of the International Military Tribunal*, 9:92; cited in Maser, *Legend, Myth and Reality*, p. 299.

246. Maser, *Legend, Myth and Reality*, p. 303.

247. Schramm, *Hitler*, p. 132.

248. Waite, *The Psychopathic God*, p. 461.

249. Liddell Hart, *History of the Second World War*, 1:75.

250. Waite, *The Psychopathic God*, p. 463.

251. Liddell Hart, *German Generals Talk*, p. 133. Next to Guderian, General von Thoma was the most notable commander of Hitler's Panzer divisions.

252. Bullock, *Study in Tyranny*, p. 585.

253. Ibid., p. 586.

254. Waite, *The Psychopathic God*, p. 462.

255. Maser, *Legend, Myth and Reality*, p. 292.

256. Trevor-Roper, *Blitzkrieg to Defeat*, p. 38.

257. Bullock, *Study in Tyranny*, p. 679.

258. Waite, *The Psychopathic God*, p. 465.

259. Ibid. The Hestons believe that Hitler was compromised by amphetamines during this period. *Medical Casebook*, p. 134.

260. Bullock, *Study in Tyranny*, p. 651.

261. Waite, *The Psychopathic God*, p. 464.

262. Quoted in ibid., p. 403.

263. It is interesting to speculate, as Waite has done, whether Hitler may have acted under the influence of a Wagnerian opera in making that fateful decision. The reader will recall that some episodes of psychomotor epilepsy may be triggered by music (see page 167 above). On July 23, 1940, the Fuehrer attended a performance of *Die Götterdämmerung*, that "somehow reassured Hitler and confirmed his conviction of heroic destiny. . . . He left [the performance] composed, his mind made up. Within the week he issued the orders that would lead to his own *Götterdämmerung*." Waite, *The Psychopathic God*, p. 464.

264. Bullock, *Study in Tyranny*, p. 629.

265. Blumentritt, *Fatal Decisions*, pp. 74, 52. General Günther Blumentritt underscored the differences dividing Hitler from his General Staff: "The difference between Hitler's point of view and that of the Army High Command remained unsolved when the battle began. This was to have . . . the most unfortunate consequences." Blumentritt, *Fatal Decisions*, p. 53.

266. Bullock, *Study in Tyranny*, p. 654.

267. Ibid., p. 655.

268. Maser, *Legend, Myth and Reality*, p. 298.

269. Toland, *Adolf Hitler*, p. 687.

270. Waite, *The Psychopathic God*, p. 472.

271. Ibid., p. 473.

272. Bullock, *Study in Tyranny*, pp. 679–80.

273. Ibid., p. 680.

274. Maser, *Legend, Myth and Reality*, p. 304.

275. Bullock, *Study in Tyranny*, p. 715.

276. Maser, *Legend, Myth and Reality*, p. 307.

277. Ibid., p. 307.

278. Toland, *Adolf Hitler*, p. 841.

279. Ibid., p. 716.

280. Maser, *Legend, Myth and Reality*, p. 303.

281. Langer, *Mind of Adolf Hitler*, p. 73.
282. Trevor-Roper, *Last Days of Hitler*, p. 298.
283. Wertham, *A Sign for Cain*, p. 79.
284. Ibid., p. 78.
285. Ibid.


# REFERENCES

**MEDICAL**

American Medical Association. Council Report. "Aspects of "Amphetamine Abuse." *Journal of the American Medical Association* 240 (1978): 2317–2319.

Arieti, Sylvano, ed. *American Handbook of Psychiatry.* 2d ed. 6 vols. New York: Basic Books, 1975.

Baker, A. B., and L. H. Baker, *Clinical Neurology.* 5th ed. 3 vols. Hagerstown, Md.: Harper and Row, 1976.

Bear, David, and George Arana. "Nonfunctional Disorders of Emotion." In *Neurology and Neurosurgery*, edited by Peritz Scheinberg, 1:12 pp. 2–8. Princeton, N.J.: Biomedia, 1978.

Benson, D. Frank, and Norman Geschwind. "Psychiatric Diseases associated with Focal Lesions of the Central Nervous System." In *American Handbook of Psychiatry*, 2d ed., edited by Sylvano Arieti, 4:208–43. New York: Basic Books, 1975.

Bradley, K., D. Easton, and J. Eccles. "An Investigation of Primary or Direct Inhibition." *Journal of Physiology* (London) 122 (1953): 474–88.

Cohen, Maynard M., and George C. Flora. "Cerebral Intoxication." In *Clinical Neurology*, 5th ed., edited by A. B. Baker and L. H. Baker, 2:20, pp. 1–66. Hagerstown, Md.: Harper and Row, 1976.

Costellani, S., E. Ellingwood, and M. Kilby. "Behavioral Analysis of Chronic Cocaine Intoxication." *Biology and Psychiatry* 13 (1978): 203–15.

Davis, Loyal, ed. *Christopher's Textbook of Surgery.* 9th ed. Philadelphia: W. B. Saunders and Co., 1968.

DePalma, J. R., ed. *Drill's Pharmacology in Medicine.* 3rd ed. New York: McGraw-Hill Book Co., 1965.

Feldman, R., M. Albert, and A. Willis, "The Subcortical Dementia of Progressive Supranuclear Palsy." *Journal of Neurology, Neurosurgery, Psychiatry* 37 (1974): 121–27.

Forrest, W., B. Brown, et al. "Dextroamphetamine with Morphine for the Treatment of Postoperative Pain." *New England Journal of Medicine* 196 (1977): 712–15.

Forster, Francis M., and Harold E. Booker. "The Epilepsies and Convulsive Disorders." In *Clinical Neurology*, 5th ed., edited by A. B. Baker and L. H. Baker, 2:24, pp. 1–45. Hagerstown, Md.: Harper and Row, 1976.

Gastaut, H. "So-called 'Psychomotor' and 'Temporal Epilepsy.'" *Epilepsia* 2 (1953): 59–96.

Gibbs, E. L., F. A. Bibbs, and B. Fuster. "Psychomotor Epilepsy." *Archives of Neurology and Psychiatry* 60 (1948): 331–39.

Gilroy, John and John S. Meyer, eds. *Medical Neurology.* 2d ed. London: Macmillan Co., 1969.

Goodman, Alfred, Louis Goodman, and Alfred Gilman. *The Pharmacological Basis of Therapeutics.* 6th ed. New York: Macmillan Co., 1980.

Guerrant, J., W. Anderson, and A. Fischer. *Personality in Epilepsy.* Springfield, Ill.: Charles C. Thomas, 1962.

Harrison, T. R. *Principles of Internal Medicine.* 5th ed. New York: McGraw-Hill Book Co., 1966.

Heston, Leonard L., and Renate Heston. *The Medical Casebook of Adolf Hitler: His Illnesses, Doctors and Drugs.* Introduction by Albert Speer. New York: Stein and Day, 1979.

Kaplan, Harold, Alfred Freedman, and Benjamin Sadock, eds. *Comprehensive Textbook of Psychiatry.* 3d ed. 3 vols. Baltimore: Williams and Wilkins, 1981.

Kubic, V. and M. Anders. "Metabolism of Dihalomethanes to Carbon Monoxide." *Drug Metab. Dispos* 3 (1975): 104–12.

L'Etang, Hugh. *The Pathology of Leadership.* New York: Hawthorn Books, 1970.

McDowell, Fletcher E., and John E. Lee. "Extrapyramidal Diseases." In *Clinical Neurology,* 5th ed., edited by A. E. Baker and L. H. Baker, 20:26, pp. 1–53. Hagerstown, Md.: Harper and Row, 1976.

McDowell, Fletcher E., John E. Lee, et al. "Treatment of Parkinson's Syndrome with L-dihydroxy-phenylalanine (levodopa)," *Annals of Internal Medicine* 72 (1970): 29–35.

MacRae, D. "Isolated Fear: A Temporal Lobe Aura." *Neurology* 4 (1954): 497–505.

Martin, Eric, ed. *The Hazards of Medication.* Philadelphia: J. B. Lippincott Co., 1971.

Merritt, Houston. *A Textbook of Neurology.* 6th ed. Philadelphia: Lea and Febiger, 1979.

Poskanzer, David C., and Robert S. Schwab. "Cohort Analysis of Parkinson's Syndrome: Evidence for a Single Etiology Related to Subclinical Infection about 1920." *Journal of Chronic Disease* 16 (1963): 961–73.

Robbins, A. "Depression in Patients with Parkinsonism." *British Journal of Psychiatry* 128 (1976): 141–46.

Schenck, Ernst-Gunther. Interview. *American Medical News.* American Medical Association. October 11, 1985. pp. 1, 34–43.

Serafetinides, A., and D. Falconer. "Speech Disturbances in Temporal Lobe Seizures." *Brain* 86 (1963): 333–46.

Shy, G. M., and G. A. Drager, "A Neurological Syndrome Associated with Orthostatic Hypotension." *Archives of Neurology* 2 (1960): 511–20.

Sleisenger, Marvin, and John Fordtran. *Gastrointestinal Disease.* Philadelphia: W. B. Saunders Co., 1973.

Stevens, J. R. "Psychiatric Implications of Psychomotor Epilepsy." *Archives of General Psychiatry* 14 (1966): 461–71.

Todd, E., and S. Sanford, eds. *Clinical Diagnosis by Laboratory Methods.* 17th ed. Philadelphia: W. B. Saunders Co., 1984.

Walters, John. "Hitler's Encephalitis: A Footnote to History." *Journal of Operational Psychiatry* 6 (1975): 99–111.

PRIMARY

Assmann, Heinz. "Some Personal Recollections of Adolf Hitler." *United States Naval Institute Proceedings* 79 (1953): 1289–95.

Boldt, Gerhard. *Die letzten Tage der Reichskanzlei.* Hamburg: Rowohlt, 1947.

———. *Hitler: The Last Ten Days.* New York: Coward, McCann and Geoghegan, 1973.

Goebbels, Paul Joseph. *The Goebbels Diaries.* Edited by Louis Lochner. Garden City, N.Y.: Doubleday and Co., 1967.

Keitel, Wilhelm. *The Memoirs of Field-Marshal Keitel.* Edited by Walter Gorlitz, and translated by David Irving. New York: Stein and Day, 1966.

Kreipe, Blumentritt, et al. *The Fatal Decisions*. Edited by Seymour Freiden and William Richardson, and translated by Constantine Fitzgibbon. New York: Berkley Publishing, 1956.

Guderian, Heinz. *Erinnerungen eines Soldaten*. Heidelberg: Plesse Verlag, 1951.

Hanfstängl, Ernst. *Hitler, The Missing Years*. London: Eyre & Spottiswoode Ltd., 1950.

Hitler, Adolf. *Mein Kampf*. Translated by Robert Manheim. Boston: Houghton Mifflin Co., 1943.

Kubizek, August. *The Young Hitler I Knew*. Boston: Houghton Mifflin Co., 1983.

Speer, Albert. *Inside the Third Reich*. Translated by Richard and Clara Wilson. New York: Macmillan Co., 1970.

*Trials of War Criminals Before the Nuremberg Military Tribunals Under Control Council Law No. 10*, October 1946–April 1949. 15 vols. Washington: U.S. Government Printing Office, 1946–49.

PERIODICALS AND NEWSPAPERS

*News and Leader* (Springfield, Missouri). December 10, 1983.

SECONDARY

Bullock, Alan. *Hitler: A Study in Tyranny*. rev. ed. New York: Harper and Row, 1962.

Bracher, Karl Dietrich. *The German Dictatorship: The Origins, Structure, and Effects of National Socialism*. Translated by Jean Steinberg. New York: Praeger, 1970.

Braunmuehl, Anton. "War Hitler krank?" *Stimmen der Zeit*. 79 (1954): 78–89.

Conway, J. S. *The Nazi Persecution of the Churches, 1933–45*. New York: Basic Books, 1968.

Frischauer, Willi. *Himmler: The Evil Genius of the Third Reich*. London: Macmillan Co., 1953.

Gutman, Robert G. *Richard Wagner: The Man, His Mind, and His Music*. New York: Harcourt, Brace, and World, Inc., 1968.

Haffner, Sebastian. *The Meaning of Hitler*. Translated by Ewald Osers. New York: Macmillan Publishing Co., 1979.

Heer, Friedrich. *Der Glaube des Adolf Hitler: Anatomie einer politischen Religiosität*. Munich: Bechtle, 1968.

Irving, David. *The Secret Diaries of Hitler's Doctor*. New York: Macmillan Publishing Co., 1983.

Karlen, Arno. *Napoleon's Glands and Other Ventures in Biohistory*. New York: Little, Brown and Co., 1984.

Langer, Walter C. *The Mind of Adolf Hitler: The Secret Wartime Report*. New York: Basic Books, 1972.

Lefebure, Victor. *The Riddle of the Rhine: Chemical Strategy in Peace and War*. New York: The Chemical Foundation, 1923.

Liddell Hart, B. H. *History of the Second World War*. New York: G. P. Putnam's Sons, 1972.

———. *The German Generals Talk*. New York: William Morrow and Co., 1948.

Maser, Werner. *Hitler: Legend, Myth and Reality*. Translated by Peter and Betty Ross. New York: Harper and Row, 1973.

Mueller, Hans. "Der pseudoreligiose Charakter der Nationalsozialistischen Weltanschauung." *Geschichte in Wissenschaft und Unterricht*. 6 (1961): 339.

Picker, Henry. *Hitler's Tischgespraeche im Fuehrerhauptquartier, 1941–42*. Introduction by Percy E. Schramm. Stuttgart: Seewald, 1965.

Rauschning, Hermann. *The Voice of Destruction*. New York: G. P. Putnam's Sons, 1940.

Schramm, Percy Ernst. *Hitler: The Man and the Military Leader.* Translated and edited by Donald S. Detwiler. Chicago: Quadrangle Books, 1971.

Toland, John. *Adolf Hitler.* Garden City, N.Y.: Doubleday and Co., 1976.

Trevor-Roper, H. R. *The Last Days of Adolf Hitler.* 3d ed. New York: Collier Books, 1962.

———. *Blitzkrieg to Defeat: Hitler's War Directives, 1939–1945.* New York: Holt, Rinehart and Winston, 1964.

Waite, Robert G. L. *The Psychopathic God: Adolf Hitler.* New York: Basic Books, 1977.

Wertham, Fredric. *A Sign for Cain: An Exploration of Human Violence.* New York: Warner Books, 1969.

*I was terrified when I saw the President's face. I felt certain he was going to
die. . . . It was gray, gaunt, and sagging, and the muscles controlling the lips
seemed to have lost part of their function.*

*John Gunther*
*Inauguration Day, 1945*

# 4

# *Roosevelt: Structuring the Aftermath*

Franklin Delano Roosevelt's extraordinarily long tenure as President of
the United States assured him a variety of public images. Initially proclaimed "Dr. New Deal" during the thirties, he enhanced his reputation
as "Dr. Win-the-War" after America's entry into World War II in 1941.
Yet his detractors ultimately pinned a negative image on the man that has
endured—the "Sick Man of Yalta." Early developments during the Cold
War era were so distasteful to Americans that an acknowledgment of
Roosevelt's ill health was offered as one explanation for the reversal of
free-world fortunes at war's end. This impression is accepted today as
much as any other image of the Roosevelt years.

If Yalta was in one sense the culmination of Roosevelt's life's work,
the tragic memory of Woodrow Wilson a quarter of a century before
brings to mind a distressing historical parallel. Had we fought two destructive wars, dwarfing all previous conflicts, only to lose at the negotiating table what we had gained on the battlefield? Is history truly
cyclical? To utilize the hackneyed phrase, were we not familiar enough
with our recent history to avoid being condemned to repeat it?

Such are the ironies of history. After skillfully leading the nation to victory under extraordinarily trying circumstances, two of the strongest American presidents of the twentieth century had fallen prostrate with exhaustion while attempting to write similar political epitaphs as world peacemakers. At Versailles and at Yalta, Wilson and Roosevelt raced against the biologic clock to complete the one task that consumed them in the twilight of their careers—a world organization created to prevent the tragedies they had just endured. That both seemingly compromised a great deal for the attainment of their goal was but one of the similarities they shared.

Further parallels come to mind. Diplomatically, Wilson's Saar and Rhineland foreshadowed Roosevelt's Poland and China. Physiologically, Wilson's progressive organic brain syndrome was echoed by the effects of hypertension and chronic lung disease on Roosevelt's behavior. Professionally, Dr. Cary Grayson's duplicity presaged Dr. Ross McIntire's denial of his own patient's failing health. And whereas Woodrow Wilson enjoyed the protection of his wife as personal guardian, so too was Franklin Roosevelt shielded by his daughter's unflagging concern. In the end, both presidents attempted to orchestrate their grand finales in face-to-face encounters with allies who countered American idealism with specific national interests of their own. Under the circumstances, these opponents measured the limitations of their American counterparts in a telling fashion. Just as Georges Clemenceau had proposed at Versailles that "too much activity had dulled Wilson's mental processes," Joseph Stalin observed at Yalta that "if I had known how tired [Roosevelt was] I would have agreed to meet along the Mediterranean."[1]

In large measure, both Clemenceau and Stalin succeeded in achieving most of what they were seeking in exchange for postulated world peace-keeping organizations. Yet insofar as Versailles and Yalta alone were concerned, the parallels diverge in one important respect. Whereas Wilson was undoubtedly a progressively compromised individual at Versailles, Roosevelt was not so afflicted while at Yalta—despite the fact that occasionally before the Conference, and almost continuously after it, he was stricken by frequent periods of unawareness (termed encephalopathy)[2] on the basis of high blood pressure and chronic pulmonary insufficiency.

True, both individuals were fatally compromised by neurologic disease. Their respective illnesses, however, were by no means identical insofar as they impacted on leadership capabilities. Wilson was afflicted in a progressive fashion, as has been argued in an earlier chapter; Roosevelt's illness manifested itself only intermittently, with clear intervals of skillful political and diplomatic leadership otherwise. There are, to be sure, several examples in the Roosevelt record where serious illness played a negative role in his executive conduct. Yet at Yalta, events were much more the product of political circumstances. Indeed, one might even credibly support William Manchester's assertion that at Yalta Roosevelt got more from Stalin than the President had a right to expect. [3]

There is much more to the Roosevelt medical record that has not been placed in proper perspective. Certainly the clarity of that record has only been muddled by the self-serving memoirs of Dr. Ross McIntire. [4] Prior to 1970 this was the only source of medical data made available by those entrusted with Roosevelt's care. [5] Nonetheless, enough data now exist to offer a detailed explanation of the President's medical afflictions. In chronicling these, one once again encounters the distressing theme of physician-sanctioned duplicity and denial that characterized these unique physician-patient relationships.

Franklin Roosevelt was a very ill—and dying—man during his last year in office. No pious memoir of his physician can dispel that obvious fact. Yet the ironic conclusion remains: despite the fact that Roosevelt was more severely stricken by a number of interrelated diseases—and nearer to death—than any of the seven other leaders discussed in this work, and despite the fact that his illness has been more widely (if incorrectly) publicized than any of the others, the lasting effect of poor health on his leadership, while significant, was probably the least among the eight men.

The noted scholar of the Roosevelt era James MacGregor Burns has suggested an incisive theoretical basis for analyzing political leadership in a chapter appended to his distinguished work *Roosevelt: The Lion and the Fox*. The core of that consideration rests with the following assessment by Burns. In analyzing the effectiveness of leaders in terms of the larger political environment, one must take into account a wide variety of factors including three other guidelines than those traditionally discussed in the study of political leadership:

(1) The traditional and desirable attention to the shaping of personality in childhood must be complemented by attention to developments in late adolescence and indeed through adulthood; . . . (2) The environmental political factors that affect the leader's personality should . . . be treated . . . in terms of that leader's *perception* of their existence and of their relative importance; . . . (3) The concept of *role-taking* is of central importance in analyzing political leadership in a fluid, variegated society. . . . The analyst of an important political leader must try to differentiate [these] roles from the central core personality. [6]

This review will expand upon the first point in particular, by emphasizing that the shaping of personality in the later stages of adulthood is

*Franklin Delano Roosevelt, 1943*

inextricably linked to the health of the individual. This is a critical influence, inasmuch as national leadership is usually gained and exercised during this later period of life; the changes that occur in the central nervous system of an aging leader at that juncture may well be the dominant factor in determining his behavior. Not only may cognitive and psychological changes be expected to alter that individual's perception of the environmental factors to which Burns refers, but an identification of these changes is instrumental in unveiling the core personality as it evolves with age.

A defensible interpretation of the neurologic changes affecting Roosevelt during his last years in office has not been presented to date. The historiography of the matter encompasses three separate arguments, embodied by critical journalistic accounts on the one hand[7] and the defensive memoirs of his physician on the other.[8] Professional historians, representing a third viewpoint, acknowledge Roosevelt's ill health but resist assuming any cause-and-effect relationship between it and the decisions he made during his last two years in office. The more correct interpretation lies between these disparate poles of thought and can only be understood in relation to the specific disease states that afflicted Roosevelt during this critical period.

Jim Bishop's work is a valuable source for an otherwise unavailable medical record,[9] unless one chooses to accept the contradictory account of McIntire, who for obvious reasons chose to present a far more sanguine narrative. The publication of *White House Physician* in the year 1946 is significant in itself. It was written to dispel both the rumors that Roosevelt was far more seriously ill than was known at the time and the suggestion that McIntire withheld this information from the American public.[10] Certainly one cannot accuse Roosevelt's senior physician of inconsistency. A. Merriman Smith spoke for most contemporaries of Roosevelt in asserting: "To his credit, McIntire never lied about Roosevelt's condition. He told the truth, but in language that could easily be misleading."[11] This *modus operandi* is readily apparent in the doctor's memoirs.[12] Smith spotlighted the issue as it confronts historians today: "The world had the word of three distinguished medical men for the cause of the President's death. . . . But the record does not seem as unquestionable on reports of his health in advance of the President's death."[13]

Any attempt to clarify the record must begin in December 1943 shortly after the Teheran Conference. Rexford Tugwell observed on Roosevelt's return that the President seemed to be a "bone-tired man. He gave the impression of being exhausted."[14] Samuel Rosenman's observation supported this claim. Acknowledging Roosevelt's usual show of vitality, Rosenman confided: "I had seen that expression many times before; but except for a few exhilarating moments during the campaign of 1944 . . . I never saw that same expression again."[15] Plagued by a persistent cough and headaches, the President, Burns wrote, "seemed strangely tired even in the morning hours."[16]

Alarmed, Roosevelt's family demanded that McIntire have a detailed physical examination performed. The Bethesda Naval Hospital was chosen, and Roosevelt's physician enlisted the services of a young cardiologist, Lieutenant Commander Howard Bruenn, to perform the evaluation. This was on March 27, 1944. The disturbing findings of the examination would be enough to distress the most complacent observer—if the results had been made known to anyone outside the tight-lipped medical circle hastily convened in its aftermath. Rosenman's account reflected the prevailing attitude and limited knowledge available concerning Roosevelt's condition:

> Teheran seemed to me to be the turning point of his physical career. . . . The President developed some sort of bronchial affliction in Teheran which gave him a racking cough. . . . Dr. McIntire called in some medical consultants, but they found no unusual condition for a man of his age except his cough and his sinuses. [17]

This was the only information regarding Roosevelt's medical condition that McIntire offered to family and close confidants at the time, a position that his later memoirs did not refute: "The results [of the examination] showed a moderate degree of arteriosclerosis, although no more than normal for a man his age; some changes in the cardiac tracing; cloudiness . . . in his sinuses; and bronchial irritation." He was asked to speak frankly to the correspondents, in view of the rumors circulating regarding the President's health. "I can say to you," McIntire assured them, "that the check-up is satisfactory. When we got through, we decided that for a man of sixty-two we had very little to argue about, with the exception that we have had to combat the influenza plus the respiratory complications that come along afterward." [18] Just how incorrect, if not deceitful, that assertion proved to be has been revealed by Dr. Bruenn's subsequent revelations concerning the examinations of March 27–28. He was alarmed to discover that for the previous four months the President had experienced recurrent upper respiratory tract infections and had felt unduly fatigued. And by now Roosevelt's physical deterioration had become distressingly obvious on appearance alone, reflecting his cardiopulmonary compromise. His face was ashen gray, his fingernails and lips blue (cyanotic), and his respirations labored in the lying position. There was also a noticeable tremor of his hands. Bruenn discovered that the President had experienced difficulty for some time in sleeping supine. Several months earlier Roosevelt had had four-inch-thick boards placed under the head of his bed to alleviate his respiratory distress at night. [19]

Roosevelt also had moderately severe diastolic hypertension; his blood pressure on this occasion was 186/108 mm Hg, the normal value for a man this age being 140/85 mm Hg. Furthermore, a review of McIntire's records (which Bruenn noted he had some difficulty in obtaining) reflected the presence of this condition as early as 1941, even though no acknowledgment of it (not to mention treatment) had been made. Bruenn's fundiscopic examination of Roosevelt's eyes likewise revealed arterial-venous nicking of the vessels of the retina, an ominous effect of longstanding hypertension. [20]

The President's blood circulation time was prolonged. Signs of congestive heart failure were evident, including a markedly enlarged left ventricle, which was forced to expel its contents against increasing resistance in the systemic circulation. This was made worse by clinical evidence for dysfunction of both the aortic and mitral valves of the heart. Basilar rales in the chest were noted, a further sign that the reduced pumping capacity of the heart was causing fluid to back up into the lungs. The cyanosis implied a striking compromise in the lungs' ability to oxygenate the slowly circulating blood. Electrocardiograms as early as 1941 demonstrated clear inversion of the "T" waves on the tracings, a dependable sign of lack of oxygen to the heart. Of significance, too, was the unexplained iron deficiency anemia recorded in McIntire's notes in 1941; the level of hemoglobin in the blood on this occasion had been alarmingly low (4.5 grams per 100 cc, as compared to a normal value of 14–16 grams per 100 cc), even though no cause for this had been described. [21]

In summary, Roosevelt's first complete in-hospital detailed examination confirmed the diagnoses of "hypertension, hypertensive heart disease, failure of the left ventricle of the heart, and acute bronchitis." [22] He had suffered from severe anemia in the past; now he had unmistakable findings of well-advanced and longstanding hypertension, severe restrictive and chronic obstructive pulmonary disease (COPD), and congestive heart failure (CHF). Each of these disease entities undoubtedly had been present for some time—though not acknowledged or treated by his original physician.

The essence of this potpourri of clinical findings in relation to Roosevelt's leadership capacity is immediately obvious to any physician remotely familiar with the effects of diastolic hypertension, anemia, COPD, and CHF on the neurologic system, and hence on cognitive and emotional function. These conditions are in fact the very factors known to precipitate what is termed "secondary metabolic encephalopathy," which results when diseases outside the nervous system interfere with brain metabolism. Early symptoms include acute confusional states. [23] Yet even such a skilled clinician as Bruenn appears to have ignored this important association. Bruenn made no reference to an examination of the nervous system per se (except an acknowledgment of the profound atrophy in the President's legs as a consequence of polio years before). Nor did he ask Roosevelt any carefully directed questions aimed at uncovering past examples of fleeting aberrations in thought processes or neurologic function (i.e., "transient ischemic attacks," or prestroke warnings), possibly because of the restrictions McIntire had placed on Bruenn, coupled with the President's perplexing tendency not to volunteer information. [24]

This restricted access to a critical portion of the medical history obtainable directly from Roosevelt ignored a well-accepted clinical precept: the most important findings in any medical examination invariably come *from the history taken* and not the physical findings by themselves. Given Roosevelt's seeming indifference to the proceedings, and acknowledging the restrictions placed upon his examiner, it is not surprising that the most important aspect of this examination and all others to follow appears to have been sadly neglected. It is in the medical history that the skillful physician uncovers telltale warning signs of potential disasters to come.

A discussion of the origins and implications of metabolically-induced encephalopathy is essential to our understanding of Roosevelt's behavior during his last two years in office. The foremost medical experts in the field of stupor and coma today, Drs. Fred Plum and Jerome Posner, recognize the most prevalent cause of secondary metabolic encephalopathy to be "subacute chronic diffuse hypoxia of the brain." They have found that hypoxia of the brain (a lack of oxygen) is almost invariably a serious manifestation of systemic disease that limits oxygen supply diffusely. Interestingly enough, the four most common causes of chronic diffuse hypoxia to the brain Plum and Posner describe are the *same four conditions* found to have been afflicting Roosevelt either prior to or at the time of his examination in March 1944. In their classic medical work *Diagnosis of Stupor and Coma*, Plum and Posner relate the following:

> Subacute or chronic diffuse hypoxia occurs with severe anemia, . . . congestive heart failure, and pulmonary disease. . . . Multifocal cerebral ischemia or hypoxia [also occurs] in hypertensive encephalopathy, where it presumably originates from focal vasoconstriction in cerebral vessels. . . . Any of these conditions can produce metabolic stupor. . . . Judgment slips away early, and confusion, disorientation, and lethargy emerge. [25]

Not only did Bruenn's examination implicate each of these four factors in the medical record of the President, but concern about the very symptoms later described by Plum and Posner had been precisely the reason for such a detailed examination in the first place. Bishop notes that "a lassitude had overcome the President. . . . The oyster circles under the eyes were deepening, the mouth often hung open unconsciously, and thought processes were sometimes left unfinished, with sentences dangling." [26] This is a typical description of transient encephalopathy. There are many more in the Roosevelt record.

More telling still is the interrelationship of these disease processes to one another in producing such a clinical picture:

Encephalopathy is seldom caused by a change in one of these functions [of anemia, hypertension, CHF, and COPD], and it most often results from a *combination* of several. . . . In all of the above abnormalities . . . there is a similar neurologic picture consisting of delirium or stupor . . . frequently combined with . . . transient or fleeting multifocal neurological signs. [27]

Roosevelt not only experienced frequent episodes that fit the description of this behavior pattern, but he had the precise combination of diseases most frequently observed to account for them. What he did not have was a physician's awareness of the problem, and neither tincture of time, nor the obligatory calls for slowing his pace, would vitiate its effect on his leadership.

Certainly Dr. Bruenn was deeply concerned over the grave combination of physical findings disclosed both in his examination of Roosevelt and in Roosevelt's previous medical record. To his surprise, however, McIntire did not appear unduly alarmed by the news. Rather, Bishop notes, he merely asked Bruenn "if he would like to serve under [him] as the President's physician-in-attendance. The implication was clear: Bruenn would be under the authority of McIntire at all times, . . . would not be permitted to discuss Roosevelt's physical condition with the patient or the First Family . . . and would obey orders." [28]

McIntire quickly called a conference of some of the nation's leading physicians to deal with the data Bruenn had uncovered. Conspicuous by their absence were the services of a neurologist, who would undoubtedly have advised the group of the implications of Roosevelt's constellation of diseases from the neurologic perspective. Guided by the restrictive hand of Ross McIntire, moreover, the group originally refused to consider even the minimum of available treatment Bruenn recommended. After all, as Bishop wrote, "McIntire had been examining the President for years and had not noted any alarming pathology." [29] Nonetheless, Bruenn held firm, and in the face of his threatened resignation over the issue, the group finally recommended the administration of digitalis for the symptoms of heart failure; prescribed a 2,600-calorie, low-fat diet; and suggested that Roosevelt get at least ten hours of sleep a day. [30]

It was likewise agreed that the President should be given full knowledge of his condition, but it was uncertain who was to relay the news. Everyone assumed that McIntire had the responsibility and would exercise it, but as James McGregor Burns later observed, "there is no indication that he ever did." Burns postulated three possible motives to account for McIntire's lack of action: perhaps he lacked confidence, or perhaps he was too timid, or perhaps he believed Roosevelt would accept neither the information given him nor the recommended treatment prescribed. [31] Jim Bishop was far more blunt in his assessment:

> As a physician, McIntire understood the situation but denied it. His daily reports from Bruenn became Navy secrets. The Admiral's dominance over [Commander Bruenn] was complete. McIntire could have revealed the President's grave condition to FDR in April 1944. If this had not stopped Roosevelt from running for the fourth term, the Admiral, as a physician of integrity, could have retired or requested other duty. . . . The researcher is left with the assumption that McIntire was lying—not only to the world but to the President himself. [32]

Evidence presented below will demonstrate that this assertion can be readily substantiated. Yet Bishop's indictment of the physician is even stronger still, implying a flagrant breech of medical ethics: "The Admiral remained the physician-in-residence, but he treated only the sinuses and pounced on Bruenn's daily reports, read them and *hid or destroyed* them. [italics mine]"[33] Given McIntire's philosophy of what a president's physician should be, and considering the circumstances involved in his being chosen for the job, his position at least had the dubious merit of being consistent. Interestingly enough, he had been recommended for the post of White House physician by none other than Dr. Cary Grayson—who, it may be remembered, believed that one of the most important functions of a physician in this position was to protect the political health of the President. He must restrict public access to only those matters deemed absolutely necessary to reveal.

McIntire admitted that his appointment as White House physician had come through Dr. Cary Grayson. "There is no embarrassment in the confession" McIntire stated. "As one of Franklin Roosevelt's oldest and dearest friends, [Grayson] had become a White House intimate after the 1932 election, and thought of me when the President asked him about a physician." That McIntire shared Grayson's perception of his proper role in this unique physician-patient relationship is reflected in his statement that "through long-established custom it is the habit of Presidents to select either an Army or Navy doctor. . . . These men are officers and can be counted on to keep a closed mouth about what they see and hear."[34]

Still, McIntire had some understandable reservations about his selection as Roosevelt's White House physician. "What could an eye, ear, nose, and throat man possibly have to offer a victim of infantile paralysis?" he asked his benefactor, Grayson. "The President [Grayson responded] is as strong as a horse with the exception of a chronic sinus condition. . . . That's where you come in."[35] This cavalier assessment of Roosevelt's condition in 1933 may have been true then, but it would prove to be far off the mark a decade later, and his physician would be ten years further removed from the wider range of experience that private practice affords in the treatment of such common ailments as congestive heart failure, chronic obstructive pulmonary disease, and hypertension.

The age of Wilson and Grayson, to be sure, had been an era in which illness still held some moral connotation of possible divine punishment for bad conduct. Nor had public perception of disease advanced far beyond that even by Roosevelt's time. Just as Grayson had before him, McIntire believed it essential to obscure any suggestion that such an esteemed individual as the President of the United States might be afflicted by serious diseases so prevalent among "lesser men" in this same age group. "There was the advantage," McIntire wrote, "that journeys to the [Bethesda] Medical Center could be made without exciting comment. . . . A visit of the President to the Mayos or Johns Hopkins [on the other hand] even for a routine checkup, was bound to have been played up as big [and politically damaging] news." It is not at all surprising, therefore, that when legitimate "big news" finally did surface with Bruenn's landmark examination, McIntire softened its impact with pious assurances that "for a man his age, the President was in good physical shape."[36]

Many observers close to Roosevelt were unconvinced from the beginning by McIntire's optimistic press releases. Rexford Tugwell recounted: "It soon appeared that [Roosevelt] was desperately ill . . .

McIntire called in consultants several times; they found no chronic troubles except the bronchitis and the sinuses he had fought for years, but the symptoms refused to clear up. . . . The well-known resilience was gone. . . . He fell sometimes into unaccustomed reverie, from which he awoke with a start.[37]

It is highly unlikely that the physical ailments that Bruenn uncovered in March had been absent four months earlier at Teheran. Indeed, Tugwell's suggestive description of periods of unawareness were all too obvious to others at the time—Winston Churchill included. McIntire alluded to an observation Churchill was said to have made at Teheran, but dismissed it out of hand: "Mr. Churchill is . . . reported to have said that he noted signs of deterioration in the President at Teheran, although I have never been able to find any direct statement."[38] Churchill did in fact make such an observation, and James McGregor Burns referred to it in his work *Roosevelt: The Soldier of Freedom:* "Had the President said much in the conference? someone asked. Churchill hesitated. 'Harry Hopkins said that the President was inept. He was asked a lot of questions and gave the wrong answers.'"[39]

Was anything lost, then, by the United States at Teheran because of illness? Probably not, for several reasons. McIntire, of course, never even considered the possibility: "I can say that the decisions made there were due in large measure to the President's superb handling of a delicate situation. . . . It was the President . . . who reconciled differences and found basis of agreement."[40] More to the point, the very format of discussion at Teheran emphasized merely preliminary introductions to a wide range of issues involved with the war and its aftermath. Teheran was the first substantial and lengthy meeting of Roosevelt, Churchill, and Stalin, and cautious appeasement (as well as appraisal) was the order of the day.

There is no doubt that a cordial relationship developed between Roosevelt and Stalin while there. If the President found himself at odds with Churchill in support of Stalin's call for opening a two-front war through France (as opposed to the Prime Minister's preferred route through the soft underbelly of the Mediterranean), most experts agree that there were sound military considerations for doing so. Aside from the settling of this thorny question, Teheran still remained a forum more for presenting views than for reaching solid agreements. As such, this meeting of East and West lacked much potential for significant gains or losses. Edward Stettinius, who was later named Secretary of State following Cordell Hull's resignation, underscored this point in his dicussion of Teheran:

> Although no agreements had been reached, the three leaders had discussed in a preliminary way such problems as the treatment of Germany, the future of Poland, General de Gaulle and France, Russian participation in the Far Eastern war, a warm-water port for the Soviet Union, colonial empires, Turkey's entrance into the war, and the founding of an organization of nations. Actual progress on these and related issues did not occur, however, until Yalta. [41]

Nor did the President's health have any substantial impact on events as they transpired at Teheran. Cognitive manifestations of Roosevelt's illness were (and would remain) only *intermittent* phenomena. Accordingly, McIntire registered false confidence with his observation that "my examination at the close of the conference found him so fit, both mentally and physically, that I did not think it necessary to urge any change."[42]

Nevertheless, a "normal" physical examination ignores the characteristic feature of intermittency of bouts of encephalopathy on a metabolic basis. In the condition of chronic or subacute diffuse hypoxia, the clouding of consciousness that occasionally results often disappears as quickly as appears. As with Roosevelt, individuals so afflicted may enjoy lengthy periods of normal behavior, only to be tipped over into a tran-

*The Commander in Chief, 1942*

sient period of unawareness or clouding of consciousness with a temporary exacerbation of one of the four predisposing illnesses cited. Yet a
careful review of the record at Teheran fails to reveal any event suggesting the occurrence of an episode of encephalopathy during that conference. Nothing of significance, therefore, was lost by the United States at
Teheran due to Roosevelt's illness.

This conclusion does not negate the fact that Roosevelt was still a
critically ill man. Following the Bethesda examination, the ailing President was packed off to Bernard Baruch's plantation in South Carolina for
a much-needed rest. The trip in itself generated a great deal of controversy regarding his health. Although the American public knew virtually nothing of the real results of the examination that prompted this
forced respite, the secrecy surrounding the trip south aroused suspicions
among many. Merriman Smith asserted that it was precisely "Roosevelt's
intense desire for seclusion [there] that made the reporters wonder
why."[43] This fact, coupled with the obvious change in his appearance,
was enough to swing the rumor mills into action.

Correspondents were witnessing the decline firsthand. "The first in-
kling I had that Mr. Roosevelt was slipping was in the spring of 1944,"
Mr. Smith recounted. "The longer [he] lived, the less productive became
his news conferences. He became listless and poor of voice . . . [and]

became increasingly quarrelsome about petty things." [44] Even McIntire began to sense a change in the public attitude on the matter:

> It was during the South Carolina stay, when bronchitis was the President's *one and only trouble* [italics mine] apart from fatigue, that the country filled with every variety of wild and reckless lies about his physical condition. . . . It became common knowledge that the President had suffered a paralytic stroke, that he was being treated for cancer of the prostate, that he was the victim of a mental breakdown, and, favorite whisper of all, that his heart had played out. [45]

Given the disclaimers of Roosevelt's private physician in the face of obvious changes in the President's physical appearance—not to mention the secrecy enveloping his retreat to South Carolina—what else would one expect from an American public that was soon to consider the nomination of this man for an unparalleled fourth term as the nation's Chief Executive? Questions were raised, but they remained largely unanswered. McIntire's memoirs reflect the medical naiveté (or duplicity) he had earlier demonstrated in the face of these rumors. If nothing else, one detects a telling degree of defensiveness in his assertions:

> In not one of these remarks was there a grain of truth. The President never had a stroke, and *never had a serious heart condition* [italics mine]. . . . I am adjudged as having deliberately deceived the people of the United States by the issuance of statements that the President was sound organically and in fairly good health. . . . It was on the strength of repeated examinations, made under my direction by competent specialists, and on the basis of reports rendered by distinguished consultants, that I issued my statements to the press in the spring and fall of 1944 [that Roosevelt] was "in excellent condition for a man his age." *I stand by that judgment today without amendment or apology.* [46]

Was Howard Bruenn not considered a "distinguished consultant"? More important, was McIntire guilty of selectively editing the record? He attempted to mount a defense by citing shortly thereafter that on May 1 Roosevelt's "blood pressure was within a normal range." This echoed his earlier revelation in January 1943 that "the blood pressure readings were well within a most satisfying range," and immediately after Roosevelt's return from South Carolina, when he found the "blood pressure dropping." [47] Strangely enough, in his account McIntire included no specific blood pressure values. The cynic, with good reason, wonders why.

What was "a most satisfying range," and what was really implied by McIntire's statement that Roosevelt's blood pressure was dropping? Had the real values been made available (remembering of course that no mention was made of hypertension at all in McIntire's press releases) moderate concern would have burgeoned into alarm. It is one thing for a physician empowered with protecting his patient politically to whitewash the facts; it is quite another to carry that assertion to the grave in one's memoirs—particularly in view of the fact that others have given us specific values with which to assess meaningfully the degree of Roosevelt's diastolic hypertension. McIntire asserted in passing that "our records prove that the malignant whisperings after Teheran have no solid ground."[48] In truth, they proved nothing insofar as they were presented in this physician's memoir.

This last assertion can be defended on two grounds. First, there is the record of Bruenn to contradict McIntire's account. During the month of April Roosevelt's blood pressure consistently ran between 210/110 to 230/130. By September nothing had changed; on one occasion his pressure readings were as high as 240/130.[49] These values signify a bona fide medical emergency, necessitating immediate hospitalization. *Cecil's Textbook of Medicine*, a revered medical text for over fifty years and published in numerous revised editions, is emphatic on this point: "Accelerated hypertension is a medical emergency, because this condition is causing progressive damage to the blood vessels in vital organs [including the brain]. . . . When the diagnosis is made, the patient should be admitted to the hospital at once for blood pressure reduction."[50] Yet Roosevelt was not hospitalized; rather, he continued a very delicate phase of negotiations at Quebec concerning proposals for postwar Germany.

Second, even if some of the blood pressure readings might have been in "a most satisfying range," as McIntire asserted (though no values are presented from this period to substantiate this), his observation ignores the distressing variability of blood pressures in patients afflicted with accelerated, or malignant, hypertension.[51] A sudden sharp rise of blood pressure in the best of circumstances may still predispose the sufferer to encephalopathy. In the worst, it may result in a massive cerebral hemorrhage of the sort Roosevelt experienced at Warm Springs, Georgia, in April 1945.

The impact of hypertensive encephalopathy on cognitive and emotional responses to environmental stimuli may be striking. Drs. Plum and Posner refer to those episodes during which it is obvious that intellectual impairment, if not overt unawareness, is prominent: "The attacks can take several forms. One consists of progressive delerium and stupor. . . . Typically, the neurological signs last minutes, hours, or days, then disappear, leaving little or no residua." A second observation highlights the frequent difficulty in making the diagnosis:

> Typically, the patients are moderately or severely hypertensive, and have suffered a *recent abrupt rise* in blood pressure [italics mine]. The thing that often makes diagnosis difficult is that many deviate from this rule, and the blood pressure sometimes drops to near normal soon after a severe attack. [52]

Countless descriptions of the President confirm that he suffered from frequent episodes of what physicians call a "quiet" delirium or stupor during his last two years in office. Most of these behavioral aberrations lasted minutes rather than hours or days. While a few heretofore perplexing and unexplained decisions may have been made during such attacks, discussed below, there nonetheless is no convincing evidence that Roosevelt suffered from significant dementia of a permanent nature on account of this disease.

This does not negate the probability that a modest degree of intellectual impairment did occur. The natural history of hypertension (and other illnesses Roosevelt had) supports this claim in relation to brain function. Dr. Michael D. O'Brien, Senior Lecturer of the Department of Neurology of Guys Hospital in London, cites abundant medical evidence to that effect: "A higher incidence of intellectual impairment has been found in patients with heart disease, hypertension, reduced pulmonary function, and peripheral atherosclerosis, [even] without obvious evidence of cerebrovascular disease." [53] Recognizing that Franklin Roosevelt was afflicted by every one of the disease processes O'Brien mentions, it is probable that some degree of intellectual restriction accompanied them, even if the record does not truly suggest as clear a progressive course as we have witnessed in the case of Woodrow Wilson.

What the record does reveal was a plethora of brief periods of unawareness, which were strikingly similar in presentation despite being described by a wide range of observers. Grace Tully's disconcerting observation in June 1944 is well known to, and often quoted by, Roosevelt's detractors: "It was in the last year that I found the Boss occasionally nodding over his mail or dozing a moment during dictation. . . . As it began to occur with increasing frequency I became seriously alarmed." [54] One may argue that this description is more compatible with generalized fatigue than a medically recognizable encephalopathy. Nevertheless, she described his appearance as a "condition" by this time, and her subsequent comment warrants a critical examination: "But it was before this condition reached an evident state that the decision was made that the Boss should run for his fourth term." [55] Others would not agree, having witnessed transient behavioral changes in the President long before June 1944. Tugwell's comment just after the Teheran Conference has already been acknowledged: "He fell sometimes into unaccustomed reverie, from which he would awake with a start." This was during the same period (March 1944) that Bishop recorded how "his mouth often hung open, his thoughts unfinished, and his sentences dangling."[56] Burns noted that Roosevelt occasionally nodded off during conversation; "once he blanked out halfway through signing his name to letter."[57] This occurred before his examination in March.

Thereafter, convincing episodes of a temporarily clouded sensorium blot the otherwise impeccable medical portrait McIntire was laboring to paint for the press and the American public. In July 1944 Roosevelt ventured to Hawaii to meet with General Douglas MacArthur and Admiral Chester Nimitz regarding military and naval strategy in the Pacific. While there, he delivered a short speech. At one point, according to John T. Flynn, "he faltered and paused, his eyes became glassy, and consciousness drifted from him. He had to be shown his place."[58] There is no record of Roosevelt's blood pressure during his sojourn in Hawaii, yet the vignette is highly suggestive of encephalopathy, with possible coincident cortical blindness, which often occurs during brief accelerated levels of hypertension. This is believed to be caused by spasm of blood vessels supplying the visual cortex in the posterior portion of the brain. Although cortical blindness is often a permanent condition, it may be temporary in the severely hypertensive state, and thus categorized as a transient ischemic attack.

It is disconcerting to recognize that at this conference the President, as Commander in Chief of the Armed Forces, was trying to resolve a dispute between MacArthur and Nimitz over the strategic conception of the remaining Pacific campaign. Not only did he have no military experience, but he also chose to weigh the merits of the contrasting arguments alone, without asking for further counsel from either General George C. Marshall or Admiral Ernest J. King.[59] The abrupt manner in which he made the final decision in MacArthur's favor suggests a degree of flippancy, perhaps brought on by fatigue or impatience. Having initially overruled MacArthur in Nimitz' favor as the Joint Chiefs had advised,[60] he suddenly reversed his position shortly thereafter, as the debate between the two military men wore on:

> It was close to lunchtime, and Roosevelt was still listening. The debaters began to repeat themselves. . . . The President waved his hands for both sides to stop. Without comment, he said he approved the MacArthur plan and would expect Nimitz to assist in the recapture of Luzon and the other islands.[61]

McIntire's account of the three-day conference in Hawaii is brief but to the point, however specious that point proved to be: "The three days . . . stand as a convincing answer to the charges that the President was a sick man. . . . There was not one who failed to comment on the vigor of his mind and the clarity of his thought."[62] Nevertheless, MacArthur (who had every reason to be happy with the result of the conference) was bothered enough by what he had seen of Roosevelt while there to predict that "the President would be dead within a year."[63]

Burns' assessment of Roosevelt's conduct in this brief encounter was mixed. He lauded the tactical finesse with which the President placated both adversaries by "steering the discussion away from absolutes." But he faulted Roosevelt's conduct as Chief Executive and Commander in Chief in failing to recognize the strategic implications of his decision. "To the extent that Roosevelt immersed himself in the role of the soldier and of the Commander in Chief, he was unable to take that balanced and comprehensive view of things that properly arrayed the military against the political, the short-run against the long.[64]

Interestingly enough, illness other than Roosevelt's played some part in agumenting the isolated position he chose for himself while arriving at such a momentous strategic decision. Not only had he apparently neglected the advice of the Joint Chiefs on the issue; he likewise had lost the services of Harry Hopkins in any advisory capacity due to the latter's accelerated illness and evident exhaustion during this period.[65] Given the President's medical condition, it is possible that the rashness of his decision, which reversed a judgment made just a few hours earlier, may have been influenced by fatigue and one-dimensional thinking. Both are known to afflict the severely hypertensive patient on an intermittent basis. If this cannot be established in Roosevelt's case with the available evidence, MacArthur's assessment of Roosevelt's physical appearance is at least enough to raise the suggestion—not to mention contradicting McIntire's deceiving assertion of the President's vitality.

This was an election year, and many observers of the day viewed the trip as politically motivated and inspired. Yet if political considerations were the order of the day, evidence indicates they were in uncharacteristically short supply for a man who owed his longevity before the public eye to the voting process. Roosevelt's associates were alarmed over his lack of interest in the game he had played so well heretofore. They worried less about Republican presidential nominee Thomas E. Dewey than they did about what Burns called their chief's uncharacteristic lack of interest in political detail.[66]

Meanwhile, those who should have been worried about Roosevelt's physical well-being were too immersed in political considerations to recognize the danger signals that were so prevalent during this period. On his return from Hawaii, Roosevelt had made a stopover at the Bremerton, Washington naval yard, during which he gave a speech on board ship. While speaking he was gripped by a searing chest pain characteristic of cardiac angina that his physician subsequently ignored. McIntire's account of the incident was either deceitful or exceedingly naive: "A stiff wind was blowing, and there was quite a slant to the deck, two things that called for bracing on his part. . . . As a result he finished up with considerable pain [which was] purely muscular as it turned out."[67] No further reference was ever made to what others have correctly described as an attack of coronary insufficiency.[68]

This was in August 1944. Even the President now confided in a weak moment that he might be dangerously ill and that he was having difficulty executing his job efficiently.[69] In September, this self-realization became transiently apparent to others at the Quebec Conference, during which Roosevelt endorsed a poorly supported plan to convert Germany into a pastoral state at war's end. This was the controversial Morgenthau Plan, authored by its namesake, Henry Morgenthau, then Secretary of the Treasury and a longtime friend of the President. The plan was both harsh and vindictive, and it initially enjoyed the support of virtually no one, even Churchill.[70] After the Conference, moreover, public opinion regarding its acceptance was negative. Within the month, wrote Burns, everyone would repudiate it, "and Roosevelt would quietly back away."[71]

Yet why did the President accept it in the first place? Had he been cognitively compromised at the time? This might be inferred from Dr. Bruenn's notation on the second day of the Conference that his patient's blood pressure had reached the distressing level of 240/130.[72] Certainly these levels were at or above those required to induce transient bouts of hypertensive encephalopathy. Had Roosevelt been so unaware of his actions as to agree to a proposal that others found inexplicable and unsupportable? On the surface at least, some of the evidence appears to support this. Roosevelt later admitted to others his unawareness of the act. Bradley Smith asserted that "FDR claims not remembering having signed the Morgenthau memo."[73] Henry Stimson had been informed by his chief that he did not know "'how' he had initialed the Quebec agreement. 'It must have been done . . . without much thought.'"[74] And in reply to Cordell Hull's protest, he first denied the agreement, then seemed "'frankly staggered' . . . and then insisted 'he had no idea of how he could have initialed the memorandum.'"[75] If these strikingly similar accounts may be dismissed as expressions of various anti-Roosevelt themes, the sober judgments of Rexford Tugwell cannot be dismissed so easily. "It is interesting that Franklin almost at once, but without any admission, abandoned the Morgenthau Plan. . . . At any rate, he proceeded to pretend that he knew nothing about it. Unfortunately, his initials were evidence to the contrary."[76]

Pretense may not have been involved at all, given the knowledge of Roosevelt's accelerated level of hypertension to a truly malignant level during this time. Perhaps he really was unaware when he signed the agreement—temporarily out of touch with his surroundings, or at least compromised enough to ignore the essentials of the issue in question. Tugwell suggested as much when he asserted:

> I am almost tempted to account for the *strange aberration* [italics mine] of consent to the Morgenthau plan by guessing that, as his strength failed, Franklin became more and more dependent upon those close to him, and that Morgenthau took advantage of this. Hopkins was not at Quebec. . . . He was too often ill. . . . So there was no one to object, until Stimson and Hull heard of the scheme. . . . [Yet] there is another explanation. . . . He may have initialed the plan absentmindedly. [77]

Indeed so, but not in the sense that the general public usually associates with the term. Roosevelt's absent-mindedness may in fact have been physiologically induced. His medical record includes a condition that readily accounts for the "strange aberrations" to which Tugwell referred. Others at the Conference such as Lord Moran also perceived the President's physical compromise while there. Moran suggested a degree of impairment in Roosevelt's ability to abstract by dealing with problems in an ad hoc fashion. [78] He showed little concern for preparation and resolved to dispose of issues quickly. That an overt lapse in awareness may have occurred as well under these conditions therefore deserves consideration.

It would be reasonable, then, to invoke poor health as the cause for Roosevelt's rather perplexing stand on the Morgenthau Plan. After all, his blood pressure was now running out of control, and the possibility of a recurrence of his encephalopathy was a constant threat. But a more-detailed knowledge of how that decision came about largely dispels this contention, and saves the writer from taking a fatal leap into the abyss of medical reductionism. Warren F. Kimball's analysis of the Morgenthau Plan shows how truly consistent that proposal was with Roosevelt's perception of the German problem throughout the war. Demilitarization, Kimball notes, had been the key to his thinking all along:

> In spite of steady pressure from the State Department, [the President] refused to . . . waver from his belief that all Germans, not just the Nazis, were guilty. . . . A pastoral state . . . could hardly support a modern military establishment or provide nourishment for the militant, aggressive nationalism long associated with Prussia and Germany. [79]

Consistent with this belief, Roosevelt and Churchill initialed a memorandum at Quebec on September 15, 1944, which read in part: "This programme for eliminating the war-making industries in the Ruhr and the Saar is looking forward to converting Germany into a country primarily agricultural and pastoral in its character."[80] The various alternatives for restructuring Germany in the postwar period had long been the subject of debate within the American government, but Roosevelt did not firmly commit himself until the eleventh hour to the plan Morgenthau had nurtured in private talks with him during the months of August and early September. Morgenthau had done his job well enough that in a meeting of the Cabinet committee concerning postwar Germany on September 9 (just two days before the Quebec Conference opened) the President had already agreed to support a hard-line policy despite his recognition that others present were against it.[81]

This was not a snap decision; Roosevelt had been leaning in that direction for some time. Yet did his inability to arrive at a firm decision earlier reflect a degree of disease-induced inability to unravel the complexities of the issue? Hardly so. At least three considerations favored caution, the first of which was the haunting specter of Wilson's predicament a quarter of a century earlier when his efforts to obtain a just peace had been skewered by similar secret agreements and treaties concluded before hostilities had ended. The second consideration was Roosevelt's desire to include the Russians in any decision about the reconstruction of Germany. The third condition was a personal one—Roosevelt's consistent reluctance to make concrete decisions.[82] Always with one ear to the political ground, Roosevelt typically failed to act until compelled to do so. Only on those rare occasions when he found himself on solid ground with close advisors he trusted would Roosevelt react before testing the more uncertain waters of public opinion. The decision on the Morgenthau Plan in September 1944 was one such occasion. Those who had opposed the plan did not go to Quebec. Yet Morgenthau did, as the President's chief advisor. As Bradley Smith succinctly noted: "At this point, Roosevelt was definitely in Morgenthau's pocket on the German question."[83] Only later, when the groundswell of adverse opinion threatened his political base would the President reverse his position on the vindictive memorandum he had initialed.

If the substance of the Morgenthau Plan was in accord with the President's overall view, the manner in which he struck the bargain at Quebec still raises some legitimate questions. Roosevelt's method of decision making had always been one of consensus; now he took up a position in opposition to the prevailing opinion in the State Department and the War Department—and ultimately risked political destruction in the process. Though he was consistent in his thinking on the German problem, Roosevelt was less so in the manner in which he now attempted to promote it, and this is where the issue of illness may have come into play.

It should be recalled that during the week of the proceedings at

Quebec, Roosevelt's blood pressure reached truly alarming levels. Always the chief protagonist in any issue where he could use the force of his strong personality, he was strangely subdued during the one meeting at which the signing of the agreement took place. Kimball himself noted that the President was virtually a nonentity in the discussions on that crucial day.[84] Jim Bishop noted that toward the end of the conference Roosevelt lapsed into an unaccountable "depressive lassitude."[85] McIntire nonetheless optimistically noted that "the President was in rare form throughout the week"—which stands as an ironic choice of words, as Lord Moran made clear: "It was not only his physical deterioration that caught [our] attention. He intervened little in the discussions, sitting with his mouth open."[86]

How much, then, does the medical argument apply to what transpired at the Quebec Conference? Not as much as one might assume, given the numerous descriptions of Roosevelt's poor appearance and the documentation that his blood pressure was now out of control. If he took his stand uncharacteristically firmly and seemingly at the behest of a very limited number of advisors, what he agreed to at least squared with beliefs he had held for some time. It is therefore doubtful that the result would have been much different had he been in good health.

Nevertheless, Quebec reinforced the feeling that all was not well with the President. Drowsiness and lethargy had been apparent to those close to Roosevelt at certain periods after Teheran. Now, his seeming lack of interest in political details concerned his associates. He appeared increasingly willing to deal with issues in a piecemeal fashion. Yet most distressing of all were the overt episodes of unawareness that began to appear in September 1944. Consider, then, the comments of Drs. Plum and Posner regarding such observations as they relate to the physical and cognitive manifestations of metabolic encephalopathy. Concerning the observation of drowsiness, they state:

> Initially the patient [with metabolic encephalopathy] appears preoccupied or just uninterested. . . . As the disease progresses, drowsiness becomes more apparent. . . . This pattern of drowsiness *preceding* other changes is more characteristic of secondary metabolic encephalopathy [such as occurs with hypertension, congestive heart failure, chronic obstructive pulmonary disease, and anemia] than of primary [as in dementia, for example]; demented patients [in contrast] tend to lose orientation and cognition long before lethargy ensues.[87]

Two comments are in order. First, Grace Tully's and Rexford Tugwell's observations of increasing episodes of drowsiness and lethargy were among the first signs of mental change cited by Roosevelt's associates during the first half of 1944. True cognitive changes and failures to abstract did not occur until later. This fits the characteristic description of a secondary metabolic process. Second, Roosevelt's condition offers an informative contrast to Woodrow Wilson's as an example of a primary dementing process. Few instances of drowsiness or stupor appear in Wilson's record, and observers placed more emphasis from the beginning on his intellectual and emotional aberrations. They characterized Wilson as a veritable whirlwind of vigorous (if ultimately ineffectual) activity at Versailles and thereafter until his stroke. Roosevelt, on the other hand, visibly slowed during his last year in office, even though observers acknowledged his clarity of thought and effectiveness to very near the end, if his interests were sufficiently aroused. Both were dangerously ill men, yet the effect on their respective leadership capabilities was strikingly different. Plum and Posner's observation allows a medically based understanding of why this was so.

Concerning the second observation, regarding Roosevelt's lack of interest and compromised abstractive capabilities, these same medical investigators make the following point: "Most conscious patients with metabolic brain disease are confused. . . . Their abstract thinking is defective; they cannot concentrate well and cannot easily retain new information."[88] Events like the President's rapid reversal in favor of MacArthur's viewpoint in Hawaii, and to a lesser extent his initial acceptance of the Morgenthau Plan, may have borne the stamp of some compromise in his abstract attitude.

With regard to overt periods of unawareness of one's surroundings, Plum and Posner reveal that "changes in mentation and awareness are the earliest and most reliable warnings of the more slowly developing varieties of metabolic encephalopathy. . . . Altered awareness is the first and most subtle index of brain dysfunction, especially in patients with acute or subacute metabolic disorders."[89] This observation should raise the concern of even the most cynical critics of the medical argument. Bruenn's examination in March 1944 merely identified the various physical signs of the constellation of diseases afflicting Roosevelt. Yet Plum and Posner have observed in numerous patients in their studies that changes in mentation and awareness may well *precede* other clinically apparent manifestations of such metabolic disorders as hypertension, COPD, and CHF. Mental changes, they note, are the "first and most subtle" indices.[90] That these disease processes were far advanced at the time of Bruenn's first evaluation represents a sobering observation for any scholar attempting to unravel the complexities of Roosevelt's behavior during his last two years in office.

A very ill man, then, chose to run for an unprecedented fourth term as President of the United States. If Roosevelt himself had any concern about his failing health, they were quickly dispelled by his physician, who insisted to the President that he was not sick, but "just getting over the flu and still troubled with bronchitis." The American public was similarly deceived. McIntire assured the journalists in a press conference on October 12, 1944: "The President's health is perfectly okay."[91] Thus began the campaign of deception in which the administration focused a very great effort on trying to make Roosevelt appear well. Roosevelt's disdain and genuine contempt for Dewey helped to stimulate his interest in the battle, and during much of the campaign he was his old vigorous, fighting self. As Burns related: "Fighting off campaign rumors about his condition, he had handled the exacting 'Fala' speech . . . with exquisite skill; he had driven gaily for hours through New York streets in a cold, driving rain."[92] Yet the disturbing intermittent symptoms failed to disappear, though they were effectively hidden from even the highest echelons of the Democratic party machinery. Burns acknowledged the vagaries of the President's condition, yet understandably lacked a medical understanding of the significance of the descriptions he made. Continuing the portrait quoted above, Burns admitted: "But at other times he seemed quite different. His face went slack; he slumped in his chair; his hands trembled more than ever. . . . Yet so swiftly did he shift from dullness to buoyancy that even while his friends were whispering to one another about their concern there would be fresh reports that the President was showing his old form."[93]

By late October the President was complaining of frequent headaches and seemed to experience both good days and bad. "On some mornings, the Boss looked 'awful,'" one of his subordinates recounted; "on others he appeared to be buoyant and bright."[94] Nagging bouts of encephalopathy persisted. "Shortly before the election," John Flynn wrote, "he had another one of those lapses of complete consciousness, much the same as happened to him in Honolulu."[95] McIntire, of course, made no mention of these episodes in his memoirs and was in fact surprised by Roosevelt's apparent show of vitality: "Quite frankly I dreaded the campaign," he recounted in his memoirs, "but the manner in which the President came through it made me doubt my accuracy as a diagnostician."[96] Yet if McIntire had portrayed Roosevelt as being the picture of health for a man his age, the critical observer might ask: What was he dreading, and why was he compelled to doubt his diagnostic acumen? Surely "sinuses and bronchitis" alone would be no serious source of concern for the successful completion of even the most vigorous of campaigns!

In his memoirs, McIntire sought to justify his portrayal of Roosevelt as being in good health during the 1944 campaign:

Since it is now a fixed habit of certain columnists to assert that Franklin Roosevelt was a dying man in 1944 and that his medical advisors were well aware of it, I submit this typical checkup covering the period from September 20 to November 1: 'Lungs clear; heart—no cardiac symptoms at any time. . . . Blood pressure of labile type; systolic ranging from 165–180; diastolic from 88 to 100; electrocardiogram shows no changes from that of the May examination. . . . Only small annoyances cause any rise in systolic pressure. Kidney function normal. . . . Blood picture—shows no anemia. . . . Any doctor going over it will bear out my statement, made to the press, that the President was in "good health for a man his age."[97]

It is true that this brief record, as presented, gives no undue cause for concern—with one critical exception. The notation of a blood pressure labile (that is, unstable) enough to be triggered by even "small annoyances" speaks to the extremely tenuous nature of Roosevelt's medical condition in this respect. How else can we account for Dr. Bruenn's documentation of a blood pressure recording of 240/130 at Quebec during the same period? One must either postulate a purposeful discrepancy in the record or accept an extreme lability of pressure. Dealing with the question of duplicity first, obviously Bruenn had no axe to grind from the standpoint of personal gain, certainly not enough to record spurious values. He was never made accountable to the public in his position as a subordinate of McIntire's. McIntire was accountable, yet his duplicity in the affair presumably did not extend to falsifying the medical record, though Bishop's assertion regarding the fate of some of Bruenn's reports (p. 230 above) is a sobering reminder of that possibility. On the other hand, wide variations in pressure do occur in individuals afflicted with moderately severe hypertension, so it can be accepted that such lability existed in Roosevelt's case. This should in no way give rise to complacency on the part of the physician. Certainly McIntire had to be aware of the occasional extremely high levels Bruenn diagnosed. To cite the lower values, even if they were far more common (but certainly still not normal), concealed the very real dangers that had attended the President.

The lability is of interest in itself and has a medical explanation. Certain pressure sensors in the arterial walls of the carotid artery in the neck trigger reflexes to lower the blood pressure when the force exerted against the artery's wall becomes too high. If the pressure becomes too low, the sensor transmits reflex impulses that augment heart rate and flow, thereby raising the pressure. "Denervation [or loss of sensitivity] of this sensor . . . causes extreme lability of blood pressure," *Cecil's Textbook of Medicine* states.[98] Physiologically, the most common cause of denervation is atherosclerosis, in which the thickened arterial wall dampens the stimulus to the sensor.

Roosevelt's mortician later reported that the deceased President's atherosclerosis was so severe that the embalming itself took five hours.[99] On a physiologic basis, then, Roosevelt lacked one of the primary defenses protecting him from sudden severe elevations in blood pressure. This factor, as much as any other, probably accounts for periods of hypertension-induced encephalopathy, when cerebral blood vessels go into spasm as a protective response to the increased pressure and flow. The increased resistance afforded by the spasm causes diminished flow, either focally to the region supplied by these vessels, accounting for the transient multifocal neurologic deficits seen with encephalopathy (e.g., cortical blindness), or generally, if all vessels spasm, accounting for the brief periods of total unawareness.[100]

Yet there are other causes for increased blood pressure, one of which is intimately related to the congestive heart failure Roosevelt experienced. If the body is severely depleted of salt and water, the blood pressure falls; if it is overloaded with these, the pressure rises.[101] In congestive heart failure, too much volume is present in systemic vessels due to compromise of the cardiac pump. This explains the rationale for the only treatment (aside from rest) available at the time for both Roosevelt's CHF and his hypertension—the restriction of salt, which otherwise acts as an osmotic, drawing fluid into the vessels and overexpanding them.[102]

A destructive cycle thereafter appears in individuals with this ultimately fatal combination of hypertension, congestive heart failure, and atherosclerosis. Experiments and clinical evidence have convincingly shown the importance of blood pressure as an accelerator of atherosclerosis. A systolic blood pressure of greater than 160 mm Hg or a diastolic greater than 95 mm Hg carries a *five-fold* increased risk of coronary heart disease compared to individuals with normal blood pressure.[103] Hypertension also compromises the pumping action of the heart. The presence of a high systemic arterial pressure increases the afterload of the left ventricle, and in consequence, the ventricle hypertrophies or thickens. As the pressure rises to a very high level, the ventricle dilates and eventually fails.[104]

Already then, there are sufficient grounds for indictment against the optimistic medical record McIntire presented in his memoirs. Yet Bruenn's own account repeatedly suggested Roosevelt's condition to be much worse than the record his superior cited. In the best of circumstances, McIntire recorded blood pressures ranging from 165 to 180 systolic and 88 to 100 diastolic. All of the accelerating effects on the cycle of illnesses that plagued Roosevelt are known to occur in this blood pressure range. Simply stated, these are not figures with which any physician should be content.

It also seems apparent that McIntire ignored the effect of atherosclerosis on denervating the carotid sensors responsible for controlling dangerous levels of blood pressure—despite the fact that he himself had noted the warning signs of lability. Roosevelt was therefore subject to wide swings of blood pressure, the last of which undoubtedly precipitated the fatal cerebral hemorrhage in April 1945. [105] One might argue that medical knowledge available at the time did not include an awareness of this intricate system of blood pressure control. This assertion is false, as Allen M. Scher has pointed out:

> In 1925 H. E. Herring noted that mechanical stimulation of the carotid sinus in a patient produced a reflex bradycardia [slowing of the heart rate]. This effect was due, of course, to increased firing of the receptors initiated by the mechanical stimulation. . . . In 1929 C. Heymans performed an ingenious series of experiments ending the confusion over these reflexes. His work led to a Nobel Prize in 1938. [106]

It goes without saying that the President of the United States should be afforded the best medical care available. That McIntire, Bruenn, and the consultants on Roosevelt's case were apparently unaware of what was then accepted physiology in arterial blood pressure and cardiovascular mechanics underscores what often happens to physicians entrusted with the care of important individuals. In essence, nourishing the social and political contacts necessary to bring one to the attention of a highly placed political leader often implies a reduction in time spent keeping abreast of the latest medical developments—not to mention one so well publicized as to be worthy of a Nobel Prize six short years before. This was not esoteric information buried in an obscure medical journal. Not only would it have represented front-page news for any physician at the time; by 1944 it was well-accepted medical knowledge. Yet if one would counter that McIntire was only an eye, ear, nose, and throat specialist and not well-versed in cardiopulmonary and hypertensive medicine, then the question must be raised why such an individual should be entrusted with a President's health.

This brings us to an important consideration that McIntire addressed in his memoirs. He argued that there were no indicators that might have predicted Roosevelt's death from a cerebral hemorrhage:

> As for cerebral hemorrhage, it was and is unpredictable. There are some conditions of course, in which we think we can prevent it, such as extremely high blood pressure and advanced general atherosclerosis. . . . *President Roosevelt did not have either of these* [italics mine]. His blood pressure was not alarming at any time. . . . The signs that we count on for the condition of the cerebral arteries all denied that the President would have trouble in that regard. His kidneys and liver functions were normal. [107]

Such a false assertion boggles the mind. For one thing, the liver has little if any importance as an indicator of cerebral atherosclerosis or hypertension. Moreover, not only was McIntire guilty of ignoring all the medical data that his own records and Bruenn's examination revealed, but most physicians at that time were well aware of the ultimately dangerous effects and implications of poorly controlled hypertension. According to *Cecil's Textbook of Medicine:*

> Comparing normotensive individuals with those having a pressure exceeding 160 systolic and 95 diastolic mm Hg [values with which McIntire was apparently comfortable] the [increased risk factor] is three-fold for coronary disease, four-fold for congestive heart failure, and seven-fold for stroke. The increase in risk with level of blood pressure is most striking for stroke deaths. [108]

Strokes in hypertension usually occur from hemorrhages deep within the brain substance from small arteries of the lenticulostriate group. These vessels are damaged by persistent blood pressure elevations, with the eventual formation of blisters known as Charcot-Bouchard aneurysms on the vessels. With sudden accelerations of pressure, the force becomes too great and rupture occurs—which is what probably occurred to cause Roosevelt's death (see Fig. 4.1). The importance of effective treatment, which McIntire appears to have ignored, is expressed in the following medical tenet: "The risk from cerebral hemorrhage is very greatly reduced by lowering the blood pressure, and this probably indicates that the Charcot-Bouchard aneurysms are remodeled or obliterated after a period of pressure control. [109] Restricting salt in Roosevelt's diet and slowing his pace obviously were not enough to lower the pressure below the critical levels that McIntire accepted. Much more, including hospitalization, was needed in the face of such failure. Yet the record substantiates that Roosevelt's pressures were often significantly higher (240/130 on one occasion), and frequent bouts of encephalopathy persisted, particularly during the period preceding the 1944 election.

As mentioned earlier, the President suffered from frequent morning headaches. Medical evidence affords us some idea of the relative levels of diastolic hypertension he was experiencing in relation to these during this period. It is known, for example, that patients with diastolic pressures exceeding 110 mm Hg frequently complain of morning headaches. These headaches are related to the level of the blood pressure. [110] McIntire himself noted with satisfaction that Roosevelt often looked better during later periods of the day than in the morning. He also recorded "the very interesting fact" that the President's pressure readings were lower in the evening than in the morning. [111] Finally, he failed to assess

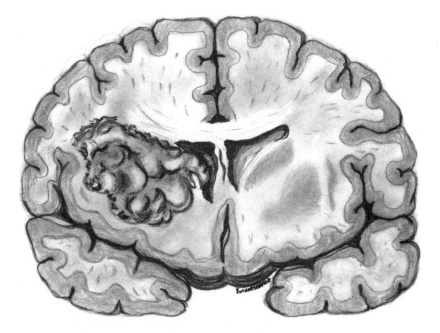

## INTRACRANIAL HEMORRHAGE

*Fig. 4.1 The large hemorrhage denotes the most frequent site of a hypertensive bleed such as Franklin Roosevelt experienced.*

the significance of Roosevelt's periods of stupor and unawareness that were becoming all too frequent. The following quote from *Cecil's Textbook of Medicine* underlines the implications of this failure:

> Patients with hypertensive encephalopathy usually present clinically with a very high level of pressure and increasingly severe headaches. These progress to general impairment of higher functions and eventually to stupor. . . . The diagnosis is a most important one to make accurately, because the patient's condition will improve rapidly if the blood pressure is reduced to a level at which cerebrovascular autoregulation is once again possible. [112]

The importance of Roosevelt's chronic obstructive pulmonary disease in the interrelationship of hypertension, congestive heart failure, and atherosclerosis should not be ignored. The President was a heavy smoker, and his physician's warnings had little impact on his habit. Furthermore, the severity of his lung compromise was documented by Bruenn's notation of Roosevelt's cyanotic fingernail beds and lips. [113] The availability of oxygen for neuron function is dependent both on the blood flow and the amount of oxygen that can be transported by red cells to the brain. Atherosclerosis progressively reduces the amount of blood delivered through narrowed vascular channels, and the diminution of available oxygen to brain cells is precisely what accounts for their dysfunction, whether generalized, as in encephalopathy, or localized, as in a transient ischemic attack or stroke. Not only did Roosevelt's smoking habit cause further deterioration in his chronic obstructive pulmonary disease, with consequent decreased oxygen available in the bloodstream; the nicotine itself accelerated the process of cerebral atherosclerosis.

Encephalopathy may be caused by chronic obstructive pulmonary disease alone or in combination with other metabolic factors, such as hypertension, congestive heart failure, or anemia. Though poorly controlled hypertension was probably the cause of Roosevelt's headaches and periods of clouding of consciousness, carbon dioxide retention due to chronic lung disease also produces these symptoms. Indeed, given the overt physical signs obvious to even the most casual observer, the latter argument may well prove to be equally convincing when applied to Roosevelt.

Recalling Bruenn's description of the President in their first encounter—a patient with a peculiar lack of interest in the examination itself, and with obvious cyanosis of lips and nailbeds, shortness of breath and rapid breathing while lying down, basilar rales in the lungs, and a persistent tremor of the outstretched hands—the image of severe pulmonary insufficiency immediately comes to mind. Drs. Austen, Carmichael, and Adams published an article in the *New England Journal of Medicine* entitled "Neurologic Manifestations of Chronic Pulmonary Insufficiency" that has become a classic treatise on the subject of pulmonary-induced encephalopathy. In the illustrative cases that they cite, the following symptoms and physical findings uniformly appear: a persistent cough, cyanosis, obvious shortness of breath, headache during the morning hours, rapid tremor of the outstretched limbs, and a mental state characterized by drowsiness, inattention, or confusion.[114] It would be difficult to construct a more representative picture of Franklin Roosevelt during the March 1944 medical examination. Compare these features to extracts taken from Bruenn's initial evaluation of Roosevelt: There was a cyanotic cast to his lips and fingernails, shortness of breath while supine, and a noticeable tremor of his hands. The year before a coffee mug twice the standard size had been ordered for Roosevelt so that he could hold it to his lips without spilling it. A soft and persistent cough as well as rales were noted on examination, indicating fluid in both lungs. Anna had been conscious of her father's soft cough for three months, and "at motion pictures, she had [also] noticed for the first time that her father's mouth hung open for long periods."[115] Only the absence of headaches keeps this description of Roosevelt from being precisely interchangeable with the illustrative cases described in pulmonary-induced encephalopathy—and headaches too would appear in abundance within two months of Bruenn's initial examination.

The parallel with Roosevelt's condition in regard to the neurologic sequelae of pulmonary insufficiency is no less convincing. Austen et al. summarized its effect on brain function in the following manner:

> *Impairment of consciousness* was noted in each patient [italics mine]. In each the principal complaint of the family and employers was that the patients were extremely drowsy and often fell asleep while at work, while eating, or while in conversation with family or friends. They were also described as being forgetful, irritable, and easily confused. . . . Many stimuli passed unheeded, and there was obvious difficulty in assimilating all the details of a situation. . . . A lack of ability to recall recent events and a failure to think quickly and coherently appeared to be the result of the inattention and reduced awareness. [116]

Grace Tullys and Rexford Tugwell's testimonials with regard to Roosevelt's lethargy and inappropriate, brief periods of sleep at work have already been cited as precisely those aspects of his behavior that alarmed them so in 1944. The other symptoms described also characterized much of Roosevelt's behavior at, for example, Hawaii and Quebec.

Thus far, this analysis has emphasized those aspects of Roosevelt's health prior to the electon of 1944 that did not warrant the optimistic appraisal McIntire's testimony affords. By November 1944 it is true that two of the four predisposing factors for chronic subacute cerebral ischemia, or encephalopathy, had been alleviated to some degree—the anemia documented in 1941 [117] and the congestive heart failure that appears to have rapidly improved with Bruenn's insistence upon salt restriction and digitalis administration. Yet the effects of hypertension and chronic obstructive pulmonary disease remained. Accordingly, the brief episodes of clouding of consciousness progressed in number, occasionally accompanied by focal neurologic deficits. For example, in January 1945 extracts from Grace Tully's recollections as recounted by Jim Bishop reflect an increasingly frequent observation:

> Some said they noticed a slight droop at the corner of his mouth. Grace Tully said she worried when Mr. Roosevelt suddenly dozed over his mail. She had witnessed it several times. In chats with political friends he frequently "drew a blank" as they listened; abashed, he had to ask what he had been talking about. After a dinner of the White House Correspondents Association, reporters who personally admired him as a great President said he seemed to have developed a slight impediment in his speech. [118]

Frequently thereafter, as one associate noted, Roosevelt was so exhausted that "he could not answer simple questions and talked what was close to nonsense." [119]

Two other symptoms that became progressive in spite of the apparent improvement in Roosevelt's cardiac condition were the persistent morning headaches and the bothersome tremor of his hands. Since these symptoms are frequently associated with hypertension, an understanding of their pathogenesis in relation to chronic obstructive pulmonary disease serves to underscore the combined influence of the two conditions on Roosevelt's recurrent metabolically induced encephalopathy. Medical articles by Westlake, [120] Davies, [121] and others echo the findings of Austen, Carmichael, and Adams: "Elevated carbon dioxide tension is probably the main factor in the development of drowsiness and impairment of consciousness." [122] Patients with COPD typically retain abnormal amounts of carbon dioxide in their bloodstreams. This also explains the prominence of headaches in these individuals, particularly in the morning. Carbon dioxide dilates the cerebral vasculature and this, stated simply, causes increased pressure on the brain within the rigid enclosure of the skull. Furthermore, carbon dioxide retention is augmented during sleep, which accounts for its more prominent pressure effects upon wakening. The cause of the twitching and tremor that are always seen in these patients is less clear, but increased carbon dioxide in the bloodstream, leading to systemic acidosis, has been considered as a possible factor in the production of this movement disorder. [123]

The implications of these various neurologic disorders foreshadow the impact illness may have had on Roosevelt's behavior and leadership. At the very least, the conclusion of Austen, Carmichael, and Adams contradicts McIntire's denial that any significant illness affected the President: "The neurologic disorder presented by these patients is not difficult to diagnose," they assert, "if it is appreciated that such seeming disparate symptoms and signs as headache, drowsiness, and confusion, as well as tremor . . . can be the manifestations of cardiopulmonary failure." [124]

It therefore appears that McIntire's medical records prior to the election, which he cited as evidence of Roosevelt's satisfactory state of health, come nowhere near to telling the entire story. [125] In fact, the appearance of bouts of encephalopathy as early as 1944, probably on both a hypertensive and a pulmonary basis, defined the longstanding and severe nature of Roosevelt's compromised health. As a respected medical textbook of the present day suggests: "The appearance of the syndrome [of encephalopathy] is associated with the end-state phase of advanced hypertensive vascular disease." [126] Franklin Roosevelt was indeed running tenuously on borrowed time, a fact of which the American voting public was unaware in November 1944.

The review to this point has examined the interval between Roosevelt's return from the Teheran Conference (approximately the point at which many observers began to note obvious changes in his appearance and behavior) through the nomination and successful campaign of 1944. The final six months of Roosevelt's tenure, including the controversial Yalta Conference, still remain to be discussed. Yet, having established Roosevelt as a President afflicted with several chronic illnesses at least as early as 1943, digression is in order to discuss how the effects of Roosevelt's compromised health influenced his third term. After all, diastolic hypertension was documented as early as 1941, and neither congestive heart failure nor chronic obstructive pulmonary disease develop overnight. Moreover, an allegation circulated that Roosevelt's campaign manager had noticed signs of mental deterioration and delayed reactions before his election for a third term in 1940, [127] and by early 1944 many newspaper reporters alleged that the President was dying. [128] Reference has already been made to at least two occasions in which the effects of illness possibly played a role during the third term—the Hawaii meeting with MacArthur and Nimitz, and the Quebec Conference. Yet these took place after Teheran. What does the record suggest of events prior to that time?

Certainly the war years took their toll on a president aging far more rapidly than simple chronology would suggest. His private secretary, Grace Tully, admitted as much: "The Boss not only grew older in the manner of all human beings, but he also faced responsibilities that intensified with the years. . . . So it was in the latter years I observed the cumulative weariness, the dark circles that never quite faded from under his eyes, the more pronounced shake in his hand . . . the easy slump that developed in his shoulders." [129] Madame Chiang Kai-shek is quoted as having been "shocked by the President's appearance" during the Cairo conferences antedating Teheran. She believed that he had "fallen off considerably" and seemed "quite ill" at the time. [130] One might suspect to find, therefore, a considerable body of evidence to implicate illness as a detrimental factor in Roosevelt's leadership during the war years. Surprisingly, there is little to suggest this prior to Teheran, as a cursory review of a few representative controversial issues shows.

On election night, November 4, 1940, the President spoke to his supporters and proclaimed: "We are facing difficult days in this country, but I think you will find me in the future just the same Franklin Roosevelt you have known a great many years." [131] Insofar as the future extended to Teheran, his assertion would prove to be true. Still, as early as 1941 there were many who began to doubt that the President was leading with the same resolution, aggressiveness, and prescience he had demonstrated over the previous eight years.

By the spring of 1941 a genuine crisis of leadership appears to have occurred, as Roosevelt appeared wavering and irresolute in directing the nation's involvement in the European war. As Burns has observed: "Most people close to the administration saw the main lack of leadership in Roosevelt himself. . . . [Felix] Frankfurter told [Harold] Ickes he was at a loss to understand the President's failure to take the initiative. . . . Roosevelt would lead—but not by more than a step. He seemed beguiled by public opinion," and he appeared irresolute.[132] David Lilienthal was reminded of the uncertain early days of 1933 when the nation willingly accepted Roosevelt's aggressive leadership and often-experimental approach to government. By 1941, however, he felt he was witnessing a very different Roosevelt: "The bold strokes of leadership, the clarion call, these aren't quite as fresh and invigorating as then."[133]

Roosevelt appeared tired, and admitted as much to others. Henry Stimson remarked to the President at one point during the impasse over entering the war that he was omitting one factor in evaluating public opinion and response to America's potential involvement in the burgeoning conflict—"the power of his own leadership." Roosevelt agreed that this was probably true but, as Burns noted, he complained that "he simply did not feel peppy enough." During this indecisive spring of 1941, "the master interpreter to the American people . . . seemed to have lost his touch."[134] Was this indecisiveness the product of illness? Acknowledging that Bruenn's perusal of McIntire's records revealed the presence of diastolic hypertension as early as 1941, there nevertheless was no hint of the episodes of encephalopathy that clearly emerged in Roosevelt's medical history by the latter half of 1944. It was not, for example, until late 1942 and early 1943 that references to Roosevelt's health even began to appear in Burns' accounts—an inference by omission of its lack of significance to that point.[135]

Perhaps more damaging in the long run was the President's inconsistent policy toward Japan, a potential adversary that at least nine months prior to Pearl Harbor had been quite inclined to seek a peaceful resolution of existing differences. In truth, Roosevelt's desire to postpone a settlement with the Japanese was consistent with his "Atlantic first" doctrine, during which time he hoped to "string things out" in the Pacific. As Burns acknowledged, however, "in Tokyo a different clock was ticking." A more moderate government under Premier Fumimaro Konoye consistently stood by its policy "not to sanction war as long as a possibility for settlement remained," and the Japanese made numerous diplomatic overtures to effect that reconciliation.[136] Yet Roosevelt remained curiously indecisive, despite warnings from the State Department that Konoye would fall unless diplomacy was given a chance. The administration remained unmoved, Konoye eventually resigned, and the militarists under the leadership of Hideki Tojo came to power. By November, the Japanese were formulating not only definite preparations for war but a precise plan for implementing a strike against the American naval forces concentrated at Pearl Harbor.

The question remains: Would the military takeover of the Japanese government have been averted at this time had diplomacy been exercised with dispatch by the United States? That question must ultimately be resolved by professional historians far more familiar with the intricacies of the issue than this brief review can afford.[137] The purpose here is to measure the impact of disease on the position taken by the President. Retrospectively, it does not seem to have carried much weight. Few, if any, close to the President of the United States during this critical year described any changes in his behavior suggesting a serious effect of illness—quite in contrast to the near-universal acknowledgment of changes in his condition remarked upon by 1944. Certainly the controversial issue of United States entry into the war was divisive enough for the most ardent critics of Roosevelt to establish a case of leadership compromise on the basis of illness if they had been able to do so. None has been forthcoming.

If illness cannot be implicated in the indecisiveness of Roosevelt's leadership at this juncture, some explanation must be tendered. James MacGregor Burns has offered the most convincing argument available: Roosevelt was waiting for a provocation. Being a deeply divided leader— "divided between the man of principle . . . crusading for a distant vision, on the one hand; and, on the other, the man of *Realpolitik*, of prudence, of narrow, manageable, short-run goals"—his strategy was "flawed by contradictions."[138] In the early going he was merely reacting to short-term circumstances while treading softly toward a military commitment to the Allies, and he needed popular support to tread that path. He was caught in the classic dilemma of the democratic leader forced to choose between the often divergent paths of what he believed was right and what was acceptable to the voting public. Therein lay one of the many contradictions Burns acknowledged: "The troubling question remained whether, in view of the critical situation abroad, he should [have been] more in advance of opinion than representative of it, . . . more of a creator and exploiter of public feeling than a reflector and articulator of it."[139]

The theme of contradiction extended to the President's character, as suggested by the title of another Burns review of the Roosevelt phenomenon, *Roosevelt: The Lion and the Fox*. Burns implied that there was much in the nature of the man that defies clear understanding:

His character was not only complex [as Robert Sherwood said], . . . it was contradictory to a bewildering degree. . . . It was not strange that he should follow Machiavelli's advice that a leader must be as brave as the lion and as shrewd as the fox. . . . But his metamorphosis from lion to fox and back to lion again mystified even his intimates.[140]

Nor did Roosevelt's most esteemed biographer find the President's behavior in regard to America's delayed entry into the war inconsistent with his role as both lion and fox:

> He felt that he understood pace and timing better than his critics did. They simply could not appreciate the web of restraints that surrounded him. It was not enough to cry out to high heaven for leadership and decisiveness. It was a matter of drawing . . . a following that could be depended on both in the day-to-day exigencies of politics and at times of national crisis and decision making.[141]

This consideration then, more than any significant influence of health, most satisfactorily accounts for Roosevelt's apparent indecisiveness in 1941. Arguably, such an approach did limit his alternatives: he was forced to await events as they unfolded, to wait for the necessary provocation. That provocation was unleashed at Pearl Harbor on December 7, 1941.[142] With that affront, both Roosevelt's method and Burns' assessment of it may have been vindicated. In the words of the historian Dexter Perkins, "No greater miscalculation has perhaps ever been made than that made by the militarists at Tokyo in December, 1941. By their own act, they unified American opinion and made their own defeat inevitable."[143] Roosevelt at last had his dependable following.

Yet if Burns emphasized a lion-and-fox dichotomy to explain Roosevelt's actions, Roosevelt nonetheless had shortcomings as a grand strategist that such a dichotomy made inevitable. This brings us to a brief discussion of the issue of unconditional surrender, a term that appeared in a pronouncement released during the conference between Churchill and Roosevelt at Casablanca in January 1943. Illness might be invoked as one reason the President made what many feel was an untimely declaration. As the historian David Shannon has defined the controversy and its implications:

> Roosevelt's critics have argued . . . that unconditional surrender caused Germany to fight on until destroyed, thereby prolonging the war and creating a power vacuum in central Europe which the Russians filled. The other side of the argument is that Roosevelt explicitly said that unconditional surrender did not mean the destruction of the German population but the end of fascism, and that a compromise with Nazism would have been immoral. But, clearly, the unconditional surrender policy did stiffen Axis resistance, and narrowed America's range of alternatives in its dealings with its allies.[144]

The suspicion that all may not have been right with the President at the time was fueled by a comment of James Byrnes, who remarked that the pronouncement concerning unconditional surrender, according to Bishop, "did not sound like President Roosevelt."[145] Nonetheless both Roosevelt and Churchill agreed to the declaration; one therefore would have to postulate some measure of communally compromised cognition to advance the thesis of ill health being causative.[146]

From the President's perspective, the declaration was quite consistent with his vengeful attitude toward Germany. His personal distaste for the German race in general and its military arm in particular strongly colored his thinking throughout the war, as a reading of his wartime letters, public speeches, and memoranda makes clear.[147] If his thinking was uncharacteristically rigid on this issue, as it would later prove to be at Quebec, it nonetheless remained a part of his personal prejudice to the end. Political considerations augmented this. The unconditional surrender policy served at least two purposes in Roosevelt's thinking: to reassure the Russians of America's resolve during the necessary delay in mounting a second front in Europe, and to guarantee a crushing defeat of German militarism. It represented, then, political glue for the wartime alliance.[148] The President was concerned most of all that a less-forceful attitude on America's part against a common foe might trigger Soviet moves toward a separate peace.[149]

One example in particular of Roosevelt's emphasizing military over political considerations laid the foundation for much of the criticism directed toward his later failure to accept Churchill's advice in pressing on to capture Berlin and Prague in advance of the Russians. This would have given him as strong a foothold in that area as possible prior to going to Yalta. Historian David Shannon has addressed the implications of this failure:

> Most people today would agree that it was a political mistake to turn south and not proceed east when the Elbe was reached. . . . By early April, the West had the better chance of reaching the cities [of Prague and Berlin] first. The decision to turn south was prompted by military rather than political considerations, although perhaps the real weakness was [Roosevelt's] failure to see clearly the relationship between the two.[150]

This last link brings us to the important consideration of the viability of the image of Franklin Roosevelt as the "Sick Man of Yalta." Chronologically, we left the story at election eve 1944 to entertain a consideration of what impact the President's compromised health had on certain controversial events as they transpired during the third term. In summary, not much of substance supports the view that illness played any role in those events—the Hawaii meeting in July and the Quebec Conference in September perhaps excepted. Nor should the indictment concerning the latter two issues come as any surprise; both occurred after documentation of the severity of the problem by Dr. Bruenn's examination in March 1944.

On the eve of embarking for Yalta, Roosevelt had already been elected for a fourth term. The severity of his illnesses and their effect on his leadership were becoming evident, though his electoral victory tended to conceal this from the American public. If McIntire's public disclosures suggested only continued improvement in Roosevelt's condition, his memoirs did not reflect the same: "It was the period between election day and the inauguration that justified concern," he wrote. Edward Stettinius echoed this sentiment:

> I had been concerned over the President ever since his inaugural address on the porch of the White House on January 20. That day he had seemed to tremble all over. It was not just his hands that shook, but his whole body as well. . . . It seemed to me that some kind of deterioration in the President's health had taken place between the middle of December and the inauguration. [151]

Even Francis Perkins was forced to acknowledge that a series of colds Roosevelt experienced during the winter of 1944 was "beyond the ordinary. For the first time since I had known him, he did not get his strength back." Though she wrote that thereafter she "did not have another moment's concern for him until the very end," her confidence was betrayed by her observation the day before the inauguration: "He looked like an invalid who has been allowed to see guests for the first time and the guests had stayed too long. . . . He supported his head with his hand. . . . His lips were blue. His hand shook." [152]

This was the period when Grace Tully registered such concern with Roosevelt falling asleep over his mail. Still, she would later assert in her memoirs that it really was not until after his return from Yalta that she noticed "the greatest and most serious bits of evidence" of his deterioration. [153] Considering her deference to her chief, whom she reverentially admired, it may be argued that her memory of events was "Gracefully selective."

Others remarked upon Roosevelt's obvious compromise before leaving for Yalta. Jim Farley recorded just before the embarkation that "Cordell [Hull] and I agreed that he was a sick man . . . and should not be called upon to make decisions affecting this country and the world." [154] Jim Bishop recounted a conversation between Vice-President Harry Truman and a confidant during December 1944: " 'Someday soon,' the friend said, 'you will be walking through the front door of that place.' . . .

'I hope not,' [the Vice-President responded.] 'I hope not,' . . . 'but I think you're right.'" [155]

His associates were also concerned about Roosevelt's predisposition to make important decisions in isolation regarding foreign affairs. As early as May 1944, Stettinius had voiced reservations concerning the President's agreement to a division of spheres of influence between Russia and Great Britain in Eastern Europe and the Balkans without consulting the State Department. Not only was the agreement "a serious mistake," in Stettinius's opinion, but the lack of coordination between the White House and the State Department was "a serious weakness," in formulating foreign policy. [156] Roosevelt's preference for making decisions on his own appeared to many to be giving Stalin a green light in Eastern Europe—with ominous implications for the future. [157]

Stettinius was also involved in another perplexing Roosevelt maneuver in January just prior to the inauguration and two weeks prior to the Yalta Conference. The President precipitously decided that his new Secretary of State and his department should be made aware for the first time of the progress of the Manhattan Project and its possible role in the future. As Bishop related: "There is no known reason why the State Department had to be made aware of the project, nor could Stettinius decipher a rationalization. . . . If there is an irony . . . [the] Vice President-elect, Harry S. Truman, to whom this subject might be of the utmost importance, was told nothing." [158] The implications of this omission for the period following Roosevelt's death are obvious.

Although unaware of the precise medical syndrome he was describing, Bishop's description of Roosevelt's appearance on a daily basis following his inauguration is significant. The episodes of encephalopathy were now so frequent as to constitute a prevailing condition rather than a transient occurrence. The bad days were now outnumbering the good. But, Bishop noted,

> in spite of the deep skeletal lines and gray complexion which McIntire at last noted, the President still arrogated to himself the right to pull himself together on occasion and enhance animation in his features, gestures and responses. He never again looked like the vigorous Roosevelt, but he could act the part and do it well. [Yet] these moments became sporadic, perhaps rare. [159]

Two separate physicians made telling comments regarding the President's condition on the eve of the Yalta Conference that lend credence to the medical indictment. Quoting Lord Moran: "To a doctor's eye, . . . the President appears a very sick man. He has all the symptoms of hardening of the arteries of the brain in an advanced stage. . . . I give him only a few months to live." Dr. Roger Lee, President of the American Medical Association, recounted: "He is irascible and becomes very irritable if he has to concentrate his mind for long. If anything is brought up that wants thinking he will change the subject." [160]

Roosevelt's confidants on board the ship bound for Yalta likewise found little solace to assuage their concerns. James Byrnes was convinced that the President had made no effective preparations for the Conference. Byrnes himself had reviewed the State Department material prepared for Roosevelt, which he felt represented "splendid studies." Yet, during the trip the President showed little interest in them; accordingly, Bishop concluded, "he did not know the solutions to problems which might have been anticipated." [161]

This lack of preparation calls to mind the first of several parallels to Woodrow Wilson on the eve of the Paris Peace Conference twenty-five years earlier. As many would have it, Roosevelt's only concerns (and hence his only preparations) were directed toward Russia entering the war against Japan and, more important, toward establishing a lasting world peace organization. Just as with Wilson, contingency plans regarding specific issues with which Roosevelt undoubtedly would be faced, and which the State Department had attempted to supply, simply were not a part of his preparation—except insofar as they could be used to bargain for Russian cooperation. Rexford Tugwell defined Roosevelt's preoccupation in a nutshell: "The real care and close attention would henceforth go to the arrangements for what he thought of as 'the peace.'" [162]

One need only recall Wilson's deep and very personal commitment to a similar ideal. Wilson had called for a New Order of diplomacy, of "ideals and principles," in lieu of Old Order considerations of national self-interest. [163] Roosevelt was now invoking the same idealistic call. As Rexford Tugwell observed: "He meant to arouse other ambitions than those of defeating the nation's enemies and taking suitable revenge for their effronteries." This same observer acknowledged: "It was a stirring call from a sick man." [164]—and a rather inconsistent one, considering Roosevelt's previously stated views of Germany's guilt.

Both Presidents had also had a personal sense of temporal urgency in their quests because of their perceived indispensability. Inasmuch as he stood as the leading supporter of the United Nations, Roosevelt felt that his continuance in office might well mean the difference between its success and failure. [165] Wilson had implied as much in the 1918 referendum in which he had warned that this was no time for divided loyalties; the American public must vote Democratic if they believed in his policies. And just as his predecessor had naively asserted that once the League was accepted, all lesser substantive matters would disappear, [166] Roosevelt believed that once the Russians agreed to the United Nations, the other problems would take care of themselves.[167]

Both leaders also faced critical problems on the domestic front, and both had a dangerous lack of concern for disruptive influences threatening their leadership. Whereas leaders of the Democratic party beseiged Wilson for guidance on vital domestic issues ("there is no Democratic Party; he is with you in Paris," they had complained),[168] Jonathan Daniels noted that Roosevelt "seemed to leave behind an almost disintegrating government at home. New feuds erupted and old grudges were indulged in as war dangers diminished."[169]

The error Wilson had made in failing to secure constructive publicity concerning the Versailles Conference was repeated by Roosevelt at Yalta. Daniels related in his memoirs that "no American reporters had been permitted at Yalta. . . . The understanding was that they could make no reports until after the President's return to Washington."[170] Educating the public early on as to what transpired at Yalta might have averted much of the criticism Roosevelt's image later suffered. People wondered about the requirements for secrecy. Was there something to hide? Had there really been a sell out?

The parallel extends to the two leaders' relationships with their allies. One may recall Clemenceau's skillfully presented agenda of specific items concerning French interests, in contradistinction to Wilson's program of general principles. The French Premier had pursued his nation's limited preoccupations in a tenacious and often successful fashion. This same discipline was alluded to by James MacGregor Burns in relation to the Russian Premier at Yalta: "Stalin far more than Roosevelt linked his wartime decisions to a strategy for long-run security, a strategy to which he adhered with a steel-like tenacity."[171]

As a fitting finale to their life's work, the two Presidents labored in a common sense of desperation against the biologic clock. Both efforts have often been roundly criticized by posterity and, not surprisingly, for similar reasons. Just as Wilson's failure paved the way for untethered aggression by a new power that arose to fill the void in Central Europe, so too, it has been argued, did Roosevelt's actions both before and during Yalta nurture the seeds of Soviet aggression in Eastern Europe.

One final parallel can be drawn between the two in relation to the efforts made to shield their respective infirmities from potentially critical observers. One of the instruments effecting that result has already been alluded to—the physician-patient relationship, which provided an ironic link between the two physicians involved. Yet there was a second instrument that shielded the two leaders both from key subordinates in government and from the American public. If Woodrow Wilson benefitted from the isolation his wife Edith afforded (a point that is open to question), so too did Franklin Roosevelt come to depend upon his daughter Anna for the same thing. Jonathan Daniels' description of that relationship, and Bruenn's role in it, is a mirror image of the relationship Wilson experienced with his wife, also on the advice of his physician:

> It is becoming increasingly clear that [Anna] means to be . . . a sort of special secretary close to the President, handling details for him and serving as intermediary. . . . She had been greatly concerned about the strains on her father. She told [Daniels] that Dr. Howard Bruenn had told her that he must greatly restrict his activities. So she had a plan. The President should see very few people. Insofar as possible, [Daniels] was to see those who wished to see him, and then pass on the matters presented . . . to Anna and her husband for decision without burdening the President with any but the greatest matters.[172]

The tragic theme of restricted access, sanctioned by a physician and exercised by a closely positioned woman, inflicted itself once again upon the office of the American presidency. If Anna's impact on events was arguably less than was Edith Wilson's, one cannot avoid a disquieting sense of déjà vu. Indeed, Daniel's description so closely parallels what had occurred twenty-five years earlier that the names of Grayson, Tumulty, and Edith might almost be interchanged with McIntire, Daniels, and Anna. Daniels himself drew the obvious parallel: "I knew than that no such plan could possibly work. It would have amounted only to something like the almost regency which Mrs. Wilson and Dr. Cary Grayson had assumed."[173]

Yet, in effect, the plan did work on most occasions. If it sometimes failed to disguise the obvious, it was not for lack of effort by the protagonists, as the following vignette reveals. James Byrnes had become so disturbed by the President's deteriorating condition that he registered his concern with both McIntire and Anna on the way to Yalta. Byrnes made it clear he did not believe Roosevelt's wasted appearance could be due to "sinus flare-ups and a cold" as had been implied by his physician. Anna, for her part, acknowledged what was now a frequent appearance in her father of periods of unawareness. She agreed that "his open mouth made him look bad," but countered optimistically that it "helped him breathe easier." And McIntire remained maddeningly consistent to the end, implicating only a combination of "sinus infections and a cold."[174]

On the very day of Roosevelt's arrival in the Crimea, other individuals' worst suspicions appeared to be confirmed. "The President looked old and thin and drawn," Churchill's physician recalled. "He sat looking straight ahead with his mouth open, as if he were not taking things in. Everyone was shocked by his appearance."[175] Later Lord Moran would confide to Churchill: "I doubt, from what I have seen, whether he is fit for his job here."[176] Jonathan Daniels' apologia serves to bolster Moran's case. "I was perhaps guilty," he later wrote, "and I have since been charged, of deluding the American people by releasing only the least tragic pictures of the face of Franklin Roosevelt taken there. Those were sad enough."[177]

Many of these descriptions, and others, have been used by critics of the course of events at Yalta to suggest that the President was a tragically compromised leader there—with consequent harm to American interests. Consistent to the end, the journalists again led the way in outlining the indictment against Roosevelt. *Life*, in its September 6, 1948, issue, launched the revisionist campaign against the Yalta agreements and the stricken President's role in them, by quoting William C. Bullitt:

> Roosevelt, indeed, was more than tired. He was ill. Little was left of the physical and mental vigor that had been his when he entered the White House in 1933. Frequently he had difficulty in formulating his thoughts, and greater difficulty in expressing them consecutively. But he still held to his determination to appease Stalin.[178]

The combination of compromised cognitive functions and Chamberlain-style appeasement, it was charged, was the source of the failures there. If Roosevelt staked the outcome of the proceedings on face-to-face encounters with Stalin, their evidence suggests the Russian leader clearly recognized the President's potential weaknesses. Many have wondered whether Stalin's predilection for dealing more with Roosevelt than with Churchill stemmed from his belief that he could ultimately get more of what he wanted from the obviously debilitated President.[179] Roosevelt, for his part, continued to relish his role as mediator between the two, in spite of his compromised credibility. Perhaps unknowingly, however, he advanced Stalin's bargaining position through his own personal influence on the Prime Minister. As such, there may have been self-serving motives behind the Russian Bear's affection, which some close to the President failed to perceive.[180]

Others have proposed that Roosevelt's position was compromised by far more than just his failure to dominate Stalin in their interpersonal exchanges. James MacGregor Burns, for example, concluded that the ailing President labored under the optimistic assumption that "better days must lie ahead." Yet this belief, he wrote, incorporated "one colossal—though understandable—miscalculation. His plans assumed that he, as President of the United States for another four years, would be around to keep the fact of one world alive . . . to mediate between Stalin and Churchill."[181] From the standpoint of later Cold War developments this assumption would prove to be Roosevelt's most significant miscalculation at Yalta.[182] Truman's inheritance of the office at Roosevelt's death ushered in a period of dramatic changes in Soviet-American relations. David S. McLellan alluded to the significance of this transformation in his work *The Cold War in Transition:*

> Truman lacked Roosevelt's incentive to avoid a rupture with the master of the Kremlin. Almost from the beginning he regarded Soviet breaches of agreement as just that—breaches of agreement—and refused to make any more concessions for the sake of preserving amicable relations or to concede anything that was not already within the Soviet orbit of power. As cooperation . . . weakened, the relationship inevitably turned into competition and rivalry.[183]

Yet as for the course of the Yalta conference itself, Roosevelt's critics later fostered the charge of tactical mismanagement.[184] Even such a neutral observer as Burns suggested as much, but only on the strategic level. Burns found the President's tactical focus to be the product of shortsightedness in strategic considerations:

> Had Roosevelt, the man who boasted of his prowess as a "hoss-trader," finally been outbargained? . . . A verdict must take account of the different operating methods of the two men. . . . [Roosevelt,] as usual, . . . was almost wholly concerned about the immediate job ahead—winning the war. . . . Stalin, on the other hand, was thinking already of political arrangements in the postwar period.[185]

This brings us to the crux of the issue regarding Yalta and Roosevelt's conduct there. Far removed from any consideration of the President's admittedly failing health, the results of that conference appear to reflect instead the different aims the participants brought with them to Yalta. Comparing the divergent goals of East and West is like comparing apples and oranges. Up to that point, the war had temporarily solidified the tenuous bonds between the two, patching them up with economic aid, the call for unconditional surrender, and the struggle against a common foe. But now Stalin was staking his claims on the principle of Russian security, while Roosevelt was still addressing issues related to completing the war and establishing the United Nations. It is therefore not surprising that both felt they had gained their respective goals at Yalta, though Roosevelt was soon to discover that their goals were not the same.

To better understand the argument, a clear delineation of the issues involved at Yalta is in order. It is instructive, for example, to contrast McIntire's summary of what Roosevelt was seeking with what actually transpired during the negotiations there. Briefly stated, Roosevelt wanted

*Roosevelt and Churchill conferring at Yalta, 1945*

*Yalta: Churchill, Roosevelt, and Stalin, February 1945*

to bring Russia into the war against Japan, to end Russian support for the Communists in China, to obtain full sovereignty for Poland, and to gain Russian assurances of participation in the United Nations.[186] Yet other issues received equal attention at the negotiating table. James Byrnes afforded the most succinct chronological treatment of the issues discussed, and some were rather far removed from Roosevelt's main interest in Russian entry into the war and acceptance of the United Nations.

From the beginning, Stalin made it clear that he wished first to discuss the terms of German surrender, the future form of the German state, the amount and type of reparations due, and the allocation of a zone of occupation to France. This was followed by a consideration of the Polish question, which Stalin perceived as a Russian security problem—far removed from Roosevelt's idealistic preoccupation with full sovereignty for Russia's neighbor to the west. Next came a lengthy discussion about a declaration of policy on liberated areas in general. The participants reached an agreement on this, but it is not surprising that, given their different aims, it was later frustrated by the self-serving interpretations the parties gave to it. The concept of the United Nations boiled down to the narrow issues of the formula for voting in the proposed Security Council and the question of who should be invited to join the United Nations itself. The meeting then concluded with a secret agreement over concessions for Russia in China and the Pacific as the price to be paid for her participation in the remaining war effort.[187]

If the course of the discussions appears at first glance to be at great variance with the goals that Roosevelt brought to Yalta, does this necessarily imply that much was lost to the United States in the transition? Certainly Roosevelt's detractors would have it so. Yet a review of the record simply does not support this contention, and still less were the results a product of Roosevelt's compromised health, as some have implied. Above all, two principal American participants in the Conference—Byrnes and Stettinius—found little fault with Roosevelt's conduct while at Yalta.

Yet John T. Flynn, a severe critic of Roosevelt's actions at Yalta, actually utilized Byrnes' account almost exclusively in building his argument.[188] Today, Flynn's account is not taken seriously by any critical historian. But the impact of its publication so soon after Yalta significantly influenced the popular perception of Roosevelt's role while there. In light of the public's suspicions regarding Roosevelt's rapid physical decline prior to the Conference, it is not surprising that a wave of protest concerning the President's conduct at Yalta arose following the publication of Flynn's work. Since Flynn depended heavily on James Byrnes' account of Yalta, one might expect the latter to be a highly critical appraisal of Roosevelt's efforts. Yet just the opposite is the case in James Byrnes' book *Speaking Frankly.*

The discrepancy between Roosevelt's general goals and the actual content of the discussions has already been outlined. Byrnes acknowledged the necessity for considering the German question first, in lieu of Roosevelt's plan for beginning the discussions with the United Nations proposal, simply because of the changing circumstances, which the President was still flexible enough to recognize. "The rapid advance of our armies required that urgent consideration be given to European political and military problems," Byrnes observed.[189] The proposed zones of occupation in Germany were an integral part of these problems. Far from surrendering this issue to Stalin, Roosevelt was able to secure Russian agreement for France to gain both control of one of the zones and a seat on the Allied Control Council—the latter of which Stalin had originally opposed.[190]

With regard to the voting formula in the Security Council, the proposal agreed upon was made not by Russia but by the United States. Byrnes specifically outlined the Soviet demand: "All decisions in the Security Council must be by unanimous vote."[191] The United States proposal, on the other hand, which was accepted by the Russians at Yalta and adopted in substantially the same form at San Francisco, was the following: "Unanimity would be required for all categories of decisions except one: in those decisions involving promotion of peaceful settlement of disputes, a permanent member of the council would not cast a vote if it were party to the dispute in question."[192] This was a far cry from the original Soviet position.

Concerning the setting of Poland's boundaries, both Roosevelt and Churchill supported the so-called Curzon Line. It therefore was not the compromised President by himself who handed over eastern Poland to the Russians as his critics have charged. Nor was it in fact "handed over." This territory was already controlled by Russian forces—a fact which was abundantly clear to people at the time and to later historians.[193] Roosevelt could not take from Stalin what in effect was already his. Nor, to follow James Byrnes' argument further, did Roosevelt attempt to compensate Poland with German territory during the Conference per se. This question would remain open, as the agreed protocol specifically stated.[194]

Concerning the question of free elections for Poland, it is easy to question Roosevelt's alleged naiveté in accepting Stalin's assurances of free and unfettered elections within the month. Yet Roosevelt should not necessarily be faulted for what transpired after Yalta. Byrnes made this clear both in regard to this specific issue and the general policy on liberated areas. His following appraisal emphasized this theme, though perhaps Roosevelt did fail to grasp Stalin's intent:

> Agreement was quickly reached among the Big Three. At least, we thought there had been a meeting of the minds, but ever since, there has been continual disagreement . . . as to its proper interpretation.
> "Poland will be the first example of operating under this declaration," Roosevelt told Stalin. "I want the election in Poland to be beyond question, like Caesar's wife . . ."
> Stalin replied, "It was said so about Caesar's wife, but in fact, she had certain sins."

Byrnes was later compelled to observe: "I only hope the lady had fewer sins than . . . this declaration had violations." "It seems to me there is no question as to the [original] intention of the parties to the agreement."[195]

Concerning the reparations issue, both Roosevelt and Churchill were in fact aware of the dangers inherent in the Russian demand for $20 billion. Events following World War I had demonstrated the limitations, if not potential disasters, of such a plan. The specific sum was not in fact agreed to by Roosevelt, only the acceptance of Russia's creation of a reparations commission. The sum itself was suggested by Roosevelt only as "an initial basis for discussion."[196] Edward Stettinius' account clarified the situation:

> Stalin again insisted that there was no commitment on the amount, and that the figure mentioned was to be "used as a basis for discussions. . . ." [But] the Prime Minister again insisted that the British could not agree to a sum being mentioned, and Marshal Stalin gave in and proposed the following formula [which was ultimately adopted]:
> *(1) that the heads of the Governments had agreed that Germany must pay compensation for the damages caused to the Allied nations as a result of the war and*
> *(2) that the Moscow Commission be instructed to consider the amount of reparations. . . .*
> [President Roosevelt replied,] "Judge Roosevelt approves and the document is accepted."[197]

The protocol, which is included in the appendix to Stettinius' account, substantiates that there was absolutely no commitment to the sum appended. Only after the President's death were the Russians to claim that Roosevelt had agreed to their figures.[198]

Nor is it at all certain that Roosevelt personally agreed to the use of forced labor as one aspect of the reparations settlement. Indeed, Byrnes' only recollection of the matter suggested that the President was opposed to the concept.[199] What is certain is that the language incorporating the concept was added by the Soviet representative and subsequently agreed to by the other delegations.[200] Roosevelt's role in this remains controversial. Nevertheless, this issue does appear to be one instance in which Roosevelt may not have been fully aware of the implications of what his delegation had accepted. After all, the President had pointed out "that the United States did not desire reparations in the form of labor, and he was sure that Great Britain held the same view."[201] In fact, Stettinius' account suggests that the Russians were attempting to work around Roosevelt's stated views on the subject. "Molotov replied [to Stettinius] that they needed to study the matter further and were not prepared to discuss it at the Conference. He agreed that it should be discussed by the reparations commission in Moscow."[202] It was in fact Anthony Eden of Great Britain who later suggested a redraft of the original American proposals on reparations, in which the phrase "use of German labor" was interjected for the first time. This phrase ultimately did appear in Section 5 under the final protocol.[203] The fact that Roosevelt agreed to it, given his known feelings on the subject, suggests the possibility of either neglect or failure of the abstract attitude—perhaps on the grounds of cognitive compromise. On the other hand, perhaps he merely did not feel strongly enough about the proposal to make an issue of it.

On the question of Roosevelt's secret territorial concessions to Russia as the price paid for clarifying "the political aspects of Russian participation" in the war against Japan, which his critics have emphasized, Byrnes admitted that such secrecy was justified. He stated:

I did not know of the agreement, but the reason is understandable. At the time I was not Secretary of State . . . [and] had I been in Yalta that day it is probable I would have learned of it.

In considering the wisdom of these Pacific agreements . . . one should be fair enough to consider the circumstances. . . . Neither the President nor anyone else at that time knew how long the Germans could hold out and how many casualties we would suffer before they surrendered. The President had with him at Yalta the Joint Chiefs of Staff. They knew the situation.

The evidence is clear that the agreement was, in great part, a military decision. . . . Once Stalin knew our plans for invasion [of Japan] were under way, he knew that we would want his armies, and he could demand more for them.

Nor should President Roosevelt be criticized for keeping the agreement secret. The Soviet Union was party to a treaty with Japan and we could not announce Russia's intention to go to war with her. Furthermore, Russia's military strength was then concentrated on the German campaign. Any hint of an agreement would have been an invitation to the Japanese. . . . It was in the interest of all of us to allow the Soviets ninety days after Germany's surrender to transfer troops from the European front.[204]

Far from demonstrating inconsistency, compromise, or duplicity, Roosevelt was in fact being entirely consistent with his strategic design (though it may have been flawed) by emphasizing military objectives to the exclusion of political considerations. In one respect, however, the President's intermittent cognitive decline did show itself. He essentially forgot to inform Byrnes of this development, which transpired on the last day at Yalta. This omission might have had distressing implications for the future, as Byrnes realized: "I [had] to know how many IOU's were [still] outstanding."[205]

The final point, concerning Russian demands for three votes in the General Assembly, which Roosevelt's critics have focused on, eventually became moot. Yet Byrnes' account of how the essentials of an agreement evolved suggest that, after some delay, Roosevelt got what he wanted from Stalin, rather than the other way around. Initially Stalin had asked for sixteen votes in the General Assembly. That demand had been pared down to three, with Byelorussia and the Ukraine having voting status. Churchill supported the Russian position. Although Roosevelt was personally opposed to the concept, Eden and Stettinius agreed to the arrangement in committee and advised the President of the action. Roosevelt therefore announced its acceptance. Byrnes was both surprised and troubled by this revelation, and he convinced Roosevelt through Harry Hopkins to withdraw his agreement regarding the two Soviet republics unless Russia agreed that the United States should also have three votes. Roosevelt thereafter gained Stalin's agreement on this issue, which appears to have represented a solid achievement on the part of a compromised President. In essence, the voting ratio between the two superpowers would remain one to one, as opposed to the original sixteen-to-one ratio proposed by the Soviet Union.[206]

To suggest, therefore, that Roosevelt demonstrated poor judgment because of illness in his dealing with the Russians on any issue while at Yalta, as many of his critics have asserted, does not square with the record. This is a major theme of Edward Stettinius' recollections of the Yalta Conference: "Throughout this give-and-take, [Roosevelt's] mind functioned with clarity and conciseness, furnishing excellent proof that he was alert and in full command of his faculties." Stettinius also concluded that, lacking any prior briefing by the State Department, the President's skill during these exchanges attested to his flexibility and intelligence. He added that in all issues discussed at Yalta, Roosevelt "continued to explain the American position skillfully and distinctly," while serving as a "moderating influence when the discussions became heated."[207]

One other major theme of Stettinius' account should be considered in assessing the impact of Yalta: Many of its implications for Europe's future resulted not from events that transpired there, but from the later failure of the Russians to honor the agreements made. Indeed, during the negotiations themselves, Stettinius wrote, "the Soviet Union made more concessions to the United States and Great Britain than were made to the Soviet Union by either the United States or Great Britain."[208] In his concluding chapter, "Appeasement or Realism?" Stettinius balanced the ledger against Roosevelt's critics. Important in countering the charge of submissive behavior on the part of the President is the acknowledgement made by all participants there that only Joseph Stalin was speaking for the Soviet Union. No other opinions mattered. Therefore, Roosevelt had to deal with Stalin. Stettinius argued that he had already done so in a manner that was beneficial for thawing relations in the earlier wartime conferences. Given the precedent established, the President was later obliged to accept Stalin's intentions as aboveboard while at Yalta. He, or any other negotiator in a similar situation, could do no other. Yet what he had gained in the short run was impressive in Stettinius' view. Consider the following achievements:

(1) All parties (including the Soviets) agreed to the concept and working function of the United Nations basically as outlined by the United States at Dumbarton Oaks. Accompanying this were gains made for American interests in all remaining questions on that organization. First, the Soviet Union accepted the American formula for voting in the Security Council, including the veto power. Second, the Russians withdrew their original request for sixteen votes in the General Assembly, and eventually Roosevelt was able to gain parity with the Soviet voting bloc (even if this would later be abrogated at San Francisco). Finally, Russia agreed to the American specifications for countries to be invited to attend the San Francisco Conference. All nations admitted were to have the right to be heard, as Roosevelt had initially envisioned.[209]

(2) Roosevelt obtained coordination of Russian and Western military activities.[210] Bringing the Soviet Union into the war at the appropriate time, along with acceptance of the United Nations, were the two goals Roosevelt sought. Both were achieved to America's satisfaction. If Roosevelt's critics were later to point out that the United States coerced China into accepting the decision as the price for the Russian agreement, even though China had not participated in it, the President nonetheless had gained Stalin's agreement to recognize Chiang Kai-shek's regime as a corollary. Above all else, one had to consider the pessimism of the time. Japan's surrender was not expected before 1947, and then only at the cost of perhaps "hundreds of thousands" of allied casualties.[211] Then too, the Battle of the Bulge raised legitimate questions as to when Germany itself would crack. Continued Russian involvement

was essential to a successful culmination of the war effort.[212] James Mac-Gregor Burns has weighed the evidence with regard to the relative merits of Russian participation in the war compared to what Roosevelt surrendered at the time, and his view compares favorably with Stettinius' assessment: "Stalin—and probably Roosevelt, too—knew that the fact of Soviet participation was not the vital point. It was the timing and strength of the intervention that were crucial."[213] The implication is clear: Here, as in other areas, Roosevelt had achieved as much as circumstances allowed.

(3) Soviet acceptance of the American-proposed "Declaration of Liberated Europe" in a broad sense implied Soviet acquiescence to Western philosophy and principles. More damaging to the Russian image in the long run was its later disavowal of many of the essentials of that declaration. Poland is a case in point. The establishment of order in postwar Europe, according to the Declaration, was to rest with the liberated nations' opportunity to choose their own democratic institutions. The Declaration further specified that the nations were to form interim governments that would be "broadly representative of all democratic elements in the population," assured through elections at the "earliest possible" time.[214] In essence the agreement was an acceptance by Russian authority of the intent of the Atlantic Charter. There was, then, no sell out of democratic Poland; Stalin specifically agreed to "free and unfettered elections" within the month. That this was later abrogated by the Soviets could only weigh against them in the balance of world opinion.

In the final analysis, these were impressive concessions by a Soviet regime that appeared to hold many of the trump cards as the conflagration in Europe was drawing to a close. Considering this, in the words of Edward Stettinius, "President Roosevelt did not 'surrender' anything significant at Yalta which it was within his power to withhold."[215] Most historians today would ascribe to this view.

In spite of these largely supportive primary sources, many observers nevertheless have refused to surrender the popular misconception of Roosevelt at the Yalta Conference. Jim Bishop devoted 150 pages to the Yalta issue, but insofar as Roosevelt's conduct while there is concerned, his indictment lacks the credibility that other aspects of his work possess. Perhaps this is largely because the fitful bouts of encephalopathy and clouding of consciousness that characterized periods of Roosevelt's behavior before Yalta—and increasingly so afterward—were simply not in evidence during the week spent at the negotiating table. None of those present at the Conference made reference to any such telling episodes, apart from Moran's observation upon Roosevelt's arrival at the airport (p. 427), and Anthony Eden's notes in his diary after dinner on the same day: "Dinner with Americans; a terrible party I thought. President was vague and loose and ineffective."[216] Indeed, the evidence suggests that precisely at this interlude the President seemed to rally for one last vigorous stand before going rapidly downhill thereafter. It is true, as Burns acknowledged, that Churchill recorded in his memoirs that Roosevelt's face had a "transparency, . . . and often there was a far-away look in his eyes." Churchill then follows this description of a physical appearance possibly suggestive of an encephalopathic state with an important disclaimer regarding the President's cognitive skills: "But even at Yalta . . . his mind moved as quickly and acutely as ever over the great range of problems that the conference considered."[217] Edward Stettinius also believed that Roosevelt held his own during the proceedings: "I wish to emphasize that at all times from Malta through the Crimean Conference . . . I always found him to be mentally alert and fully capable of dealing with each situation as it developed."[218] According to Stettinius, British Foreign Secretary Anthony Eden agreed that "the President looked better . . . than when he had last seen him."[219] Ross McIntire, of course, argued the same in addressing his comments to the "malicious rumors" after Roosevelt's death: "Never once was there a loss of vigor or clarity. . . . Had he been 'dying on his feet' at Yalta, I, as one bound by his professional oath, could not and would not have permitted the President to have poured out his energies in day and night sessions."[220]

It might be assuring to have the President's physician on one's side in this particular argument, but given his proclivity for stretching the truth, a few observations regarding these last statements are in order. First, in comparison with his evident deterioration during the months prior to (and then after) the Conference, Roosevelt may not have been himself at Yalta after all—at least insofar as his close associates had come to know him during the despairing, antecedent period of deterioration. It may be argued that he was not himself simply because he was better! This may not be what McIntire had in mind, of course, but it is precisely what the record suggests. Second, the whispers at Teheran and after were not as "false and baseless" as McIntire implied. Finally, it is poignantly ironic that this physician would invoke the defense of professional ethics on this occasion, when the record demonstrates how seriously he violated them on other occasions.

McIntire's argument was echoed by Samuel Rosenman: "The wild tales being circulated today by some of the more fanatical anti-Roosevelt haters . . . that Roosevelt was mentally unfit at Yalta are just so much nonsense."[221] McIntire and Rosenman's arguments might be viewed as attempts to circle the wagons, much as the defenders of Woodrow Wilson had done following his stroke in 1919. Yet much more impartial opinions support the impression that the President was in fact an effective spokesman for his nation's interests while at Yalta. Averell Harriman, another participant in the Conference, admitted that Roosevelt was not in good health, but argued nevertheless that the President carried on the negotiations at Yalta "with his usual skill and perception."[222] Dr. Howard Bruenn, who remained for so long the lone messenger of distressing news regarding Roosevelt's health, nonetheless acknowledged that his patient's clinical condition stabilized during the trip to Yalta—albeit transiently so: "Despite the demands made upon him, his mental clarity was truly remarkable. His memory for past and recent events was unimpaired."[223] This observation does not negate, of course, the potential for transient bouts of pulmonary or hypertensive encephalopathy to have interrupted that stable condition. Yet, for that one week at least, nothing in the record suggests that this occurred. Burns recognized that the Americans working with Roosevelt there gave him high marks for his efforts. Perhaps unconsciously, he underscored why this may have been so: "Nor was Roosevelt ill during these February days in the Crimea. . . . His blood pressure [remained] unchanged." Burns cited as evidence the observations of Eden, who had been criticial of the President's health in the past. The Foreign Secretary conceded later that ill health had not altered Roosevelt's judgment.[224]

Given what has been described concerning Roosevelt's illnesses in general in this review, and acknowledging the natural history of hypertensive encephalopathy in particular, this apparent contradiction is not necessarily surprising. The extreme variability of Roosevelt's blood pressure has been alluded to, and it is only during periods of striking elevations in pressure that episodes of confusion or clouding of consciousness occur. It may therefore be proposed that the President was fortunate not to have experienced any noticeable periods of malignant hypertension while there.[225] Despite the record for at least one year prior to the Yalta Conference, Roosevelt's accomplishments while at Yalta were on the whole positive, given the political and military circumstances that he faced.

Yet if the President's deteriorating health played no significant role in events there, the same cannot be said for the period following. Yalta represented Roosevelt's last contribution as a statesman and as a President. The transition into his last desultory days began almost immediately, as Samuel Rosenman's observations about Roosevelt's return voyage attest:

> The hard voyage to Yalta, and the shattering responsibilities of the conference seemed to have sapped a substantial part of the President's remaining reserves. . . . All the buoyancy of the campaign, all the excitement of arranging and preparing for the conference, had disappeared; in their place was gray fatigue—sheer exhaustion.[226]

Roosevelt thereafter showed no appetite for work, and the death of his longtime intimate Edwin "Pa" Watson during the voyage home triggered a depression that augmented this lethargy. Rosenman lamented: "I could not get the President to go to work on the speech [concerning what had transpired at Yalta]. . . . In fact, though the speech was scheduled to be delivered immediately upon his return, almost a week went by before I could get him to give any serious attention to it." [227]

The March 1 speech reflected the poor attention the President had given it. Roosevelt's presentation also reflected his grave physiologic compromise that was obvious to every observer. Burns agreed that he was obviously ill during his speech to Congress concerning Yalta, citing as evidence Roosevelt's slurred speech and trembling hands. [228] Rosenman admitted to being "dismayed at the halting, ineffective manner of delivery. . . . He ad-libbed a great deal. . . . Some of his extemporaneous remarks were wholly irrelevant, and some of them almost bordered on the ridiculous." [229] Jonathan Daniels referred to Rosenman's dismay over the presentation: "Sam was terribly distressed after the President finished his speech. He had a feeling the President's ad-libbing had made a mess of [it all] and that some of the things he had put in were going to have a very bad reaction. William Hassett and Grace Tully felt the same way . . . and I must say I agreed with them." [230] Burns recognized the speech as symbolic of the President's behavior during his final weeks in office. What Burns described as a condition by this time precisely mirrored the descriptions of encephalopathy witnessed less frequently at an earlier date:

> Roosevelt's voice was strangely thick and blurred as he told Congress about Yalta. . . . At times his face and words flamed with the old eloquence, [only] to ebb away. Thus it was constantly in the final weeks. . . . His gray-blue eyes clouded, his face went slack, his head hunched over. Then, suddenly, miraculously, the old gayness and vitality would return. [231]

If Burns stressed the symbolic significance of the speech, [232] Rosenman drew attention to one of the uncharacteristic political mistakes it contained. Roosevelt had not divulged the existence of the agreement between Russia and the United States regarding votes in the General Assembly, and Rosenman felt this would have been an appropriate time to do so:

> His decision not to disclose it in his speech was the kind of mistake he had never made before, and I have never been able to understand the reason for it. . . . Had he taken the American people into his confidence he could have explained how unimportant a concession this was; but having kept it from them, he never was able adequately to justify his action. [233]

This was but one error which fueled public suspicions that, in Daniels' words, "perhaps he has given away everything, particularly to Russia. . . . And sometimes, wearily, he did not seem to care to contradict them."[234] Roosevelt's apparent lack of interest in placing his efforts at Yalta in a proper and favorable perspective for the public was highlighted by a vignette Daniels recounted about this period. Apparently he and Archibald MacLeish had prepared a statement for Roosevelt to approve concerning the misleading interpretations that were already beginning to circulate about what had really happened at Yalta. Having presented the statement to Roosevelt, Daniels observed that "with seeming precision he made a slight change in the first paragraph and pushed the paper back to me. We departed in haste [only to find that] the change he had made in the first paragraph turned into confusion the rest of the statement [which] he obviously had not bothered to read."[235]

By this time the President had neither the interest to study statements made in his name nor apparently the capacity to prepare them himself. Almost all of the correspondence during his last month in office was written and transmitted by others and often dispatched without his approval—even when, as the above vignette makes clear, his subordinates did make efforts to obtain it. Those with whom he corresponded, however, were not fooled. Winston Churchill acknowledged, "Although I had no exact information about the President's state of health, I had the feeling that . . . the telegrams he was sending us were not his own."[236]

Churchill's observation implied a much graver concern than a mere acceptance either that the character of the President had changed in such a way that his communications no longer bore the indelible Roosevelt stamp or that others in fact were speaking for him. On a larger scale, the British were desperately in need of American support in dealing with Russian duplicity after Yalta. Therein lay the tragic implications for Europe. Roosevelt had the power to orchestrate that support but no longer appeared to know—or care—how to exercise it. Churchill described in his memoirs the critical impasse that appeared to be evolving rapidly:

> As the weeks passed after Yalta it became clear that the Soviet Government was doing nothing to carry out our agreements . . . . At this critical time [late in February] Roosevelt's health and strength had faded. . . . The President's devoted aides were anxious to keep their knowledge of his condition within the narrowest circle, and various hands drafted in combination the answers [to Churchill's telegrams] which were sent in his name. . . . These were costly weeks for all.[237]

This, then, is the real indictment against Roosevelt's health as it impacted on postwar events—far removed from what had transpired at

*Tired warrior: Roosevelt with Truman, August 1944*

Yalta, which, taken by itself, had been an exemplary beginning. Rather, it was the absence of staying power on Roosevelt's part *after* that conference that effectively precluded a successful continuation of the hopeful initiative. It is significant in itself that during these costly weeks between Yalta and Roosevelt's death in April that Churchill began referring to the President of the United States as both Franklin Roosevelt and Harry Truman:

> We can now see the deadly hiatus which existed between the fading of Roosevelt's strength and the growth of President Truman's grip of the vast world problem. In this melancholy void one President could not act and the other could not know. Neither the military chiefs nor the State Department received the guidance they required. . . . The indispensable political direction was lacking at the moment when it was most needed.[238]

It is immaterial to the argument whether Truman actually was partly responsible for conducting executive affairs during this dark interlude prior to the President's death. The record, in fact, suggests that he was still very much precluded from any participation in that role. Roosevelt attempted—albeit only fitfully—to maintain control of the helm of his ship to the very end. The important observation to emphasize is Churchill's indication that he at least believed it probable that Truman was involved, but that he was uncertain who was in fact really accountable for United States actions—or lack of them—at the time.

Observers closer to the President were now as one in attesting to Roosevelt's sharply varying intellectual capacity. According to Bishop, "Wide vacillation, within hours, of peak form alternated with periods of apparent incomprehension. His signature became indecipherable, and he often lost the train of his thought midway through a sentence. All had agreed that Franklin Roosevelt 'looked dead on his return from Yalta!'"[239] No resurrection was forthcoming, as events were left to drift unattended in darkening international waters. Grace Tully acknowledged Roosevelt's manner during the last weeks to be that of "a man to whom little is important; everything could wait."[240]

The behavior of Roosevelt's physicians was instrumental in fostering a pattern of isolation. On Ross McIntire's orders, Bruenn's access to the family remained restricted, as did their access to him. Nor could Bruenn even warn the President of his precarious health, although by now Roosevelt most assuredly was aware he was living with a biologic clock that was rapidly winding down. Anna intensified her efforts to cloister her father away from disagreeable encounters. "In addition to her kindness and devotion she had wisdom and tact and had learned how to guide difficult situations," Edward Stettinius observed. "She was most skillful, when a conversation at the dinner table seemed to be disturbing her father, in quietly suggesting another topic."[241]

Where was Ross McIntire in all of this? And what of public awareness, beholden as it was to press releases from the President's physician-in-attendance? McIntire simply continued to issue the usual denials of the obvious. "Vital was the right word for the President," McIntire wrote later. After returning from Yalta "his checkups continued to be satisfactory, showing *no evidence of organic ailment* [italics mine]. . . . The manner in which the President came through furnished further disproof of the charge that he was suffering from a coronary thrombosis, cancer, kidney infection, premature senility and everything else that occurred to the minds of malicious gossips."[242] McIntire's disclaimers of the specific diseases he mentioned may be true enough, but Roosevelt *was* suffering, much more significantly, from malignant hypertension, congestive heart failure, and chronic obstructive pulmonary disease—all of which his physician failed to mention. Close observers of Roosevelt would doubtless have been astonished to learn what he later attributed to them: "All agreed that he was never in better form," McIntire related.[243] Grace Tully, for one, would have denied this; she wrote about Roosevelt's last day in Washington prior to leaving for Warm Springs: "We had been waiting for the Boss in the Oval Study, and when he was wheeled in I was so startled I almost burst into tears. In two hours, he seemed to have failed dangerously."[244] This sharply contradicts McIntire's account that Roosevelt appeared the picture of health prior to going to Warm Springs. The measure of McIntire's effectiveness as purveyor of optimism is underscored, moreover, by the genuine shock and disbelief that swept the country upon hearing of the President's death shortly thereafter.

Jim Bishop has addressed the salient dilemma of compromised leadership and its implications during this final interlude after Yalta. Roosevelt could not challenge Stalin to honor the Yalta agreements; but he could not fail to challenge him either. After Stalin attempted to reverse the score by accusing the Allies of treachery in turn, the President's reply was uncharacteristically weak. As Bishop noted, at an earlier time such an accusation would have raised him to a fever pitch; now he only responded that he would not allow it to depress him. The response was left to someone else.[245]

It would in turn be left to Samuel Rosenman to comment on the effect of the decline of Soviet-American relations in precipitating Roosevelt's death. His comment may lack proven medical credibility, yet it substantiates the suspicion prevalent among physicians that once an individual loses his sense of self-worth and purpose, the will is lost to defend against the inroads of a fatal illness. Rosenman concluded, "The gradual breaking down of the close cooperation that had developed at Yalta had a depressing effect on the President. I am sure it hastened his death."[246]

One of the most extraordinary aspects of Franklin Roosevelt's presidency was the unparalleled longevity of his tenure in office. Historians have developed an understandable preoccupation with how this individual used power to serve his interests in such an enduring fashion. Most have examined the issue from a static perspective, assuming that recognizable, characteristic features of his leadership remained inviolate from beginning to end. This assumption all but ignores the transitions in style, personality, and most significant, health that would naturally be expected to occur over a twelve-year period of time. The record suggests that in matters of health, in fact, a relatively abrupt transition occurred approximately one year prior to Roosevelt's untimely death.

The effects of this transition were perhaps magnified by the close public scrutiny given to a President who was entrusted with conducting the largest war effort in history and preparing for the aftermath of that conflict. Any deficiencies in leadership uncovered during this critical period would naturally spur an examination to assess their significance. The turn for the worse in Roosevelt's condition after Teheran in March 1944 is now nearly universally accepted, yet its impact on specific events after that time has remained an open question. Historians have acknowledged that serious illness existed, but perhaps through a lack of familiarity with the subject, they have declined to weigh its significance with conviction. The few writers who have taken a firm stand have treated the subject as an all-encompassing, pervasive influence on nearly every action taken and decision made by the stricken President. Yet no medical opinion has addressed the impact of each disease specifically or the degree of its effect on isolated issues. Roosevelt was a chronically ill man, and Yalta occurred in the twilight of his career. Therefore it has been incorrectly assumed by those who perceive all disease as a relentless continuum rather than an intermittent phenomenon that what transpired at the Yalta Conference must have been influenced adversely by its effects.

In regard to the specific disease entity that affected Roosevelt's conduct—metabolically induced encephalopathy—its effects were by definition intermittent rather than constant. It is precisely this intermittency of disease effect and resultant unevenness of personal performance that have perplexed investigators of Roosevelt's last year in office—enough so that some have doubted the significance of illness altogether. They have chosen instead to emphasize more familiar themes to explain the apparent duality of Roosevelt's character during these critical months.

Raymond Moley addressed the issue of the "mental intoxication" that comes with power exercised in isolation over long periods. What he observed of Roosevelt's character during the earlier stages of his working relationship with him may be applied to Roosevelt's later years in office— but with one critical addition. Moley wrote:

> Until the very end of my association with Roosevelt I hoped that his quality of pragmatism would keep some of the windows of his mind open. I finally found . . . that he himself was slamming shut windows. He developed a very special method of reassuring himself of his own preconceptions. . . .
>
> Ultimately, of course, a man closed off by one means or another from free opinion and advice suffers a kind of mental intoxication. He lives in a world of ideas generated only by himself, a world of make-believe. . . . That is why the problem of restraining power has always been the central problem of government. . . . Power is dangerous. It grows by what it feeds upon, dulling the perception, clouding the vision, imprisoning its victim, however well-intentioned he may be in that chill of isolation of a self-created aura of intellectual infallibility which is the negative of the democratic principle.[247]

The evidence presented in this review now suggests the need for some important qualifications to Moley's observations. That is to say, the longevity and isolation Roosevelt enjoyed over the years may have set the stage for a later critical denial of his own increasing physiologically induced fallibility. In the end, some windows of Roosevelt's mind had been slammed shut simply by periods of unawareness implicit in the encephalopathy from which he suffered. The mental intoxication and world of make-believe may, on occasion, have been the product of disease-induced cognitive aberration. The isolation to which Moley referred was accentuated by the actions of a concerned daughter and a self-serving physician. Indeed, something other than power itself in the end dulled the perceptions and clouded the vision in a far more literal sense than Moley intended. Ultimately, the aura of intellectual infallibility that had become dimmed by late 1944 may have served to negate even further the democratic principle.

James MacGregor Burns takes this last concept of the democratic principle one step further in defining it as a classic dilemma intrinsic to all democratic leaders. "To some extent Roosevelt succumbed to [this dilemma]" he argued. "He must moralize and dramatize and personalize and simplify in order to lead and hold the public, but in doing so he may arouse false hopes and expectations, including his own, the deflation of which in the long run may lead to disillusionment and cynicism."[248] Might Roosevelt have succumbed to the dilemma in part for reasons of neurologic compromise? On the basis of illness, he had become in the end even less effective in dramatizing, personalizing, and especially simplifying for the public, creating even more false hopes and expectations than would have been anticipated—only to face greater disappointment in the end. Was it not in fact the disillusionment and cynicism that resulted from Roosevelt's having misread the intentions of Stalin so completely that led to the public outcry regarding his health in the first place? Had he been more aware of the implications of certain of his actions than his illness afforded, he might have avoided the deflation of expectations that occurred so resoundingly at war's end.

To bring the argument full circle back to the issue of power in isolation that Raymond Moley addressed, let us examine the argument of the esteemed Roosevelt scholar Frank Freidel, cited in the introduction to Jonathan Daniels' work, and then apply it to the medical argument:

> There was power in the White House which in its global dimensions surpassed that in any earlier administration. . . . And because the effective use of that power required secrecy to protect great projects, it was power for which the President did not need immediately to account to either Congress or the public.[249]

Had this precedent been extended to the motivations of Ross McIntire in justifying his own betrayal of the requirement to remain accountable? Among other secret projects, Roosevelt's deteriorating health had become one of the most closely guarded secrets during the last year of his tenure in office. It was ironic indeed that precedents set by the President himself may have served to condone the efforts of others to conceal the increasingly ineffective use of his power. Congress and the American public relinquished their demands for accountability in the executive sphere, only to realize too late that what they had acquiesced to was now a drastically changed entity. Bluntly stated, McIntire may have taken advantage of the precedent afforded him.

It is only by the addition of the medical argument to the perceptive observations of Moley, Burns, Freidel, and others concerning the exercise of power in the democratic state that the reader may appreciate some of the implications beyond what these observers have made. As such, this review has directed its attention to one prevailing influence on Roosevelt's exercise of power that the writer felt qualified to address— much as others have directed their investigations to their own particular spheres of knowledge. No assessment by any one investigator should be construed as possessing a monopoly on the truth. It is only by assimilating data from very disparate viewpoints that a more comprehensive understanding of Franklin Roosevelt's successes and failures can be had. Viewed in this perspective, the medical argument does not judge Roosevelt as harshly as the label "the sick man of Yalta" implies, nor as lightly as Ross McIntire's memoirs asssert.

## NOTES

1. George and George, *Wilson and House*, p. 97; Bishop, *FDR's Last Year*, p. 378.

2. The term "encephalopathy," medically defined, means "clouding of consciousness" and may occur due to metabolic alterations in the body or structural changes in the brain. Plum and Posner, *Stupor and Coma*, p. 144.

3. Manchester, *Glory and Dream*, p. 425. Unfortunately, much of what was achieved was easily turned aside after Roosevelt's death.

4. McIntire, *White House Physician*.

5. In that year Dr. Howard Bruenn, the cardiologist in attendance on Roosevelt's case, wrote his own account of his examinations and treatments of the President; see Bruenn, "Clinical Notes," 72:579–91. It contrasted sharply with that of McIntire.

6. Burns, *Lion and Fox*, pp. 484–86.

7. Flynn, *The Roosevelt Myth*; Lane, *I Saw Poland Betrayed*.

8. McIntire, *White House Physician*. Another physician, Dr. Hugh L'Etang, has studied the data. His conclusions are reflected in the title to his chapter "A Puzzling Diagnostic Problem" in *The Pathology of Leadership*, pp. 86–102.

9. Bruenn apparently felt compelled to write his own account for a peculiar reason: "[Roosevelt's] original hospital chart . . . was kept in the safe at the U.S. Naval Hospital, Bethesda, Md. After the President's death, this chart *could not be found*." See "Clinical Notes," p. 580. This article was one source to which Bishop referred in reconstructing a medical record which other unidentified parties apparently felt compelled to suppress.

10. McIntire, *White House Physician*, pp. 15–16.

11. A. Merriman Smith, *Thank You, Mr. President*, p. 134.

12. Other primary source materials reflect similar biases, which only serve to compromise their credibility. For example, Frances Perkins begins her account by acknowledging that "this book about Roosevelt . . . is biased in his favor. . . . I am bound to him by ties of affection, common purpose, and joint undertakings. All doubts have been resolved in his favor." See Perkins, *Roosevelt I Knew*, p. 4.

13. A. Merriman Smith, *Thank You, Mr. President*, p. 201. Smith was referring to Drs. Ross McIntire, James A. Paullin, and Frank Lahey, all of whom had both examined Roosevelt and reviewed the available records and current tests. Paullin is cited as an expert on hypertension in a contemporary medical textbook; see *Cecil's Textbook of Medicine*, 6th ed., 1944, p. 1035.

14. Tugwell, *Democratic Roosevelt*, p. 635.

15. Rosenman, *Working with Roosevelt*, p. 411.

16. Burns, *Soldier of Freedom*, p. 448.

17. Rosenman, *Working with Roosevelt*, p. 411.

18. McIntire, *White House Physician*, pp. 183–84.

19. Bruenn, "Clinical Notes," pp. 580–83.

20. Ibid.; Bishop, *FDR's Last Year*, pp. 4–5. Diastolic hypertension (elevation of both the higher and lower numbers) signifies a more severe condition than systolic alone (elevations of the upper value only).

21. Bruenn, "Clinical Notes" pp. 580–83; Bishop, *FDR's Last Year*, pp. 4–5. Bruenn believed Roosevelt's anemia was due to bleeding hemorrhoids. "Clinical Notes," p. 583.

22. Bishop, *FDR's Last Year*, p. 6.

23. Plum and Posner, *Stupor and Coma*, p. 144.

24. Bishop, *FDR's Last Year*, pp. 6, 4. This is not necessarily an indictment against Bruenn. Specialists are prone to concentrate on their area of expertise in taking a medical history. That frank communication between the physician and his special patient may have been lacking is suggested by McIntire's order to Bruenn not to discuss the nature of his findings with the President. Ibid., p. 6.

25. Plum and Posner, *Stupor and Coma*, p. 170. This is not new information. The sixth edition of *Cecil's Textbook of Medicine*, published in 1944, refers to "hypertensive encephalopathy," in which headaches, retinal changes, and other cerebral manifestations occur on the basis of "alterations in the cerebral circulation due to vascular spasm or actual damage" (p. 930). Despite his detailed account, Bruenn did not acknowledge the possibility of encephalopathy.

26. Bishop, *FDR's Last Year*, p. 2.

27. Plum and Posner, *Stupor and Coma*, pp. 170–71. With reference to the tremor described in Bruenn's initial examination, one such multifocal neurologic sign of metabolic encephalopathy that these investigators describe is tremor—"a prominent manifestation of metabolic brain disease." *Stupor and Coma*, p. 161.

28. Bishop, *FDR's Last Year*, p. 6.

29. Ibid., p. 8.

30. Burns, *Soldier of Freedom*, p. 449. Phenobarbital and salt restriction were also prescribed for his hypertension; Bruenn, "Clinical Notes," p. 580.

31. Burns, *Soldier of Freedom*, pp. 449–50.

32. Bishop, *FDR's Last Year*, pp. 201–2.

33. Ibid, p. 202. In McIntire's defense, it should be acknowledged that this accusation is not further substantiated; on the other hand, it has not been disproven either. Bruenn admitted that the records later disappeared. Perhaps they were lost or destroyed. If destroyed, and not at the family's request, McIntire may indeed have been guilty of a breech of medical ethics.

34. McIntire, *White House Physician*, pp. 55–58. This is substantiated by Jim Farley, who claimed he received McIntire's recommendation from Dr. Grayson for the post primarily because McIntire believed Roosevelt's doctor "should be one who would not talk." *Jim Farley's Story*, p. 108.

35. McIntire, *White House Physician*, p. 57.

36. Ibid., pp. 67, 22.

37. Tugwell, *Democratic Roosevelt*, p. 635. This same observer then bolstered his own case by citing the views of A. Merriman Smith, one of three journalists assigned to cover the White House during the Roosevelt and Truman years. Smith wrote: "All of the Big Three [Roosevelt, Stalin, and Churchill] . . . were sick old men at Teheran. . . . The correspondents had for a year watched Franklin 'die before their eyes.'" *Democratic Roosevelt*, p. 635n.

38. McIntire, *White House Physician*, p. 175.

39. Burns, *Soldier of Freedom*, p. 409. The "someone" referred to was Churchill's physician, Lord Moran, who had posed the question to Churchill at the Conference. Moran, *Diaries*, p. 150.

40. McIntire, *White House Physician*, p. 171.

41. Stettinius, *Roosevelt and the Russians*, p. 8.

42. McIntire, *White House Physician*, p. 175.

43. A. Merriman Smith, *Thank You, Mr. President*, p. 137.

44. Ibid., pp. 135, 25.

45. McIntire, *White House Physician*, pp. 187, 137.

46. Ibid., pp. 15–17. It bears repeating that a neurologist was not among the specialists and consultants McIntire enlisted.

47. Ibid., pp. 186, 20, 185.

48. Ibid., p. 20.

49. Bruenn, "Clinical Notes," pp. 584, 587. It was at this point that the divergent viewpoints of Vice-Admiral McIntire and Lieutenant Commander Howard Bruenn were so apparent. "McIntire insisted that Roosevelt was in good health; Bruenn kept penning his grave findings about the President's health, . . . aware that the hypertensive heart disease was irreversible." On November 14, for example, McIntire wrote to Dr. Harold T. Hyman of New York: "I am glad to tell you that all of these fancy diagnostic charges are false. The President is in *excellent health.* [italics mine]." See Bishop, *FDR's Last Year*, p. 201; Bruenn, "Clinical Notes," p. 584.

50. Beeson et al., *Cecil's Textbook of Medicine*, p. 1204. Lest one would argue that this is new information of which Roosevelt's physicians were unaware, consider this opinion recorded in the 1944 edition of this same text: "In malignant hypertension, the systolic blood pressure is excessively high, 200 to 250 mm, and the diastolic pressure is correspondingly elevated. Retinal hemorrhage . . . and congestive heart failure commonly complicate the clinical picture and cerebral vascular accidents are not infrequent. The condition is invariably fatal." *Cecil's Textbook of Medicine*, p. 1037.

51. That Roosevelt suffered from truly malignant hypertension is beyond question. Bruenn later disclosed that Roosevelt had a systolic blood pressure on one occasion of 300 mm Hg! L'Etang, *Pathology*, p. 93.

52. Plum and Posner, *Stupor and Coma*, p. 171.

53. O'Brien, "Vascular Disease and Dementia," p. 79. For a more detailed review of this argument, see Obrist, "Cerebral Physiology of the Aged."

54. Tully, *FDR: My Boss*, p. 274.

55. Ibid.

56. Tugwell, *Democratic Roosevelt*, p. 635; Bishop, *FDR's Last Year*, p. 2.

57. Burns, *Soldier of Freedom*, p. 448.

58. Flynn, *The Roosevelt Myth*, p. 403.

59. The Joint Chiefs of Staff, King and Marshall among them, had begun to question MacArthur's proposed plan of approaching Japan by way of the Philippines. They suggested instead to bypass the Philippines by invading Formosa, and had advised Roosevelt of this before the President left for Hawaii; see Potter and Nimitz, *Seapower*, p. 771.

60. Bishop, *FDR's Last Year*, p. 120.

61. Ibid.

62. McIntire, *White House Physician*, p. 198.

63. Bishop, *FDR's Last Year*, p. 121.

64. Burns, *Soldier of Freedom*, pp. 488–89, 495.

65. Ibid., p. 495. Hopkins suffered from peptic ulcer disease, which eventually necessitated surgical removal of a portion of his stomach. Cancer was found in the surgical specimen. The reader is referred to Hugh L'Etang's account of the pervasiveness of disease and infirmity among Roosevelt's associates, which further enhanced his isolation. *Pathology*, pp. 104–21.

66. Burns, *Soldier of Freedom*, pp. 508–9.

67. McIntire, *White House Physician*, p. 202. It is true that Bruenn had considered the possible diagnosis, but dismissed it on the basis of an EKG tracing obtained immediately after the episode, which allegedly demonstrated no change. In fact, the EKG is not entirely reliable in either supporting or ruling out the suspicion of angina. The diagnosis is made most accurately again by the clinical history, and the ischemic changes Roosevelt already had on his previous EKGs may have masked its occurrence here.

68. James MacGregor Burns asserted that during the speech Roosevelt "suffered his first and only attack of angina pectoris." *Soldier of Freedom*, p. 508.

69. Bishop, *FDR's Last Year*, p. 113. Bishop cited as evidence an interview with Roosevelt's son, James.

70. It is true that a few individuals of lesser standing did support the plan, among them Bernard Baruch, James B. Conant, and Lord Cherwell. According to Warren Kimball, Lord Cherwell was largely responsible for ultimately convincing Churchill to favor the plan. See Kimball, *Swords or Ploughshares?* p. 38. Other historians believe that the Prime Minister finally agreed to the distasteful proposal only in exchange for more Lend-Lease aid and postwar financial assistance for Great Britain. Ibid.

71. Burns, *Soldier of Freedom*, p. 521. Some have argued that Roosevelt withdrew support of the plan on account of his reelection bid. According to H. B. Westerfield, "The Republican Party would have taken great delight in defeating Roosevelt over this [unpopular] issue." *Foreign Policy and Party Politics*, p. 135. Warren Kimball agreed that this was the President's motive for reversing himself; *Swords or Ploughshares?* pp. 42–43.

72. Bruenn, "Clinical Notes," p. 587.

73. Bradley Smith, *Reaching Judgment at Nuremberg*, p. 31.

74. Bishop, *FDR's Last Year*, p. 153.

75. Flynn, *The Roosevelt Myth*, p. 383.

76. Tugwell, *Democratic Roosevelt*, p. 657.

77. Ibid.

78. Moran, *Diaries*, p. 192.

79. Kimball, *Swords or Ploughshares?* pp. xiii, xiv, 3.

80. U.S. Department of State, *Foreign Relations of the United States*, pp. 466–67, 1972.

81. Kimball, *Swords or Ploughshares?* p. 32.

82. Ibid., pp. 40–41, 6. Stimson later implied that poor health had affected Roosevelt's attitude toward Germany. But as Kimball points out: "That ignores the thrust of Roosevelt's thinking toward the Germans since the start of the war. FDR's . . increas-

ingly frequent lapses of memory . . . probably stemmed from his cardiovascular illness, but his poor health does not change his earlier condemnations of Germany in general." Ibid., p. 33.

83. Bradley Smith, *Reaching Judgment at Nuremberg*, p. 23.

84. Kimball, *Swords or Ploughshares?* p. 40.

85. Bishop, *FDR's Last Year*, p. 142.

86. Moran, *Diaries*, p. 239.

87. Plum and Posner, *Stupor and Coma*, p. 150.

88. Ibid., p. 162; see also *Cecil's Textbook of Medicine*, 6th ed., 1944, p. 930.

89. Plum and Posner, *Stupor and Coma*, p. 149.

90. Ibid.

91. Bishop, *FDR's Last Year*, pp. 156, 157. James Roosevelt certainly refused to absolve McIntire of his responsibility for perpetrating this ruse. With reference to the decision to run for a fourth term, he asserted: "I never have been reconciled to the fact that Father's physicians did not flatly forbid him to run." Roosevelt and Shallett, *Affectionately, FDR*, p. 313.

92. Burns, *Lion and Fox*, p. 468.

93. Ibid.

94. Bishop, *FDR's Last Year*, p. 199.

95. Flynn, *Roosevelt Myth*, p. 404.

96. McIntire, *White House Physician*, p. 209.

97. Ibid., p. 204.

98. Beeson et al., *Cecil's Textbook of Medicine*, p. 1206.

99. Bishop, *FDR's Last Year*, p. xiii.

100. Simply stated, if the resistance increases in a conduit such as a blood vessel, the flow decreases.

101. Beeson et al., *Cecil's Textbook of Medicine*, p. 1207. This work is used in the discussions as a representative text. Any currently published medical text gives the information recorded in this review.

102. See Bruenn, "Clinical Notes," p. 580. Digitalis was available at the time, and only upon Bruenn's insistence was it prescribed to Roosevelt. The drug acts by increasing the efficiency of the pumping action of the heart. It is significant that within three days of its initiation, the edema in Roosevelt's lungs perceptibly improved, although his blood pressure remained high. Effective antihypertensive medication was not available at the time. Only with the introduction of the thiocyanates in 1949 and reserpine in 1951 did drugs show any usefulness in treating that condition.

103. Beeson et al., *Cecil's Textbook of Medicine*, p. 1219. Coronary heart disease is caused by thickening, and later occlusion by atherosclerosis, of the vessels supplying the heart.

104. Ibid., p. 1206.

105. Another physician, Dr. F. M. Massie, has built an intriguing, if unproven, case for Roosevelt's death having been caused by a malignant melanoma that had spread to the brain. He argues that the disappearance of a pigmented mole over Roosevelt's eye after 1943 (implying its surgical removal), in conjunction with the President's profound loss of weight during his last year in office, suggested the presence of a widespread cancer by 1945. See Massie, *Modern Medicine*, March 6, 1961, p. 211. Hugh L'Etang found this argument intriguing enough to surmise that an autopsied brain from the year 1945 containing a melanoma deposit in the right hemisphere among specimens in the Walter Reed collection may have been the President's. *Pathology*, p. 95. To the present day it is denied that an autopsy was performed on Roosevelt. It is true that melanomas of the brain have a propensity to bleed, and the rapidity of Roosevelt's death speaks strongly to

a profound hemorrhage as the cause. But to postulate a bleed into a tumor is to suggest a second and far more rare cause for cerebral hemorrhage, when the record documents the presence of a much more common etiology for the fatal bleed. Then, too, one need not attribute the President's wasted appearance to cancer when it is well known that patients in the end stage of chronic obstructive pulmonary disease demonstrate similar degrees of weight loss. More germane to the present review, even assuming that cancer did in fact exist, its presence in most cases does not impact on the cognitive skills of the sufferer. Could it have accounted for Roosevelt's appearance? Perhaps. Did it impact on his leadership skills? Unlikely. Massie's thesis, then, with all the intrigue and ingenuity in investigative reporting it entails, remains speculative. Dr. Bruenn was certain Roosevelt died of a hypertension-related hemorrhage and affirms that no autopsy was performed; "Clinical Notes," p. 591.

106. Scher, "Control of Arterial Blood Pressure," p. 664.

107. McIntire, *White House Physician*, p. 239. The relation of hypertension to cerebral thrombosis or hemorrhage was common medical knowledge at the time; see *Cecil's Textbook of Medicine*, 6th ed., 1944, p. 1034. The precise relationship was more rigidly defined in later editions of the same text; see note 108 below.

108. Beeson et al., *Cecil's Textbook of Medicine*, p. 1203. If the exact ratios in regard to risk factors related to hypertension were not yet available in 1944, the cause and effect relationships and relative risks were still well known. The reader is referred to any standard medical text of the time; see, for example, the 1944 edition of *Cecil's Textbook of Medicine*, in which an estimate is made that 20 percent of hypertensive patients suffer strokes (p. 1034).

109. Ibid., p. 1218.

110. Ibid., p. 1205; Harrison, *Principles of Internal Medicine*, p. 1479.

111. McIntire, *White House Physician*, p. 185; Bruenn, "Clinical Notes," p. 584.

112. Beeson et al., *Cecil's Textbook of Medicine*, p. 1205. This is not to suggest that other physicians of his day would necessarily have been any more successful in their treatment, given the limited alternatives available (see *Cecil's Textbook of Medicine*, 6th ed., 1944, pp. 1036–37, for recommended therapy of that time). What does deserve indictment was McIntire's seeming indifference to the problem, apparently for the sake of preserving his reputation.

113. Bruenn, "Clinical Notes," pp. 580–83; Bishop, *FDR's Last Year*, pp. 11, 4.

114. Austen, Carmichael, and Adams, "Neurologic Manifestations of Chronic Pulmonary Insufficiency," p. 585.

115. Bishop, *FDR's Last Year*, pp. 4–11.

116. Austen et al., "Pulmonary Insufficiency," p. 585.

117. Although McIntire assumes credit for having successfully treated the anemia of unknown etiology with iron replacement, Roosevelt's worsening COPD may have contributed paradoxically to an improvement in this condition. As lung disease becomes progressive, and oxygenation more compromised, the red cells multiply in a compensatory fashion as a physiologic response to enable more oxygen transport in the bloodstream. This is termed "polycythemia," and such high blood-count levels are in fact often seen in the end stages of COPD.

118. Bishop, *FDR's Last Year*, pp. 263–64.

119. Manchester, *Glory and Dream*, p. 398. Statement attributed to John Gunther.

120. Westlake, Simpson, and Kaye, "Carbon Dioxide Narcosis in Emphysema."

121. Davies and MacKinnon, "Neurologic Effects of Oxygen in Chronic Cor Pulmonale."

122. Austen et al., "Pulmonary Insufficiency," p. 588.

123. Ibid.

124. Ibid.

125. Again, alleged lack of available medical knowledge of this condition at the time cannot be used as a defense for McIntire. The influence of increased carbon dioxide on both brain structure and neurologic function was outlined as early as 1930; see, for example, Wolff and Lennox, "Effect on Pial Vessels," as well as the 6th edition of *Cecil's Textbook of Medicine*, printed in 1944.

126. Beeson et al., *Cecil's Textbook of Medicine*, p. 662.

127. Flynn, *The Roosevelt Myth*, p. 410.

128. See A. Merriman Smith, *Thank You, Mr. President*, p. 134. Such pessimism was not confined to the journalists. Roosevelt's son asserted that "the fourth-term race in 1944 was my father's death warrant. . . . I realized with awful irrevocable certainty that we were going to lose him." *Affectionately, FDR*, p. 311.

129. Tully, *FDR: My Boss*, p. 254.

130. McIntire, *White House Physician*, p. 175.

131. Burns, *Soldier of Freedom*, p. 4.

132. Ibid., pp. 65–66.

133. Ibid., p. 119.

134. Ibid., pp. 133, 98.

135. Ibid., p. 332.

136. Burns, *Soldier of Freedom*, pp. 145, 138.

137. One historian, Dexter Perkins, downplays the significance of Roosevelt's indecisiveness in Japanese political developments; see Perkins, "Coming of World War II," p. 383. For contrasting views of the issue, the reader is encouraged to review the arguments of Paul Schroeder and Dexter Perkins in "The Coming of World War II: Avoidable or Inevitable?" in *Interpretations of American History*, pp. 347–84.

138. Burns, *Soldier of Freedom*, pp. vii–viii.

139. Ibid., p. 133.

140. Burns, *Lion and Fox*, p. 472.

141. Burns, *Soldier of Freedom*, p. 119.

142. A sizeable body of conflicting data has recently emerged in regard to Roosevelt's involvement in, and knowledge of, the Japanese attack. Viewed as another controversial occurrence within the time frame of the third term, the scope of the argument lies outside the realm of this review, as illness obviously had nothing to do with that controversy.

143. Perkins, "The Coming of World War II", p. 383.

144. Shannon, *Twentieth Century America*, 3:488.

145. Bishop, *FDR's Last Year*, p. 133.

146. Nor did Churchill's physician, Lord Moran (who never hesitated to comment on changes in the health and appearance of world leaders he met), give any indication that Roosevelt appeared ill or compromised during the Conference. It was not until five months later during their visit to Washington that he made the first notation in his memoirs of a change in Roosevelt's condition; *Diaries*, p. 103.

147. Kimball, *Swords or Ploughshares?* p. 18. The depths of his feeling can be summed up by his declaration on August 14, 1944: "You either have to castrate the German people or you have got to treat them . . . so they just cannot go on reproducing people who want to continue the way they have in the past." Ibid., p. 96.

148. Ibid., p. 18.

149. Bacher, *Decision to Divide Germany*, p. 28.

150. Shannon, *Twentieth Century America*, 3:497.

151. McIntire, *White House Physician*, pp. 211, 22; Stettinius, *Roosevelt and the Russians*, pp. 72–73.

152. Perkins, *Roosevelt I Knew,* pp. 390–93.

153. Tully, *FDR: My Boss,* p. 353.

154. Bishop, *FDR's Last Year,* p. 270.

155. Ibid., p. 228. It is significant that Truman was assigned further Secret Service protection during this period.

156. Stettinius, *Roosevelt and the Russians,* pp. 10–12. Many, in fact, suspect that Stettinius was appointed Secretary of State simply because Roosevelt believed it would be relatively easy to influence him, and hence to keep exclusive control over the affairs of state for himself—an accusation that McIntire, of course, vigorously denied; *White House Physician,* p. 213.

157. Stettinius' concern over this one exemplary issue in particular appears to have been justified. In May the agreement had been made temporary as a three-month trial. By October, however, Churchill and Stalin had extended the arrangement indefinitely; Stettinius, *Roosevelt and the Russians,* p. 12; Burns, *Soldier of Freedom,* p. 537.

158. Bishop, *FDR's Last Year,* p. 249.

159. Ibid., p. 247.

160. Ibid., pp. 294, 295.

161. Ibid., pp. 284, 283. Byrnes asserted in his account of Yalta that "I am sure the failure to study them while in route was due to the President's illness." *Speaking Frankly,* p. 23.

162. Tugwell, *Democratic Roosevelt,* p. 636.

163. Daniels, *Wilson Era,* p. 479; Baker, *Wilson and World Settlement,* 1:193. In Roosevelt's defense, it should be noted that he was at least aware of Wilson's previous failure to allow adequate Republican representation among his advisory ranks at Versailles. See Daniels, *White House Witness,* p. 262. That Roosevelt was poignantly aware of the historical parallels only heightens the irony in the negative similarities that nevertheless evolved. This included his health. As Manchester concluded: "Yalta will be recalled because the President sacrificed much of himself there." *Glory and Dream,* p. 440.

164. Tugwell, *Democratic Roosevelt,* p. 643.

165. McIntire, *White House Physician,* p. 193.

166. George and George, *Wilson and House,* p. 214.

167. Bishop, *FDR's Last Year,* p. 296.

168. Walworth, *Woodrow Wilson,* p. 336.

169. Daniels, *White House Witness,* p. 255.

170. Ibid., p. 261.

171. Burns, *Soldier of Freedom,* p. 551.

172. Daniels, *White House Witness,* p. 266.

173. Ibid.

174. Byrnes, *Speaking Frankly,* p. 22. Perhaps conscious deceit was not McIntire's only motive. In his defense, medical specialists are prone to emphasize those diagnoses with which they are familiar.

175. Moran, *Diaries,* p. 234. Well they should have been, for they were witnessing yet another episode of encephalopathy first hand. This would, however, be the last notation of such behavior in the record until Roosevelt's return to the United States.

176. Ibid., p. 239.

177. Daniels, *White House Witness,* p. 3.

178. *Life Magazine,* September 6, 1948; quoted in Stettinius, *Roosevelt and the Russians,* pp. 5–6. Referring to his colleagues' appraisals of Roosevelt, the journalist A. Merriman Smith asserted: "They wanted to believe he was dying. And he was. But they didn't know how right they were." *Thank You, Mr. President,* p. 134.

179. Bishop, *FDR's Last Year*, p. 378.

180. For example, see McIntire, *White House Physician*, p. 215.

181. Burns, *Lion and Fox*, p. 470.

182. John D. Feerick alluded to this when he wrote: "The extent to which . . . Roosevelt was disabled, *if at all* [italics mine], during the last years of his life is unclear. . . . What is clear is that the President refused to acknowledge his medical condition lest his goals of ending WWII and of establishing an organization for world peace be thwarted." *Twenty-Fifth Amendment*, p. 15.

183. McLellan, *Cold War in Transition*, p. 7.

184. Flynn, *The Roosevelt Myth*, pp. 388–90.

185. Burns, *Lion and Fox*, p. 469.

186. McIntire, *White House Physician*, p. 196.

187. Byrnes, *Speaking Frankly*, pp. 24–43.

188. Flynn, *The Roosevelt Myth*, pp. 388–90.

189. Byrnes, *Speaking Frankly*, p. 24.

190. Ibid., p. 25.

191. Ibid., p. 34.

192. Ibid., p. 37.

193. Samuel Rosenman stated that "concerning the treatment of liberated European countries . . . Russia could have taken whatever she wanted." *Working with Roosevelt*, pp. 533–34. Burns concluded on this issue that Roosevelt "had reached the limit of his bargaining power. . . . Russia occupied Poland." *Soldier of Freedom*, p. 572. Edward Stettinius underscored the critical point in the issue: "By February 1945, . . . Poland and all of the eastern Europe, except for most of Czechoslovakia, was in the hands of the Red Army. . . . The United States was in no position at Yalta to change the Russian attitude." *Roosevelt and the Russians*, p. 301.

194. Byrnes, *Speaking Frankly*, pp. 30–31.

195. Ibid., pp. 33–34.

196. Ibid., pp. 28–29.

197. Stettinius, *Roosevelt and the Russians*, p. 266.

198. Ibid., p. 267.

199. Byrnes, *Speaking Frankly*, p. 29.

200. Ibid.

201. Stettinius, *Roosevelt and the Russians*, p. 130.

202. Ibid., p. 168.

203. Ibid., p. 345.

204. Byrnes, *Speaking Frankly*, p. 43.

205. Ibid.

206. The United States would later surrender this point at San Francisco in choosing not to ask for as many votes as Russia had obtained. Roosevelt, of course, could not be held accountable for this; he had already died.

207. Stettinius, *Roosevelt and the Russians*, pp. 203, 267.

208. Ibid., p. 6.

209. Ibid., p. 296.

210. Ibid., p. 298.

211. Feis, "A Military Necessity," p. 244.

212. Stettinius, *Roosevelt and the Russians*, p. 305.

213. Burns, *Soldier of Freedom*, p. 575.

214. Stettinius, *Roosevelt and the Russians*, pp. 302, 343.

215. Ibid., p. 306. Burns listed the trumps Stalin held in his hand: "Russia occupied Poland. Russia distrusted its allies. Russia had a million men who could fight Japan. Russia could sabotage the new peace organization." *Soldier of Freedom*, p. 572.

216. Bishop, *FDR's Last Year*, p. 322.
217. Burns, *Lion and Fox*, p. 469.
218. Stettinius, *Roosevelt and the Russians*, p. 73. Stettinius believed that Roosevelt had shown some signs of deterioration even before the inauguration of January 20 (p. 73). Yet his comment regarding the President's conduct at Yalta once again attests to the intermittency of Roosevelt's symptoms even at this late date.
219. Ibid., p. 72.
220. McIntire, *White House Physician*, p. 24.
221. Rosenman, *Working with Roosevelt*, p. 522.
222. Harriman, "Military Situation in the Far East," p. 3330.
223. McIntire, *White House Physician*, p. 28; see Bruenn, "Clinical Notes," p. 591.
224. Burns, *Soldier of Freedom*, pp. 573, 574.
225. Lacking a detailed understanding of the disease processes that afflicted Roosevelt, some sought to reconstruct telling episodes of compromise at Yalta—assuming incorrectly that what illnesses he had would be manifest on a daily basis. This has led on more than one occasion to some rather bizarre medical non sequiturs in the absence of medical data to substantiate them. For example, on one occasion at Yalta Bruenn is described has having detected "something new, 'pulsus alternans'—a pulse which skipped beats. No matter what the technical terms, it was a syndrome of senility," it was asserted. (Bishop, *FDR's Last Year*, p. 383). It represented nothing of the sort! There is no direct relation between intermittent irregularities of the heartbeat and senility. The latter is confined, in medical terminology, to the aging of cortical neurons with consequent changes in mentation and behavior. A shallow understanding of medical terms is a poor servant in assessing the impact of disease on Roosevelt's leadership.

Other examples are readily apparent. Recalling Lord Moran's educated guess that Roosevelt was suffering from the adverse effects of atherosclerosis to an advanced degree, some attempts to offer medical clarification for the reader's benefit have proved spurious: "It is a medical fact that when an insufficient supply of blood reaches the brain, impaired powers of reasoning and concentration result. . . . Deprive the cerebrum of nourishment . . . and the ability to think faces irreversible damage." This statement has merit as far as it goes. Yet what follows dangles as a useless appendage of alleged medical fact:

In human beings arteries age slowly, moderately or swiftly. In the case of President Roosevelt, a chronic wheelchair patient who could not indulge in normal exercise, the aging process was swift. Overwork, flaccidity of musculature and chronic fatigue induced a speeding up of plaques forming inside arterial walls; this reduced the amount of blood pumped by a tired heart and increased the blood pressure because of narrowed venous walls. (Bishop, *FDR's Last Year*, p. 295).

Simply stated, there is no evidence to support the contention that confinement to a wheelchair, lack of exercise, flaccid musculature, or chronic fatigue accelerates the process of atherosclerosis. Nor is increased blood pressure the result of "narrowed venous walls." Nor, for that matter, does atherosclerosis significantly affect the venous side of the circulation in the first place!

This indictment of one medical explanation of Roosevelt's health is not intended as a pompous gesture on the part of a physician to berate an otherwise informative writer for a lack of medical sophistication that he should not be expected in any event to possess. Yet to pass such statements off as a credible medical clarification of the disease process that afflicted Roosevelt does a disservice to the record, and it only muddles our understanding of the issue in relation to the President's compromised health.
226. Rosenman, *Working with Roosevelt*, pp. 522–23.

227. Ibid., p. 523.
228. Burns, *Soldier of Freedom*, p. 581.
229. Rosenman, *Working with Roosevelt*, p. 527.
230. Daniels, *White House Witness*, p. 267.
231. Burns, *Lion and Fox*, pp. 470–71.
232. There was more than symbolism in it. His slurred speech is described by the term "dysarthria," which in this case refers to one of the transient focal neurologic deficits so often seen during episodes of encephalopathy.
233. Rosenman, *Working with Roosevelt*, p. 537.
234. Daniels, *White House Witness*, p. 276.
235. Ibid., p. 277.
236. Winston Churchill, *Second World War*, 6:377.
237. Ibid., pp. 367–68.
238. Ibid., p. 399.
239. Bishop, *FDR's Last Year*, p. 499. Cordell Hull was one who remarked on the frequency with which Roosevelt "lost the thread of the conversation" while discussing Yalta with him after his return. Bishop, *FDR's Last Year*, p. 516. John D. Feerick unconsciously corroborated the increasingly frequent episodes of encephalopathy: "He vacillated between intellectual acumen and a vacuous attitude which seemed impossible to penetrate." *Twenty-fifth Amendment*, p. 16.
240. Ibid., pp. 485, 487, 509.
241. Stettinius, *Roosevelt and the Russians*, p. 73.
242. McIntire, *White House Physician*, pp. 232, 236, 226.
243. Ibid., p. 232.
244. Tully, *FDR: My Boss*, p. 357.
245. Bishop, *FDR's Last Year*, pp. 496, 544.
246. Rosenman, *Working with Roosevelt*, p. 539.
247. Moley, *After Seven Years*, p. 397.
248. Burns, *Soldier of Freedom*, p. 550.
249. Freidel, Introduction to Daniels, *White House Witness*, p. ix–x.

# REFERENCES

**MEDICAL**

Austen, Frank K., Miriam W. Carmichael, and Raymond D. Adams. "Neurologic Manifestations of Chronic Pulmonary Insufficiency." *New England Journal of Medicine* 257 (1975): 578–85.

Beeson, P., W. McDermott, and J. Wyngaarden. *Cecil's Textbook of Medicine*. Philadelphia: W. B. Saunders Co., 1979.

Cecil, Russell L. *Textbook of Medicine*. 6th ed. Philadelphia: W.B. Saunders Co., 1944.

Davies, C. 15th ed. and J. MacKinnon. "Neurologic Effects of Oxygen in Chronic Cor Pulmonale." *Lancet* 2 (1949): 883–85.

L'Etang, Hugh. *The Pathology of Leadership*. New York: Hawthorn Books, 1970.

O'Brien, Michael D. "Vascular Disease and Dementia in the Elderly." In *Aging and Dementia*, edited by W. Lynn Smith, and Marcel Kinsbourne. pp. 77–90. New York: Spectrum Publications, 1977.

Obrist, W. D. "Cerebral Physiology of the Aged: Influence of Circulatory Disorders." In *Aging and the Brain*, edited by C. M. Gaitz. pp. 117–33. New York: Plenum Publishers, 1972.

Plum, Frederick and Jerome Posner. *Diagnosis of Stupor and Coma.* 2d ed. Philadelphia: F. A. Davis Co., 1972.
Scher, A. M. "Control of Arterial Blood Pressure." In *Physiology and Biophysics,* 19th ed., edited by T. Ruch and H. Palton. pp. 660–83. Philadelphia and London: W. B. Saunders Co., 1965.
Westlake, E., T. Simpson, and M. Kaye. "Carbon Dioxide Narcosis in Emphysema." *Quarterly Journal of Medicine* 24 (1955): 155–73.
Wolff, H. and W. Lennox. "Effect on Pial Vessels of Variations in Oxygen and Carbon Dioxide Content of Blood." *Archives of Neurology and Psychiatry* 23 (1930): 1097–1120.

PRIMARY

Bruenn, Howard. "Clinical Notes on the Illness and Death of President Franklin D. Roosevelt." *Annals of Internal Medicine* 72 (1970): 579–91.
Byrnes, James. *Speaking Frankly.* New York: Harper, 1947.
Churchill, Winston. *The Second World War.* Vol. 6, *Triumph and Tragedy.* London: Cassell and Co., 1954.
Daniels, Jonathan. *White House Witness.* Garden City, N.Y.: Doubleday, 1975.
Farley, James. *Jim Farley's Story.* New York: McGraw-Hill Book Co., 1948.
Harriman, W. Averell. *Military Situation in the Far East.* Senate Committee Hearings. Part 5, pp. 3330–331. Washington, D.C.: U.S. Government Printing Office, 1951.
McIntire, Ross T. *White House Physician.* New York: G. P. Putnam's Sons, 1946.
Moley, Raymond. *After Seven Years.* New York: Da Capo Press, 1972.
Moran, Lord. *Churchill: Taken From the Diaries of Lord Moran.* Boston: Houghton Mifflin Co., 1966.
Perkins, Frances. *The Roosevelt I Knew.* New York: Viking Press, 1946.
Roosevelt, James, and Sydney Shallett. *Affectionately, FDR.* New York: Harcourt and Brace, 1959.
Rosenman, Samuel. *Working with Roosevelt.* New York: Harper and Brothers, 1952.
Stettinius, Edward R., Jr. *Roosevelt and the Russians: The Yalta Conference.* Edited by Walter Johnson. Garden City, N.Y.: Doubleday and Company, 1949.
Tugwell, Rexford G. *The Democratic Roosevelt.* Baltimore: Penguin Books, 1957.
Tully, Grace. *FDR: My Boss.* Chicago: People's Book Club, 1949.
U.S., Department of State. *Foreign Relations of the United States. Conference at Quebec, 1944.* Washington, D.C.: Government Printing Office, 1972.

PERIODICALS

*Life Magazine.* September 6, 1948.

SECONDARY

Bacher, John H. *The Decision to Divide Germany.* Durham, N.C.: Duke University Press, 1978.
Bishop, Jim. *FDR's Last Year, April 1944–April 1945.* New York: William Morrow and Co., 1974.
Burns, James MacGregor. *Roosevelt: The Lion and the Fox.* New York: Harcourt, Brace, and World, 1956.
———. *Roosevelt: The Soldier of Freedom.* New York: Harcourt Brace Jovanovich, 1970.
Feerick, John D. *The Twenty-fifth Amendment: Its Complete History and Earliest Applications.* New York: Fordham University Press, 1976.

Feis, Herbert. "A Military Necessity." *Major Problems in American Foreign Policy.* Paterson, Thomas G., editor. Vol. 2. Lexington: D. C. Heath and Co., 1978.

Flynn, John T. *The Roosevelt Myth.* New York: Devin-Adair Co., 1948.

Kimball, Warren. *Swords or Ploughshares?* The American Alternative Series, edited by Harold Hyman. Philadelphia and New York: J. B. Lippincott Co., 1976.

Lane, Arthur B. *I Saw Poland Betrayed.* New York: Bobbs-Merrill, 1948.

McLellan, David S. *The Cold War in Transition.* New York: Macmillan Co., 1966.

Manchester, William. *American Caesar.* Boston: Little, Brown and Co., 1978.

Perkins, Dexter. "The Coming of World War II: Avoidable or Inevitable?" In *Interpretations of American History.* 2:347–84. London: Macmillan Co., 1978.

Shannon, David. *Twentieth Century America.* 2d ed. Vol. 3. Chicago: Rand McNally and Co., 1969.

Smith, A. Merriman. *Thank You, Mr. President.* New York: Harper and Brothers, 1949.

Smith, Bradley. *Reaching Judgment at Nuremberg.* New York: Basic Books, 1977.

Westerfield, H. B. *Foreign Policy and Party Politics.* New Haven: Yale University Press, 1955.

*Whither is fled the visionary gleam?*
*Where is it now, the glory and the dream?*

*Wordsworth*

# 5

# *Churchill and Eden:*
# *Epilogue after the Fall*

The respective prime ministries of Winston Churchill and Anthony Eden during the Cold War era make sad reading for a British public nurtured on the pretensions of nineteenth-century pax Britannica. In a very real sense, the fifties unmasked traditional Europe's diminished role in world affairs. No nation grieved for this loss more than Great Britain. Her diplomatic clout had been eclipsed by the onrush of events that were largely out of her control. In the aftermath of World War II, power devolved away from London and the other capitals of Europe toward two relatively new superpowers on the world stage. As such, Churchill and Eden shared a bitter inheritance.

Yet the two Prime Ministers had more in common than a shared legacy. As individuals, both were in many respects hollow reminders of the formidable kingpins they had been in an earlier age. Both were mesmerized by unwarranted assumptions concerning British power that no longer existed. Both were compromised by illness as they struggled to forge pathways toward international influence that were increasingly closed to them. And neither, in the end, fully appreciated the degree to which their poor health contributed to this distasteful circumstance.

*In 1950, returning to power at age 76*

Historians have traditionally viewed the second and final Government formed by Winston Churchill in 1951 as almost an afterthought in
evaluating his extraordinary career. Some have gone so far as to describe
his last four years in office as an exercise in opportunities lost. Until recently, little of consequence seems to have caught the historian's eye
during this period.[1] True, Churchill would remain to the end an articu-
late visionary of events as they came to pass—perhaps as much ahead of
his time in calling for detente with Russia in the mid-fifties as he had
been in 1946 with his prescient pronouncement concerning the Iron Cur-
tain falling over Eastern Europe. Yet his singular preoccupation with
mollifying Cold War realities solely with agreements arranged in face-to-
face consultations with other leaders remained an intensely personalized

perception of things as he thought they should be, and of his rightful place among them. It was a measure of Churchill's ineffectiveness in the end that, despite his exemplary visions, he failed to obtain the goals he so doggedly sought.

Viewed in perspective, Churchill's final attempts to move to center stage in consultation with the power-brokers of the world represented little more than a nostalgic appeal to recapitulate his previous genuine contributions at the end of World War II. He endured the final five years to carve his own epitaph for a career that would span the contrasting poles of great leadership. Having stood alone in the beginning as Defender of the Realm in a winning war effort, Churchill hoped in the end to embellish the feat by assuming the role of World Peacemaker under the inauspicious conditions engendered by the new threat of nuclear war.

*Churchill prior to his stroke, June 1953*

*Arriving at the Bermuda Conference, December 1953*

This pretension all but ignored the dramatic shifts of power that five short years had witnessed. Britain's sacrifices may have been instrumental in winning the war, but the price paid for participation was steep enough to assure her place thereafter as a second-rate force in international politics. Having achieved a veneer of importance as the third power to obtain nuclear armaments during the postwar era, Britain's shaky facade was weakly supported by an economy on the verge of bankruptcy.

A parallel bankruptcy of leadership existed in postwar British politics. Indeed, Labour's defeat at the hands of Churchill in 1951 was due as much as anything to the exhaustion and illness that wracked its party leadership at the critical juncture of election eve. A similar fatigue char-

*Delivering Conservative rally speech, Bedfordshire, May
1955*

acterized the Conservative party thereafter—personified most strikingly
by the Prime Minister himself. Only those issues that interested him
captured Churchill's executive attention. Economic matters were simply
not among them. What domestic successes his Government achieved
were largely due to the aptitudes of his Chancellor of the Exchequer on
the one hand, and the administrative skills of his Minister of Housing on
the other. Nor was the factor of luck to be ignored in regard to the economic recovery which occurred by 1953, because a favorable balance of
trade, induced in part by American needs in the Korean conflict, as
much as any other factor stimulated industrial growth.

On the international front, the United States and the Soviet Union
considered Churchill's efforts politely in deference to the man, but did
not, so it seems, take them seriously. The politics of drift was in the saddle
and riding the tired horse of British prestige. The reins were held by a

rapidly aging individual increasingly victimized by illness—specifically cerebrovascular insufficiency, depression, and dementia. His conduct in office was governed by a combination of these as much as by his nostalgic view of his past strengths.

Churchill's inability to have an impact on any more meaningful basis than through his past reputation actually paralleled what logically was to be expected from a British nation decimated by the war effort. Yet Britain refused to throw in her lot with the other similarly afflicted nations of postwar Europe. Churchill, like Britain, stood as an isolated and rapidly dimming beacon in the darkening twilight of increasingly tense international relations. Just as Britain remained more a worn symbol than a forceful protagonist of free-world aspirations in the early years of the

*Retirement*

Punch *cartoon, November 1954: "The Heir"*

Cold War, so did Churchill represent a symbol of the leadership of a very recent but bygone era.

Under such circumstances, preserving the appearance of his personal symbol assumed an extraordinary amount of the Prime Minister's attention. Beginning with his first cerebrovascular accident, or stroke, in 1949, Churchill became obsessed with making a good show in what public appearances he made thereafter. This was the source, however superficial, of his waning political strength. If he could but continue long enough to maintain an image of resiliency, then he might be granted that last opportunity to assume the mantle of Peacemaker.

In the interim, however, he suffered two further strokes and numerous transient ischemic attacks that were described in explicit detail in the published diaries of his physician, Lord Moran. In concert with a life-long endogenous depression, Churchill was victimized during his final three years in office by a cerebrovascular induced dementia that compromised his best intentions, if not his leadership skills. The stroke in 1949 had affected the sensation of his right arm and leg and was compatible with a hypertensive lacunar infarction deep in the brain on the left side.[2] In both 1950 and 1951 he suffered transient symptoms of atherosclerotically induced vascular insufficiency involving the two largest arteries supplying the posterior aspect of the brain.[3] In 1952 a fleeting but ominous speech disturbance occurred, suggesting partial occlusion or spasm of the left middle cerebral artery supplying the speech center of the cerebral cortex. Finally, a second hypertension-related lacunar stroke occurred in 1953, which profoundly weakened his left arm and leg.[4] The widespread involvement of both sides of the brain by the effects of atherosclerosis and hypertension effected changes in Churchill's behavior that were characteristic of an organic brain syndrome with which the reader has already become familiar. More tragic still, all of these

*John Foster Dulles, Anthony Eden, and Winston Churchill, September 1954*

*Assuming role of Prime Minister, 1955*

cerebrovascular events, except the last, were carefully hidden from the British public.

Alas, the superpowers never called for Churchill's encore on center stage, and the last two years of waiting induced him to rely upon drugs in the form of central nervous system stimulants to enhance the image he was increasingly struggling to project.[5] Nor were his people as critically aware of his true condition as they should have been, given the air of secrecy that shrouded his medical problems from view.

To his credit, Churchill compensated for the tenuous nature of his health without yielding to truly self-destructive impulses. If not much of substance was left as a legacy of those years, what resulted was at least not strikingly detrimental to British interests. His successor in office, however, wrestled with different but equally telling limitations of health while using similar pharmacologic supports. Tragically for Anthony Eden, history has recorded a rapid dissolution into the self destruction that his predecessor had managed to avoid. In fact, Churchill's role in his successor's tragedy was by no means a small one. This may be accounted for by Eden's character and temperament as they were affected by his relationship with his intransigent superior. As early as 1951, Eden's associates noted disquieting characteristics that made working with him difficult at best. Sir Roderick Barclay observed during the first year of Eden's foreign secretaryship under Churchill that his "impatience and irritability, partly no doubt due to his ill health, tended to make life difficult for his closest associates."[6] The description of impatience is the key, for Eden's unstable temperament was accentuated by his years as prime minister-in-waiting under the oppressive hand of his aging mentor.

This lengthy subordination to Churchill proved to have ominous implications for the future once Eden finally did assume the office he had coveted for so long, for somewhere along the line Anthony Eden had changed. Indeed, his personality unraveled completely during the first international crisis he was to face as Prime Minister—the Suez Canal crisis of 1956. Thereafter, contemporaries and historians alike have been left to sift through the rubble of the Suez debacle in search of illusory explanations for why he acted as he did.

After seizure of the Canal by the Egyptian President, Gamal Abdel Nasser, Eden ultimately chose to join forces with the French in a secret conspiracy aimed at recouping their loss. They reached an agreement whereby the Israelis were induced to attack the Egyptians in the Canal Zone, following which a combined "peace-keeping force" of British and French troops entered the conflict, as planned, and attempted to reassert European control over this vital lifeline in the Middle East. The entire scenario might not have seemed so out of the ordinary were it not for the fact that the British Parliament, and indeed most of Eden's own Government, were unaware of the conspiracy from beginning to end. Eden arranged Britain's role in the affair in secrecy, as the record makes clear, yet the reasons why such an invidious scheme (which ultimately led to Eden's downfall) was required in the first place have been heatedly debated on both sides of the Atlantic.

The official British argument revolves around the lack of support the United States government gave to the allies early on, when it would have assured a rapid resolution of the conflict by peaceful means. Lacking alternatives, and faced with a fascist-style Egyptian dictator, their governments were obliged to resort to force, moral or not.[7]

The American view, coinciding with British Opposition opinion, held that the British and French leadership revealed their cynicism and duplicity by engaging in an immoral conspiracy.[8] This view suggests that Eden and the French Premier Guy Mollet knew their actions could be disastrous but calculated that they could get away with a rapid strike disguised as a peace-keeping force. While ostensibly "separating the combatants," they would in effect take over the Canal Zone. By doing so, they were subconsciously seeking to reestablish waning European prestige in the Middle East.

If one fact about Anthony Eden's involvement in the Suez Crisis is

*Leaving 10 Downing Street to resign, January 9, 1957*

abundantly clear, it is the dramatic rejection of the diplomatic methods that he had so successfully employed at an earlier time while serving as Churchill's Foreign Secretary. The tragedy is compounded, then, by the realization that Eden's abilities should have been tailormade for the crisis at hand. Yet the traditional explanations embodied in the two sides of the argument simply cannot account for how a man of such proven ability failed so abysmally in 1956. As such, there is a third explanation for Suez, which historians and participants alike have largely ignored. This is the evidence that Anthony Eden's involvement with amphetamines during the ensuing crisis was partially responsible for his disreputable actions.

All accounts of the period have made passing reference to Eden's tenuous health during his years as Foreign Secretary and Prime Minister, but they refer largely to his well-known episodes of intermittent bile duct obstruction,[9] a condition which in itself would not have been sufficient to affect his judgment.[10] Bile was not the only evil humour afflicting Anthony Eden during the Suez crisis. It was left to an American writer, William Manchester, to suggest that his thought processes may also have been influenced by the effects of chronic amphetamine abuse on a naturally high-strung personality.[11] Such abuse in Eden's case is a matter of record. During the Suez crisis, he admitted that he "was practically living on Benzedrine",[12] a popular and at that time, ubiquitous brand of amphetamine, and his dramatic behavioral change reflected its influence to the letter. Prescribed for all manner of ailments in the forties and fifties, the deleterious effects of the drug became general medical knowledge only after his passing. Yet its sinister impact on Eden's conduct during the Suez crisis has not been properly emphasized by professional historians, who either have chosen to ignore, or have not been aware of, the dangerous effects of this drug on the human psyche. Manchester, however, stated the case succinctly:

> The Suez Crisis would have taxed the gifts of a Disraeli, and the householder at 10 Downing Street was no Disraeli. He was Sir Anthony Eden, once Churchill's great Foreign Secretary, and now worn to a shadow. The office of Prime Minister was simply too much for him. Struggling along with less than five hours sleep a night, he became addicted to amphetamines. Years later medical scientists discovered that amphetamines could rob a sensible man of his good judgment, and that is what happened to Eden in 1956.[13]

From the medical perspective, then, there may be more than mere historical circumstance to explain Britain's denigrated role in world affairs following the transformation of Europe effected by the two world wars. Britain's diminished status signified, in part, the end result of that evolution, in which the neurologic illnesses of such predecessors as Wilson, Hindenburg, MacDonald, Piłsudski, Hitler, and Roosevelt played a not insignificant role. There is an element of tragic irony here: Britain's leadership reflected the same physiologic compromise which contributed to the transformation that has been the subject of this review. With the political collapse of Europe assured by war, power had devolved during the fifties from the Old World to two competing nuclear colossi separated by the widest ideological gap and military might in the history of the modern world. As such, the bubonic plague may ultimately pale by comparison to the effects of a few individual examples of disease in man's attempt to rationally control his twentieth century environment.

# NOTES

1. A few investigators would take exception to this; see Seldon, *Churchill's Indian Summer.*

2. Moran, *Diaries*, pp. 355–56.

3. Ibid., pp. 358–59, 368.

4. Ibid., pp. 398, 434–38.

5. Ibid., pp. 507–509.

6. Carlton, *Anthony Eden*, p. 298.

7. Eden, *Full Circle;* Macmillan, *Riding the Storm.*

8. Robertson, *Crisis;* Thomas, *Suez;* Nutting, *End of Lesson.*

9. Eden had previously undergone unsuccessful gallbladder surgery, which had left him with a stricture of the bile duct; see Neff, *Warriors at Suez*, p. 182; Thomas, *Suez*, p. 35.

10. Thomas, *Suez*, p. 35.

11. Manchester, *Glory and Dream*, 2:935. To his credit, Donald Neff later postulated the same; see *Warriors at Suez*, p. 182.

12. Thomas, *Suez*, p. 35.

13. Manchester, *Glory and Dream*, 2:935. After the Suez crisis, his physician, Sir Horace Evans, asserted that Eden could no longer afford to depend on the amphetamines that had sustained him; see L'Etang, *Fit to Lead?*, p. 96.


# REFERENCES

**PRIMARY**

Eden, Anthony. *Full Circle: The Memoirs of Anthony Eden.* Boston: Houghton Mifflin Co., 1960.

Macmillan, Harold. *Tides of Fortune, 1945–1955.* New York: Harper and Row, 1969.

Moran, Lord. *Churchill: Taken from the Diaries of Lord Moran.* Boston: Houghton Mifflin Co., 1966.

Nutting, Anthony. *No End of a Lesson.* London: Constable, 1967.

**SECONDARY**

Carlton, David. *Anthony Eden: A Biography.* Penguin Books, Allen Lane, 1981.

L'Etang, Hugh. *Fit to Lead?* London: William Heinemann Medical Books Ltd., 1980.

Manchester, William. *The Glory and the Dream.* 2 vols. Boston: Little, Brown and Co., 1973.

Neff, Donald. *Warriors at Suez.* New York: Simon and Schuster, Linden Press, 1981.

Robertson, Terence. *Crisis: The Inside Story of the Suez Conspiracy.* New York: Atheneum, 1964.

Seldon, Anthony. *Churchill's Indian Summer.* London: Hodder and Stoughton, 1981.

Thomas, Hugh. *The Suez Affair.* London: Weidenfeld and Nicolson, 1966.

# 6

## *Implications for the Future*

Most historians would acknowledge that the political collapse of Europe was largely framed between the two world wars. Implicit in that conclusion is the recognition of a noticeable decline in the quality of national leadership during this period—part of which, at least, may now be attributed to disease and infirmities in those involved in staving off that collapse. It began with Woodrow Wilson.[1] His efforts at Versailles in 1919 represented the first attempt to reconstruct an already fatally stricken Europe. Sadly enough, he agreed to some aspects of the treaty ending World War I during an episode suggestive of encephalitis. This induced further intellectual compromise in a man who already demonstrated early signs of dementia on the basis of poorly-controlled hypertension. Not surprisingly, many of the points agreed to at Versailles remained festering sores that partially prevented Europe from rehabilitating its own unhealthy carcass. Furthermore, the potential for policing the tenets of the Treaty through the League of Nations was fatally weakened with its rejection by the United States—again largely as a result of Wilson's disease-induced frame of mind following a severe stroke.

Over the next twenty years, Europe crept inexorably toward a second and far more devastating war fostered by the unfinished business of the first. From the perspective of the principal nations involved, age and decrepitude played a larger role in the origins of that war than historians have acknowledged to date. They did so, (1) by paralyzing the government of Germany, leaving it with little alternative in the end but to allow Adolf Hitler to consolidate his position there; (2) by compromising the leadership of a nation, Great Britain, that had both the material resources and credibility to restrict Hitler's access to increasing power; and (3) by allowing Poland, a critically placed European state, to be used by Hitler to overrun Central Europe in a timetable of his own choosing.

In Paul von Hindenburg, the German government was caught in the dilemma of being reliant upon the good graces—and the good judgment—of a man obviously compromised by his advanced years. This fact was perceived by all and used cynically by some. Palace intrigue enveloped the government and its hapless father figure, which merely perpetuated the image of the Weimar Republic as ungovernable during the early thirties. Into that void of leadership stepped Adolf Hitler.

In Ramsay MacDonald's case, a lifelong endogenous depression was augmented by a break with his longstanding identity as spokesman for the Labour party. This presaged the onset of a well-defined dementia, which became apparent by 1933. Indeed, it may be argued that his depression was the first manifestation of that disease. The effect of the policies that he pursued under its influence was to place Germany on an equal footing, allowing her to redress the perceived imbalances that Versailles had created—which were, paradoxically, supposed to be Europe's guarantees for the future.

In Józef Piłsudski, the manifestations of overt senility were less pervasive; yet the effects of the natural aging process fostered inappropriate delusions concerning both Poland's military strength and Hitler's ultimate intentions. The result of the foreign policy Piłsudski rigidly followed—the German-Polish Declaration of 1934—gave the Fuehrer his first green light in Central and Eastern Europe.

The effects of aging and illness did not end with the outbreak of World War II. Marshal Philippe Pétain was ninety years of age when he served as the senile figurehead of a French government that collaborated with the Nazi regime. Adolf Hitler himself lost his thousand-year Reich after 1941 partly on the basis of decisions that bore the stamp of drug abuse and a personality disorder probably caused by the ravages of temporal lobe epilepsy. The reconstruction of Europe after World War II may have been compromised in part by Franklin D. Roosevelt, an American president assaulted during his last year in office by the deleterious effects of hypertensive and pulmonary-induced encephalopathy on his thought processes.

Nor did this dreary sequence of events cease at war's end. If one sign of Europe's political collapse was the movement of power away from the European capitals and toward the two emerging superpowers, then it might be argued that Great Britain's last hurrah as a world power occurred in the mid-1950s. England, that last vestige of international power centralized in the Old World, was forced to witness the dimming of the beacon of its influence during the second prime ministership of Winston Churchill—himself the victim of multiple episodes of cerebrovascular insufficiency, which left him but a hollow shell of the man he had once been. She saw that light go out completely with his successor Anthony Eden. Victimized by amphetamine abuse, he precipitously passed the torch of power to the Soviet Union and the United States by his ignominious involvement in the Suez Canal crisis of 1956.

Within a forty-year period, then, the peoples living under four distinctively different forms of government were subjected to compromised leadership at the highest level on the basis of neurologic disease. As disparate as the circumstances in each case may have been, two unifying threads link the protagonists discussed in this review to a common theme. The first is an acknowledgment that illnesses that lead to impaired brain function transcend national boundaries.[2] The common denominator is advancing age. For the future, the likelihood of repetitions of the performances witnessed in the first half of the twentieth century will remain, as the exercise of political power on the national level will continue to be reserved for those with years of experience.

The second encompasses the universal question of how the public deals with the unforeseen circumstance of compromised leadership. Regardless of the political context within which solutions are tendered, the problem remains the same: How does one go about effecting a solution to, first, defining disability in a medico-legal sense and, second, legitimizing the transfer of power to a more effective leader? In a word, how does a governed people protect itself against this potential, if not predictable, catastrophe?

In each case study presented here, attempts to disguise the obvious resulted as altered behavior became apparent to those closely positioned to the affected leader. Yet his physician's restriction of access to information regarding that leader's medical condition effectively precluded a satisfactory solution to the twin problems of defining disability and exercising a proper transferral of power. Fortunately for America's future, this should remain of interest only within the context of history, as media exposure today has fostered the emergence of what the esteemed political scientist Clinton Rossiter has termed "the public Presidency." As opposed to the era during which the likes of a Cary Grayson or a Ross McIntire simply withheld information believed to be politically damaging to their respective charges, the American public is now virtually assured that nothing of this nature will be kept from it. As Rossiter points out, "the palace guard now exists to feed information, not to withhold it."[3] This same circumstance would also be expected to apply in Great Britain, where the highly readable (if not always reliable) tabloid press maintains a peculiar credibility in the public eye.

Such assurances, of course, do not exist in a totalitarian state. One doubts that any greater degree of information would be made available today in such a state than was allowed in Adolf Hitler's time by officials entrusted with that leader's health. The impenetrability of the Soviet facade regarding Yuri Andropov's and Constantine Chernenko's fatal illnesses underscores this assertion. Within the context of a public's right to know, limited access to such information will remain a problem peculiar to totalitarian societies—and consequently outside the sphere of free-world influence.

Should this acknowledgment justify a lack of concern on our part? Absolutely not. The need has never been more critical to obtain and evaluate what little information can be gleaned regarding the health of leaders of any totalitarian state, whether it be the Soviet Union, with its capacity for initiating a nuclear holocaust, or a Third World nation restricted to propagating terrorist activities. If it might one day be substantiated, as a few have already suggested, that Idi Amin really suffers from tertiary syphilis (with all that admission would imply for the activities that characterized his reign of terror in Uganda), it remains more compelling still to monitor the state of health of a Kaddafi of Libya or a Khomeini of Iran. It is precisely this awareness that the medical politics of deception can still be practiced so effectively today in less-open societies than our own that gives cause for the gravest concern—if not pessimism—regarding the future conduct of their affairs.

One would hope that the principle of collective leadership that appears to be on the ascendancy in the Soviet Union today offers some buffer against an individual aberration on account of neurologic illness being responsible for launching nuclear missiles in a westward direction. We have no way of knowing for sure. Yet the recognition of what has transpired in our recent history within the context of the Hitler experience offers a sobering reminder of that possibility occurring in any totalitarian state blessed with nuclear arms. Need we recall the horror of the unstable Fuehrer's last defiant act directed against the civilian population of Great Britain? Had the V1 and V2 rockets launched indiscriminately against London in the waning days of World War II contained nuclear warheads, the outcome for civilization at that earlier point might have been considerably different.

In relation to the Soviet system in particular—a system in which leadership is gained only after an extraordinary number of years in service at lower levels—the medical argument weighs more heavily still. Without a doubt, Leonid Brezhnev was a chronically ill man for a number of years prior to his demise. That his illnesses appear to have been related more to cardiopulmonary compromise than to overt brain dysfunction is merely the luck of the draw, statistically speaking. In Andropov's case, the effects of longstanding kidney failure conceivably may have played some role in the deteriorating relations between East and West, as physicians today are well aware of the adverse neurologic sequelae that often attend this disease.[4] This must remain in the realm of speculation, as access to the medical record of Soviet leaders is nonexistent. Still, from the standpoint of deception and disguise of the facts, the United States experience vis-à-vis Wilson and Roosevelt was not so far removed from what exists today in regard to public knowledge of illness among the Soviet leadership. Considering, moreover, that the line between survival and catastrophe is so much more thinly drawn now than a half century ago only emphasizes the seriousness of the argument.

The acts of duplicity among those responsible for ministering to the medical needs of their special charges is a historical luxury present-day conditions can ill afford to sustain. As stated, this issue is now believed to be—or at least fervently hoped to be—of only historical interest from the standpoint of the United States. Our nation's experience with Dwight D. Eisenhower probably assures us of that. On three separate occasions Eisenhower was, by his own admission, ill-equipped to perform the duties of his office, on the basis of a recurrent cardiac condition. What transpired in the interim was one nation's attempt to deal through trial and error with a potentially disastrous situation for which the United States Constitution had made no adequate provision. Although the experience was a landmark of sorts in allowing the President to declare his own disability, the precedent thus set largely begs the question in relation to neurologic compromise; for this is disability of a different and far more sinister sort.[5]

The key distinction rests with the recognition that Eisenhower was at that time aware of his own disability, and therefore able to initiate a temporary solution.[6] The serious need remains, however, to set a precedent for those cases in which the nation's Chief Executive is either unaware of, or unable to acknowledge, his own disability—or more perplexing still, permanently compromised on the cognitive level, enough so as to preclude his ever resuming the powers and duties of his office. This is an issue, unfortunately, for which there are still no suitable answers. Neither Congress nor the American public has seemingly learned from the experiences chronicled in this review.

Acknowledging that fully one in four Presidents has died while in office, a number of legislative measures have been taken to deal with the anticipated succession crisis in such a circumstance. We have even gone so far as to legislate for the very unlikely possibility of the loss of the services of both the President and the Vice-President. Yet, ironically, only a less-than-satisfactory agreement has been reached on the far more likely possibility of a cognitively disabled President in office. I am referring to Section 4 of the Twenty-fifth Amendment. This deals with the implications of mental inability in the nation's Chief Executive and reads in part:

> Whenever the Vice President and a majority of either the principal officers of the executive departments [i.e., the Cabinet] or of such other body as Congress may by law provide, transmit . . . their written declaration that the President is unable to discharge the powers and duties of his office, the Vice President shall immediately assume the powers and duties of the office as Acting President. [7]

Inability is not defined in the text of the Amendment. As John D. Feerick points out, "this was not the result of an oversight. Rather, it reflected a judgment that a rigid constitutional definition was undesirable, since cases of inability could take various forms not neatly fitting into such a definition." [8] More to the point, defining disability in the medical sense of the word lies more properly outside the purview of legislative skills. Therein exists the weakness of the Amendment. Having provided the legal framework for both initiating and concluding the process, Section 4 is vague on how Congress arrives, if you will, at point B from point A. [9] Enlisting "such other body as Congress may by law provide" is simply too imprecise to be consistently effective. Medical expertise of the highest order should be mandated by law and cloaked with a higher authority transcending its current advisory capacity. [10]

Concerning the relative merits of the Twenty-fifth Amendment, Feerick concludes:

> Nothing in the record to date indicates that there is a superior remedy for dealing with the complex problems involved. . . . Under the inability procedures of the Amendment, neither the Vice-President nor Cabinet can declare a President disabled without the concurrence of the other, and if a President disagrees with their declaration, he is in a position to have the dispute resolved by Congress in accordance with procedures weighted heavily in his favor. [11]

As a legal technician, Feerick lauds the preservation of the principles of the separation of powers and of checks and balances. Yet there are potential problems inherent in the amendment that threaten both a rational, apolitical resolution of a given case and, in consequence, the best interests of the public this legislation is intended to serve. First, where do government officials and legislators obtain the necessary data to make such a decision? Second, it appears that the President even has the power to override that decision should it be unfavorable. Simply stated, we require more safeguards than current legislation affords.[12]

Modern medicine may be aware enough of the serious drawbacks of amphetamine toxicity, polypharmacy, and overt senility to avoid the pitfalls seen in European history in the future; but we are far less prepared to predict which leaders will succumb to the effects of cerebrovascular insufficiency. If the ascension of the "public Presidency" has assured the American public at least some modicum of awareness of the possibility of neurologic illness in our own Chief Executives, we remain woefully unprepared to deal with the implications of that revelation should we be faced with its occurrence.

The cases of Woodrow Wilson and Franklin Roosevelt poignantly illustrate the prevalence of the problem at hand. We learned from neither experience, largely because we had chosen (or, more correctly, had been induced) to ignore them, given the limited information available at the time. No greater irony exists than the parallels linking the two physicians who withheld the necessary information from the public in these two cases. As chronicled in this review, Ross McIntire had been recommended to Roosevelt by none other than Cary Grayson, largely on the basis of their shared belief that their respective roles as White House physicians entailed the withholding of potentially damaging information from the public. Their perception of how this might have affected their own positions close to the seat of power in American politics may well have entered into their considerations as well.[13]

Hugh L'Etang posed what he felt to be the essential question: "Does the electorate have the right to know the medical history and state of health of a candidate for high office, and does the physician have the obligation to make such information public?" Our history has taught us that both must be answered in the affirmative. Now we must ask far more important questions: How does one define disability in our leaders, and how does one remove them when they become so? L'Etang concludes that: "However binding the Hippocratic oath may be . . . Lord Moran has shown that no study of any historical period can be complete without . . . a detailed medical history of the personalities of the time."[14] Historical accuracy is one legitimate concern; what is in the best interest of a nation is still another. The need surely exists to apply the best medical thinking outside the confines of patient confidentiality to obtain the necessary detailed medical data about our leaders.

Acknowledging the often-profound personal impact these powerful men exerted on their physicians, the latter's duplicity may therefore be excused somewhat, given the traditional code of ethics that dictated then, and dictates today, that confidential information of one's patient must not be revealed. Yet this ignores the essential issue: The physician in this circumstance is ultimately accountable to the public he serves. That the nuances of this peculiar responsibility were lost on these physicians is a tragic legacy of our past. It is hoped that this will not be ignored by future physicians in similar circumstances.

The Hippocratic oath reads in part: "Whatever . . . I may see or hear in the lives of men which ought not to be spoken abroad, I will not divulge." Using this in defense of confidentiality is untenable in this unique physician-patient relationship. As L'Etang observed:

> The oath confers no priviledge on the physician, for a doctor may be compelled to give evidence in a court of law. . . . [Similarly], if the health or safety of the community is involved he may use his discretion . . . to disclose information which in his patient's view "ought not to be spoken abroad." [15]

One may rest assured that in those instances where it has applied in twentieth-century history, such information was certainly not "spoken abroad." More germane to the discussion, confidentiality is simply no longer the issue. How best to determine and then reveal that medical information is the key.

Yet are we making too much of all of this in our recent history? The need to avoid reductionism in medico-historical analysis (and, by extension, to weigh the impact of a physician's duplicity with caution as it contributed to events) must remain paramount in any investigator's outlook when embarking on such a task. L'Etang notes that "retrospective analyses of events . . . often seek a facile or face-saving explanation which the illness of an individual provides. Analysis of successful government might show that affairs can be usefully conducted even by sick statesmen." [16] Roosevelt at Yalta is a case in point. The need therefore exists to document beyond a reasonable certainty that illness and its concealment have resulted in bad decisions and imprudent conduct in high office.

With regard to the individual leaders discussed, this review speaks for itself. The implications of physician-sanctioned duplicity for twentieth-century history have been bothersome enough: Permitting a President to continue to participate in delicate negotiations during a systemic viral infection; refusing to certify disability in a Chief Executive so ill that he could not meet with his Cabinet for seven months while, in effect, his wife ran the country; allowing another President manifesting transient behavioral aberrations on account of three serious medical conditions to run for an unprecedented fourth term of office; continuing to prescribe a staggering array of central nervous system stimulants to an unbalanced dictator driving his nation inexorably to a crushing defeat; acknowledging the effects of two separate strokes and a handful of transient ischemic attacks on an aging Prime Minister while still permitting that individual to remain at the helm past his eightieth birthday; and prescribing amphetamines to a temperamental successor who managed to embroil himself in a deceitful scheme so distasteful to his own government that he would be forced from office.

This is the tragic litany for which modern medicine bears partial responsibility in the first half of the twentieth century under the guise of the sacred physician-patient relationship. It is to be hoped that during the second half of the century this pretention has been laid to rest. For this is the least of our problems in relation to the issue at hand. The remaining two—the issues of defining disability and assuring a legitimate succession under the circumstances—deserve further consideration in concluding this review.

We are indebted to Clinton Rossiter's cogent analysis of the problem insofar as it reflects the pessimism he assumes in dealing with it. In the revised edition of *The American Presidency* he asserted:

> The problem of disability is, then, a real problem, real in history and even more real in the threat of demoralizing chaos it constantly poses. . . . Our continued failure to come to grips with it is not, I am sure, a product of carelessness or petty politics. It is, rather, our left-handed way of acknowledging how slippery a problem it really is.[17]

Hugh L'Etang stated the problem another way:

> History teaches us that it is difficult to remove a statesman from office when he has some knowledge of the nature of his disability; when his condition removes any insight about the disability the task of management may be well nigh impossible.[18]

In a very real sense, we have successfully dealt with that other great calamity in American politics on too many occasions already: the death of a President while in office. Experience has been an adequate teacher, and the transfer of power to the Vice-President in such circumstances has been legitimized in practice over the years. This issue, then, and its corollary of losing both leaders during the same period, are no longer critical matters to address. Experience has led the way with the former, and the latter is simply less pressing than previously acknowledged on the basis of the unlikelihood of its occurrence. *Yet the chances are good that the real emergency will come in the area of presidential neurologic disability, either temporary or permanent.* It has arisen on at least three occasions already in the twentieth century,[19] and none of these men was as old at the time as our current President.

The most direct encounter with obvious disability was the case of Woodrow Wilson. The specific question of certifying disability was addressed—and then ignored. The obvious individual to assume that responsibility abrogated it, and no governmental instrument was as yet established to fill the void. That situation remains inadequately provided for today, and it represents one of the gravest dangers threatening the stability of the executive branch. Certainly Dr. Grayson had an ample definition of the term as it related to presidential function. Article 2, Section 6 of the United States Constitution outlines both a broad definition of the term "disability" ("inability to discharge the powers and duties of the said office") and what must therefore follow under the circumstances ("the same shall devolve on the Vice-President . . . [who] shall act accordingly until the disability be removed"). The critical issue that the framers of the Constitution ignored (either intentionally or unintentionally) was to define the precise authority empowered to determine that disability. Lacking any other mandate, that determination should have been left to Wilson's physician, as Robert Lansing clearly perceived. If Grayson admittedly felt uncomfortable in preempting this responsibility for himself, at the very least he could have presented data to an appropriate authority to make that determination. Failing to do either, he went the other directon in clear disregard of medical judgment.

Nothing of substance regarding that question was learned in the process. Twenty-five years later, a similar if less exacting case occurred, and Ross McIntire behaved in precisely the same manner as his predecessor. If he viewed Grayson's experience as a precedent (and there is substantial reason to believe he did) the evidence indicates that he made a poor decision. American interests were served no better in the second case than they had been in the first. Grayson had been relatively shielded by his position as a physician, while twenty-five years later McIntire was far less isolated and far more subject to public scrutiny. This was the period in which the public presidency of which Rossiter speaks began to evolve, as journalists in particular began to demand accountability to the American people more forthrightly. Eisenhower's experience a decade later legitimized that evolution in public awareness. That McIntire felt immune to its pressures even as early as 1944 signified a sad miscalculation on his part.

Perhaps Lord Moran was aware of just how far this process of increasing public awareness had evolved—enough to prompt a full disclosure of the record in retrospect, even if his nation's best interests had not been served before he made the facts known. Theodor Morell, on the other hand, had no accountability to anyone other than the Fuehrer. This is shown by the attempt of other physicians to challenge his authority in an open forum, with the result that they lost face in a resounding fashion. This result speaks to the influence of the totalitarian state under which they labored, legitimized by the Fuehrer Principle. In such a society, the physician had no other accountability than to its leadership. This does not, however, negate the impact upon the members of that society.

So the principle of having the physician determine disability and make his judgments known was rejected in each case. Nonetheless, this professional remains the only instrument with sufficient credentials to assume the role. The fact that these men failed to perceive this does not justify our continuing to ignore that possibility. Certainly in matters of disability determination in contemporary medical practice it is the physician who makes that appraisal based on a uniform standard.[20] It is true that in some instances an instrument of the judicial system reviews the facts in the case and makes a disposition based on the data presented by a physician. The system works today, and there is no reason why such an arrangement should not translate to the presidency. Determining disability is a responsibility of today's physician, who admittedly has to deal with such an issue more often than he would like, but it is a responsibility nonetheless, and a workable one at that.

Certainly such investigators as Clinton Rossiter have found other alternatives uninviting. In his chapter on "The Firing, Retiring, and Expiring of Presidents" Rossiter reviewed the possibilities, including a determination by the Vice-President, the Cabinet, the Secretary of State, Congress, the Supreme Court, the governors of the fifty states, or a panel of eminent private citizens. All are found wanting, and for obvious reasons, the most obvious of which is the inescapable political entanglement of the decision. Further, assessing the medical data required to determine disability as it relates to the President's capacity to lead is an exacting science requiring far more expertise in pathophysiology than any government official or private citizen without medical training would be expected to possess. It is easy enough to document paralysis, for example; the physical signs are all too obvious to even the most casual observer. Its occurrence, however, does not necessarily imply the inability to lead. Similarly, the reason why Dwight Eisenhower and his heart attacks and John F. Kennedy and his Addison's disease were not included in this study should be obvious: these ailments in themselves did not affect their decision-making ability and hence their leadership capacities. This is also why Franklin Roosevelt's polio affliction has been ignored in this account.

Rossiter is left with what he feels is the only acceptable alternative, and yet he admits some understandable discomfiture in proposing it. Citing the Eisenhower experience as a precedent, Rossiter concludes: "Although almost every method proposed for determining that disability exists has also been proposed for determining that it has come to an end, once again the chief responsibility is pinned on the President himself. His announcement that he was ready to reassume his powers would, in the nature of things political and constitutional, be conclusive." It would not, however, necessarily be medically conclusive, as this author's appended caveat declares: "I am assuming, of course, that a deranged President would not be permitted to announce anything to anyone . . . I could be wrong."[21] Indeed, we could all be wrong, as a careful reading of our recent history outlined in this review would suggest. For there is no assurance that the very President who is allowed to exercise the power to declare his own disability is necessarily of sound mind; and he would not have to be "deranged" as such. Cognitive compromise and emotional aberrations on a much more subtle level might still preclude his making a rational decision on that issue—not to mention the natural proclivity to be somewhat self-serving, if not defensive, when the credibility of one's intellect is questioned.

Dr. Rossiter's proposal for dealing with this circumstance entails the following:

> In the event of an inability which would prevent the President from communicating with the Vice-President, the Vice-President, after such consultation as seems to him appropriate under the circumstances, would decide. . . . The President, in either event, would determine when the inability has ended.[22]

From the medical perspective, such a proposal lacks credibility, and Sections 3 and 4 of the Twenty-fifth Amendment have attempted to redress the potential for abuse. Not only would a Vice-President's decision be construed, correctly or incorrectly, as politically motivated,[23] but there is nothing to suggest in a typical Vice-President's qualifications (or those of a Cabinet member) the capacity for determining disability with the degree of medical acumen one would hope such a weighty determination would deserve. Then, too, leaving the resumption of office to the President's decision leaves us with the same problem encountered in his initiating the process. Should a man of compromised intellectual abilities on the basis of neurologic illness in the early going be allowed later to declare that such an impairment has been resolved? I think not. Does Section 4 of the Twenty-fifth Amendment provide a tenable solution to the heretofore unresolved issue? Not completely. Only an impartial medical determination of the process of recovery can legitimately answer that question. Just because a President might have the physical stamina to meet with his Cabinet, for example, does not necessarily imply that his cognitive impairment has improved accordingly, at least to the point of resuming the arduous duties of the highest decision-making office in the land.

Nor does Rossiter's proposal acknowledge the very real possibility that a President's capacity to declare that his improvement is sufficient for him to return to office may be an open-ended circumstance; he may never improve to a degree sufficient to make that pronouncement. And who is to determine the permanency of that condition? The Vice-President again? The Supreme Court? This writer, for one, hopes not. This is an impartial physician's domain, and it is a task he encounters every day of his professional life. Rossiter asserts that a judgment of presidential disability would be "a political decision—a determination of high policy, and thus a task for [politicians] . . . who are permitted to practice their art under the most favorable circumstances."[24] If such be the intent, we would be guilty of perpetrating the same injustice imposed on the public in our past experience. Was it not, in fact, political considerations that retained the likes of a Wilson, a Roosevelt, a Hitler, or a Churchill in the critical position of decision making long after their respective skills, if not their mental capacities, had faded? If politics is the game, the least those who are subjected to its results should expect is a leader whose mental health is equal to the task. If Rossiter would plead for allowing those "to practice their art in the most favorable circumstances," this medical reviewer would plead the same for allowing the skills of his profession, in an impartial fashion, to be exercised in kind.

Given the proper application of an appropriate instrument to determine disability, I do not share Rossiter's conclusion that, in a certain sense, "the problem of disability is quite insoluble."[25] What I propose as a workable solution is the concept of a Presidential Disability Commission restricted to physicians empowered to speak prospectively. That is to say, rather than accepting Rossiter's assertion that physicians should "speak only when spoken to,"[26] and therefore be asked to act after the fact (and hence in a sense retrospectively), a panel of physicians should be chosen or appointed before the inception of the incoming administration. Its duties should be limited to making an objective recommendation based on the data it gathers. It should not be empowered directly with the ability to remove the President from office. Emphasis should be placed on the expertise of those skilled in neurologic illness, as this is precisely the medical realm of a President's health that should interest us most in relation to the capacity for rational leadership. Nor should the physicians on the panel be entrusted with the day-to-day care of the President, to avoid conflict of interest or the constraints of the physician-patient relationship.

Empowering such a panel before the next presidential election, and dividing it equally with regard to party affiliation, should largely circumvent the probability of political allegiances coming into play—at least in gathering the data and making its recommendations known. Neither, for that matter, would too much time be required in compiling the evidence, as some might fear. Judging disability impartially, which in properly trained hands requires in nearly every case merely a proper history and physical examination, is a straightforward matter.

Certainly a determination of disability could be had forthwith if such a committee utilized the definition proposed by Dr. Ruth Silva. Disability would be defined as "any *de facto* inability, whatever the cause or the duration, if it occurs at a time when the urgency of public business requires executive action."[27] Such an approach would largely circumvent the objections of Dr. L'Etang regarding an individual physician's responsibility in determining disability:

> Great men are different from you and me. . . . The role of the doctor in regard to this small and select group of patients is unique, and most practitioners have neither personal experience, nor second hand knowledge from experienced colleagues, of the correct approach and of the special problems that are involved. . . . Would any doctor care to decide whether the crippled Woodrow Wilson was any less effective than his inept Vice-President? Would any physician care to decide whether the crippled Churchill was more or less effective than the younger, but ailing, Eden? Certainly all three had disorders which at a lower executive level would lead most doctors to recommend rest, a change of occupation, or early retirement.[28]

This is precisely why we need *collective* responsibility for the decision by those so skilled. Nor would a Disability Commission be required (or empowered) to judge the relative merits of a prospective successor, or even to pass judgment on the political ramifications of the recommendation it makes. The sole concern here is to gather the data in an objective and apolitical fashion. Having established the medical merits of a given case, they might then be presented to a suitable political forum as outlined in the Twenty-fifth Amendment. The political process would still have its day, but we would at least be allowed the comfort and protection of knowing that the medical details of the question would be divorced from the vagaries of that process.

The theme and the proposal of this review, then, dovetail in a rather ironic fashion. Having acknowledged the medical profession's failure, if not duplicity, in determining disability and effecting the necessary transfer of power in the past, we are calling now for that same instrument to be empowered with these duties in the future. The key distinction rests with divorcing that role from the individual physician-patient relationship.[29]

The determination of disability now urgently requires that same legislative or statutory effort that has already been applied to the issue of presidential succession. The Twenty-fifth Amendment alone is unequal to the task; an apolitical, prospectively selected panel of physicians should represent the heart of that effort.

This discussion of disability and succession has largely centered upon our own form of government, virtually to the exclusion of other forms similarly affected by the universal historical impact of disease. There is no reason to expect that a similar proposal could not be effected within a parliamentary form of government as in Great Britain. We cannot speak, of course, for the totalitarian state, but only can hope that their awareness of the problem at least parallels our own. Certainly both a parliamentary system and a totalitarian state have every reason to be concerned about the perplexing implications of the succession problem—perhaps more than ourselves. The experiences of Great Britain and Germany dramatize the restrictions their peoples experienced when faced with compromised leadership.

In the British system, the Prime Minister may so structure his Government's activities along noncontroversial lines that he may be able to avoid almost indefinitely (within a five year limit) the necessary censure by vote of no confidence in the Commons to force him from office.[30] If little of a concrete or revolutionary nature resulted from Winston Churchill's last years in office, an awareness on his part of the importance of avoiding the controversial may have played a larger role in his longevity in office than his supporters would probably admit. Ironically, his successor perpetrated such a disservice upon his own Government that controversy was unavoidable. Not surprisingly, Eden's tenure was strikingly brief compared to Churchill's.

The disparate results of Churchill's and Eden's encounters with neurologic disability reflect the difference in the disease processes that afflicted the two. If Churchill's dementia, induced by cerebrovascular insufficiency, compelled him to be extremely cautious, if not desultory, the extraordinarily unremarkable (and uncontroversial) record of his administration would be precisely what a medical reviewer would expect. Yet the impetuous, unpredictable, and above all unrealistic pattern that characterized Anthony Eden's tenure in office reflects in a similar manner what one would anticipate from a leader under the influence of amphetamines. If Eden, at least as Prime Minister, could be viewed as a tempestuous funnel cloud in British politics, Churchill could be appropriately described as a stagnant pool. Eden personified the thunderstorm that rapidly dissipated; Churchill, the shallow puddle which slowly evaporated. In this one sense, perhaps, the Prime Minister in a parliamentary system may exercise a more immediate impact on his own political viability than is found in the American system. To date, barring the extremes of disability or political malfeasance, the American public largely remains committed to a four-year experience with its elected leadership.

In a dictatorship, the succession problem is more perplexing still. How does a people subjected to the consequences of unrestricted yet compromised leadership remove that leader from power? Germany's experience with Adolf Hitler illustrates the only viable alternative in that system—his removal from office by force. As such, the assassination attempt in the Fuehrer's bunker in 1944 represented the only means that those who were aware of the problem could employ. When the conspirators failed, Germany was left to live with its predicament—a potential circumstance that undoubtedly will remain for similar societies in the future. There are, quite simply, no easy answers here.

National leadership will in all probability continue to remain within the purview of the aged. How various peoples are empowered to deal with the potential problems of disability, duplicity, and succession inherent in such a circumstance will remain crucial to the viability of their nation-states. In the United States, with the burgeoning powers of the evolving modern presidency, these problems will remain particularly vexing as the office becomes even more personalized in the future. Richard E. Neustadt has identified this trend in his compelling work *Presidential Power.* Several observations by this distinguished scholar are worthy of emphasis in order to define the magnitude of the problem. Neustadt warns that "Presidential power has been at times dangerously personalized. . . . If one wants effective policy from the American system, danger does not lie in our dependence on *a* man; it lies in our capacity to make ourselves depend upon a man who is inexpert."[31] After digesting the message implicit in this medical review, one might reasonably add "or who is mentally disabled."

Neustadt then compares the British system to our own, acknowledging the universality of the problem:

> The British cabinet system tends to cover up the weaknesses and to show up the strengths of the top man; ours tends to do the opposite. . . . But Britain . . . has not lacked for inexpert heads of government, albeit quite professional, and British policy has paid a heavy price for them, most recently in Eden's case.[32]

What Neustadt does not acknowledge are the physiologic changes that might affect previously expert and professional leadership. No one remotely familiar with the earlier careers of Eden, Churchill, or Mac-Donald could accuse any of the three of being inexpert. Their records prior to assuming their respective prime ministerships reflect a high degree of professional leadership skills. Simply stated, choosing the expert is no assurance that the skill that brought him there will remain. The vagaries of age and illness may exercise such an influence that leadership may become not only inexpert, as in MacDonald's case; it also may become dangerous, as Anthony Eden's brief tenure attests.

Long before falling victim himself to the stress of the office he endured while chronically ill, Woodrow Wilson made the following prescient observation: "Men of ordinary physique and discretion cannot be Presidents and live, if the strain be not somehow relieved. We shall be obliged always to be picking our chief magistrates from among wise and prudent athletes—a small class."[33] Neustadt felt compelled to make some revisions in this observation, given the evolution of the office and the even greater stress that Presidents must now endure. "If we want Presidents alive and fully useful," he concludes, "we shall have to pick them from among experienced politicians of extraordinary temperament—an even smaller class."[34] Acknowledging the implications of this medical review, we now are compelled to offer even further revisions, the most obvious of which is that even the wise and the athletic are subject to the aging process and compromised health. Picking leaders from this "smaller class" is simply not enough. The question of how to monitor them and to remove them if necessary, is equally important.

Sound temperament is essential, as the cases of Adolf Hitler and Anthony Eden tragically demonstrate. Yet even an experienced leader blessed with extraordinary temperament is still subject to the biologic clock. Even the best leaders change with age and are eventually conquered by its vicissitudes, as the careers of Wilson, Roosevelt, and Churchill demonstrate. If Neustadt warns future Presidents to follow "the dictates of common prudence," namely, to stretch personal control and judgment "as wide and deep as he can make them reach,"[35] those entrusted with his health should be implored to be wary of the constraints the aging process places on the exercise of that judgment. We simply have been too *timid* in the past to acknowledge red flags when they appeared. This is the greatest lesson to be learned from a reading of these pages.

The public must not fall into the trap of entrusting its fortunes to first impressions of the individual we put in office. Our recent history suggests that we part with the initial public images of our leaders only grudgingly.[36] This has important implications, the most obvious of which is the danger inherent in believing that the initial image will remain inviolate, rather than recognizing the changes in character or behavior that may evolve. America's peculiar fascination with image and labels was readily understood by Roosevelt himself, who made a point of assuring the public in 1940 that, though he was entering his ninth year in office, we would "find him the same man we had known these many years." This consummate manipulator of public opinion understandably derived no small amount of satisfaction in accepting the popular labels of "Dr. New Deal" and "Dr. Win-the-War." And his physician undoubtedly saw the merits both for himself and his President in leaving those images untarnished, despite very obvious signs to the contrary in the end.

This reluctance to relinquish images appears to have also smitten some historians to a distressing degree. Perhaps this as much as anything explains the proclivity to define our past in themes that essentially redeploy hackneyed images we have embraced from the beginning. This may account for why Woodrow Wilson's rigidity was viewed to the end as an outgrowth of his Calvinist background of morality and righteousness rather than the progressive dementia such obstinacy also implied; or why Winston Churchill was seen as a remarkable visionary rather than as an aging stroke victim struggling to recapture a previously receptive audience with an encore on center stage; or most peculiar of all, how Adolf Hitler's bizarre behavior and unprecedented decisions and actions after 1940 were viewed as an irrational "disdain for the experts" (among other perplexing qualities), rather than recognizing the profound impact of a worsening personality disorder accentuated by an astounding combination of drugs.

Returning for the moment to the issue of stress in office, Neustadt proposes that "if a President is to assist himself through the vicissitudes of four long years, or eight, his sense of confidence must make him capable of bearing . . . sadness with good grace." [37] This review would emphasize the equal importance of good health to see him through—for it is precisely the qualities of humor and perspective to which Neustadt refers that are lost with cognitive compromise of whatever sort. With regard to humor per se, one cannot be certain that either Wilson or Hitler ever had it. But certainly the British politicians typify the argument. The elements of confidence, humor, and above all perspective were precisely what Ramsay MacDonald lost under the influence of premature brain aging. Anthony Eden lost the same qualities under the influence of amphetamines and obstructive cholangitis. The pitiful surrendering of Churchill in his last years to his old nemesis—the "Black Dog" of depression—as dementia enveloped him requires no further amplification. If, as Neustadt says, "the great separator" between the average and the extraordinary leader—temperament—is truly a "human resource not discovered every day among . . . politicians," [38] consideration must now be given to the realization that even those few who possess it run the risk of losing it while in office on account of rapid aging or illness.

The analogy of failing to utilize the abstract attitude presented in Woodrow Wilson's case can be applied equally to the other subjects in this review. Nothing underscores this faculty, which a leader in the modern world must employ, than the plethora of different functions he is called upon to administer. The noted American historian Arthur Schlesinger has referred to this as the "balance of administrative power," which Neustadt interprets to include a "balance of political, managerial, psychological, and personal feasibilities."[39] The final word is the key; it implies an abstractive ability to recognize and weigh alternatives. A failure to employ the abstract attitude in the long term renders one's leadership ineffectual—a feature that characterized each of the eight leaders at the close of their careers.

Woodrow Wilson's failure to abstract evoked an increasingly rigid and dogmatic view of the world. Franklin Roosevelt's failure left him awash in unconcern for the office after Yalta and may have contributed to a few disturbing decisions before that time. Ramsay MacDonald's inability to utilize the abstract prevented him from recognizing the errors implicit in pacifying a deceitful foe. Paul von Hindenburg was blind to the palace intrigues swirling about him, just as he failed to gauge his successor's intentions realistically. Józef Piłsudski proved unable to grasp the new essentials of modern warfare. Winston Churchill was unable to accept that time had passed him by; he assuaged his vanity by invoking past methods in an attempt to remain a member of the leadership elite. Adolf Hitler and Anthony Eden, of course, were so disrupted by the influences of unstable temperament augmented by drugs that powers of abstraction were totally lost to them. Their respective conditions represent the most extreme illustrations of the compromised abstract attitude.

One final point: Neustadt argues that a governed people's perception of a leader's effectiveness is reflected in what is happening to them during the time he holds office.[40] The consequences have been immense, if the first half of the twentieth century is any indication. The corollary danger that Neustadt fails to address, however, is the following: The public's perception of their leader should also include an awareness of what is happening to *him*. A more direct accountability by those charged with overseeing his health is required. The medical profession left us with a disturbing legacy in our recent past. Blinders must never be worn again, either by those charged with this important duty or by the public they serve.

## NOTES

1. There is an intriguing disclaimer to this assertion. One could argue that it had all begun in Germany thirty years earlier. Frederick III became Emperor of Germany in 1887. The year before, he had developed cancer of the larynx. The diagnosis was missed by Sir Morell Mackenzie, a distinguished English laryngologist who had been asked to

consult in the case. Frederick died four months after succeeding to the throne, and his impetuous son, William II, succeeded him at the age of twenty-nine. Not only did Frederick's successor have a love for the navy that found expression in the extensive build-up of Germany's surface fleet to compete with Great Britain (one cause of the burgeoning conflict leading to World War I), but he was also correctly perceived as being immature and impatient. As Dr. Ned I. Chalat described the possible impact of this missed medical diagnosis on the course of history: "Had Frederick remained Emperor and encouraged Bismarck to continue a more liberal government and constitutional monarchy; had he continued the non-aggression treaty between Russia and Germany; had he honored his pledge to [Queen] Victoria of a 'close and lasting friendship between our two nations,' how differently our history might have been written." See Ned I. Chalat, "Sir Morell Mackenzie Revisited."

2. As one medical investigator has observed: "If illness occurs in all countries at all times, the ill-effects should in the long term affect all countries equally; though it could follow that one country, more appreciative of this hazard, might take steps to ensure that any unfit representatives were summarily removed from the firing line." L'Etang, *Pathology*, p. 11. One proposal for effecting this end is discussed in this concluding chapter.

3. Rossiter, *American Presidency*, p. 214.

4. For the best current review of the neurologic sequelae of chronic renal failure, the interested reader is directed to Raskin and Fishman, "Neurologic Disorders in Renal Failure." Encephalopathy in this condition is secondary to uremia, an accumulation of urea in the bloodstream that would normally be filtered out through healthy kidneys.

5. It is perplexing that the precedent should be set in this case, when the neurologic disabilities of two earlier Presidents were far more relevant to decision making than was Eisenhower's coronary insufficiency. Perhaps this peculiar circumstance underscores the effectiveness of the deception exercised by Grayson and McIntire.

6. Subsequent legislation was passed in 1967 to provide for similar situations in the future. Section 3 of the Twenty-fifth Amendment deals with the potential case of a President acknowledging his own inability, either on the basis of illness or physical separation from the office precluding his administration of it. He may choose to suspend his power and duties temporarily. In the words of John D. Feerick, who has studied the Amendment in detail, such a decision would involve "a personal judgment on the part of the President." *Twenty-fifth Amendment*, p. 198. We have seen this applied by President Ronald Reagan during his operation for a colon cancer.

7. *United States Code*, 1970, "Organic Laws," 1:liii.

8. Feerick, *Twenty-fifth Amendment*, p. 197. Some observers saw the merit of being more precise. During Senate debates on the Amendment, Senator Birch Bayh outlined his definition of the words "inability" and "unable," which he asserted should refer to "an impairment of the President's faculties [in such a sense] that he is unable either to make or communicate his decisions as to his own competency to execute the powers and duties of his office." He went on to say: "The Cabinet, as well as the Vice-President and Congress, are going to have to judge the severity of the disability and the problems that face our country." *Congressional Record*, 1965, 111:3282, 15381. Certainly the last consideration should remain within the purview of government officials. Its corollary, however, that they should also be called upon to "judge the severity of the disability," would represent a dangerous (and unskilled) exercise of power. The burden of that particular responsibility should rest with medical experts.

9. Under Section 4 any declaration of inability is perceived to be a joint responsibility of the Vice-President and the Cabinet. An agreement between the two for determining disability or recovery is necessary for either question to be considered by Congress. "Thereupon Congress shall decide the issue" by two-thirds vote within twenty-one days.

If a preliminary agreement is not reached, then "the issue is not appropriate for Congress to decide, and the President then resumes his powers and duties." Feerick, *Twenty-fifth Amendment*, pp. 203, 200.

10. "In deciding the issue [of inability], Congress can proceed as it thinks best. . . . Thus it may request that the President undergo medical tests and examinations or submit to questioning at hearings." Feerick, *Twenty-fifth Amendment*, p. 205. Experience has shown that Congress almost invariably thinks politically—and not necessarily on the basis of right and wrong. There is enough potential for political gerrymandering in the text of the Amendment to make it mandatory that establishing the data should not be subject to such vagaries.

11. Feerick, *Twenty-fifth Amendment*, p. 238.

12. Other scholars apparently share this concern. During the fall of 1985 the Miller Center of Public Affairs at the University of Virginia sponsored a series of forums and public lectures dealing with problems of presidential disability not adequately provided for by the Twenty-fifth amendment. *Miller Center Report*, Fall 1985, 2 : 1.

13. We are not indulging in idle speculation here nor are we necessarily impugning the motives of either Grayson or McIntire with charges of self-aggrandisement. Human nature might well compel similar individuals of like capacity to behave precisely as they did. This cannot be ignored. Their guilt can be further assuaged by Hugh L'Etang's empathetic observation: "In treating the elect the doctor may be unable to avoid an element of self interest. . . . If his patient remains in power he basks in reflected glory; if his patient resigns he may return to the shadows with his political master." *Pathology*, p. 214. We should not fail to note, however, that his professional reputation would still have been immeasurably enhanced by the association regardless of the outcome.

14. L'Etang, *Pathology*, p. 2.

15. Ibid., p. 3.

16. Ibid., p. 9. To paraphrase Arno Karlen: Nearly every medical biohistorian has at one time or another posited his own theory concerning the maladies of history's tyrants. Each reaches for his part of the medical dinosaur. If our subject had been the extinction of the mighty brontosaurus with its walnut-size brain, would I, as a neurosurgeon, have been guilty of imparting too much significance to the influence of neurologic disease in its demise? Perhaps. Yet we are speaking now of mortal giants of a very different age than prehistoric times, and here the evidence is far more substantial. The ultimate question rests with the extent of the influence of neurologic disease; see Karlen, *Napoleon's Glands*, p. 46.

17. Rossiter, *American Presidency*, p. 204–5.

18. L'Etang, *Pathology*, p. 53.

19. William McKinley lingered in coma for eight days following an attack by an assassin. The cases of Wilson and Roosevelt have been detailed.

20. The American Medical Association publishes a manual that physicians refer to in defining "disability of the whole man" on a percentage basis.

21. Rossiter, *American Presidency*, p. 208.

22. Ibid., p. 209.

23. Indeed, his choice of appropriate consultants might well be anticipated to be politically motivated in itself.

24. Rossiter, *American Presidency*, p. 211. With the passage of the Twenty-fifth Amendment, Congress has apparently accepted Rossiter's view that the determination be a political one if the President alone is unable to define his own disability.

25. Ibid., p. 213.

26. Ibid., p. 212.

27. Rossiter, *American Presidency*, p. 205.

28. L'Etang, *Pathology*, p. 211.

29. L'Etang strikes at the heart of the matter: "Little or no attention has been given to the attitude and personality of the few select physicians who are called upon to treat the elect. . . . Their judgment or advice may be swayed . . . by factors that bear no relation to strictly professional or ethical questions; and as a consequence, they may exert more political influence than they realize or desire." L'Etang, *Pathology*, p. 213–14.

30. A current member of the House of Lords, Lord Crowther-Hunt, aptly described the potential dilemma for Great Britain: "There is no way to 'pick off' a Prime Minister by himself. If he doesn't resign the only recourse is a call for a vote of no confidence— which would be suicidal for the whole party. One would therefore have to rely on extreme personal pressure to get the job done." Personal communication with the author, August 4, 1985.

31. Neustadt, *Presidential Power*, p. 193.

32. Ibid., p. 193.

33. Wilson, *Constitutional Government in the United States*, pp. 79–80; quoted in Neustadt, *Presidential Power*, p. 195.

34. Neustadt, *Presidential Power*, p. 195.

35. Ibid., p. 200.

36. Ibid., p. 94.

37. Ibid., p. 182.

38. Ibid., p. 182.

39. Ibid., p. 184.

40. Ibid., p. 95.

# REFERENCES

MEDICAL

L'Etang, Hugh. *The Pathology of Leadership.* New York: Hawthorn Books, 1970.
Raskin, N. H., and R. A. Fishman. "Neurologic Disorders in Renal Failure." *New England Journal of Medicine* 294 (1976): 143–48, 204–10. January.

PRIMARY

*Congressional Record.* 1965. Washington, D.C.
*United States Code.* 1970.

SECONDARY

Chalat, Ned I. "Sir Morell Mackenzie Revisited." *Laryngoscope* 94 (1984): 1307–10.
Feerick, John D. *The Twenty-fifth Amendment: Its Complete History and Earliest Applications.* New York: Fordham University Press, 1976.
*Miller Center Report.* Newsletter of The White Burkett Miller Center of Public Affairs. Vol. 2:1–6. Fall 1985.
Neustadt, Richard E. *Presidential Power.* 4th ed. New York: John Wiley and Sons, 1964.
Rossiter, Clinton. *The American Presidency.* New York: Harcourt, Brace, and World, 1964.
Wilson, Woodrow. *Constitutional Government in the United States.* New York: Columbia University Press, 1908.

# APPENDIX 1

# Comments on the Medical Historiography of Woodrow Wilson

Explanations of Woodrow Wilson's health have been plagued by inconsistency. For example, Gene Smith used an imprecise definition of the terms "stroke" and "thrombosis" in his examination of Wilson's last years. Smith contended that a "thrombosis is not the same thing as a stroke, in which the blood vessel ruptures, but the symptoms are similar."[1] To be more precise, the word "stroke" suggests a nonspecific reference to alterations in an individual's cerebrovascular system, manifested by varying degrees of changing mentation, with or without deficits in sensation or motor skills. As such, it may imply either an occlusion of a blood vessel supplying the brain or the rupture of it, with resultant hemorrhage. Such lack of medical sophistication lends little credibility to Smith's subsequent statement that "in April, 1919, in Paris, the President of the United States suffered, from all the available evidence, . . . a thrombosis in his brain."[2] Not only was Smith in error with regard to his understanding of the concept of stroke, but the statement that Wilson had suffered a thrombosis in April 1919 during the Paris Peace Conference is likewise without merit.

This incorrect assumption was also suggested in 1970 by Dr. Edwin

Weinstein, who postulated the diagnosis in an article published in the *Journal of American History*.[3] A decade later Weinstein altered his original conclusions when he published a more detailed study of Wilson's medical condition.[4] This physician was among the first to suggest that a series of strokes on the basis of cerebral arteriosclerosis afflicted Wilson over a period of many years prior to his assuming the presidency. In Weinstein's opinion, Wilson's medical history can be divided into three interdependent states. From 1896 through 1907 Wilson suffered at least four strokes causing injury to the left side of the brain and the left eye, followed in September 1919 by permanent right hemisphere damage on the basis of a well-documented cerebrovascular accident (stroke) in Pueblo, Colorado. Thereafter Wilson experienced changes in symbolic organization, which often occur with right-sided brain injury, leading in his case to ineffective and occasionally irrational political behavior.[5] Weinstein is to be credited with drawing proper attention to the significant role of neurologic illness in the conduct of Wilson's presidency. Yet a few shortcomings in his thesis are apparent and need to be addressed. Certainly the underlying cause of the cerebrovascular accidents has been open to question. Some have wondered if they occurred at all.

The four principal events in Wilson's early medical history (the strokes that Weinstein alleges to have occurred in 1896, 1904, 1906, and 1907) have generated a great deal of controversy. Essentially, two contrasting views have been proposed in the literature:

1. Edwin Weinstein and Arthur Link subscribe to the belief that in 1896 Wilson suffered pain and weakness in his right arm on the basis of a stroke from an occluded vessel in the left half of the brain arising from the carotid artery in the neck. They contend that another stroke from the same carotid artery occurred in 1906, causing permanent visual loss in the left eye, and that in both 1904 and 1907 Wilson had a recurrence of the first condition, which again affected his right arm. The latter three strokes in particular are said to account for some changes in Wilson's behavior during his term as president of Princeton University (1902–1910), and later similar events supposedly affected his conduct as President of the United States.[6]

2. Michael Marmor believes there are inconsistencies in the above thesis and proposes that the episode of 1896 may have been nothing more than peripheral nerve entrapment, or perhaps a case of "writer's cramp," while the partial blindness Wilson suffered in 1906 was due to a retinal hemorrhage. Neither event, he claims, nor those of 1904 and 1907 that were merely recurrences of the first, were related at all to carotid, or large-vessel, disease. Alexander and Juliette George strongly support his contention,[7] as do physicians such as Robert Monroe and Jerrold Post. Monroe, in fact, thought a pinched nerve in the neck due

to cervical disc disease may have caused Wilson's difficulties with his right arm.[8]

The battlelines have been drawn and numerous skirmishes have been fought between the two opposing camps. Yet there is one area in which the two apparently diametric views coincide. They agree that hypertension was documented as early as 1906. Link, Weinstein, et al. believe it to be "a very significant fact that [the Georges and Marmor] and we agree on the crucial fact that there is conclusive evidence that Wilson suffered from hypertension and advancing arteriosclerosis."[9] The reference to hypertension is more significant than either group of investigators recognizes. For here is the very underlying disease necessary to account for the presence of small-vessel lacunar infarctions that I believe *did* occur and *did* impact deleteriously on Wilson's later political conduct (a partial defense of the Link-Weinstein thesis). Hypertension was also the probable cause of the retinal hemorrhage in 1906, as Marmor and others suggest. Within this context, the present review addresses the need to suggest certain critical revisions in the Link-Weinstein argument, but not to dismiss it altogether, as others have done.

The first shortcoming in Weinstein's thesis relating to the April 1919 allegation of a stroke in Paris has been previously referred to and later corrected by that investigator. This demonstrates the limitations of applying ill-fitting medical facts to a preconceived synthesis. Nor is it now by any means certain that Wilson in fact suffered a branch left middle cerebral artery occlusion in 1896. Weinstein notes that in this episode Wilson experienced "weakness and loss of dexterity of his right hand, a numbness in the tips of several fingers, and some pain in the right arm . . . the symptoms and manner of onset indicating . . . an occlusion of a central branch of the left middle cerebral artery."[10] But Weinstein may have ignored other clinical possibilities. First, pain in the extremity is an extremely rare manifestation of a middle cerebral artery thrombosis, and might suggest alternative possibilities that are as plausible as disc disease in the neck with nerve root entrapment leading to the right arm pain and weakness. Indeed, the fact that Wilson later suffered a "painful neuritis" in his shoulder speaks to this possibility, as this is a very frequent clinical presentation of a cervical disc syndrome.[11] Other possibilities, such as entrapment of the median nerve in the wrist, or even writer's cramp, have also been suggested.[12]

Second, compromise of the hand *without* facial weakness on the same side is somewhat atypical for even branch middle cerebral artery occlusion, as the cortical centers for control of face and hand are juxtaposed to one another and are usually affected in concert. The absence of lip and tongue involvement resulting in thick speech (dysarthria) likewise militates against this for similar reasons. By way of example, with

Wilson's later undisputed cerebral thrombosis in September 1919, dysarthria and face, arm, and leg weakness were observed.

Third, this condition affecting the right arm was to plague Wilson for years, even though permanency of deficits other than those which occur with overt *major* branch-vessel occlusion is unusual, due to the abundance of collateral circulation supplying the same areas of the cerebral cortex. If one postulates either internal carotid embolism or branch middle cerebral artery occlusion as having occurred in 1896, then the above caveats involving the face and tongue (not to mention the absence of any speech deficit, termed dysphasia)[13] argue against the certainty of either having been the etiology of the postulated stroke in this case.

One further clinical possibility does exist, however, which not only fits the symptomatology described in 1896 and 1907, but also might more readily account for Wilson's later medical history—while still falling within the framework of the Link-Weinstein thesis of intellectual and personality deterioration in Wilson's case during later years on the basis of cerebrovascular disease. Weinstein himself alluded to, but apparently dismissed, the possibility of what he termed "little strokes" to account for Wilson's recurring cerebrovascular insufficiency, such as described by Dr. Walter Alvarez in 1946.[14] Other protagonists in the debate on both sides of the question have also ignored this very significant and plausible consideration. Link, Weinstein, et al., paint themselves somewhat into a corner after correctly dismissing the considerations of cervical disc disease, peripheral nerve entrapment, and writer's cramp, by unequivocally stating: "We are reduced to the *only* [italics mine] cause which could have produced Wilson's condition in 1896–1897—as Weinstein puts it, 'an occlusion of a central branch of the left middle cerebral artery.'"[15]

Unfortunately, their list of differential diagnoses is incomplete—in spite of unequivocal evidence of hypertension acknowledged as early as 1906.[16] This is the very disease that gives rise to these "little strokes" known as lacunar infarcts. That Wilson's hypertension may have been under far poorer control than was recognized at the time is supported by the fact that he suffered a retinal hemorrhage in that year, which was related to that condition and not to large-vessel carotid disease (see page 6).

Michael Marmor also ignored the possibility of repeated lacunar infarcts. His argument for doing so lacks validity, given present-day medical knowledge. He states:

> Could Wilson have had "little strokes" accumulating over the years? One would be hard pressed to argue firmly one way or the other, but current monographs on stroke avoid discussion of such "little strokes," and emphasize that a correlation between lacunar lesions and specific behavioral changes is problematic.[17]

Actually, many current monographs detail in a precise fashion the clinical syndromes associated with specific types of lacunar infarcts.[18] Indeed, perhaps the most esteemed neurologist dealing with stroke and cerebrovascular disease, Dr. C. Miller Fisher, asserts that these clinical syndromes of lacunar infarction are so recognizable as to preclude any further evaluation, including angiography, for their cause other than to document the presence of hypertension.[19] The evidence is simply too compelling, and the presence of the very predisposing factor for their occurrence is too well accepted, to ignore the consideration of lacunar infarctions as contributing to the President's behavior years later. As such, Marmor's conclusion dismissing the possibility of strokes having occurred prior to Wilson's assuming office in 1913 must be rejected.[20] On the contrary, the plausibility of strokes can be defended, but not of the sort Weinstein has postulated and Link has defended.

The syndromes associated with lacunar infarcts are recognized today as a very common clinical presentation of stroke in the older individual with high blood pressure.[21] These "little strokes" are synonymous with the modern-day term "lacunes," which occur deep within the brain in hypertensive individuals on the basis of small-vessel arteriosclerosis. These strokes are different from large-vessel atherosclerosis and embolism, in which the more superficial cortex supplied by the middle cerebral artery is usually involved. Although routine blood pressure measurements were not available in 1896, medical evidence as early as 1906 confirmed the existence of hypertension in Wilson's medical history.

Occurring repeatedly over time, these tiny infarcts often lead to a typical syndrome, termed the "lacunar state," in which cognitive and emotional aberrations become manifest in concert with other motor system symptoms. This is not a steadily progressive course, but rather a series of sudden episodes of focal neurologic disturbances that clear with variable residua. These later lead to disturbances in judgment, orientation, memory, and cognitive function. This process, properly termed a "subcortical dementia," is usually superimposed on bilateral motor signs, such as muscle rigidity and spasticity.[22]

The evidence suggests that prior to his documented large-vessel cerebrovascular accident in September 1919 in Pueblo, Colorado, on the basis of a probable right internal carotid artery thrombosis, Woodrow Wilson's altered mental and physical state may have been due more to lacunar insults related to markedly elevated systemic blood pressure than to overt atherosclerotic thrombosis or embolism. Such an hypothesis fits more comfortably into the Weinstein thesis than does that author's own attribution of significance to large-vessel disease allegedly occurring very early in Wilson's medical history.

Neurologists and neurosurgeons alike will point to some deficiencies in the record in support of the "lacunar" over the "large-vessel" hypothesis. Certainly the characteristic later stage of the lacunar state from the standpoint of motor-system involvement did not evolve full-blown in Wilson's case—that of "pseudobulbar palsy"[23]—even though some motor-system compromise was obviously manifest. Nor did the specific symptomatology of 1896, for example, fit precisely into any one of the four distinct syndromes of lacunar strokes Dr. Fisher has described.[24] In fact, only one of the four syndromes described by Fisher involves single extremity compromise—the so-called and rather rare "dysarthria-clumsy hand syndrome."[25] The absence of noticeable dysarthria (slurring of speech) in Wilson's case weighs against this specific syndrome. Invoking the more commonly occurring syndrome of "pure motor hemiplegia"[26] would likewise be inappropriate on the basis of an absence of face or leg involvement, and pain does not characteristically occur in this entity.

Nonetheless, variations of these syndromes do occur, and the neuroanatomist is well aware of the juxtaposition of thalamus and internal capsule deep within the brain in the region of the basal ganglia,[27] a small lesion of which might involve the internal capsule (accounting for the motor weakness) in conjunction with thalamic injury (accounting for the discomfort Wilson experienced). Damage to the thalamus is well known to cause pain, as this structure is a sensory relay station to higher cortical centers in the brain. Further militating against branch middle cerebral artery occlusion on the basis of large-vessel disease is the fact that *unilateral* cortical infarcts (strokes) alone as a rule do not result in cognitive alterations suggestive of early dementia or personality changes, and Weinstein is emphatic that behavioral aberrations characterized Wilson's personality following the 1896 episode and its aftermath at Princeton in the following decade.[28]

Weinstein also alluded to the remarkable ambidexterity Wilson demonstrated after the 1896 incident in learning almost immediately to write with his unaffected left hand. According to the acknowledged authority today on language disorders, Dr. Norman Geschwind, the learning of such a left-handed skill so rapidly is unusual, in that lesions of the motor cortex of the dominant left hemisphere generally interfere with learned movements of the ipsilateral *left* arm as well for a period of time.[29] Indeed, movements of the left extremities are usually clumsy initially, in concert with the paralyzed contralateral right extremity. Weinstein asserts that Wilson's accomplishment may have been due to an uncommon "bilateral cerebral representation of language and graphological skills" known as "developmental dyslexia."[30] It might be postulated, on the other hand, that the 1896 paralysis was on the basis of a lacunar (and not a cortical) infarction, in which case the synergistic effect on coordination of the opposite extremity affected would not be observed. Nor would language skills be affected, as the speech center is not located in the basal ganglia.

The available evidence also suggests that Weinstein's interpretation of ophthalmic artery occlusion (the blood vessel supplying the eye) as the cause of Wilson's sudden onset of blindness in the left eye on May 28, 1906 (which Weinstein again used to substantiate his thesis of long-standing left internal carotid artery disease)[31] may not be correct. Certainly Marmor and others have argued as much.[32] The testimony of the ophthalmologist Dr. George de Schweinitz, who examined Wilson's retina on this occasion, undermines the notion of blood vessel *occlusion*. Schweinitz suggested retinal hemorrhages, "caused by a bursting blood vessel in the eye."[33] If they occur in the region of the macula (the visual focal point of the retina), such lesions are known to affect vision profoundly. Schweinitz diagnosed the malady as a *ruptured* vessel in the retina, but incorrectly ascribed this to a probable embolus from the internal carotid artery traveling to the ophthalmic artery.[34] More to the point, retinal hemorrhages are usually found accompanying high blood pressure, and are *rarely* seen in occlusion of either the carotid artery or its tributaries to the eye, the ophthalmic or retinal arteries. As Drs. John Gilroy and Sterling Meyer have observed: "Thrombosis or embolism with occlusion of the ophthalmic artery or the central retinal artery produces a pale retina, with thin, white threadlike vessels that do not contain blood."[35] This does not correlate at all with what Dr. de Schweinitz described.

A second ophthalmologist, Dr. Edward D. Gifford, later documented the presence of hypertensive retinal hemorrhages and exudates (scars on the retina) in Wilson's medical record, accompanied by spasm of the retinal vessels.[36] This only adds to the argument that hypertension, rather than vessel occlusion, was the cause of the eye illness in 1906. These observations by Gifford, diagnosed while Wilson was President, would have been indicative of progressive impairment had they been known at the time, as they were, in Weinstein's words, "harbingers of cardiac, renal, and diffuse cerebrovascular disease,"[37] all known to be accelerated by the effects of hypertension.[38]

Reference has already been made to the initially incorrect assumption that Wilson suffered significant brain injury from a stroke on April 3, 1919, in Paris. Originally Weinstein asserted that Wilson sustained an injury to his right hemisphere in April 1919, enough to warrant the assumption that he now had bilateral cerebral damage in concert with the 1896 episode presumably involving the left hemisphere. This second insult would be enough to affect Wilson's emotional and social behavior more than would have been the case with strictly unilateral lesions. Weinstein later corrected this early conclusion to implicate influenza, and possibly encephalitis lethargica, into a thesis of generalized brain dysfunction on a transient basis, the effect of which would be enhanced by the presence of cerebrovascular disease.[39] I support this view.

If all of this may seem to be an academic (and perplexing) exercise in splitting hairs, it is nevertheless necessary if the reader is to gain proper insight into the investigation regarding Wilson's conduct in office. That he suffered from documented hypertension, and that subsequent episodes in his medical history, both ophthalmologic and neurologic, suggested a hypertensive etiology for these, does not prove the lacunar state argument, but it at least raises the possibility of other causes for Wilson's decline than the large-vessel atherosclerotic thesis proposed by Weinstein. The various technical medical caveats notwithstanding, the record largely supports Weinstein's overall thesis that Wilson's cognitive and emotional functions were significantly compromised—but only during the crucial years of the latter half of his administration.

## NOTES

1. Smith, *When the Cheering Stopped*, p. 100. Nor does this writer strengthen the credibility of his medical knowledge in attempting to relate various unrelated symptoms Wilson was known to have experienced in an attempt to explain the effects of a "thrombosis" to the unfamiliar reader. Smith asserted: "Some of the symptoms of a thrombosis in the human brain are violent upsets—which are at first often diagnosed as resulting from indigestion or influenza and hitherto unexperienced insomnia, twitching of the face, . . . headaches, great weakness, and paralysis of one side of the body." Smith, *When the Cheering Stopped*, p. 100. Only the last statement regarding paralysis can be applied correctly to cerebral thrombosis in general, and Woodrow Wilson in particular. Blockage of a blood vessel supplying the brain is rarely confused with indigestion or influenza. Inability to sleep is not characteristic of the stroke patient; if anything, lethargy is more often apparent. Facial twitching is rarely seen in an acute thrombosis, and it certainly had nothing to do with Wilson's affliction of hemifacial spasm. Nor are headaches a common accompaniment of stroke unless an intracranial hemorrhage has occurred, which, again, did not apply to Wilson. Such lack of precision compromises any contribution by Smith to a medical understanding of Wilson's health.

2. Ibid., p. 100.

3. Weinstein, "Woodrow Wilson's Neurological Illness."

4. Weinstein, *Woodrow Wilson: A Medical and Psychological Biography*. Some aspects of this work were enlargements of a theme originally proposed in the medical literature by Dr. Walter J. Friedlander; see "Woodrow Wilson's Cerebral Arteriosclerosis" and "About Three Old Men," both published in the medical journal *Stroke*.

5. Weinstein, "Wilson's Neurological Illness," p. 325.

6. Weinstein, *Woodrow Wilson*; Link, Weinstein, et al. "Communication to Editor." pp. 945–55.

7. Marmor, "Wilson, Strokes, and Zebras"; George, Marmor, and George, "Issues in Wilson Scholarship."

8. Monroe, "Comments on 'Woodrow Wilson's Neurological Illness' by Dr. E. A. Weinstein;" Post, "Woodrow Wilson Re-examined: The Mind-Body Controversy Redux and Other Disputations." 4:229.

9. Link, Weinstein, et al., "Communication to Editor," p. 953.

10. Weinstein, *Woodrow Wilson*, p. 141. Link later clarified for the record that Wilson experienced "soreness," not pain, in his arm. "Communication to Editor," p. 946.

11. Robert T. Monroe asserts that "today, this affair would likely be treated as pinched nerves in the neck (cervical arthritis) with stretching and a collar." Monroe, "Comments on 'Woodrow Wilson's Neurological Illness,'" p. 1. This claim is admittedly difficult to refute altogether. For one thing, there is the abrupt onset that Link and Weinstein cite as evidence for a stroke: "The onset of paralysis was sudden. One day Wilson could use his right hand; the next day he could not." Link, Weinstein, et al., "Communication to Editor," p. 948. But this is not agreed to by all. Marmor counters by stating that "there is no documentation that the symptoms had a sudden onset." As early as 1884 Wilson had made frequent reference to pain in his hand while attempting to write; his own physician had referred to the condition as a "writer's cramp or neuritis." Marmor, "Wilson, Strokes, and Zebras," p. 529. Link's rejoinder is not entirely convincing; he asserts that a pinched nerve in the neck almost invariably causes excruciating pain, "and it would have been 'remarkable' indeed that such a serious situation in the neck would have righted itself in eight months." Link, Weinstein, et al., "Communication to Editor," p. 948. Yet pain does not have to be excruciating, nor does it have to occur at all; see Charles A. Fager, "Cervical Disc and Spondylotic Lesions," p. 228, for a description of the "painless segmental syndrome". Also, spontaneous remissions often occur with cervical nerve root impingement, though symptoms usually recur in time.

The argument for a cervical etiology for Wilson's symptoms from 1896 through 1907 is suggestive, then, but by no means unassailable. The most significant evidence arguing against it is the fact that the hand is *rarely* the predominant site of the patient's complaints (aside from numbness in the fingers) in cervical disc disease. Moreover, Wilson experienced both arm and leg compromise in 1906; see Baker, *Life and Letters*, 2:201. "Neuritis" of the leg should not be ascribed to pathology in the neck, but in conjunction with arm involvement on the same side, might suggest a variant of a lacunar infarct, termed a "hemisensory stroke;" see Fisher, "Pure Sensory Stroke," 15:76–80. Then, too, if some would argue that Wilson's frequent headaches may have been caused by muscle tension associated with cervical arthritis, the evidence suggests that the headaches were due more to sustained elevations in blood pressure. The fact that Wilson suffered ten straight days of headache just prior to his documented stroke in September 1919 supports this contention (see pages 46–48 in the text). Finally, even if temporary remissions in cervical nerve root compressions occur, the aging process usually assures a progression of this disease that is not apparent in Wilson's medical history, especially during his second term in office.

12. Median nerve entrapment in the wrist, like disc disease in the neck, deserves consideration in the differential diagnosis. Its symptoms are aggravated by continual usage of the affected hand or by activities requiring forced flexion at the wrist. Writing, therefore, might be considered to promote the condition, as Marmor and others have suggested. Nonetheless, Link, Weinstein, et al. are correct in asserting that the condition is usually progressive without treatment, and atrophy of the thumb muscles is often seen in longstanding cases, neither of which Wilson demonstrated; Link, Weinstein, et al., "Communication to Editor," p. 948. Characteristically, too, patients complain of being awakened at night by painful numbness in the hand. No such complaints were registered in Wilson's descriptions of his malady.

13. The term "dysphasia" implies inability to express or comprehend speech. "Internal carotid embolism" signifies the breaking off of a small clot in this artery, situated more proximally in the neck, that subsequently is propelled to a more distal branch of this vessel supplying the brain—in this case, the middle cerebral artery.

14. Alvarez, "Cerebral Arteriosclerosis."

15. Link, Weinstein, et al., "Communication to Editor," p. 948. Emphasis added.

16. Wilson went to the Royal Infirmary in Edinburgh on August 31, 1906, where one of the few instruments in the world capable of measuring blood pressure documented the presence of hypertension in his case. It was significant enough that medication to treat the condition was prescribed. See Link, Weinstein, et al., "Communication to Editor," p. 950.

17. Marmor, "Wilson, Strokes, and Zebras," p. 532. Most neurologists do not ascribe to Marmor's opinion. Dr. Walter Freidlander, for example, believes that "repetitive 'small strokes'" exaggerated Wilson's underlying premorbid personality; see "Three Old Men," *Stroke*, 3:467.

18. See note 24 for a summary of these.

19. Fisher, "Pure Sensory Stroke Involving Face, Arm and Leg," p. 77.

20. Marmor, "Wilson, Strokes, and Zebras," p. 533.

21. Fisher, "Lacunes: Small, Deep Cerebral Infarcts." See note 24.

22. Ibid. These physical findings are also suggested in Woodrow Wilson's medical history. At a much later date, on Wilson's return from Paris aboard ship prior to his major stroke in 1919, he was observed to stumble repeatedly over an iron ring on the deck. L'Etang, *Pathology*, p. 50. Increasing spasticity with rigidity is often manifested by a gait disorder, the subtle nature of which at this time may have been magnified by walking on a surface as unsteady as the deck of a ship at sea.

23. The term "pseudobulbar palsy" denotes a disorder manifested by slurred speech, difficulty in swallowing, and emotional lability, usually seen in the end stages of the lacunar state. (Significantly enough, these symptoms *did* appear after Wilson's stroke in September 1919.) Cognitive changes, however, are usually detected before the appearance of these other symptoms.

24. These are, in decreasing order of the frequency of their occurrence in clinical practice: (1) pure motor hemiplegia, (2) hemisensory stroke, (3) dysarthria-clumsy hand syndrome, and (4) ataxia-crossed paresis. The reader is referred to a brief synopsis of the four in Merritt, *Textbook of Neurology*, p. 196.

25. Fisher, "Lacunar Stroke." In this entity, slurred speech and incoordination of one arm are observed.

26. Fisher and Curry, "Pure Motor Hemiplegia of Vascular Origin." Face, arm, and leg paralysis on one side of the body occurs without loss of sensation.

27. Deep within the brain, neural tracts and aggregates of cells connecting sensory pathways (the thalamus) and motor pathways (the internal capsule) that run between the cortex of the brain and the spinal cord converge in close proximity to one another. This is termed the "basal ganglionic region."

28. Weinstein, "Wilson's Neurological Illness," pp. 336, 348–49.

29. Geschwind, "The Apraxias: Neural Mechanisms of Disorders of Learned Movement"; cited in Weinstein, *Woodrow Wilson*, p. 142.

30. Weinstein, *Woodrow Wilson*, p. 142.

31. Ibid., p. 165. Dr. Freidlander also invokes this implausible diagnosis. "Three Old Men," 3:468.

32. According to Marmor, the importance of this distinction between a clot (embolus) and a hemorrhage is that the sudden blindness that characterizes unilateral carotid obstructive disease is caused by arterial occlusion, not by intraocular hemorrhage. "Evidence of intraocular hemorrhage essentially rules out the diagnosis of acute stroke." Marmor, "Wilson, Strokes, and Zebras," p. 531. I agree.

33. Weinstein, "Wilson's Neurological Illness," p. 334. Wilson wrote to his wife, "I have just had the misfortune to suffer a hemorrhage of one of the blood vessels of my left eye." Wilson, *Papers*, 16:413.

34. Weinstein, *Woodrow Wilson*, p. 165; Wilson, *Papers*, 16:413.

35. Gilroy and Meyer, *Medical Neurology*, p. 12. Marmor correctly asserts that "spontaneous retinal hemorrhage . . . produces a strikingly hemorrhagic fundus picture that cannot be mistaken for arterial occlusion." Marmor, "Wilson, Strokes, and Zebras," p. 531.

36. Weinstein, *Woodrow Wilson*, pp. 296–97. Dr. Gifford saw Dr. de Schweinitz' records of Wilson's eye examinations dating back to 1906. It was recorded that Wilson "suffered from *very high blood pressure* [italics mine] and his fundi showed hypertensive vascular changes with advanced angiosclerosis." Unfortunately, Dr. Gifford did not specify the year in which these profound changes first appeared. Marmor, "Eyes of Woodrow Wilson," p. 463.

37. Weinstein, *Woodrow Wilson*, p. 297. Wilson suffered from all three during his second term.

38. Although Marmor correctly identified hypertension as the cause of the retinal hemorrhage in 1906, he failed, as all others have done, to emphasize its significance. He acknowledged only that "ample evidence indicates that Wilson had hypertension . . . in 1906. [It] may indeed have taken a toll from Wilson over the years, and may be [a] factor to consider in evaluating his overall mental and physical abilities." Marmor, "Wilson, Strokes, and Zebras," pp. 531–32. More to the point, it *is* a factor to consider, which no one has done prior to this review. Marmor then added that "this is hardly equivalent to implying that discrete strokes affected Wilson's behavior and personality at specific times in his career." Marmor, "Wilson, Strokes, and Zebras," p. 531. He argued that one cannot document cause and effect relationships of behavioral changes in Wilson's case immediately after a proposed stroke had occurred. This is correct, but Marmor ignores the cumulative effect of such ischemic insults, which may well account for Wilson's perplexing behavior and character transformation during his second term. Such delayed effects of hypertension and lacunar infarcts are precisely what are to be expected in this disease state.

39. Weinstein, *Woodrow Wilson*, p. 338. Michael Marmor does not subscribe to the opinion that Wilson suffered from viral encephalitis in April 1919, as Weinstein asserts and the present review suggests. "Weinstein's diagnosis of viral encephalopathy is highly speculative," Marmor states, "and it is *inconsequential otherwise* [italics mine]. [Wilson's symptoms] are so common with viral disease that although calling them a resulting encephalopathy may be correct pathophysiologically, it carries no implication of residual impairment." Marmor, "Wilson, Strokes, and Zebras," p. 532. Marmor is perhaps unaware that most cases of viral encephalitis do not result in the "severe encephalopathy" he appears to require in order to accept the hypothesis. Even in systemic infections not directly involving the brain, disorders of perception may be frequent and attention spans are limited. Nor is he at all correct in stating that the disease "carries no implication of residual cerebral impairment" (p. 532).

## REFERENCES

MEDICAL

Alvarez, Walter. "Cerebral Arteriosclerosis with Small Commonly Unrecognized Apoplexies." *Geriatrics.* 1 (1946): 189–216.
Fager, Charles A. "Neurologic Syndromes of Cervical Disc and Spondylotic Lesions." In *Clinical Neurosurgery.* 25:218–44. Baltimore: Williams and Wilkins Co., 1978.
Fisher, C. Miller. "Lacunes: Small, Deep Cerebral Infarcts." *Neurology* 15 (1965): 774–84.

————. "Pure Sensory Stroke Involving Face, Arm, and Leg." *Neurology* 15 (1965): 76–80.

————. "A Lacunar Stroke: The Dysarthria-Clumsy Hand Syndrome." *Neurology* 17 (1967): 614–17.

Fisher, C. Miller, and H. B. Curry. "Pure Motor Hemiplegia of Vascular Origin." *Archives of Neurology* 13 (1965): 30–44.

Geschwind, Norman. "The Apraxias: Neural Mechanisms of Disorders of Learned Movement." *American Scientist* 63 (1975): 180–95.

Gilroy, John, and Sterling Meyer. *Medical Neurology.* London: Macmillan Co., 1969.

L'Etang, Hugh. *The Pathology of Leadership.* New York: Hawthorn Books, 1970.

Marmor, Michael. "Wilson, Strokes, and Zebras." *New England Journal of Medicine* 307 (1982): 528–35.

————. "The Eyes of Woodrow Wilson." *Ophthalmology* 92 (1985): 454–65.

Merritt, Houston. *Textbook of Neurology.* 6th ed. Philadelphia: Lea and Febiger, 1979.

Monroe, Robert T. "Comments on 'Woodrow Wilson's Neurological Illness' by Dr. E. A. Weinstein." 1971. Arthur Walworth Papers. Yale University Library, New Haven, Connecticut.

Post, Jerrold M. "Woodrow Wilson Re-examined: The Mind-Body Controversy Redux and Other Disputations." *Political Psychology* 4 (1983): 289–306.

Sandok, Burton A. "Organic Mental Disorders Associated with Circulatory Disturbances." In *Comprehensive Textbook of Psychiatry.* 3d ed., edited by Harold I. Kaplan, 2:1392–405. Baltimore and London: Williams and Wilkins, 1980.

Weinstein, Edwin A. "Woodrow Wilson's Neurological Illness." *Journal of American History* 57 (1970): 324–51.

————. *Woodrow Wilson: A Medical and Psychological Biography.* Princeton, N.J.: Princeton University Press, 1981.

PRIMARY

Wilson, Woodrow. *The Papers of Woodrow Wilson.* 49 vols. to date. Edited by Arthur Link. Princeton, N.J.: Princeton University Press, 1966–.

SECONDARY

George, Juliette L., Michael F. Marmor, and Alexander L. George. "Issues in Wilson Scholarship. References to Early 'Strokes' in the *Papers of Woodrow Wilson.*" *Journal of American History* 70 (1984): 845–53.

Link, Arthur, E. A. Weinstein, et al. "Communication to the Editor." *Journal of American History.* 70 (1984): 945–55.

Smith, Gene. *When the Cheering Stopped: The Last Years of Woodrow Wilson.* New York: Time Incorporated, 1964.

# Comments on the Medical Historiography of Adolf Hitler

An examination of the historiography of Adolf Hitler's health demonstrates some inadequacies of interpretation. Alan Bullock's appraisal typifies the problem: "For my part, the more I learn of Adolf Hitler, the harder I find it to explain and accept what followed. Somehow the causes are inadequate to account for the size of the effects."[1] His summary of the Fuehrer's health in his biography of Hitler included the following observations:

> During the course of 1943 Hitler began to suffer from a trembling of his left arm and left leg. . . . Professor de Crinis believed that these were the symptoms of Parkinson's disease, but he never had the opportunity of examining Hitler, and other specialists believed they had an hysterical origin like the stomach cramps from which he had suffered for some time. It has also been suggested that Hitler's . . . symptoms in the last years of his life may have been those of a man suffering from the tertiary stages of syphilis. . . . Until 1943 he actually suffered very little from ill health.[2]

Frankly, this synopsis contains both tenuous innuendoes and overt errors. First, that Hitler suffered from Parkinson's disease should no longer be doubted.[3] Second, the abdominal symptoms referred to were hardly manifestations of hysteria, but were, rather, typical exacerbations of chronic inflammation of the gallbladder.[4] If Hitler's preoccupation with his stomach pain suggested a hypochondriacal neurosis, this observation still ignores the fact that even hypochondriacs are subject to real disease on occasion. Third, history is replete with assertions by political enemies and historians alike that undesirable behavior is a product of syphilis, that plague of mankind that inflicts itself only upon the morally destitute and insane among us! An examination of Hitler's neurologic abnormalities hardly substantiates this specious suggestion. Finally, the assertion that Hitler suffered very little from ill health prior to 1943 simply does not fit the facts.

Werner Maser, to his credit, was willing to attribute greater significance to ill health in his authoritative treatment of Adolf Hitler.[5] His account was among the first to document the numerous pharmacologic poisons to which the Fuehrer was subjected by Theodor Morell. Recent available data, however, have undermined many of Maser's conclusions regarding other aspects of Hitler's health. For example, Maser discounted the probability of Parkinson's disease for three reasons: first, Morell's examination did not reveal it; second, the tremor waxed and waned; and third, the tremor was initially unilateral.

The first argument is without merit on the basis of Morell's demonstrated limitations as a diagnostician. Morell originally believed the possibility of this diagnosis was excluded by what Maser calls "his analysis of the activity of the central nervous system and the major reflexes."[6] He was the same physician who had erroneously tendered the diagnosis of syphilis and "creeping paralysis," but at the same time made the incongruous observation that Hitler's "cerebrum was normal and the cerebellum and spinal cord were free of disease."[7] Individuals with tertiary syphilis hardly demonstrate a normal neurologic examination! Furthermore, Morell's edited diary substantiates that during the last weeks prior to Hitler's death, he had in fact considered Parkinsonism as a possibility; he even treated Hitler in the end with the medication then being used for that disease.[8]

The second and third reasons cited by Maser as evidence against Parkinsonism should be dismissed on the basis of the author's understandably limited knowledge of this disease. Parkinson's syndrome often, and in fact characteristically, initially presents as a unilateral tremor, and may be the only symptom of the disease for months or even years. Furthermore, the tremor is often accentuated by stress or emotion, which (in conjunction with Hitler's known proclivity to conceal his left-sided infirmity) is enough to account for the alleged "waxing and waning" nature of the tremor.[9] Since Hitler developed the entire symptom-complex of Parkinson's disease by 1943, the cause of his earlier tremor may have become apparent in retrospect.

Then, too, Maser bears some responsibility for perpetrating the belief that Hitler suffered from viral encephalitis at Vinnitsa in the summer of 1942. Maser based this on Morell's description of an illness Hitler suffered then, but Morell's inadequate description of the nature and extent of that sickness does not really suggest that viral encephalitis was the real culprit. The data supplied in his diary are simply not substantial enough to warrant tendering that diagnosis. This is but one example of how certain accepted myths in the medical history of Hitler are perpetuated without sufficient evidence.[11]

Maser nevertheless placed great importance on Hitler's poor health, which is a milestone in the historiography of the Fuehrer in itself, even if some of the illnesses he alluded to were less than significant, as cited by Robert Waite:

> As a result of [a] monumental head cold [in 1942] Hitler and history were transformed: all at once the Fuehrer became "suspicious and distrustful," "began to repeat himself," started to concoct "fantastic, unreal projects"; he now reacted "obstinately to situations that displeased him." This was also the time he gave orders for the massacre of the Jews, and "now too occurred the catastrophe of Stalingrad."[12]

Such a sweeping assertion, quite frankly, boggles even the most creative medical imagination.

To enlarge upon the theme of how errors are made and repeated, examine Hugh Trevor-Roper's contribution to an understanding of the negative role Morell played in Hitler's deteriorating health.[13] There are two shortcomings in Trevor-Roper's work. The first concerns the time frame in which disease is said to have occurred. Trevor-Roper stated that "in 1943, the first symptoms of physical alteration [in Hitler's appearance] became apparent."[14] A review of the medical record substantiates that physical alterations and behavioral changes occurred at a much earlier date, at least as early as 1941.

Second, Trevor-Roper expressed doubt as to whether disease existed at all. How is one to explain his comment that "in his last days, *though he suffered from no organic disease,* [italics mine] Hitler had become a . . . physical wreck"? The author embellished this non sequitur by describing Hitler's "gray complexion, his stooping body, his shaking hands and foot, his hoarse and quavering voice, and the film of exhaustion covering his eyes. His look was staring and dead."[15] Despite Trevor-Roper's assertion that Hitler suffered from no organic disease, this one brief description is enough to draw attention to at least three separate conditions, among them: (1) the effects on complexion of medications and/or episodic jaundice; (2) recurring polyps of the vocal cords, from which Hitler was known to suffer; and (3) several physical features of Parkinson's disease.

Two paramedical works deserve mention as representative of a plethora of efforts directed toward a psychiatric evaluation of Hitler's behavior, foreshadowing the enthusiasm for psychoanalytic history of today. Early in the war, the Office of Strategic Services commissioned Walter Langer to write a psychoanalytic examination of Adolf Hitler.[16] Langer had never spoken to, much less examined, Hitler, and the dubious conclusions he drew from interviewing German emigrés compromise the book's usefulness. If many of Langer's observations were plausible, and perhaps even descriptively correct, the author still ignored the possibility that organic disease may have precipitated the psychiatric symptomatology he described. He postulated: "As far as we know, Hitler is in fairly good health, except for his stomach ailment which is in all probability a psychosomatic disturbance."[17]

Langer's complete dependence on a Freudian psychoanalytical approach weakens his analysis. Freudian psychology has repeatedly been called into question by modern psychiatric thought; indeed, its limitations were addressed by Robert Waite in the afterword he wrote to Langer's book. Waite correctly perceived that organic disease may in fact have played a greater role than Langer knew. According to Waite, "Hitler suffered either from advanced Parkinson's Syndrome, or from localized degenerative brain damage to lower brain centers."[18] The specific disease entity Waite was postulating by the latter imprecise description is unclear, but his observation at least serves to underscore the inadequacies of the Langer account on this point.

Unfortunately, Waite's own account of the Hitler phenomenon, *The Psychopathic God: Adolf Hitler*, itself relies too heavily upon popular psychoanalytic biographical technique to the exclusion of medical evidence. Waite was correct in underscoring the difficulty in diagnosing any specific neurologic disease influencing Hitler's conduct, given the fact that many of the suggested organic diseases show similar symptoms. But such an undertaking, though difficult, is by no means impossible.

Let us examine, for the moment, Waite's arguments against any neurologic illness being implicated in Hitler's behavior. Waite discounted Parkinson's syndrome on the basis of the same inadequate understanding of the disease that plagued Maser. Even if Hitler demonstrated some features of Parkinson's, Waite said that he nonetheless "failed to show others." Citing a textbook published in 1943, Waite accepted the deceiving assertion that the Parkinsonian tremor must be "relentlessly progressive."[19] Modern medical understanding of this disease dispels the notion that the tremor cannot be dampened on occasion, as previously discussed. More important, if that symptom in Hitler's case was intermittent, it nonetheless proved to be progressive. By 1944 all four extremities were involved.

Similarly, Waite's argument suggesting an absence of "pill-rolling movements" lacks validity.[20] Not only was Hitler prone to disguise all his physical infirmities, but such a clinical finding may be recognized only when a clinician has a high enough index of suspicion to look for it. Just because it was not mentioned by Morell does not necessarily signify its absence. Waite, in fact, acknowledged that no comprehensive psychiatric examination record exists in Hitler's case. The same may be said for the absence of a thorough neurologic examination by a trained neurologist. Both Erwin Giesing and Theodor Morell made limited examinations, but the former was an ear, nose, and throat specialist and the latter was a self-proclaimed skin and venereal disease expert.

With regard to the polypharmacy issue, Waite acknowledged that drugs contributed to Hitler's deterioration. Yet he buried the observation in a paragraph concerned with disproving Maser's assertion that a severe head cold could account for the transformation of Hitler's behavior.[21]

Thereafter Waite suggested a diagnosis of *diffuse* atherosclerosis, a condition he inferred from ischemic changes others had described in Hitler's electrocardiograms (EKGs).[22] That Hitler suffered from coronary atherosclerosis is not in dispute. This condition would have limited blood supply to the heart. The available data does not, however, substantiate Waite's inference that Hitler had *generalized* atherosclerosis, which would have limited blood supply to his brain as well. No episodes of transient ischemic attacks, the *sine qua non* for cerebrovascular insufficiency, are found in Hitler's medical record.[23] Waite also accepted that large-vessel, generalized atherosclerosis can cause "tremors, insomnia, slowness of motion and confusion of thought." This is not really medically defensible today without evidence of previous strokes or transient ischemic attacks occurring either in the past or in concert. Waite also cited Wechsler's outdated textbook to assert that "delusions of grandeur, paranoid tendencies, and moral aberrations" result from this same disease process.[24] Today physicians know that these manifestations are exceedingly uncommon, and occur only when that disease has reached its most severe, chronic form.

Waite appropriately dismissed the syphilis argument, both on the grounds that no documentation of Hitler's ever being treated for it exists and that blood tests for the presence of syphilis were negative. Nor are the clinical descriptions of Hitler in relation to syphilis specific enough to raise that consideration in the differential diagnosis.[25] Yet by 1942 Hitler's changed behavior and altered physical appearance were noticeable enough to prompt Heinrich Himmler to investigate the Fuehrer's health. This was the period during which the false assumption was raised by both Felix Kersten and Theodor Morell that he might be suffering from the neurologic consequences of venereal disease.[26] A modern description of the disease entity known as "paretic neurosyphilis" does much to dispel this myth.

> Paretic neurosyphilis is first and foremost a *dementing* illness or organic psychosis [italics mine]. Focal neurologic signs such as transient hemiparesis [weakness or paralysis of one side of the body] are often observed. Physical and mental examination may reveal little except evidence of an organic dementing process [changes of mentation including disorientation to person, place, or time, inability to learn new material, and overt disorders of perception]. Personal habits are likely to deteriorate. Speech is characteristically altered, with difficulty in enunciation. . . . Laboratory diagnosis rests on positive serologic reactions in the blood and spinal fluid, *and are almost always positive.* [italics mine][27]

The absence of a profound dementia and the negative serology for syphilis documented in Morell's diary are evidence enough to discredit the possibility of this disease in Hitler's case.

Historians are prone to exhibit a keen interest in the "two-brain theory"—that the two hemispheres of the brain have separate functions and act independently—and Waite dealt with it as another possibility for explaining Hitler's behavior. The argument runs as follows: If an individual suffers injury or damage to one hemisphere, the opposite hemisphere assumes predominant control over the patient's actions. Simply stated, the left hemisphere governs speech and analytical thinking, whereas the right hemisphere controls emotional and creative activity. Although some recent experiments suggest that there may be a modicum of credibility in this hypothesis, the argument in Hitler's case is not nearly as clear-cut as the papers Waite cited would suggest, both of which, it should be noted, were unpublished.[28] Indeed, as he acknowledged, Hitler did not fit the hypothesis proposed by Martindale et al. These investigators proposed that Hitler's right hemisphere was abnormally active because the left half was defective and underdeveloped. They erroneously cite evidence referrable to the *left* side of Hitler's body, such as a "missing left testicle and a defective left leg."[29] Such right cerebral dominance might then have accounted for his emotional, impulsive behavior.

Since the right side of the brain controls the left side of the body (and vice versa), these investigators implicated the wrong hemisphere! If the theory can be applied at all to Hitler, his early left extremity tremor would suggest abnormalities in the *right* hemisphere—thereby contradicting the theory. More to the point from the neurophysiological perspective, this division of labor by the brain is more apparent than real. The interdependence of the two hemispheres is too dynamic to place much emphasis on the independent functions of each. In the final analysis, the less acknowledgment given this theory the better, insofar as a medically defensible understanding of Hitler is concerned.

Finally, the possibility of psychomotor seizure activity was not included in Robert Waite's list of medical illnesses. This is a critical omission when one considers his conclusion that:

> the student of Hitler's psychological development from infancy must reject the main argument made by the proponents of a neurologic explanation of his behavior—namely, that nerve and brain damage was responsible for sudden and dramatic changes in Hitler's personality during the last years of his life.[30]

It is now recognized that one-fourth to one-third of all psychiatric illness can be accounted for by undiagnosed physical disease. This is precisely the reason why physicians today often take psychoanalysts grounded in Freudian disciplines to task—their inability to acknowledge, on the basis of a skewed diagnostic approach, how organic disease may cause the very psychiatric aberrations of which they speak.

Waite in fact believed that no transformation of Hitler's character occurred, that Hitler's behavior was consistent from beginning to end. With regard to the argument for temporal lobe epilepsy in Hitler's case, its occurrence does not necessarily imply a dramatic change or transformation of character. Typically occurring first in childhood or in the young adult years, the afflicted individual often bears the indelible stamp of its effects on his personality by middle age. This is in fact what occurred in Hitler's case. The thesis, then, that one must view a clear change in behavior when organic neurologic disease becomes manifest, as suggested by Waite, is not at all correct in relation to the effects of psychomotor seizures.

Finally, to complete this historiographical review it must be acknowledged that a few writers still refuse to accept the thesis of physical illness in Hitler's case at all. One eminent German historian, Joachim Fest, has asserted that "medical findings throw little light on the matter. . . . We now [as of 1973] have the files of his medical examinations and these reflect *no condition* [italics mine] that would have justified his worry. We must be content with positing psychogenic causes."[31] This call for a psychoanalytic approach to the problem underscores the limitations of an author whose own brief discussion of the disease alternative reflects unfamiliarity with medical precepts. He cited the works of both

Werner Maser and H. R. Trevor-Roper, but dismissed their arguments: "It would be a mistake to attribute the symptoms of degeneration, the crises and the fitful outbursts on Hitler's part, to structural changes in his personality. . . . However shadowy he looked outwardly . . . he was still the man he had once been."[32]

Fest's dismissal of Parkinson's disease, for example, is superficial: "The principal symptom of both Parkinson's disease and the Parkinson syndrome, namely the shaking arm or leg, can also be caused by many other diseases."[33] Nor does he even address the other salient features of Parkinson's—all of which Hitler demonstrated. Fest's treatment of the drug issue was equally simplistic: "Quite rightly, Hitler attributed his remarkable energy to Morell's efforts, overlooking the extent to which he was consuming his physical reserves. . . . In the euphorias produced by his drugs he seemed to glow like a wraith."[34] The first statement is so imprecise as to be meaningless from the medical perspective. The second is a colorful description, but sadly deficient in addressing the drugs' real significance. In the final analysis, Fest surrenders the field of available data by ignoring it.

Admittedly, it might appear at first glance to be a suicidal literary venture for a writer with far fewer academic credentials than such authoritative historians as Bullock, Maser, Trevor-Roper, Waite, or Fest to take such an unabashedly critical stance towards them. Yet a review of their works, and others, suggests an urgent need to augment the historiography of the man with a properly conceived medical evaluation. This review has suggested certain limitations of Hitler's main biographers as regards the issue of his health, and it is hoped that some clinical expertise in medical neurology may make the counter-arguments acceptable to future historians.

## NOTES

1. Bullock, Foreword to the English edition of Franz Jetzinger, *Hitler's Youth*, p. 10.

2. Bullock, *A Study in Tyranny*, p. 717. Maximilian de Crinis was a professor of psychiatry and neurology at the Charité Hospital in Berlin.

3. The Hestons discount Parkinson's disease on the basis of a few thoughtful arguments, but there are some bothersome aspects of the question that even they acknowledge: "Having eliminated Parkinson's disease, however, we are embarrassed by the fact that the progression of Hitler's tremor from limb to limb is typical of Parkinson's tremor *and no other* [italics mine]." Heston and Heston, *Medical Casebook*, p. 122. They attempt to tie up this loose end with the pervasive argument of amphetamines. Yet this ignores that Hitler had experienced the tremor long before his encounter with this central nervous system stimulant (which does in fact cause tremor in toxic states). They also state that "the period of recovery would seem to exclude Parkinson's disease; once established, the signs of Parkinson's disease persist with little variation." (p. 122) But the

symptoms of the disease might be expected to be ameliorated by effective treatment—which Hitler was inadvertently, if fortuitously, receiving in Dr. Koester's anti-gas pills for his gastrointestinal condition. These pills contained significant amounts of atropine, one of the drugs used today to treat Parkinson's disease (see pp. 183–84). Furthermore, observations by many contemporaries of Hitler suggest that his illness was truly progressive (see pp. 153–54), even though periods of remission (more apparent than real) can occur with this disease.

4. I am in complete accord with what the Hestons have to say regarding this diagnosis. See Heston and Heston, *Medical Casebook*, pp. 105–13; pp. 157–58 in text.

5. Maser, *Hitler: Legend, Myth and Reality.*

6. Ibid., p. 231. Taken from Morell's deposition. The major reflexes are *not* affected in Parkinson's disease.

7. Ibid., p. 23. Taken from Morell's deposition.

8. Irving, *Diaries of Hitler's Doctor*, p. 271. The Hestons incorrectly assert that "not one of the six physicians mentioned that he even suspected Parkinson's disease." *Medical Casebook*, p. 122. Morell's diary entry published in Irving's more recent account dispels that contention.

9. Robert Waite suggested what I believe to be a fatuous motive for Hitler's tendency to clasp his right hand over his left "in front of his crotch" during periods of tension or excitement: "a childhood habit of clutching at defective genitals," as Waite termed it. See Waite, *Psychopathic God*, pp. 177–78. I believe Hitler did this to conceal his tremor from the camera.

10. Maser, *Legend, Myth and Reality*, p. 232.

11. David Irving also accepted Morell's diagnosis. Arno Karlen refers to this as the Law of Repetition, which accounts for much inherited error in historical analysis. "A historian . . . may worshipfully buy what any doctor says on a medical point," Karlen charges. "Instead of rechecking and seeking verifications, he repeats the first "authority," he reads;" see *Napoleon's Glands*, p. 45.

12. Cited in Waite, *The Psychopathic God*, p. 409. This is an excerpt taken from Waite's review of the original German version of Maser's work entitled *Adolf Hitler: Legende-Mythos-Wirklichkeit.* The phrase "eine schwere Kopfgrippe" Waite translates as "a bad head cold." In Maser's English translation, reference is made to Hitler "again [being] afflicted by some form of influenza. . . . In a very short space of time he became quite literally a changed man." *Legend, Myth and Reality*, p. 217.

13. Trevor-Roper, *The Last Days of Hitler.* pp. 120–29.

14. Ibid., p. 124.

15. Ibid., p. 132.

16. Langer, *The Mind of Adolf Hitler.*

17. Ibid., p. 209. This ailment, now believed to be cholecystitis, first afflicted Hitler in 1929; see Irving, *Diaries of Hitler's Doctor*, p. 258.

18. Langer, *Mind of Adolf Hitler*, p. 235.

19. Israel Wechsler, *A Textbook of Neurology* (London, 1943), p. 600; cited in Waite, *The Psychopathic God*, p. 408.

20. The phenomenon of "pill-rolling" is a frequent observation made in the Parkinsonian patient, whose hands demonstrate a fine tremor in which the movements suggest the patient to be rubbing pills between his fingers.

21. Referred to in Waite, *The Psychopathic God*, p. 409. Waite's review of Maser's original German version is found in *Central European History* 2 (1974): 90–94.

22. Waite, *The Psychopathic God*, p. 409. "Ischemic changes" means lack of oxygen secondary to inadequate blood supply occurring on the basis of atherosclerosis (cholesterol deposits partially occluding the lumina of blood vessels).

23. The Hestons make vague reference to "two vascular disorders" from which Hitler may have suffered—an alleged "possible myocardial infarction" in 1943, and "at least one small stroke" in February 1945. They further claim: "But he may well have had several, and indeed, his rapid decline from this time onward suggests widespread vascular disease." Heston and Heston, *Medical Casebook*, p. 141. There is no further reference, either in their account or any others, to specific descriptions of any such events sufficient to substantiate the claims made. Indeed, both poorly documented events are advanced to support the Hestons' arguments regarding yet another result of the perfidious amphetamine problem. They postulate that the intravenous administration of amphetamines caused diffuse blood vessel constriction, which may have had some cause-and-effect relationship with these otherwise poorly described vascular events. True, Hitler's amphetamine abuse was a very real cause of his decline, as was his rapidly developing Parkinson's disease and personality disorder consistent with longstanding temporal lobe epilepsy. Such postulated strokes, however, either on the basis of amphetamine-induced vasoconstriction or unsubstantiated claims of diffuse peripheral vascular disease, probably did not occur at all.

24. Waite, *The Psychopathic God*, p. 409.

25. Ibid., pp. 409–10. Werner Maser agrees; see *Legend, Myth and Reality*, p. 218.

26. Heinrich Himmler's masseur, Felix Kersten, became convinced "beyond a shadow of a doubt" that Hitler was suffering from progressive paralysis associated with neurosyphilis after he examined secret Gestapo files concerning his health. Waite, *The Psychopathic God*, pp. 409–10.

27. Schmidt and Gonyea, "Neurosyphilis," 2:19, pp. 8–9.

28. Waite, *The Psychopathic God*, p. 411. Waite refers to the following studies: David Galin, "Implications for Psychiatry of Left and Right Cerebral Specialization: A Neurophysiological Context for Unconscious Processes"; and Colin Martindale et al., "Hitler: A Neurohistorical Formulation."

29. Waite, *The Psychopathic God*, pp. 411–24.

30. Ibid., p. 412.

31. Fest, *Hitler*, p. 535. Morell's diaries were not available in 1973.

32. Ibid., p. 673.

33. Ibid., p. 807.

34. Ibid., p. 673.

# REFERENCES

**MEDICAL**

Heston, Leonard L., and Renate Heston. *The Medical Casebook of Adolf Hitler: His Illness, Doctors, and Drugs*. Introduction by Albert Speer. New York: Stein and Day, 1979.

Schmidt, Richard, and Edward Gonyea. "Neurosyphilis." *Clinical Neurology*. 7th ed., edited by A. B. Baker and L. H. Baker. 2:19, pp. 1–20. New York: Harper and Row, 1976.

Wechsler, Israel. *A Textbook of Neurology*. London, 1943.

**SECONDARY**

Bullock, Alan. *Hitler: A Study in Tyranny*. New York: Harper and Row, 1962.

Fest, Joachim D. *Hitler*. Translated by Richard and Clara Winston. New York: Harcourt Brace Jovanovich, 1973.

Irving, David. *The Secret Diaries of Hitler's Doctor.* New York: Macmillan Publishing Co., 1983.

Jetzinger, Franz. *Hitler's Youth.* Foreword by Alan Bullock, translated by Lawrence Wilson. London: Hutchinson Co., 1958.

Langer, Walter. *The Mind of Adolf Hitler.* New York: Basic Books, 1972.

Maser, Werner. *Hitler: Legend, Myth, and Reality.* New York: Harper and Row, 1973.

Trevor-Roper, H. R. *The Last Days of Hitler.* 3rd ed. New York: Collier Books, 1962.

Waite, Robert G. L. *The Psychopathic God: Adolf Hitler.* New York: Basic Books, 1977.

Waite, Robert G. L. "Review." *Adolf Hitler. Legende-Mythos-Wirklichkeit* by Werner Maser. *Central European History* 7 (1974): 90–94.

# Index

*Acknowledgment is made for permission to quote from the following works.*

*Woodrow Wilson and World Settlement* and *Woodrow Wilson: Life and Letters*, by Ray Stannard Baker. Reprinted by permission of Judith M. MacDonald.

*The Myth That Will Not Die: The Formation of the National Government, 1931*, by Humphry Berkeley. Reprinted by permission of Littlefield, Adams & Company.

*FDR's Last Year*, by Jim Bishop. Copyright © 1974 by Jim Bishop. Used by permission of William Morrow & Company.

*The Path to Dictatorship, 1918–1933*, (articles by Bracker, Krausner, Morsey). Used by permission of Frederick A. Praeger.

*Hitler: A Study in Tyranny*, by Allen Bullock. Used by permission of Harper and Row Publishers.

*Roosevelt: The Lion and the Fox* and *Roosevelt: The Soldier of Freedom*, by James MacGregor Burns (excerpts slightly abridged and adapted). Reprinted by permission of Harcourt Brace Jovanovich.

*Speaking Frankly*, by James F. Byrnes. Used by permission of Greenwood and Harper and Row, Publishers.

*Anthony Eden*, by David Carlton. Reprinted by permission of David Carlton and Allen Lane Publishers.

*Memoirs of the Second World War*, by Winston S. Churchill. Copyright © 1959 by Houghton Mifflin company. Reprinted by permission of Houghton Mifflin company and Cassell & Co.

*White House Witness*, by Jonathan Daniels. Copyright © 1975 by Jonathan Daniels. Reprinted by permission of Doubleday & Co., Inc.

*The Wilson Era: Years of War and After*, by Josephus Daniels. Copyright 1946 by The University of North Carolina Press. Reprinted by permission of the publisher.

*Foreign Policy of Poland, 1919–39*, by Roman Debicki. Reprinted by permission of Frederick A. Praeger.

*Poland in the Twentieth Century*, by M. K. Dziewanowski. Copyright © 1977 by Columbia University Press. Reprinted by permission of the publisher.

*The Memoirs of Anthony Eden: Full Circle*, by Anthony Eden. Copyright © 1960 by The Times Publishing Co., Ltd. Reprinted by permission of Houghton Mifflin Company and Cassell & Co.

*Jim Farley's Story*, by Jim Farley. Reprinted by permission of McGraw-Hill Book Company.

*The Twenty-Fifth Amendment: Its Complete History and Earliest Application*, by John D. Feerink. Reprinted by permission of Fordham University Press.

*The Fatal Decision*, edited by Seymour Frieden and William Richardson. Reprinted by permission of Berkley Publishing.

*Woodrow Wilson and Colonel House*, by Alexander George and Juliette George. Copyright © 1956 by A. L. and J. L. George, renewed 1984. Reprinted by permission of the publisher.

*The Memoirs of Field Marshall Keitel*, by Walter Gorlitz. Copyright © 1961, 1965 by Walter Gorlitz. Reprinted by permission of Stein and Day, Publishers.

*Woodrow Wilson: An Intimate Memoir*, by Carry T. Grayson. Reprinted by permission of the Grayson family.

*Interpretations of American History*, vols. I, II, edited by Billias Grob. Used by permission of the Free Press and Macmillan and Co.

*The Meaning of Hitler*, by Sebastian Haffner, translated by Ewald Osers. Copyright © 1979 by Ewald Osers. Reprinted by permission of Macmillan Publishing Company and Weidenfeld & Nicolson, Ltd.

*Germany Tried Democracy*, by S. William Halperin. Reprinted by permission of Anchor Books.

*The German Generals Talk*, by B. H. Liddell Hart. Reprinted by permission of the Putnam Publishing Group.

*The Medical Casebook of Adolph Hitler*,

by Dr. & Mrs. Leonard L. Heston.
Copyright © 1979 by Dr. & Mrs.
Leonard L. Heston. Reprinted
by permission of Stein and Day,
Publishers.

*Mein Kampf*, by Adolf Hitler, translated
by Ralph Manheim. Copyright 1943,
copyright © renewed by Houghton
Mifflin Company. Reprinted by permission of Houghton Mifflin Company
and Hutchison Publishing, Ltd.

*The Political Collapse of Europe*, by Hajo
Holborn. Reprinted by permission of
Alfred A. Knopf, Inc.

*The Ordeal of Woodrow Wilson*, by
Herbert Hoover. Copyright © by
McGraw-Hill Book Co. Reprinted by
permission of the publisher.

*Forty-Two Years in the White House*, by
I. H. Hoover. Copyright © 1934 by
James Osborne Hoover and Mildred
Hoover Stewart. Copyright © re-
newed 1961 by James Osborne
Hoover. Reprinted by permission of
Houghton Mifflin Company.

*The Secret Diaries of Hitler's Doctor*, by
David Irving. Copyright © 1983 by
David Irving. Used by permission of
Macmillan Publishing Company.

*Piłsudski: A Life for Poland*, by Wacław
Jędreszejewicz. Reprinted by permission of Hippocrene Books, Inc.

*Swords or Ploughshares?*, by Warren
Kimball. Used by permissionn of
Harber and Row, Publishers.

*The Young Hitler I Knew*, by August
Kubizek. Copyright 1954 by Paul
Popper and Company; copyright ©
renewed 1983 by Paula Kubizek and
William Guttman. Reprinted by permission of Houghton Mifflin Company
and MacIntosh & Otis, Inc.

*The End of Glory: An Interpretation of the
Origins of World War II*, by Lawrence
Lafore. Reprinted by permission of
J. B. Lipincott and Harper and Row,
Publishers.

*The Mind of Adolf Hitler*, by Walter C.
Langer. Copyright © 1972 by Basic
Books, Inc. Reprinted by permission
of the publisher.

*The Pathology of Leadership*, by Hugh

L'Etang. Reprinted by permission of
E. P. Dutton and Hawthorne Books.

*The Goebbels Diaries*, translated by Louis
Lochner. Copyright © by Fireside
Press, Inc. Reprinted by permission
of Doubleday & Company, Inc.

*The Glory and the Dreams*, by William
Manchester. Reprinted by permission
of Little, Brown, and Company.

*Ramsay MacDonald*, by David Marquand. Reprinted by permission of
David Higham Associates, Ltd.

*Hitler, Legend, Myth and Reality*, by
Werner Maser. Reprinted by permission of Harper and Row, Publishers.

*White House Physician*, by Ross T.
McIntire and George Creel. Copyright © 1946 by Ross T. McIntire
and George Creel. Reprinted by permission of the Putnam Publishing
Group.

*The Cold War in Transition*, by David S.
McLellan. Copyright © 1966 by
David S. McLellan. Reprinted by
permission of Macmillan Publishing
Company.

*After Seven Years*, by Raymond Moley.
Reprinted by permission of DaCapo
Press, Inc.

*Presidential Power: The Politics of Leader-
ship from FDR to Carter*, by Richard
Neustadt. Reprinted by permission of
John Wiley & Sons, Inc.

*Churchill: Taken from the Diaries of Lord
Moran*, by Kird Niran. Copyright ©
by the Trustees of Lord Moran,
Nutley Publications, Ltd., 1966. Re-
printed by permission of Houghton
Mifflin Company and William
Heinemann, Ltd.

*The Politics of Reappraisal*, by Gillian
Peale and Chris Cook. Reprinted by
permission of St. Martin's Press and
Macmillan Press Ltd.

*The Roosevelt I Know*, by Frances Perkins. Reprinted by permission of
Penguin Books.

*Affectionately, FDR*, by James Roosevelt
and Sidney Shalett. Reprinted by
permission of Harcourt Brace Jovanovich, Inc. and Harold Matson.

*Working with Roosevelt*, by Samuel

Rosenman. Reprinted by permission of DaCapo Press, Inc.

*Hankey, Man of Secrets*, by Stephen A. Roskill. Reprinted by permission of Collins Publishers.

*The American Presidency*, by Clinton Rossiter. Reprinted by permission of Harcourt, Brace and World, Inc.

*Hitler: The Man and the Military Leader*, by Percy Schramm. Reprinted by permission of Quadrangle Books, Inc.

*Twentieth Century America*, by David A. Shannon. Reprinted by permission of David Shannon.

*Post-War Britain*, by Alan Skeed and Chris Cook (Pelican Books, 1979). Copyright © 1979 by Alan Skeed and Chris Cook. Reprinted by permission of Penguin Books, Ltd.

*Thank You, Mr. President*, by A. Merriman Smith. Reprinted by permission of DaCapo Press, Inc.

*Reaching Judgment at Nuremberg*, by Bradley F. Smith. Copyright © 1977 by Basic Books, Inc. Reprinted by permission of the publisher.

*When the Cheering Stopped: The Last Years of Woodrow Wilson*, by Gene Smith. Used by permission of Time, Inc.

*Clementine Churchill: The Biography of a Marriage*, by Mary Soames. Copyright © 1979 by Thompson Newspaper, Ltd. Reprinted by permission of Houghton Mifflin Company and Curtis Brown.

*Starling of the White House*, by Edmund Starling. Copyright 1946. Reprinted by permission of Simon and Schuster, Inc.

*Roosevelt and the Russians*, by Edward Stettinius. Copyright 1949 by the Stettinius Fund, Inc. Reprinted by permission of Doubleday & Company, Inc. and Harold Ober Associates, Inc.

*Sixty Years of Power; Some Memories of the Men Who Wielded It*, by the Earl of Swinton, with James D. Margach. Reprinted by permission of the Century Hutchinson Ltd.

*England in the Twentieth Century*, by David Thomson (Pelican History of England, 1965). Copyright © 1965 by the estate of David Thomson. Reprinted by permission of Penguin Books, Ltd.

*Adolf Hitler*, by John Toland. Copyright © 1976 by John Toland. Reprinted by permission of Doubleday & Company, Inc.

*The Last Days of Hitler*, by H. R. Trevor-Roper. Reprinted by permission of A. D. Peters & Co. Ltd.

*The Democratic Roosevelt*, by Rexford G. Tugwell. Reprinted by permission of Russell & Volkening, Inc.

*FDR: My Boss*, by Grace Tully. Reprinted by permission of People's Book Club.

*Woodrow Wilson as I Know Him*, by Joseph Tumulty. Copyright 1921 by Joseph P. Tumulty. Reprinted by permission of Doubleday & Company, Inc. and William Heinemann, Ltd.

*The Psychopathic God: Adolf Hitler*, by Robert G. L. Waite. Copyright © by Basic Books, Inc. Reprinted by permission of R. Waite and Basic Books.

*Woodrow Wilson: A Medical and Psychological Biography*, by Edmund Weinstein. Copyright © 1981 by Princeton University Press. Reprinted by permission of E. Weinstein and Princeton University Press.

*The Tragedy of Ramsay MacDonald*, by L. MacNeill Weir. Reprinted by permission of Martin, Secker & Warburg, Ltd.

*A Sign for Cain*, by Fredric Wertham. Copyright © 1966 by Fredric Wertham. Used by permission of Macmillan Publishing Company.

*Action This Day* and *Hindenburg: The Wooden Titan*, by John Wheeler-Bennett. Reprinted by permission of Penningtons and St. Martin's Press.

*The Nemesis of Power: The German Army in Politics 1918–1945*, by John Wheeler-Bennett. Reprinted by permission of Macmillan and Co. and Russell Press.

*America in Search of Itself: The Making of the President 1956–1980*, by Theo-

*Permission to reprint photographs is acknowledged as follows.*